Hel
Mis

This book and its contents are neither authorised by, nor do they have the sponsorship or endorsement of, the United Nations or any member, department or organisation within the United Nations. The publisher does not intend to assert by the publication of this book any affiliation with or endorsement by the United Nations.

Hello Missus
A Girl's Own Guide to Foreign Affairs

Lynne Minion

HarperCollins*Publishers*

HarperCollins*Publishers*

First published in Australia in 2004
by HarperCollins*Publishers* Pty Limited
ABN 36 009 913 517
A member of the HarperCollins*Publishers* (Australia) Pty Limited Group
www.harpercollins.com.au

HarperCollins*Publishers*
25 Ryde Road, Pymble, Sydney, NSW 2073, Australia
31 View Road, Glenfield, Auckland 10, New Zealand

National Library of Australia Cataloguing-in-Publication data:

Minion, Lynne Maree.
Hello missus : a girl's own guide to foreign affairs.
ISBN 0 7322 7967 4.
1. East Timor – Politics and government. 2. East Timor – History – Autonomy and independence. 3. United Nations – East Timor. 4. Political atrocities – East Timor. 5. East Timor – Social conditions. I. Title.
959.87

Cover photography by Stephen Oxenbury, 2c Management Pty Ltd
Cover design by HarperCollins Design Studio, internal design by Louise McGeachie
Map by Laurie Whiddon, Map Illustrations
Typeset in Minion 11.5/14.5 by HarperCollins Design Studio
Printed and bound in Australia by Griffin Press on 70gsm Bulky Ivory White

9 8 7 6 5 4 3 2 1 04 05 06 07

To Maria Pelech, my grandmother, who continues to inspire me.
Anton Pelech, my grandfather, at peace now.

Acknowledgements

I thank all of the following for their immense support during a remarkable journey, in the Third World and the First: Olga and Darrell Minion, Brett Minion and Samantha Thompson, Margaret Minion, Kelly Minion, Libby Douglas, Ged Griffin, Jen Worthington, the Horta family, Ercia Madeira and Baby, Ruth, Betty and Dudu, Asim Salkanovic, Gina Kelly and Electra Aitchison, Sharon Stone and Bruce Bennett, Andrew and Bill Heather, Marc Williams, Jacinta Tynan, Kevin Roberts, 'J-Lo Travel', Rosa Gomez and the staff of the Esplanada, Ali Urquhart, Shona Martyn and, of course, Mary Rennie.

Contents

Wetar
Kisar
Moa
Adonara
Lomblen
Alor
Atauro
Baucau
Com
Leti
Lakor
Liquica
DILI
Los Palos
Solor
Pantar
Balibo
Maubisse
EAST TIMOR
Oecussi
INDONESIA
Rote
INDONESIA
Bali
DILI
EAST TIMOR
Darwin
AUSTRALIA

Glossary

Alin	Younger person
Atelogu	See you later
Bondia	Good morning
Bonoite	Good evening
Botardi	Good afternoon
Bulak	Crazy
Diak	Good
Diak ka lae?	Good or not? (in greeting, similar to: How are you?)
Diskulpa	Sorry
Ikan bot	Big fish, in this case referring to an inflatable killer whale beach toy
Kapas	Nice
Kolegas	Colleagues/friends
Lae	No
Lae problema	No worries
Malae	Foreigner
Neba	Over there
Nebe	Where
Parabens	Congratulations
Obrigado/a	Thank you (masculine/feminine)
Obrigado/a barak	Thank you very much
Sin	Yes

Arieia Branca	Beach outside Dili where Timorese onlookers line the fence, buff Portuguese peacekeepers play soccer, and the GNR (see below) patrol frequently; soundtrack and refreshments provided by the Caz Bar over the road
Capacity-building	Mentoring Timorese employees (and ideally roosters) in the skills required to be independent
City Café	Meeting place of the international population and a hub of local commerce, with a special black-hair signature garnish with every dish
Crocodile Alley	UN military base in Dili, featuring the Dengue Bar
Diana's	Restaurant on the beach and Dili's premier first-date venue
DSRSG	Deputy Special Representative of the Secretary-General (of the UN)
ETPS	East Timor Police Service, now TLPS or Timor-Leste Police Service
GNR	Portuguese Republican National Guard, or very special police unit
Hotel Timor	Luxury hotel and conference facility with satellite TV showcasing the considerable talents of Portugal's game-show hosts
Maubisse Pousada	Former Portuguese mansion, now a hotel with a children's swing in the manicured garden designed for romantic protestations
Obrigado Barracks	Main UN base in Dili, a licensed establishment and the site of free

	essential services, such as enthusiastic dentists
OCPI	UN Office of Communication and Public Information
Poy Cholor	Preferred nightclub of the Prime Minister of East Timor
Purple Cow	(also known as the Mad Cow) Hip oceanfront nightclub, populated by weapons of mass erection and Dili Princesses, until a riot transfers popularity to Poy Cholor (see above)
SRSG	Special Representative of the Secretary-General (of the UN)
The Espy	The Esplanada Hotel, providing gourmet food, friendly staff and a cocktail bar all in a sumptuous environment showcasing Balinese architecture and the beauty of Dili Harbour (clothes optional pool)
TVTL	Televisaun Timor Lorosa'e
UNDP	United Nations Development Programme
UNAMET	United Nations Assistance Mission in East Timor
UNHCR	United Nations High Commission for Refugees
UNMISET	United Nations Mission of Support in East Timor
UNPOL	United Nations Police
UNTAET	United Nations Transitional Administration in East Timor

And then there's the Prime Miniature's Shoe and Handbag Emporium . . .

1

BRIGHT LIGHTS, PIG CITY

Every now and then in life the universe conspires to lend humility. So I emerge from the arrivals area and into the humid heat to find that my worst-case scenario is, in fact, true. Other travellers' faces are lighting up in recognition, backs are being slapped, a kiss on each cheek in welcome; *bemvindo!* One after another they leave while I remain rooted to my spot, with no idea of where to go, as a group of jostling East Timorese stare with curiosity at the white woman rigid with fear.

Count to ten, suppress any desire to calculate your financial wherewithal, Lynne, and hold in the sobs; it'll be okay, just count to ten, twenty, a thousand, whatever it takes.

My impulsiveness is to blame. The job I'd expected here had fallen through days ago but I'd decided to take a chance. Anyway, I was already committed — the furniture was in storage, accounts had been closed, mail was redirected and there was a lot of self-talk about believing strongly in realising dreams.

Realising dreams comes with risk, I'm telling myself again on the forecourt of Dili International Airport. After all, that's what makes them dreams, otherwise they'd just be occurrences. Yes, realising dreams requires bravery . . . but at this moment I'm wondering if they also require enormous fucking stupidity.

The Timorese teenagers can't contain their intrigue any longer, 'Dollar Missus?' comes the chorus as they descend on me. They are desperately poor, they are certainly filthy, and they give some perspective to my circumstances. I might be arriving in Dili in a rather foolhardy manner but I certainly won't be going hungry tonight, unlike them. I just wish they wouldn't swarm around me as they're doing, and I wish they wouldn't keep asking me 'Where you go Missus?' because I have absolutely no idea.

Would it be uncharitable of me to think of them as dirty urchins? 'Where you go Missus?' Then they try to reach into my handbag and cop a feel of my bum and I'm wondering if it would be unhumanitarian of me to just elbow them away on my first day here. Great, now is *not* the time to realise I have no compassion to give these desperate innocents with the big, wide brown eyes beseeching me 'Dollar Missus?' because they have none and I have a relative fortune.

Although, I am currently homeless, like them. Where do I go? I doubt they can advise me. The sun starts to set and the sky turns a shade of pink and the children continue to mob the ivory-coloured statue, scattering only when it moves and dials a mobile phone.

'Hello,' I say into the receiver.

'Hello Missus!' they yell and mob me again. Damn it. Voice-mail.

I had hoped my impulsiveness would be offset by high-level contacts in this country, an arguable benefit when they can't be contacted I'm thinking, as my white-knuckled hands grip a trolley that carries a monstrous pile of luggage. Yep, my life is contained in a trolley — five pairs of shoes, only one with stiletto heels, indicating the extraordinary sacrifice I've made in coming here; a $300 pair of Scanlan & Theodore dry-clean-only pants, which may have been an ill-advised inclusion but after a wine-soaked goodbye lunch they seemed essential; a lace bustier, because my mum said it's too nice to languish in storage; a collection of pretty sun frocks in various tropical hues; and four handbags in a kaleidoscope of colours designed for best feats of coordination. See, I had felt that just because I'd be living in a Third World country I didn't have to *look* as though I was living in a Third World country.

Right now, however, I glance at the duty-free bag holding my new Chanel lip gloss, mascara, powder foundation (all with in-built sunscreen in deference to the context) and my frown lines deepen alarmingly as I consider that all these fundamentals could very well be heading back to the First World sooner rather than later. And to think of the energy I expended today begging at check-in counters for the 20-kilogram limit to be overlooked on the grounds of gender discrimination because men generally weigh more than me to the precise value of my additional luggage weight.

Three hundred and fifty-four, three hundred and fifty-five . . . I'm still counting yet panic rises . . . three hundred and . . . 'Hello, do you need a lift?'

I turn around amid a crowd scattering again, expecting to see an angel complete with wings. 'Oh, yes please.'

'Where do you want to go?'

'I, um, don't know.'

'You don't know?'

'Well, I arranged to be met here and I haven't heard a word and I don't know where to go so I suppose I should get a hotel room.'

'Okay, which one?'

'Um, don't suppose you know of one? Not too expensive would be great because I don't have very much money.'

'O-kay.' I can tell she thinks it is all rather peculiar; meanwhile in me my fear mingles with relief.

How did it all unravel? It had been so well planned. Job, a lift on arrival, accommodation. Seems I had placed my developed world expectations into the chaos of a developing nation, which leaves me to ponder: Is this idealism or is it madness?

Guardian angels these days travel by car, so I sink into the passenger seat and she directs us towards the capital city of East Timor. She surveys me curiously out of the corner of her eyes and I pretend to be a Very Sane Person despite my apparent lack of prospects. Chattering away, I look out the window and we move into the outskirts of Dili. Why isn't she taking me on a more scenic route, I'm thinking, as we negotiate pigs and potholes beside the remnants of burned-out buildings in the dust. Knowing of the billions of dollars of aid that have made their way to this nation in the last couple of years it strikes me as peculiar that the city hasn't been rebuilt. Was I expecting shopping malls and boulevards? No. But I'm wondering why the place for the most part remains razed to the ground.

The prevalence of vandalism on the partial walls, which stand as a reminder of the destruction of 1999, suggests to me that illiteracy could be combated with the provision of spray paint. And while I appreciate the attempts at English, it takes me a while to realise it is actually that: 'Otonomi, yes . . . !'

The East Timorians — as George W. Bush called them — are all short, skinny, malnourished frames with dark brown skin, darker than I'd anticipated. The women lope slowly with a rhythmic swinging movement, small groups of them, arm in arm, in tight jeans and bright T-shirts, black hair swaying down their thin backs. The men squat on their haunches in the shade of frangipani trees, picking their noses in what seems to be the national sport, dressed in the civilian uniform of thongs, bandanas and military fatigues.

Scrawny dogs with their ribs displayed and coats covered in

festering sores interrupt the journey whenever they walk straight out onto the roadway. UN Land Rovers overtake us at tremendous speed.

The car parks in front of the Hotel Dili 2000. I run across and request a room. 'Finish, maybe tomorrow,' the attendant tells me and my face drops. 'Missus try Hotel Dili 2001,' and I know I'm running out of options given that it is now the beginning of 2002.

I feel about ready to release my inner princess complete with tiara. Yes. I have a tiara with me but even I didn't include that in my luggage by design. Leaving my apartment with its views of Sydney Harbour, it'd been placed on my head to protect it as removalists packed up my furniture and I'd promptly forgotten it was there. Much later, when I'd remembered, I'd appreciated the sweet irony of the tiara coming along with me, as had the three friends who were sitting on my suitcase, drinking champagne and debating the merits of hairspray in the developing world. But it's right now bittersweet to discover that a tiara's usefulness really is relative when I have nowhere to sleep. Keep counting, Lynne.

So we drive along the oceanfront, past the magnificent proportions of a United Nations building that presides colonially over its surroundings, then past the fish market with its wooden tables displaying produce emitting a stink that reaches my nose as we motor by while the locals sit behind their fare, slowly waving the flies away or nose-picking, on a needs basis I assume. Meanwhile, I continue my rapid outpouring of words. 'So, you're Timorese?' I observe astutely.

'Yes, but I lived in Darwin during all the struggles. My family is still there. Three months I'll stay here.'

'Ah, children still there?' I'm happy to focus on someone else's problems.

'Yes, daughters. It's so hard. One month I've been in Dili.'

'Two to go, I'm sure it'll fly.' Competent, Sane, Wise I am.

'Yes, I'll visit my family one time so it's not too bad. It's hard but I have to rebuild my country.'

The car slows to let a family of goats meander by, then we come upon a little twisting part of the road, over a bridge with, to the left, an expanse of sea and, to the right, a slum littered with naked children and wandering piglets. In the distance, in the diminishing light, I can see the outline of the massive Christo Rei, the statue of Jesus *à la* that in Rio de Janeiro, all Catholic majesty surveying His Creation. And in this pocket of the world, all that seems to have been created are squalor, salmonella and giardia.

I'm deposited in pitch darkness at the Hotel Dili 2001 and a Timorian bellhop manages to carry a suitcase bigger than him to my room — a converted shipping container complete with steel walls. All for the bargain price of US$38. I calculate that at this rate I'll hardly reach my objective of being here until the true emancipation of this nation — Independence — which lies months away. Despite my bravado, that amount of time sounds interminable as I leave yet another voicemail message and tug simultaneously at a zip on my baggage; it bursts open.

Making every effort to relax, I step into the shower and move towards the trickle of water that promises comfort and with a jolt I realise it's not the advertised hot water. 'Goddamn it!' I curse my continuing First World naivety. This is all going well I think to myself, as I emerge, the walls vibrating in concert with the loudly grumbling generator next door, and I take a swig of duty-free vodka, put on my tiara, power up my laptop, and I type:

> 'DAY ONE. Have I made a horrible mistake? Will this dream come true or will I find myself back in Sydney, money-less, home-less, job-less, all round less than before I ever entertained the idea of

> racking off to this place that has no real connection to me? Why do I care so much about this country? What on earth can I contribute? Is it worth the risk to my perfectly fine life in the developed world? And what is the dream? Is it merely the indulgences of those of us with opportunity? Is it indulgent to alleviate First World guilt and come here believing my skills will assist these people when a short car ride has shown me that all they really need is food, education, jobs, sanitation and I'm not skilled in the provision and sustainable development of any of these?'

Sweltering in the oppressive heat, with beads of sweat running between my breasts and down the backs of my calves, my long hair refusing to dry in the humidity and the shipping container preparing for take-off, I contemplate my dreams versus those of the Timorese, and I know that not even in their wildest dreams would they dare to hope for the life I have just left behind.

Even still, despite these reminders of my own luck, I lie down on the lumpy, sex-stained bed and cry. Because I may be comparatively rich and educated and fortunate, but in this room on this night I am (unlike previous occupants) the loneliest individual in the world . . . and inexplicably, despite the opportunities handed to me in life, I clearly *am* fucking stupid.

2

THE GUILT-EDGED GATES

Chain smoking at the crack of dawn isn't the most constructive thing to do given my circumstances, but it's due to my circumstances that it's my chosen pastime, so I sit with my back against the wall of a large grotto to the Virgin Mary and stare out at the sea, pondering my alternatives which currently number zero.

Timorese children wander past me, slowly, staring at the peculiar sight: a white woman, on their beach, sitting in the filthy sand and adding cigarette butts to a pile she's created on her right. 'Malae, malae,' I hear them say as I light up again and I wonder what it means. Maybe it's Tetum for alien? Or tasty? Scrawny dogs come by to have a sniff. I feel as forlorn as they look. That's all I need, to be eaten by starving dogs when no one knows where I am and the remnants of my body will lie unidentifiable, slowly biodegrading into this beach, just another piece of smelly debris.

I may want to assist in eradicating poverty in this country but food aid is not my area of expertise so I stub out my cigarette, quickly throw off my frock and dash for the sea, clad only in my bikini. Diving under the surface of the bath-warm water and feeling a sense of weightlessness is the cure to my self-absorption. I am mermaid hear me roar. I float along the top of the water and survey the lush, towering mountains, the city of Dili, the UN helicopters overhead and the Christo Rei with His arms outstretched just like mine, embracing this place.

Yes, I'd wanted to come to this place, but, more to the point, I'd wanted to contribute to the rebuilding of a nation which had never lost sight of its dream of freedom, persevering for twenty-four long years of struggle. And I will persevere too and make whatever contribution I can here — here, yes, I've made it, I'm here! And right now, I am convinced that every problem has a solution: theirs and mine.

Imbued with renewed determination and confidence I end my reverie and stand up in the thigh-high sea water and, appalled, I plunge back under the surface again. Oh, no! I've noticed a Timorese audience, which has accumulated to rather large proportions, and I realise the spectacle is me. Men have sat themselves on a rock wall to catch glimpses of a skin colour they're familiar with predominantly from pornos. Wanting to end the display I dart back onto the beach and easily find my remarkable pile of butts all right but, hello, standing there in this season's Hawaiian-print red cossie with applause rising from the crowd, I discover that my clothes are no longer here. Oh shit, this is rather vulnerable. Perhaps I should take a bow? I spot my room key half buried beneath that worldwide beach accoutrement, an empty VB stubbie, and I have no choice but to run across the road, past the hotel reception and into my shipping container. *Bemvindo* to East Timor, indeed!

This is all going well, I think to myself, pledging to be fully clothed for any remaining time I may have in Timor, although now it seems unlikely that mere finances will see me leave this country; instead I imagine I will be immediately expelled for displays of public indecency. On cue, it seems, there is a knock on the door. Toothbrush in mouth I open it, expecting hotel management or immigration. Instead, it's the solution to my problems.

Dulce is the matriarch of the Horta family and niece of the freedom fighter turned Nobel Peace Laureate turned Foreign Affairs Minister in East Timor's transitional administration, José Ramos-Horta — the man who was the recipient of my phone calls of the day before. I had first met José in 1996 when I'd interviewed him and I'd been preoccupied with the East Timorese cause ever since. The Hortas are part of the ruling elite in Timor, a formidable and well-connected 'Portuguese' family. 'Come!' she says and I am swallowing toothpaste, stuffing clothes into luggage and picking it up with a strength previously unknown, all while resisting the urge to yell *yes!* and I'm thanking God or whomever was listening to a sleepless night's worth of prayers.

Retracing the road of the night before we turn left at a pig, right at a goat then left again at a burned-out building until we enter a fenced compound where we stop. Two houses and a few shacks make up the accommodation for a confusing tree of relatives: 'Lynne, this is my sister-in-law; that is José's cousin; she is my cousin; sister, how do you say, mother-in-law, husband's sister . . .'

My room has walls fixed with religious iconography, including a large glo-in-the-dark Jesus on His crucifix over my bed, which I consider ingenious contraception, and I unpack the sheets I've brought along — white cotton with satin piping. A maid, Elsie, puts them on as I fill my wardrobe. Oh, I could get very accustomed to all this developing nation hardship.

Most rooms open onto a long veranda with bamboo furniture and a view past the generator and roosters on to high green mountains. East Timorese police officers patrol the compound, children run past screeching with laughter, and my explorations take me down to the kitchen which is a little house of its own. More faces which I'm yet to meet are in here and they baulk to see me, 'Mana! Mana!'

Dulce appears, 'Yes, Lynne, you want something?' Oh dear, I'm obviously not supposed to be here where servants sweat over wood stoves roughly constructed of concrete, within walls black with soot. Working away, they peer at me. I can see only the whites of their eyes in the dark room and I feel a bit too glo-in-the-dark myself thanks to the whites of my eyes, teeth, skin.

'I just came to say hi and have a look. They say the kitchen is the hearth of every home,' I laugh awkwardly.

'You want something to eat? Some coffee? We bring it to you on veranda.'

'No, no. Um, I'm fine thank you. I was just looking around for no good reason really.' And my voice tapers off. Alrighty, I'm being segregated by a complex class structure I don't understand except that my colour has apparently spirited me to the very uppermost echelons, which I think is frightfully unfair because I want to spend time amongst the chatter and activity down here.

'Wow! Did you see that?' says cousin Eduardo, who is leaning against a bench, sipping espresso. 'Did you see that? That was a big ah . . . that was a big ah . . . how do you say in English?'

'I'm not sure what you mean.'

'That was a big ah . . . oh my English . . . a big ah . . . mouse!' he says triumphantly.

'Ah, that'd be a rat,' and I get the point, leaving, quickly, suppressing a look of horror lest I offend Dulce with my absolute white-skinned detestation of vermin! I leap onto a veranda chair, suppressing also the desire which is overtaking me to have a cigarette and some of the duty-free vodka which is hidden in the bottom of my wardrobe. It's a human rights abuse but I know that women shouldn't indulge in these things in Timor and this, if anything today, indicates my complete commitment to behaving with decorum here.

I'm battling the onset of withdrawal symptoms when a motorcade arrives and lovely, firm bodyguards launch themselves out of moving vehicles and, as the tyres crunch to a halt in the gravel, a door is opened to reveal José. 'Where have you been?'

'Hello Minister.'

'Where have you been? You were expected last night.'

'I was at the Hotel Dili 2001.'

'Why didn't you come here? Food was prepared, inconvenience for everyone and you go elsewhere.'

'Well, there was no one at the airport. Your phone was off. I didn't know where to go. I thought it best to go to a hotel.'

'And what are you wearing? You come to this country and you dress like a prostitute in Darlinghurst.' Jesus Christ, I was dying for a fag *before* I was described as a Darlinghurst prostitute, now I have to hold my hands together to override the hand-to-mouth compulsion — my fist, his mouth.

'What! I am wearing lilac. In all the years you've known me have I ever worn lilac? I borrowed these clothes specifically to be culturally sensitive!'

'Culturally sensitive? What culture are you being sensitive too? A brothel's? We are going to Sergio Vieira de Mello's house for dinner and you can't be seen like that, put on a stole.'

'A stole? I'm sorry but I didn't pack my pashmina.' How dare he presume me to be a person who'd pack luxuries of such a kind to come to this poor, poor nation. 'If my grandmother saw me dressed like this she'd think I was going to Mass.'

'God, Mass? What kind of church does your family go to?

You think you can tell me what is appropriate to wear here just because you are Catholic? This Catholic country does not have women go to church half naked!'

'Half naked!'

'We have to go. If you refuse to change then you will just have to go dressed like a prostitute.'

'Refuse to change! I don't have anything more appropriate than this. I have only packed pretty frocks!' I think it best not to mention the black lace bustier.

'Did you really come to my country with no thought to the customs?'

'I put a *lot* of thought into this. What is wrong with this dress?'

'The shoulders, of course! Now, we have to go.'

Oh, of course, that well-known erogenous zone. How silly of me, I mean shoulders just scream XXX and here I am exposing them through strips of fabric like a brazen, yet frightfully fashionable, hussy. Still, I rush into my room and throw open the doors of the recently arranged wardrobe and toss out item after item of clothing (ooh, a lovely beige halter neck, perhaps not), shoes (stilettos aren't quite appropriate), frenziedly, looking for anything which covers my naughty shoulders and illustrates that I have put thought into cultural sensitivities. Nothing! And I'm going to the house of the man who heads the United Nations in East Timor, the transitional leader of the country! Okay, I will at least look perfectly groomed and I carefully apply fabulous new Chanel cosmetics that promptly slide off in the humidity. Great.

Exiting my room, sweaty, half naked, mascara down my cheeks and lip gloss down my chin, and a car door is opened for me. I sit in the back dressed in my lilac frock, with frightfully well-coordinated little mother-of-pearl coloured shoes and handbag, my hair up in a chignon . . . I think I look like I should be going to a Country Women's Association meeting and yet I apparently look like a hooker in this part of the world. I don't want a stole at this moment, I want a poncho, preferably hooded. I am mortified!

The motorcade spirits us through the streets and along the oceanfront again and the dust and dogs and pigs of daylight are well hidden by the poncho of darkness, making Dili Harbour as picturesque as can be. Into the seaside residential compound of Sergio Vieira de Mello, and the bodyguards launch themselves (oh, lovely), the tyres crunch to a stop again, doors are flung open and, as we dismount, out from the casa he bounds, all soap-star-esque tan, big teeth and crisp blue shirt. 'Bonoite, Aze!' And Sergio herds us in, hands in smalls of backs, smiling in a rather *Truman Show* manner. Dazzled by shiny welcome I can't help but look left and right for television cameras which surely must be pointed at us.

Inside and the shine and dazzle continue in opulent style. Big-screen TV and DVD equipment, plush sofas, Timorese waiters carrying trays of food and frightfully posh white people talking in English about their scuba diving, as I stand with my hands on my shoulders and wonder what country we are in. Did the motorcade take a short cut to the Hamptons?

No, I'm not in the *Truman Show*, am I? I'm in an episode of *Dynasty* and, continuing on that theme, in walks the most beautiful girl in the world, who makes a beeline to Sergio's side. Hang on, isn't he married? Aren't we in a Catholic country with an abundance of cultural, class and moral standards that I seem to have been flagrantly stumbling around all bloody day, despite my good intentions? And what is she wearing? I look over to see that she's resplendent in a tight, short green dress with spider straps proudly showing her tanned, toned cleavage, back and *shoulders*! Cultural sensitivity seems to be a matter of interpretation.

Right! I drop my hands and proceed to devour hors d'oeuvres and down champagne with an abandon which I feel is rather Richard Carleton of me but I've had a day of failing at adapting to the Third World and so I'm gunna be First World right now . . . and get pissed, inspired by a United Nations of flamboyant lifestyles and jet-setting international careers. And just as the Timorese could only dare to dream about the life I've left behind in Sydney, these humanitarians have eclipsed my most affluent fantasies. *Bemvindo* to Timor, indeed.

So tonight I happily avail myself of the hospitality of nations united in the value of international affairs. And sipping from a glass of personality, I expect to hear someone toast the proletariat at any time; after all, we are here thanks to the devastating poverty of the masses out there beyond the guilt-edged gates.

3

COCK-A-DOODLE DOO

I awake. Pillow over my head. The roosters, don't they know they are only supposed to crow at dawn and not all night long? God, even the fauna here needs capacity-building.

I can hear the deep tones of the Foreign Affairs Minister in the dining room. I drag myself from bed, put on the required coverage and join him.

'Good morning, Minister.'

'So what are you going to do for work?'

'Um, yes, there lieth the $2.50 question. I thought I'd approach the television station.'

'I won't be responsible for this. And I won't be responsible if you get malaria or dengue.'

'Well, I will take responsibility if I succumb to malaria or dengue or consumption or whatever, and I certainly take responsibility for getting a job.' Smile benevolently. 'You know my work and I think I can contribute something worthwhile.'

'Do you? We'll see.'

How pleasant this discussion is. And to think I would have settled for: 'Good morning, Lynne, welcome to East Timor, thank you for wanting to assist in rebuilding my country.'

'Yes, we'll see,' I offer generously. 'So, how is the rebuilding of a country going?' His phone rings.

In comes a sister, cousin, niece, in-law? Oh, I don't know. Hang on, yes, it's the maid, Elsie. She discards her thongs at the doorway, 'Bondia,' and serves us bread rolls, fried eggs (I'm glad those chooks have a purpose but I'd prefer a rooster's head on a plate, actually), coffee, mango. He shouts in a language I don't understand to the person on the other end, simultaneously eating and taking his digestion tablets. I play with my food and look around the walls at faded photos of an enormous extended family, wincing as his voice rises in fury. I recognise José as a boy with brothers and sisters who look like him, some of whom are long gone now, killed during the Indonesian invasion and decades of occupation. And there's José with Bill Clinton. José with Harrison Ford. The telephone conversation reaches its crescendo suddenly and ends, as does ours.

'I'm going to work. Gabriella Carrascalao runs the television station. She is my sister-in-law. Here is a note of introduction. I will not be responsible.' He writes words that are foreign to me. He leaves. Okay then. And I stab a yolk.

I get up and clear the table, taking the plates down to the kitchen where servants rush to unburden me of my load. 'It's okay. Really.' If only they knew that I am not particularly high in the class structure. I mean a Timorese man has just patronised me resoundingly, which suggests that colour does not buy class and class does not give, well, class. I try out my language skills to help lend clarity and suggest egalitarianism, 'Diak, hau diak'. Indeed, whatever the fuck that meant they are giggling and I presume I didn't hit my mark. I probably said bite my fat arse and if that's the case I'll use it on the Minister next time I see him.

'Lynne,' it's Dulce, 'you know, we go shopping. You come?' Clearly, my wardrobe issues are a matter for public concern.

Still, I am thankful for the solution, so I reply, 'Sin, obrigada.' More giggles, this time drowned out by the whump, whump, whump of a UN helicopter close overhead, and that's when I see, out of the corner of my eye, an arresting sight. It's a sight that gives me a cardiac arrest, for hanging on the clothesline are a few pairs of José's stretch boxers in black and white. As shocking as that is, it'd not the cause of my alarm. Rather, interspersed with the underwear of a world leader are some gorgeous lace G-strings in colours that exclude lilac. Hence my dive to them, then to my room.

I'm starting to suspect that sovereignty and self-determination, while ambitions for East Timor, need to be relinquished by me for the duration of my stay, and so, together with quite a number of women and children, I bundle into a 4WD that heads to the shopping district of Dili. There we walk into a shop to be met by a rooster leaving. I look at the racks of clothing in a department store the size of an average Sydney corner shop and The Family brings appropriate selections to me. Lilac. More lilac. I'm having a job interview, not an audience with the Pope, but I guess I should capitulate to those who know. But do I really have to wear an outfit with lilac ribbon at the neckline too? How old am I? Although I do find a fake Fendi handbag to match, which lifts my spirits considerably.

Browsing, I am surrounded by a proliferation of short, squat, muscular peacekeepers in combat fatigues, each with Portuguese flags on an arm, and they are all holding large guns while they stand within my personal space. I move. They follow. I move. They follow. How odd that these men are interested in female hygiene products, children's toys, women's clothing, all the products I stand before. I move. They follow. I turn around quickly. They pretend nonchalance. Is that a gun in your pocket or are you pleased to see me? It's both, I can see.

Out on the street, I pass an ANZ bank and head to the little shop next door, stepping carefully over the broken footpath and around stall-holders with their wares displayed on the ground amid the rubbish. The crowd of peacekeepers follows my path. I feel like a tour guide. The roadway is packed with UN Land Rovers and men in uniforms bearing flags, many of which I don't even recognise. These men all tower over the Timorese — and the Portuguese peacekeepers — and they are black, white, Asian. I listen to a melange of languages, including the Timorese refrain: 'Hello Missus?' 'Phonecard Missus?' 'Telstra Missus?' And all eyes follow me and my retinue of admirers. Is my fly down? My top gaping? What on earth is the appeal?

I duck into a fitting room with an array of pubescent-style ensembles. Can we diversify colourwise? Apparently not. I prefer dressing like a Darlinghurst prostitute . . . well I would but for the extraordinary interest that style seems to have generated outside my cubicle. I am starting to appreciate the need for the female dress code, and I suspect it is not only a cultural sensitivity of Timor but a multicultural one, given that I couldn't see any other white woman on the street, in a country filled with male peacekeepers and UN police officers. I doubt that dressing like a schoolgirl will deter them, quite the contrary. 'Um, Dulce, do they sell ponchos here?'

I beckon a sales assistant. 'Bondia, do you speak English?'

'Yes.'

'Do you have this in any colour besides lilac?'

'Yes.'

'Do you have blue?'

'Yes.'

'Could I ask you to get it for me?'

'Yes.'

'Alrighty, could you get it for me in blue please?'

'Yes.'

'Rather quickly would be great because there are some men leering into the fitting room right now.' I draw the curtain closer around me.

'Yes.'

Oh, hang on. 'Right, do you have it in red?'

'Yes.'

'Puce?'

'Yes.'

'With vomit-coloured polka dots?'

'Yes.'

'I think not, no.'

'Finish, maybe tomorrow.'

It appears I'd best learn their language quickly. In the interim, I accept defeat and choose the lilac. Taking my purchases, I exit, running the gauntlet of eyes that burn holes in my butt (that'll explain the cellulite) and I am relieved to get into the car and obscure it from view. 'Hello Missus!' 'Phonecard Missus?' 'Telstra Missus?' Timorians crowd around the car as it takes off.

'Lynne, you know, there are many men in Timor. Many, many men,' says Dulce.

'Yeah, clearly.'

It's a surprise to me. I hadn't expected this side of a peacekeeping mission and, thinking about it right now, it makes complete sense. And on further thought I can't see a problem with it really. I mean, hey, I've just left the gay heartland of Australia and years lamenting the lack of good (straight) men out there. Now I have found myself in a smorgasbord of them. Ooh, yes, maybe the struggle required in coming here was worthwhile. And suddenly I'm rather pleased I packed the hairspray, shoes, handbags and various shoulder-baring items which I'd been tempted to think were redundant.

Things are looking up, I'm thinking, as I get ready to go to the local TV station about a job, singing in the cold-water shower at the top of my happy lungs to the Kylie Minogue CD playing on my laptop and I'm spinning around. Soon I'm heading out wearing my new lilac outfit, feeling buoyed by the beat of the music and, as I'm walking out the gate of the compound, I hear wolf whistles and I turn around to see the uniformed police charged with responsibility for maintaining the security of the compound having a perv. 'Oh, for God's sake.' And I'm not even showing my shoulders.

I stand in the dust on the side of the busy road, extend my arm in First World style and one of many Timor taxis stops in front of me. It has no doors but it has the most extraordinary volume on the stereo, 'FREEZE! I'm Ma Baker — put your hands in the air, gimme all your money' . . . Boney M, that's a flashback to times past. Why would Boney M have made it to contemporary Timor? If you were in a newly free country, no longer oppressed, would you choose to listen to Boney M? Still, over the booming noise I yell the destination, 'BA TVTL! BA TELEVISION STATION! OBRIGADA!'

The Tetum language skills are already impressive, I'm thinking, as we drive around purposefully for half an hour at 30 kilometres an hour with the driver honking his horn and waving at his mates. 'Ma Ma Ma Ma — Ma Baker' . . . Is this song on repeat? I was told the destination was just down the road. It all only costs US$1 so it's not a fiscal consideration. I just wonder how many unlicensed fourteen-year-old boys in Australia would drive at 30 kilometres an hour if they were behind the wheel of a car, until I realise he is pretty pleased to be seen about town with the white woman in his cab.

I reach the destination eventually and within ten minutes I have a job with the United Nations and I can hardly believe my luck, as the head of TVTL, Gabriella Carrascalao, announces that she has been looking for a person to train her news journalists and, even more so, she is particularly happy to defy her brother-in-law and his note which apparently said 'I will not take responsibility for this' in Portuguese. She takes me on a tour of the station and I am introduced to my new colleagues who all shake my hand, but I am aware of the predisposition to nose-picking here so I discreetly wipe my hand on my thigh at intervals. Still, I HAVE A JOB WITH THE UNITED NATIONS so they could blow their noses on my hand and I would remain the happiest girl in the world! I HAVE A JOB WITH THE UNITED NATIONS!

I rush out onto the road and jump into a taxi with another fourteen-year-old boy at the wheel and his enormous collection of bouncing dogs on the dashboard and I point them all towards my home, which is actually just 300 metres down the road and, as we come towards it, I try to get him to stop, 'Parabens!' Why won't he stop? 'Parabens! Parabens! Parabens!' I don't want to be taken on another tour of Dili, I am bursting with my news, 'Parabens!' And he finally brings the car to a halt and turns around, beaming at me. I consult the phrasebook as I am hurrying towards the gates of the compound to see '*para* = stop'. What did I yell at that boy with such vigour? '*parabens* = congratulations', which obviously complimented his appalling driving skills profoundly and I think it's very subliminally appropriate of me.

'I have a job! Parabens to me!'

'Do you? Well, let's see how good a contribution you make,' says the country's top diplomat.

'Thank you for your note to Gabriella. It obviously did the trick, with those effusive compliments about my professional background.' I smile sweetly.

He stares back. 'Did it? I won't be responsible.'

I can feel the stress of days rising up inside my body and I am unable to contain the inner princess a moment longer: 'Right! I've had enough! What on earth is all this about? Why am I feeling unwelcome? You know perfectly well that I can make a contribution and you should be flattered and pleased that people come here and sacrifice everything they have in Australia because they want to help the Timorese!'

'God. Flattered?'

'Yes, flattered, pleased, whatever, but you shouldn't be dismissive. My arrival here was horrible. Do you have any idea how devastating that was?'

'Devastating? Sacrifice? Big deal.'

'Big deal?' Political assassination wouldn't be a great capacity-building measure on my part and I'm sure it contravenes my new employment contract in some way, however . . .

'Lynne, I'd love to humour your self-indulgence . . .'

'Well then do humour it, it could do with some humouring right now, let's humour it for a while.'

'. . . but this has been a very hard week for me professionally.'

'No. Wrong. Not you. We're humouring me right now.'

'The nominations have just closed for presidential candidates and Xanana has been saying he wouldn't run. The people want him as the president and the UN want him to run.'

'O-kay, I'll allow a short detour away from me for a minute. Why doesn't he want to be President?'

'After all the years of struggle he has a family now and he wants to be a photographer or grow pumpkins.'

'Pumpkins? Lucrative.'

'He fought in the mountains, spent years in prison. He says he is tired now and he wants to live his life.'

'Fair enough. Anyway, examples in other countries suggest that former guerrilla fighters usually don't make the best politicians. So did he register? Is he going to run?'

'After a lot of discussion, yes. It was important for me because, if he'd refused to run, then someone else had to run so the election could be democratic.'

'Xanana can't be the only person in Timor capable of being President.'

'Well, if he didn't run, according to the UN, the person who had to run had to be me.'

'There you go. Wouldn't that have been great?'

'Lynne, I have no plans to be President. For the next five years of my life, every ambition I had for my own life would have ended. I have fought for my country for years now. I am tired. I am not a government politician. There are other things I want to do, that I enjoy doing.'

'Pumpkins?'

'No, you know, there are many things that can be done for this country without being President.'

'I imagine East Timor has the distinction of being the only country in the world where no one wants the top job.'

'So you can see that while you were having this "devastating" experience there were other important issues going on, more important than yours.'

'And that's not to negate my circumstances and extraordinary bravery, Minister, I'm sure.'

'I am leaving. I have to go to the airport,' he says, and the back door of his car is opened for him and he heads towards it.

'Where are you going?' I ask as he gets in.

'Oh, I'm going on a long trip, official visits . . . and I'm going to the Oscars.' Finally, he smiles.

'Of course you are.'

'And Lynne . . .' I turn back towards the car to see him pointing at me, 'the outfit is much improved, very chaste. But, really, I don't think the colour suits you.'

The car door closes and the lovely, firm bodyguards jump into various vehicles in the motorcade and the tyres crunch as they all head away, roosters scattering, and I watch them disappear from my spot on the veranda and, with the coast clear, I light up a cigarette in parabens to the end of struggle. Then five Timorese children run up to me, 'Bonoite, diak ka lae!' and I click PLAY on my laptop — hit it Kylie — and in the early night-time, as the Southern Cross shines above us, we all dance and sing along, 'La, la, la. La, la, la, la, la . . . ', no need for English language skills, 'La, la, la. La, la, la, la, la . . .' Yes, parabens on the end of struggle.

4

THE MALAE SYNDROME

A UN Land Rover moves into the compound in the dark. It is an unusual arrival and so The Family and I, we all come out to greet it. Inside is a lovely, firm bodyguard, a Brazilian, and he announces that he has come to talk to me.

He has dropped his 'principal' off at the airport and it appears he now sees a window of opportunity. Oh dear. This is very uncomfortable in a Catholic country where I am supposed to be the Virgin Mary, played out under the gaze of a public gallery.

'Hello, Lynne, how are you?'

'Good . . . good.'

'That's good.'

'Yes, good. Um, and you?' Go away. Shoo. He may be firm and lovely, but I really don't want to be picked up right here, right now.

'Oh, I'm good, thank you.'

'Good.' Many Timorian faces are watching this display, fascinated.

'So, Lynne, things are good?'

'Yes, good. Look, I have to go and pray or something similarly moral so . . .'

'Oh good, yes, well, have you eaten?'

'Yes, I have.'

'Oh, good, how was that?'

'Good.' Go a-way, away, now, quickly.

'Good. Well, anyway, Lynne, I was wondering, would you like to go out sometime, maybe this week?'

'Okay, yes, fine, must go now.'

'Let me give you my number.' Eek! Where does this idiot think he is? Rio?

'No,' I speak quietly and quickly. 'Pick me up Thursday night at 6 pm in front of TVTL, don't come into reception, I'll find your car. Must go.' Oh God, I've just made a date with a Brazilian UN police officer. 'Thanks for popping by,' I chirrup loudly for the benefit of the onlookers and vanish into the house with my halo only slightly askew.

I'm doomed to never get eight hours' sleep in this place. And this time the roosters have competition, from the East Timor police who patrol the compound. With their principal away they feel the security risk diminished to the point where it is appropriate to sit in the garage with loud music booming while engaged in ths building of their capacity for playing cards. Unfortunately the garage adjoins my room. Meanwhile, a terrorist cell has probably driven a semitrailer into the compounds and is spending hours noisily constructing a bomb under José's bed. 'IS THIS YOUR WORKPLACE OR A SOCIAL CLUB?' I try to ascertain at 3 am to be met with howls of laughter, as these professionals in the course of their duty roll on the ground with uniforms akimbo.

Thank God Timor produces coffee because my consumption is increasing each morning commensurate with the decreasing slumber I manage to achieve each night. And, sure, I may be tired but I'm sick and tired of being isolated to the upper-class dining room, served by the maid

— I'm not Lady Muck, and I'm homesick. So with a royal flourish I pick up my coffee and head down into the kitchen and sit down.

The community down here is somewhat startled but I can see they are fascinated with this display too, 'Bondia, Lynne, you want something?' says Dulce.

'Bondia. Well, actually, I'd like to eat with your family if that's okay.'

'Okay, please, sit, eat, Lynne.' They are, I think, pleased. They certainly tolerate me and so they resume their morning-time routines, Dulce icing cakes to be served in Eduardo's Portuguese restaurant, Elsie opening cans of sweetened condensed milk, the children staring at me as they tentatively reach into the bread basket on the table in front of me before running off screeching with laughter. Meanwhile other servants are moving to and fro burdened with a load of something or other. I listen to the women chattering away in a Tetum and Bahasa Indonesia blend, and at intervals Dulce emits 'Ay!' in exclamation.

I chase away the festering dogs in Tetum (they don't understand English: '*sai* = rack off now before your diseases jump species'). Even the privileged families here seem to have no access to a vet, which I realise, of course, is a First World luxury. There is a clock on the wall with Xanana's face as the face, although it doesn't work; alongside me is a wall constructed of bamboo to shoulder height and otherwise the view of the mountains dotted with shacks around us (here comes the 7 am UN helicopter on schedule, whump, whump, whump); the floor is rough concrete and the roof is corrugated-iron, making the area an oven even at this hour of the morning.

'Atelogu,' I say, walking out of the compound to the requisite wolf whistles from the police — they really shouldn't test me given my sleep deprivation issues — and out on the street there is a remarkable level of activity as the dilapidated taxis honk and groups of men point at me, 'Malae, malae.' 'Hello Missus, fuck, fuck.' The latter I can comprehend, the former I want to understand so I open the phrasebook: '*malae* = foreigner'. Yes, I am a bit conspicuous, no other white woman is walking this road, 'Malae, malae.' 'Hello Missus,' and I arrive, dusty, harassed and drenched in sweat, at the UN's Office of Communication and Public Information, vowing to do the taxi tour of Dili from now on.

The OCPI is housed in a large white rundown building, and it comprises Televisaun Timor Lorosa'e together with Radio UNTAET and a publications unit producing magazines and public information materials like posters for distribution around the nation. I expect a dynamic and high-tech hub of ground-breaking independent journalism but the immediate impact is the pong from the loos — a remarkable stench emanating from a place beside reception I will never venture into, which requires repeated and well-timed breath-holding throughout a workday.

TVTL is the television station established by UNTAET, the United Nations Transitional Administration in East Timor, for the broadcasting of Tetum language programming, replacing the highly controlled media that existed under the Indonesians and was destroyed two years ago. Yet the programs are now produced with equipment no self-respecting American would take on holiday. The crews here use handheld digital cameras of appalling condition, scratched, dirty, bits pulled off. I am surprised the UN gave such second-hand cast-offs to this national broadcaster, until it is pointed out to me that the contributions were in mint condition not that long ago, and I wonder at the folly of the Timorese in ruining technology they would not be able to self-fund; surely that kind of disregard is reserved for rich white kids with new toys on Christmas Day?

The computers are in similar condition but they perform as required, I note as I turn on a monitor, which springs to life with images of men and women performing extraordinary sexual acts. I find my head turning sideways, intrigued, to examine feats of physical contortion I didn't know my body could perform. I can understand, now, the fascination the Timorese men have with white women if Internet porn is their exposure to our culture. Realising my colleagues are watching on, I clear my throat, cross my legs and reboot.

My job is within the newsroom. I am charged with the task of capacity-building the Timorese news journalists in editorial skills, particularly in the coverage of the upcoming presidential election campaign and the transition to Independence. It is an essential element in any democracy, especially a new one, that people know what is happening and changing in their nation, that they learn how to participate in democratic processes such as elections, and that they understand the endemic domestic violence, sexual abuse and hygiene issues here.

The morning editorial meeting is held in Tetum, which clearly impacts on my ability to contribute. Afterwards I attempt to talk to my '*kolegas* = colleagues', all of whom can speak some English but choose to do so with varying enthusiasm. The boss of the newsroom just ignores me; he is unwilling to accept advice from a malae. One kolega is patently unable to focus on my discussion with him thanks to the distraction provided by my tits, which are unfortunately positioned at eye-level for most Timorese men. The women peer at me with curiosity and whisper amongst themselves.

My mobile phone rings. I am relieved at the thought of an easy dialogue for the first time in days and I eagerly move outside, past reception, holding my nose. 'Ello.'

'Hello, remember me? It's your mother calling from the wealth and comfort of the lucky country.' She laughs.

Around me as I talk are Timorian employees in common repose — smoking clove cigarettes, squatting on their haunches. They try to see up my skirt but otherwise they're not particularly pleased to see me. Already I am aware that '*malae* = scab foreigner', the more accurate phrasebook translation, for it is not a popular beast here. We are a novelty at best, but generally we are perceived as the cultural imperialists, the colonisers. We are privileged, rich, educated, independent. The malae, according to the Timorese, have come to their country, earned a fortune, cavorted with sexual abandon, worn indecent clothing, made little effort to learn the local languages, and flaunted their wealth and opportunity with activities out of Timorian league, such as chatting on mobile phones. 'Um, Mum, can I call you back later?'

Back in the newsroom I notice my handbag is clearly not where I left it. Instead of sitting discreetly beside my chair it now sits on top of a desk in clear view, and among the disturbed contents is my purse, which sits open. I look to see that US$100 has disappeared — the money I intended to give Dulce for my room. Now, it's okay, I have perspective, I know the thief could do with the money *but* I do feel rather unwelcome in my new workplace. It is clear that it's Us versus Them. Still, I won't make a complaint and, by reacting in this way, I hope the money is an investment that shows my kolegas I am a loyal member of the newsroom. Despite the examples of malae behaviour that must have come before me, I see it as my personal ambition to change the stereotype because some of us genuinely want to help them attain our level of opportunity. But a hundred bucks! Man, I hope they attain our level of opportunity quickly.

Charitably stoic, I join the news crew as they head out onto the road to chase their stories for the day and everyone piles into the one TV crew car. And what is remarkable is not how many people can fit inside one five-seater vehicle, it is the type of vehicle — the Indian version of a Lada, this one called a Tata — which resembles the Popemobile with its box-like shape, parsimonious detailing, windows free of tinting and lack of functional features (including brakes, it seems). And, in keeping with Timorian tradition, every optional extra has been looted, leaving empty receptacles and wires hanging from the dash. The Tata even has a logo for the Timorese Government on the doors — 'Governu' — which wouldn't imbue many with confidence in the independence of the broadcaster. So the one crew car drives away with its cargo of six journalists, attendant cameramen and sound recordists (and me), all arms, legs, handicams, tripods, handbags, clove cigarettes and chatter, combining to create a wonderful Third World chaos as we strive to be there as the news happens.

I work with men called José. The women who work at TVTL are named mainly in honour of Timor's favourite saints. And all of them, like many Timorese, have difficulty with my name — it is completely foreign to them; to them it is merely a sound: Lim? Line? Leeen. That'll do.

The Josés and the saints all news-gather with an organic style. The cameramen have an aversion to using tripods, creating an artistic wobble effect, and occasionally they are satisfied to shoot the profile or back of head to lend variety. Colour balance isn't held in high regard and thus the sky is a bright white in the background of any shot. Sound is a random thing, it comes and goes, leaving the viewer to guess the goings-on. There is no effective archiving of material, which sees footage of consequential events recording the history of this nation just disappearing into the ether. Pictures are used repeatedly throughout a bulletin, meaning the same billowing flag shot can be showcased four times in half an hour. The voiceovers have a special style without pause in a breathless speed that is actually impressive. The practice of writing to pictures is just seen as a quaint malae hobby, and instead at TVTL the words and vision have no association, giving the stories a clever cryptic quality. But even more compelling is the unwillingness of the journalists to present each side of a story.

'So then, Fatima, will we go now to get so-and-so's reaction to being called a murderer and autocrat? No? Of course not, how silly of me, it's lunchtime. Oh well, not to worry, the accusations will merely be broadcast around the nation. I'm sure he won't mind.'

Thus, the Timorese put their news to air each night, the first at 6.30 . . . or 7.15 . . . or 8.00, whenever it's ready, with presenters wearing suits in a country without Armani or Zegna, and an impossibly hot climate. Watching the broadcast of one strobing ensemble that needs a warning to epileptics, it strikes me that the dress should be in keeping with the normal style of Timor: Che Guevara top and combat pants? Or what about the popular Osama bin Laden T-shirt that gets around town?

Anyway, what would I know? Any instruction I contribute goes unheeded, as the Timorese assert their authority. The United Nations has been rebuilding Timor's institutions since '99 and now responsibility is being handed over to the locals in time for Independence, but they're not quite skilled yet. UN staff are employed in mentoring during the handover but the Timorians want the malae to 'go home' — a refrain heard often here. God, and I've only just arrived.

In fact, I've arrived at a time when the Malae Syndrome has been aggravated by a recent influx of foreigners into East Timor; people who have flown in to work on readying the nation for Independence; people from all over the world who knew someone in the UN. The old adage is true here: it's who you know that gets you the job, which would be fine if you were known for your professional experience, but shared taste in beer, nationality or familial ties don't assure of the appropriate qualifications. Thus, there seems to be a lot of capacity-building of the malae required, which somewhat defeats the purpose. 'I've never worked in a radio station before so I am pinching myself!' crows one successful British candidate, unaware of the pathos of her statement.

Ignorant of it also is a Peruvian colleague, who contends with the frustrations of being unheeded by raising his voice in tempers, which do nothing to endear him to the locals. 'You people are stupid! You produce the worst news service I have ever seen! Why do you refuse to learn?' None of this serves to endear him to me either and so, after his morning outburst, every day he goes to the pub. And we all wish he'd just go home.

'Lynne, you are a journalist, you must write a book on all this! People must know!' says Gabriella Carrascalao, my Timorian boss who spent her exile years in Australia and has been newly ensconced in the top job at TVTL. An inexperienced manager in an unenviable position straddling a cultural clash.

Still, we have months until Independence to overcome the Malae Syndrome and create a quality, free media, I say to myself every night as I return to The Family and a cultural exchange of a no less peculiar yet happier kind. '*Mai han* = come eat', and I am pleased these days to be ensconced down in the kitchen, with a buffet of food on the table — whole fish with a sauce of shallots and tomatoes, '*ai manas* = chilli', an enormous colander of rice, a broth of chicken and vegetables, a stew of beans and pork. In accordance with the class structure, I serve myself in the first wave together with Dulce and her husband, next come the adult relatives, then their children, then the children of the servants, then the servants have their own echelons determining access to whatever is left.

'I love the fish!' Blank looks, blink, blink. Okay, 'Kapas, nice,' pointing at plate, 'Diak.' Sure, I can't contribute to the conversation in here but I don't have any friends in this country and it is nice to have company, especially such generous company. Saying that, I am always loath to take too much food. What if I load my plate and Elsie goes without at the other end of the procedure? I feel terrified that I could compound the poverty here. Anyway I am losing weight, a benefit that comes from living in a developing nation, a benefit only a person from the developed world could enjoy.

And we eat, all of us balancing our plates on our knees, sitting on the plastic chairs which have proliferated to tremendous numbers in Timor, and we watch South American soap operas dubbed into Indonesian on satellite TV, with Bahasa-speaking sexy Latinos and their groaning cleavages and passionate trysts that leave me sweating — mind you, that could be the ai manas, or the corrugated-iron roof: is there ever a respite from the heat?

Seeking out a respite on this Wednesday night, I adjourn to the veranda and start applying nail polish in preparation for my date the following eve. Women are not supposed to have painted nails here but I figure I am prepared to make the remarkable compromise of merely painting my toenails as a balance between custom and my own standards of vanity — particularly as I want to wear my new pair of slip-on sandals. But the nail polish doesn't dry in the humidity. Catastrophe! Now this is hardship. But it's okay, I will adapt, I am adapting. So much so that I am losing the vestiges of my First World perspective, proven today when I purchased my new shoes at the US$4 price tag, then went into a shop across the road, saw the very same shoes discounted by 25 per cent and said, 'Shit,' out loud.

I run the gauntlet of the malodorous reception area and emerge from TVTL in the late hours of the day. I walk outside the gates and locate the UN vehicle idling at the side of the road. I hop in.

'Hello, Maluco*.' An awkward kiss on each cheek.

'Hello, Lynne. How are you, are you good?'

'Yes, I am good.'

'Good.'

'And you, are you good?'

'Yes, Lynne, I am good.'

'Good, Maluco.' Stop it, Lynne, stop it!

The car moves away from the kerb and onwards towards the oceanfront. 'I want to watch the sunset,' I say.

'Good, Lynne. I want to take you to the Central boat, do you know it?'

'No, I don't. Is it good, Maluco?' Lynne! Stop it now!

To be honest, I am petrified. I loathe first dates. They make me completely insecure. On this occasion, the UN police radio provides a diversion and I am fascinated to hear the Timorian police officers communicating on the official police communications tool: 'Meow.'

'What on earth are they doing?'

'Oh, it drives me crazy but the Timorese police officers like to play games with the radio. They don't see how important it is, so they do things like meow.'

'Meow. Okay. It's cute but not constructive in the game of catching bad guys, I imagine.'

'No, I complain but they don't want to listen to me so what more can I do?'

The meowing stops and these pillars of Timorese society, the enforcers of law and order, start singing. I turn on the Land Rover's generic radio and, sure enough, they are singing along to the song playing on Radio Falantil, 'Who Let the

* For legal reasons the name of this character has had to be replaced with a pseudonym.

Dogs Out'. 'Woof, woof, woof, woof,' they bark. Animal noises are a motif it seems.

We turn into a carpark that skirts the sea, wander up the long gangplank and onto the luxury hotel in Timor. A floating palace. A cruise ship docked in Dili Harbour complete with suites, restaurants and a cocktail bar at the stern. We find our way to the back deck and sit down. A Timorian waiter attends us. 'I'll have a margarita.'

'No worries,' and he grins at his multilinguistics and I do too. The night has started well. And thus I sit and watch the bobbing yachts moored nearby and the island of Atauro just out there as the sun sets over the horizon, with a margarita in my hand. Hardship? Bullshit. I *am* Lady Muck.

'This is very, very good, Maluco.'

'No worries, Lynne.' And he, too, adopts the language of my country.

'Ah, you speak Australian?'

'Well, I try. There are so many Australians here I try to learn it. Gee-day maaate.'

'Close.'

'But, Lynne, sometimes I talk to Australians and I can't understand what they are saying.'

'Yes, you see, it is a special language of its own.'

'You can teach me.'

'No, I think it'd be much more constructive for you to teach me Portuguese.' Thought bubble: 'In that lovely accent of yours.'

'Oh, okay. Muito gusto.' Palpitation from me. 'Tem olhos verdes lindos.'

'See, this is much better than "Beauty bonza, you little ripper", although that phrase applies.'

'I'm sorry? I told you that you have beautiful green eyes.'

'Even better. I like Portuguese, it has many merits.'

'I'm sorry, Lynne, I don't understand.'

'Oh, no worries, please continue. And I think you should teach me about Portuguese wine too as a relationship builder between our two nations.'

'Oh, yes, let's see. I think we should have a bottle of the Planalto or the Casal Garcia. Have you tried these wines?'

'No, but I intend to do so as a diplomatic gesture.'

Brazilians speak with a Shakespearean-style English. 'Speak-ed, walk-ed, liv-ed,' and so, just as Maluco can bring on palpitations in me when he speaks his own language, he can bring on palpitations when he speaks mine too.

'I lov-ed your green eyes the first time I saw you.'

'Alack.'

'Lynne, you are okay, you lik-ed the wine?'

'Don't mind me, just a heart palpitation, verily' (caused by Latino men).

'Oh . . . good.'

'So you are a police officer in Brazil I assume.'

'No, I am a fireman.'

Palpitation. 'A fireman, you say?'

'Yes, in Brazil our emergency services are not separated like yours and so I am a fireman in Brazil but I am part of the same system as the police so I can come here and work for UNPOL.'

The United Nations Police, or UNPOL, is the police service responsible for law enforcement and the training of the East Timor Police Service (ETPS). Thousands of police officers from all over the world are in East Timor wearing the uniforms of their home forces, creating a parade of differing outfits in various hues of blue, all emblazoned with flag badges and the embroidered UN symbol. Unlike the peacekeepers (who are soldiers), the UNPOL officers can choose to live in houses rather than barracks, they can eat in the restaurants, and they have autonomy once they finish their shifts. Which means that this particular UNPOL officer can drink Casal Garcia on the back deck of the Central with me.

Tonight Maluco is wearing civilian clothes — jeans and a shirt untucked over the gun attached to his belt in its holster. A gun. I've never really seen a gun. A pistol. Loaded. In close proximity to me, which I find rather exhilarating.

'Do you have to wear your gun all the time?'

'Oh yes, Lynne. For protection. I am your own personal bodyguard tonight.'

Satisfied with that explanation I imagine I could very well require close personal protection in this dangerous country.

Thus, after an eve of building ties between the countries of Australia and Brazil, we drive home with both of us full of good spirits and I note that drink driving is *de rigueur* here, but I don't have a care in the world because the warm wind is in my hair as we drive along the waterfront and Maluco catches my eye and he and I smile and on the police radio the ETPS officers apparently sense the chemistry in the air and feeling it timely they delve into their repertoire and simulate sex.

5

SURFACE TENSION

It's a Saturday and there's no great sense of urgency amongst my kolegas even though two news bulletins will be produced today, the Sunday news, too, so everyone can have the day off tomorrow, which I think negates the value of the word 'news', and we've just been turned away from a Fretilin conference, told it's media-free, leaving us with a four-minute hole in the 'olds'. Still, in a city that is filled with stories, it is just a matter of time before some political or social issue presents itself, and so we motor slowly in the Popemobile along the streets of Dili.

It's '*manas loro-loron* = hot as always' and the chatter fills the car, as I watch the harbour peek through the shipping containers littering the foreshore. It's a shame that these monstrous iron boxes, designed for pragmatism, not aesthetics, have colonised the prettiest parts of this town, obscuring views and taking over footpaths. Who on earth put them there and there and there? Today, though, I see that trucks have arrived to take them somewhere else and, while the Dili clean-up appeals to this aesthete, she marvels that the Japanese Government can provide an 'emergency fund' to remove rusted, discarded objects and cut grass and pick up litter in time for Kofi Annan's arrival for Independence. Is this Ghanian Secretary-General of the United Nations unable to cast his eyes upon debris, otherwise it would be an emergency?

My musings are interrupted when the comedic travelling mass of humanity I'm within drives by a park just near the city centre. Ten people are standing in a circle and we slow down, curious; and we turn around, intrigued; and we pull to a stop, clambering out, arms, legs, smoking cigarettes and damaged technology, prying into their story, doubling the numbers of the crowd.

In the unkempt grass (yet to come to the attention of the Japanese emergency fund) and on the edge of the park, stands a group of women weeping while they watch a man digging. Digging for what? More men swagger around on the periphery of the pit. They move with the bravado the men feign here — chest out, cocky, uninterested, in the manner I assume was developed during years of trying to pretend to their oppressors they weren't frightened (or short). Yet all of these men, despite the attempted illusion of indifference, seem shaken by the proceedings. Whatever they are.

One of them approaches and tells me: 'A family is digging for the father. He was killed in '99. That man digging, he says he saw the murder, he thinks he knows where the body is buried.'

Ninety-nine. That number needs no more explanation. It comes laden with visual images of militia in the streets, people moving with silence and fear in the mountains, bodies dragged through dusty roads, families sheltering in the UN compound, an election that turned horribly wrong — even if it did produce a clear result. Self-determination for East Timor. The election process had been administered well by the UN, ballot papers distributed, the turnout better than expected, little vote tampering, and the numbers announced to an international audience appropriately impressed. The carnage that followed, the easily anticipated, inevitable violence, the lives lost, 80 per cent of the nation's infrastructure destroyed, that was collateral damage, the price paid for Independence; the victims, therefore, duly canonised martyrs.

'Why now?' I ask about the body of this particular martyr that has been lying under the public's feet for three years.

'They haven't been able to afford to do this before. Now he can have a funeral in Baucau, his district.'

We sequester ourselves down to wait while the digging continues. It is hard to comprehend that death lies just there, as UN vehicles whiz by and passengers hanging out of the little public buses — microlets — yell greetings to a group which is growing in size now.

'That's a leg!' in Tetum every now and then. False alarms. My kolegas giggle and play tricks with their clove cigarettes to pass the time. Meanwhile, lying in the car, insulated from the rising, falling tensions but aware of a methodical and consistent sound of digging, I'm labouring under the weight of the humidity and wondering if my hair will ever dry in this country and whether the consistent damp at my scalp will manifest in mould soon, and the heat infiltrates from outside the windows where the past continues to influence the present and a handicam immortalises it all.

Then screams rise and I scramble, along with others, onto what can no longer be perceived as a park but a graveyard. This is no false alarm, there is no possibility of confusion, a man once alive lies on the ground dead beside the earth that had entombed him for years, this man, father of these women, uncle of the others, and owner of this body, which lies here, stiffly.

The women shriek with a wail foreign to this malae, a high-pitched, horrible screech that pierces my heart and carries over the city of Dili. The gravedigger holds a dead rooster over the hole. The body is wrapped in fabric, a knot at the head, one at the feet, making it a thin, rigid package. I get down on my knees in the freshly dug dirt to take a photo of the pit between the feet of the utterly transfixed crowd but standing again I can't photograph the women as they cry out of faces contorted in grief, emitting the sound of pure pain. This pain should never be captured on film, I decide. A decision I regret. For this is the picture of Timor, the real Timor. A Timor still coming to terms with the horrors experienced here. Families still feeling the agony of loss. People still struggling to survive utter poverty. A nation still rebuilding from the ashes of '99.

Yes, this is the First Nation of the New Millennium. Clean streets will be presented to the world come Independence. But the scars and the legacies will remain, barely hidden. An hour's digging below the surface is all that's required.

6

HISTORY 101

Hooray! After weeks of homesickness and friendlessness I am going out to lunch with some of my malae kolegas and we are heading to City Café, the busy day-and-night meeting place where the international community congregates. This institution has been servicing the sequence of missions in Timor for years with a gamut of fare — coffee, cake, meals, alcohol — all in a humming environment filled with disparate uniforms, languages and tastes from the cuisines of the world.

As I sit at an outdoor table under the shade of the front awning, street children offer to wash cars at entrepreneurial prices, a wizened Timorese man demands my attention and gestures to a stick over a shoulder with pineapples tied at either end, young boys hawk cartons of Marlboro Red or pirate CDs, while others advertise they are trading the very latest in Scandinavian film-making: 'Jiggy jig?' 'Dollar Missus?' 'Hello Missus?' 'Ananas Missus?' 'Australian Missus?' 'Hungry Missus?' 'CD Missus?'

Distracted Timorese waitresses take orders that present themselves randomly. My Greek salad comes with cheddar cheese (in a touch of innovation) and a black hair for garnish.

Fighting a losing battle to eat it in the heat before it wilts into liquid form, every now and then impressive vehicles drive slowly by with the occupants leering out from behind dark sunglasses, their pumped biceps pressed against the outsides of their car doors for best effect. They are attractive men in dark blue uniforms with blue UN berets perched dashingly on the sides of their heads. What on earth is this magnetic sight?

'Fucking GNR,' says a male dining companion. The women don't share the sentiment. The Guarda Nacional Republicana is the Portuguese special police unit, the riot police. They patrol as a preventative measure, to show the Timorese they are watching, ready to activate, but really they spend most of their time patrolling the beach front and cafés watching the malae women.

The Portuguese have an influence here which harks back to the early sixteenth century, when a small band of its Catholic friars settled in an area on the sea where they built, with the generous volunteer labour of the Timorese, a monstrous fort complete with moat. The monks then embarked on a selfless quest to spread the Word, which required them, curiously, to demand control over the island. However, these God-fearing men met resistance from the empire-building Dutch, with their colonial aspirations and desire to own the valuable sandalwood covering the mountains. So the next few centuries were spent periodically in bloody skirmish until, after centuries of rivalry, a clever solution was reached in the 1859 Treaty of Lisbon, which saw them simply split Timor in half. Holland took the west and Portugal took the east along with, in a nod to sentimentality, the original landing place, the pocket of land of Oecussi, which lies smack in West Timor and contains that nice fort with its moat and the unmarked graves of the one thousand Timorese who died in its construction.

For all of its skirmishing, Portugal actually colonised Timor rather half-heartedly and the envoys sent were not from the intelligentsia of Portuguese society, but rather from the riff-raff classes in a policy which was rather *en vogue* in those days, given that it underpinned the colonisation of my country as well. Sure, these renegades were transported in order for them to pay penance for crimes committed, however in this tropical paradise they amassed riches, married local girls, and created an upper echelon that consisted of them. And, thus, history tells us, the Portuguese squattocracy sipped coconut milk, established sweeping coffee plantations and fathered children, meanwhile neglecting any responsibilities of a community sort.

Then Portugal's President Marcello Caetano was overthrown during a coup in Lisbon in 1974, which left that nation in somewhat of a hurry to get rid of its colonies. By the time the colonising administration left the East Timorese to themselves in 1975, fleeing to Atauro Island as the Indonesians advanced, 10 kilometres of road had been built and the general population remained uneducated and living a subsistence life in desperate poverty. The exceptions were the Portuguese families who, to this day, comprise the nation's elite, an upper echelon that consists of them.

Just as it was clever of their forebears to create an upper class, membership of which required what they alone had, Portuguese blood, it is clever of the elite families now to insist that membership requires the same. Chips off the old blocks. Thus, the people who now run the country represent those elite families. And they are augmenting their position by cleverly imposing an official language that only they can speak (Portuguese), while insisting on the eradication of the language the people speak (Bahasa Indonesia).

Why can't the leadership speak Bahasa? Because they were generally away in exile for the duration of the Indonesian annexation. Some in Portugal, some in Mozambique, very few in the United States, many in Australia. Now the elite are returning to Timor and, in tandem, the former coloniser is sending its elite forces to support this re-Portugalisation, which they do in the most attractive of ways — and here comes the GNR again as I push my plate away in the City Café and my swoon mixes with the cacophony: 'Jiggy jig?' 'Dollar Missus?'

Regardless of the display, I've got to get back to TVTL in time to witness the adoption of the Constitution in East Timor's Parliament House. It is an important day and I'm overjoyed at the prospect of witnessing history as it occurs.

I rush to the television station and kolegas are squatting on their haunches and smoking clove cigarettes out the front. 'Botardi! Come on! Mai!' I yell excitedly as I dart past them. Others are milling around in the newsroom, giggling. 'Let's go!' I say. They all look at me without enthusiasm. 'This is a big day!' They ignore me. 'Look, for once I really think we shouldn't be late, I doubt the parliament will wait for us to arrive.' It is a habit they have here, being late. And it is a particularly mortifying habit for journalists to have when it often means they turn up at occasions as they end. 'Come on! This is great! History is being made! Your democratic Constitution! We'll miss it!' Finally, the Popemobile is stuffed with its cargo of media representatives, and it moves towards the octagonal Australian-built parliament building. Inside there's a vast screen providing live coverage of the discussion on the floor of the chamber and direct translation via earphones for those in the public enclosure, '*tais* = traditional fabrics' representing the districts of Timor hanging from the walls, wood panelling and even a press gallery.

I run in and my kolegas dawdle, giggling, behind me and the debate in the high-tech chamber has begun between the individuals who were voted onto a committee responsible for drafting the nation's Constitution. And in addition to imposing Portuguese as the official language of the nation, they've also shown a pioneering interpretation of democratic principles and written themselves in as the first government. So the people won't get a chance to go to the polls and vote for their parliamentary representatives and, therefore, this will be a democratic government with the remarkable distinction of not having been elected as such. Yes, this is history, all right, and I'm loving the audaciousness of it all. I've got to hand it to the committee. Why go to the expense of having an election with all that inconvenient campaigning and baby-kissing bullshit when you can just ensconce yourselves as leaders of the nation? Even thought the President, on the contrary, will still be chosen by a general election, a lot of trouble for a toothless position — that's right, the Constitution states that the President will have no actual power. Well, at least the people will feel they have participated in democracy! And, thus, the first lesson of history is that it repeats itself.

The Constitution is adopted and those on the chamber floor embrace. Well you would, wouldn't you? And we all file out to find a sumptuous array of catering awaiting us. Wine, beer and tables groaning with food. I locate the TVTL journalist who's earmarked to do this story. This saint thinks she's fabulous and perhaps she is. I wouldn't have a clue given that I've never seen her do anything more productive than flirting, really. 'We have to go.'

'No! We no go!' and she resumes her activity.

'It's three-thirty, come on, there's three hours until news time.'

'No! Tomorrow, not possible tonight!' and she rolls her eyes at me and says something to an amorous new MP in Tetum which contains a word I understand, '*bulak* = crazy'. I help myself to a glass of chardonnay from a silver tray as it whizzes by and I resign myself to accepting that it's their country and it is up to them to want a questing media that reports on matters of public consequence with an appropriate timeliness.

'Can I have taste?' I am about to take a draught when a Timorese journalist asks to have a sip of my wine.

'Why mine? Do you want me to get you a glass?'

'No!' she says.

'Oh, I soooo don't want to be responsible for you developing a taste for alcohol.' Timorese women aren't allowed to imbibe and while journos generally do have a reputation for drinking, I'm not going to capacity-build her in this particular skill, despite my proven bona fides.

'Oh, come on, Leeen.'

'Oh, okay,' after all, I'm not her mother. 'A sip. Then give it back.' I pass her the glass, feeling that I'm dealing in illicit drugs.

'Do not bring your filthy Australian habits here and corrupt these girls!' Gabriella rounds on me.

'Um, I . . .'

'Just because you can behave like trash where you come from doesn't mean you can come here and teach my girls your disgusting behaviour.' All right, all right! I humbly apologise for my nationality's preponderance for disgusting, filthy conduct which makes us trashy, and Gabriella glares at me before moving off to join the saints and I hear the word 'bulak' a couple more times as they point over at me with Portuguese egg tarts in their hands and no concern for the impending TVTL news slot — and I must be crazy because it all doesn't make a great deal of sense to me, as I place the glass of chardonnay back on a passing tray.

Thus, come Friday, I need a drink, which has me at the AMOS — a ship that, like the Central, is moored on Dili Harbour. This one isn't posh, though. It's an ugly monstrosity composed of shipping containers and the scene of the local disco. It's also notorious, despite its lucrative business, for choosing not to pay tax to this poor country. I know that I am about to contribute to the burgeoning off-shore bank account of the owners of this floating pleasure palace but I need to do something more active than watching South American soap operas dubbed into Bahasa. Even more specifically, I've heard that the men are usually proposing marriage by 1 am, and right now I don't care who I've gotta pay for that pleasure.

So I walk up the gangplank and into a place that awes me. Many, many men, to use Dulce-speak, and I need a drink, which sees me at the bar, 'A vodka soda, thank you,' and suitably hydrated I, less intimidated and freer of inhibition, approach the gyrating masses. In a spot along the stern rail, there is Ignatius Jones, the Australian showman who is here to organise the Independence celebrations, and he is holding court with a scotch in a hand while he basks in the attention of a cluster of gay Timorese.

I'm on the back deck of a boat, swaying to Portuguese pop music, as twinkling surrounds me from the disco lights and the yachts on the harbour and the buildings along the shoreline and up in the mountains surrounding Dili and the stars shining above us all. There are few moments more magnificent in a life, I'm thinking, and I move my hips to the booming Latino beat with the breeze coming off the sea cooling the sweat on my skin, when, to illustrate my point, I'm engulfed by Latino men.

7

TRAINING WHEELS

I'm in a shop looking for something special. It's Corrie's twelfth birthday, an opportunity for me to repay, in some small measure, the hospitality The Family has shown me. What does one buy a pubescent girl, I wonder. I imagine she is too old for dolls and I patently refuse to buy her an outfit in lilac. Finally, I see it. A bike.

I've noticed that the boys in The Family have bikes but the girls have to walk wherever they go. The joy I felt as a child getting my new pink Dragster is unforgettable. US$60 later and I'm loading a bicycle wrapped in bubblewrap into the back of a cab and unloading it at TVTL where the Timorians all stare at this wondrous thing. You'd think it was plated in gold. They ask me if it's mine. 'Well, no. It's a bit small. It's for a Timorese girl.' They look shocked.

'A girl?' they ask me and I am worried that, once again, I may be breaking a gender rule.

I carry it into my boss's office, 'Gabriella, is it inappropriate for me to give this to Corrie for her birthday?'

Gabriella baulks. 'Um, couldn't you think of anything else?'

Uh-oh. It sits beside me in the newsroom for the afternoon, gathering reverential comment, and I am concerned now that I might be doing something really wrong, again. Still, I lug it into a taxi at the end of the day and disembark in the compound. The boys run out and stare at my burden. 'Missus Lynne! Missus Lynne!'

'Bonoite, Corrie nebe?'

They point me towards the kitchen. I walk in and Corrie looks stunned. Dulce says, 'Ay, Lynne!' as I place the bike on the concrete floor in front of her daughter, and Corrie surveys it for a little while before turning back to the South American soap opera dubbed into Bahasa on the television. 'Thank you, Lynne,' she says softly.

I'm a bit embarrassed so I go to my room, worried that I've offended her. 'Lynne, mai han!' and by the time the dinner process starts the bike leans forlornly against a wall, the bubblewrap in place. Uh-oh.

In the morning I head for work. I've foregone breakfast due to the whole situation and I'm cursing that I didn't err on the side of caution and buy her a doll in a lilac frock. Moron, Lynne, I'm thinking, as a mantra. Walking past the kitchen I can't help but look in to see if the bike remains against that wall. It does. But right now, a young girl, Corrie, is kneeling in front of it with a look of wonder on her face and she's gently, as though it's plated with gold, easing the bubblewrap from her very first bike.

Beep, beep. Beep, beep. My phone. **1 new message. He's landed.**

I reply, **It's nothing a bottle of duty-free vodka won't withstand.** I press SEND.

Beep, beep. Beep, beep. My phone. **1 new message. LOL, girl!**

Laugh out loud indeed! A deep throat within the Foreign

Affairs Ministry has taken it upon herself to alert me to José's arrival in Dili. I log on to the UNTAET internal website, go to the classifieds, search through the homes-to-rent category and find one in my price bracket:

> There is a house with two bedroom, one bathroom and one hall in safety area with UN neighbor. Now one bedroom for rent to friendly and moral lady. Decline gentleman's contact.

Perhaps that's not the best alternative to my current domicile. Ramos-Horta could have posted that ad.

As I head home in a taxi with the requisite booming Boney M and the bouncing dogs on the dashboard, I look out at the traffic around me and I'm distracted from my moody thoughts by the GNR patrol. Berets, sunglasses, biceps. Alongside them is an entire family balanced on a motorcycle, Dad driving, two little girls, and Mum breastfeeding the latest addition on the back. Beside that sight is a motorcade. Is it José's? I look for the registration plate on the white Prado in the centre of the stream of cars and see that the number is '1', which means it holds Dr Mari Alkatiri, East Timor's new Prime Minister. I marvel at the entourages that come with public office here, when I've seen Australian government ministers at airport carousels plucking off their own baggage. I suspect, anyway, that ostentations such as entourages in my country would be met with the classification 'Wanker'. Here, however, they are curiously common, a highly visible demonstration of the gulf between the elites and the great unwashed.

After dinner I shower and peruse the bookcases. There is no opportunity to buy newspapers, magazines or books in Timor and tonight I can resist temptation no longer. I help myself to the Minister's offerings, which contain a number of international relations texts and some novels including the one I bought him for Christmas last year, *Harry Potter and the Philosopher's Stone.* I choose *The Hours* by Michael Cunningham.

Covering myself with mosquito repellent, I sit on the bamboo furniture on the veranda and immerse myself in the most beautiful of words, interrupted only when the maid's twelve-year-old child sits beside me, her body pressed against mine, and she starts to read out from a book of her own, a Tetum schoolbook. It is about a crocodile, a good crocodile, and I am overcome with delight and affection as her little face laboriously says each word aloud to me and every now and then she looks up at me and smiles and, ignoring Mrs Dalloway, I try to read along aloud too, as she points at each word with a finger. And, you know, he was a very misunderstood crocodile, that crocodile. You see, he wasn't anywhere near as frightening as everyone thought he was and so the crocodile, he just wanted to be loved. Meanwhile, I keep one ear listening for the crunch of the tyres on pebbles which, in time, I hear coming towards us — Baby and me — together with the sound of many engines, and the cars pull to their dramatic stop, including the car marked on the registration plates with the number '2', and the bodyguards launch themselves, 'Hello Maluco,' and a door is opened and José emerges. The Family come running and they all greet the Minister, the principal, their uncle, happily.

'Hello, Miss Minion. You've lost weight. You're too thin,' he says as he gives me a kiss on each cheek and sits down in the spot recently occupied by Baby, and the motorcade turns and leaves, driving around Corrie, who's riding her bike in figures of eight.

'How was your trip?'

'Good, very productive. Many meetings. God, I tell you, those Americans, they love the Timorese cause. I went to an

Oscars party, I was told to wear a stupid penguin suit and I was the only person in one, I felt ridiculous, but the Hollywood celebrities, they care very much about Timor, they all came to talk to me, telling me they support Timorese Independence, they want to help.'

'Then why are you back early?'

'Well, I had to come back and sort out the problems here. Xanana saying he is independent. God, how can you be an independent candidate when you represent nine political parties?'

'Yeah, I heard about that. What's his point?'

'Well, the other candidate represents Fretilin and, of course, Fretilin is the most powerful political party in Timor. It was the party of the freedom movement.'

'And Alkatiri and most members of the government are Fretilin.'

'Yes, but Xanana doesn't trust Fretilin to run the country and he wants his popularity to break the popularity of Fretilin.'

The President of East Timor will hold a non-executive position, which means he will not actually lead the country. The Prime Minister will continue to do so. The President will be the figurehead. Xanana, however, believes that his immense popularity will force the Prime Minister and Fretilin to be accountable to more than party politics.

'But why can't he have the nine parties on his ballot paper?'

'Exactly.'

I begin to understand. He wants to be free from party politics too, even though the opposition parties endorsed his candidacy. Hence the confusion. 'I'm sitting beside one very unhappy independent Minister, I can see.'

'Yes, you know, I was in the United States and I'm having a very successful visit and I get a phone call from Sergio Vieira de Mello about all this so I have to come back. Of course I'm angry. Xanana is being difficult, causing problems. He is blackmailing the UN. He says if he can't have a ballot paper with no political parties on it then he will pull out of the presidential race.'

'That's very melodramatic.'

'Yes, it is. But this is a man with such an inflated idea of himself. But, you know, I made him. All the years of struggle and I needed a public figure for our cause and I chose him. I could have chosen countless other freedom fighters, he was no more remarkable than any of the others.'

'But you must have chosen him because he was the true leader.'

'No. But I chose him and he went on to be the face of our cause in the biggest public relations campaign, run by me, and it goes to his head.'

'That's a rather extraordinary statement.'

'Well, it's true. Anyway, enough of that stupid idiot.'

'Alrighty. Any Hollywood offers to make the movie of your life story?'

'Yes. And I told them that an Australian woman would also be a character and so there had to be a lot of sex scenes.'

'Ahem, um, so who's going to play you? Danny DeVito?'

'No! He's that short one, no?'

'Right. Of course, what was I thinking? Well, how about a brutish Latino stud, maybe Benicio Del Toro?'

'Okay, maybe.' And he laughs his characteristic laugh, all inhalations of breath.

'You could do worse, my friend. This is my area of expertise so take my word for it.' And I laugh too.

'He-he-he,' he breathes. 'Anyway, I'm tired, I'm going to bed,' he rises to leave, 'and, Miss, you should eat more.'

'Well, more than rice at least. Bonoite, José.'

'Bonoite.'

He disappears into his room and I'm happily

contemplating that José has found another person on whom to project his stress when a UN vehicle pulls into the compound. It's Maluco. He disembarks and he, too, sits himself down on the bamboo seat that José recently occupied beside me. I am flattered by this show of boldness but I have to wonder: what on earth is he doing? Is he mad? His principal's window is just there, fronting onto the veranda!

'How are you, Lynne?'

'Um, I'm good. Look, Maluco, this isn't the best time.'

'Oh, I'll only stay a while.'

'But you do realise that staff are not supposed to sit up here, don't you?'

'Oh, sure, but I'll be quiet.'

'Okay.' I'm not entirely convinced but I'm rather delighted and maybe I am being too paranoid. After all, José lived twenty-four years of exile in First World countries so he must understand my social mores.

'The Master can't mind,' he says and I smile. It's cute of Maluco to try to use Australian pronunciation but he needs to be careful with the word 'can't'.

'So tell me about your work in Brazil? Do you like being a fireman?'

'Yes, very much, Lynne, but it can be so sad. People in the slums can try to take electricity cables from out on the streets for free power to their houses and if they cause a fire then a whole slum can burn down. Many people killed. But I like being a fireman very much.'

'In Australia, firemen are very popular. I was working as a journalist during some big bushfires at Christmas . . .'

'Oh, I know about them.'

'. . . and I was talking to some ambulance officers and one of them asked me, "Why do women like firemen more?".'

Maluco laughs and he says, 'It is the same in Brazil. Actually, once I had a big success as a fireman — I was photographed, black from the smoke, leaving a burning building with a baby in my arms.'

'Yes, that wins.' Here come the palpitations again. This man is very bad for my health, but what a way to go, I'm thinking, and I try desperately to change the subject away from great feats of masculine bravery. 'So, tell me, do you still shoot street children in Brazil?' and I manage to move the topic from the sublime to the truly ridiculous.

Eventually Maluco leaves. Was he quiet? Not really. But then, diverted by my primitive urges, I must say, I forgot to care.

Emerging in the early morning and Ramos-Horta is at the breakfast table. 'Bondia, Minister.'

'Bondia,' he replies gruffly as he eats a piece of mango.

I help myself to steaming black coffee. 'I am thinking of getting my hair cut off, I can't stand it in the heat. What do you think of this?' I show him a picture of Sarah Jessica Parker's new short hairdo from an *InStyle* magazine I brought with me to Timor, a magazine I've read so much that I've almost memorised each word.

'Fine.'

'Do you think it'll suit me? I mean, it's very short.'

'Fine.' Alrighty.

'Listen, José, I wanted to talk to you about something. I heard yesterday about an attack on an Australian woman and a GNR who, apparently, almost had his arm and a leg severed.'

'So?'

'So? Well, it's pretty alarming. I think we need to talk about this. It worried me a lot but the UN won't release any details.'

'So?' He eats more mango.

'So? I have every right to know what has occurred so I can keep myself safe. If this sort of thing is happening then all the malae women in Timor need to know so they can protect themselves.'

'Well, all you need to know is that if you come to this country and act like sluts then something can happen.'

'What? So you're saying that in Timor if a woman is culturally insensitive then it is appropriate retribution for her to be gang-raped and macheted across the face?'

'If you come here then you accept the moral rules.'

'The moral rules? If it is immoral for an Australian woman to sit in a car with a man, then how can it possibly be moral for a group of Timorese men to attack her? You are being deliberately provocative.'

He is standing now. His voice is raised. 'I have provided you with a place to stay, my family has taken care of you. If you don't like it you can go!'

I stand there, silent for once, and we stare at each other across the breakfast table, until I run from the room so he can't see the tears which are welling up.

Bursting through my door and under the gaze of the glo-in-the-dark Jesus I'm sobbing as I pack my bags. Then I sit quietly waiting, wiping my nose with the wad of toilet paper in my hand, until I hear his motorcade leave for his office and, following orders, I pick up my luggage and go.

8

THE CRUSADES

Trust me. There is something disconcerting about cockroach shit on one's bed each day.

My room is infested. I wake up in the middle of the night to the sound of them scuttling around. This surpasses roosters and partying police officers, certainly, for displeasure.

Every morning I go into the bathroom and approach their nest, an uncovered drain. I only have to wait a minute, quiet and still, for them to emerge and I attack them with Mortein but it only makes them stagger. Then, once they are slowed down, drunk on poison, I stamp on the huge beasts. It's part of my daily chores. Still, it is not an effective long-term approach. I am unable to conquer them and therefore I see myself as the colonial power, meaning we cohabitate in an uneasy relationship.

Otherwise, if I don't want to see them I use an old bush trick designed to scare off snakes and I stomp as I'm entering the room to make sure the cockroaches have a chance to hide in their hole, and I continue to stomp while I hop on the loo then for the duration of my stay.

I have undergone a marked dive in my accommodation, all

for the astonishing price of US$350 a month — at the current exchange rate this is approximately the same price as I was paying for my harbour-view apartment in inner Sydney. At first sight, this room seemed pretty enough, opening out, as it does, onto a veranda that fronts a lovely garden containing an enormous grotto with a statue of Saint Philomena. And I was happy to move to Dulce's brother-in-law's, and remain part of The Family. I liked, also, that there was a private *en suite*. Problem is I didn't adequately assess the facilities therein. That's why I have a 'mandi' bucket, which must be filled with water to throw at a precise angle into the non-flushing toilet, when required, to rid it of detritus. The shower is cold water only, a trial even in this hot country. And, as the house doesn't have a generator, the electricity comes and goes at whim, an issue for seeing at night; an even greater one when the water system is linked to it.

Which means that on this eve I'm bracing myself under a cold-water shower and quickly shampooing my hair — I can wash with great speed in this place — when suddenly, without warning, everything goes black. 'Damn it.' And I've forgotten, as always, to fill my mandi. 'God Almighty!' The darkness doesn't daunt every organism, however, and so, standing stark raving nude, I'm wondering what to do when I hear it start up — the scuttling — and the creatures move . . . over my feet, around me, behind me, in front of me . . . and I run, crunch.

It strikes me that East Timor has a cost of living that rivals New York. Supply and demand has made the international consumer captive to whatever a proprietor wants to charge for whatever is required — and I can assure you that few are humanitarian in intent. So questionable products and services are proffered for five-star prices. It's no surprise that merchants charge exorbitant fees, they know the UN pays huge wages to much of its civilian staff. The Special Representative of the Secretary-General, as a case in point, enjoys a base salary over double that of the Prime Minister of Australia's, and it's tax free; he also enjoys the addition of pension, settling-in allowances, shipping costs, cars, a jet, living expenses, and other benefits. In fact, UN salaries are vastly more than many Australians are accustomed to. For those working for the UN from other countries, like Burundi where over half the population lives on less than US$1 a day, receiving salaries like these are equal to winning the lottery.

Alongside all of the monstrously overpaid civilian staff are the UNVs, or United Nations Volunteers, who perform work of the same high value as the professional ('P') level positions and are paid a stipend equivalent to an average Australian wage, thanks to current exchange rates and zero tax. I am one of them. Perfectly happy to be so.

Then there are the Timorese employees, who receive contributions that pale in comparison to anything the international *bon vivants* are living on with such aplomb; local police officers receive around US$85 a month and the Timorese Prime Minister receives US$450, for example. This is designed to make their wages sustainable once the UN leaves, and this is a commonsense objective, except that it contributes substantially to the Malae Syndrome. No surprise when they've been watching the debauchery over two missions, soon to be three: UNAMET (United Nations Assistance Mission in East Timor), UNTAET (United Nations Transitional Administration in East Timor), and soon UNMISET (United Nations Mission of Support in East Timor), which will be introduced with the biggest party of them all on 19 May.

Before we reach the Independence celebrations, though, there's another gripping event. What an election, what a campaign! I've come away from the experience full of ideas for the next Australian federal election — vote-catching stunts such as animal sacrifices would be marvellous media-attention grabbers, I've learned.

The launch of the presidential campaign saw the two candidates go head to head in a contest to lead a new independent East Timor, a free nation after decades of oppression and guerrilla warfare. A proud role? A glorious reward? Well, to those of us from the competitive enclaves of the global north, yes. To the Timorese, no, given that nobody wanted the top job, so they said.

Francisco Xavier do Amaral was President of Independent East Timor for the ten days between the end of Portuguese colonisation and the Indonesian annexation in 1974. As a result, he had job experience but he was no alternative to the hero Xanana. The old, deaf and frail Xavier knew he was in a one-horse race and he was comparatively lame. He was perfectly happy to lose, he said, he was merely running because UNTAET wanted the appearance of democracy — and apparently democracy requires choice, however unrealistic an option it may be.

What of the favourite, José Alexandre Gusmão, the man known by the nom de guerre Kay Rala Xanana Gusmão? Well, there were those pumpkins luring him away from his chance at omnipotence. Still, he capitulated to the UN and, despite continual threats to resign along the way, he, too, crossed the finish line.

There were no losers, only winners in this contest of true champions. Nah, bugger off — in politics, someone gives a Viktory speech and another concedes defeat. There ain't no silver medals in this game, even in the carefully stage-managed East Timorese Presidential Election Campaign . . .

It's a Saturday night and it's activity-filled at TVTL, with the first election debate planned for live broadcast from a burned-out building in the back yard of the station, three handicams facilitating the multi-camera shoot.

It's compelling television from the start. Xanana has to explain the questions to the 75-year-old Xavier, who isn't quite in attendance; chirping birds are audible above any political discussion as they fly around the studio; the American beside me asks, outraged, 'Why isn't this in English?'; the audio comes and goes at whim; and then there's the inevitable, the monsoon . . . and there isn't even a ubiquitous UNHCR tarpaulin in sight to use as a roof.

Chaos ensues, watched live around the nation. TVTL staff put boxes over technology (an obvious short-term solution), the audience runs to any pockets of cover (hooting with laughter), panicked advisers hold umbrellas (floral, to add charm) over candidates whose clothes are getting sodden. Xanana wipes the drops away from his face and, chuckling, he keeps talking about erudite issues of policy until Mother Nature achieves what the Indonesians could not and she dampens the spirit of people accustomed to struggling, and the pounding rain drowns out a peculiarly entertaining political broadcast.

Promptly afterwards Xavier is hospitalised in intensive care with pneumonia and a list of other ailments. I interview his doctor: 'Will you be advising Xavier to pull out of the race?'

'That's a political decision.'

'For the benefit of his health, should he pull out of the race?'

'Um, well, yes.'

'Has the campaign so far contributed to his condition now?'

'Um, yes.'

'What is required for a recovery?'

'Rest.'

'Four weeks' rest?' The remaining time of the campaign period.

'Yes.'

'If he is elected President will he live out the five-year term?'

'Um, it's unlikely, no.' That's got to be bad for one's electoral chances.

Yet the man hits the hustings again, his confidence growing with every event, despite his rather rambling manner and looking as though he's about to fall over and drop dead among the assembled masses — problem is those masses are being assembled by UNTAET, which is sending trucks to the surrounding areas, rounding up men (invariably) and dropping them off at Xavier's speeches, once again to give the appearance of democracy. Thus a megalomaniac is born.

In the town of Liquica, the site of one of the worst massacres of '99, the trucks are late and so the sparse few who turn up out of real interest in the election are entertained in the interim by the booming music preferred by the Timorese, including a catchy tune with words proclaiming a love of Indonesia and a wish for its continued presence in Timor. And there is Boney M, the soundtrack to this place.

> . . . There lived a certain man in Russia long ago
> He was big and strong, in his eyes a flaming glow
> Most people looked at him with terror and with fear
> But to Moscow chicks he was such a lovely dear . . .

Rasputin probably isn't a wise choice, lyrically speaking, but to the tiny audience, blissfully ignorant of the English words and the Russian history, it is a great contribution to their day. For a people more accustomed to dying for their politics, this new democracy business is much more fun.

Meanwhile, Xanana is touring the nation with that smile, that charisma, the croon, those arms that hug everyone. I've come to think that perhaps he could make an international career of this and be Australia's first president too. Vote 1 Xanana.

His tour sees him head to Oecussi and, proving he is a brave and statesmanlike character, he journeys through West Timor by car, stopping at the refugee camps which still house hundreds of thousands of East Timorese who fled in '99. It is an embarrassment that these people are choosing to stay in Indonesia and Xanana tells them it is safe to return. Then he hits the campaign trail again, on his way to the site of that first Portuguese settlement on Timorese soil.

I travel to Oecussi on a UN helicopter, hugging the coastline, beside a vista of mountains grand, whump, whump, whump, for over an hour, the wind rushing in the open window beside me, and, sure, the rudimentary condition of the aircraft and emergency instructions in the Cyrillic alphabet could be cause for concern but I am surrounded by every conceivable variation in uniform representing police and military worldwide, which is as close to bliss as a girl can get.

All, ostensibly, for a good cause too: producing mini-documentaries for TVTL, interviewing aid workers about their hopes and concerns for East Timor post-Independence. Oxfam's participant has lived in the area for years, has local language fluency and has made a great effort to assimilate. His white skin highlights his difference, but joining the local soccer team is designed to have him accepted. I arrive to film him on the field where play is interrupted by an errant bull, allowing an interview to take place, with a local team-mate preferring to join in. They sit on a gnarled old fallen tree trunk, side by side, the American answering his questions in Tetum, his friend staring intently into the lens of the camera, unblinking, unnerving. When finally asked about his dream for the future of Timor, the aid worker looks at his team-mate, who nods. He looks back at me and answers, 'World Cup for East Timor,' indicating the disparate personal ambitions for this nation come self-determination.

Riding around Oecussi in a UN Land Rover, one of thousands in this nation for our convenience, and it manoeuvres the uneven surface, as tranquil rice fields stretch alongside, attended by women bent over, sarongs around their knees, feet in the mud, picking; deserted beaches line the oceanfront and islands dot a shiny sea; buffalo cool off in mud ponds; then the peacekeeper-built roads wind through collections of bamboo huts leading to the Indonesian border; we are in time for a very special event. And I'd like to state for the record that I don't like animal sacrifices very much — a distaste which is apparently specific to my country. I know this because sitting in the back of a UN Land Rover, reading the program of events for a reconciliation and forgiveness ceremony, I note '10.15 am Slaughter of Animal'.

'Oh,' I say, 'I don't think I can watch the "Slaughter of Animal",' and my Timorese colleague in the front passenger seat looks at his compatriot driver and comments knowingly, 'Ah, Australian.' So a pig and a cow and two chickens have their throats slit, are bled, chopped up, cooked and promptly devoured by very old men stoned on betel nut while I watch on respectfully, through my fingers over my eyes. Pigs scream in a traumatising, agonising screech but cows just swish their ears to keep the flies away from the mortal wounds and slowly, softly, peacefully slip away from life. Chickens? By now I'm hiding in the car, adopting vegetarianism. Still, it is all a great success and the announcement is made that the lovely blue sheen of various animal spleens shows that the refugees can come back from West to East Timor, it really is safe now.

All this tranquillity and simplicity is life-affirming for me. Indeed it affirms the value of a First World life, thanks very much. I'm traumatised not only by animal sacrifice but by the hotel bathroom. I doubt that many Australian press gallery journalists have had to live like this while covering a campaign, eg: I simply will not accept that I am expected to wipe my bum with my hand. Assimilation can go too far.

Meanwhile, the advance towards the nation's Independence continues, with Xanana's motorcade moving ever closer to Oecussi on his presidential campaign trail. Anticipation rises in this enclave and, together with a group of kolegas, I drive a UN Land Rover up to a little community perched on a mount to see my beloved. And in that part of the world it is to peek into another time: tais-wearing girls performing a traditional dance with flicking kerchiefs and drums, men in elaborate medieval-style chain-mail costumes and hundreds of bells around their legs stomping a beat, Timor ponies running in procession, and (intake of breath) Xanana carried aloft on a throne for miles along winding paths lined with beautiful floral and wooden celebratory stakes, through utterly breathtaking mountains and picturesque villages as the faithful run alongside yelling in ululating tones (oh, actually, that may be me).

There is a fervour of worship. I feel they've mistaken Xanana for Jesus Christ and I expect Charlton Heston to walk into the scene at any moment. Anyway, I suspect Xanana is Jesus Christ.

And if the people believe Xanana is the Son of God then these innocent and isolated people must reckon I'm his mum. Women, particularly, come to me and they stroke the pale skin on my arms, they stare at my eyes, they say reverently, 'Botardi, Senhora.' And when this vision that resembles images they've seen of the Virgin Mary answers them, they jump and almost drop their breastfeeding babies, shocked that it speaks and, even more profoundly, that it speaks to them.

Religious analogies are completely appropriate up here, especially due to Xanana's rather cynical manipulation of the Catholic vote. So much for Him wanting to grow pumpkins;

this man has a campaign any First World candidate would envy. His poster alone clinches a landslide, with Him beaming down in a rather beatific way, a background of clouds and the light creating the sense of a halo around His head. He seems anointed to assume the role of President or Pope. And He certainly performs miracles such as managing to distribute that poster around a muddled nation. Even in Oecussi, children scamper along the roadsides beside my car, holding Xanana's poster aloft, and every single grass hut has it stuck to its front.

Back in Dili, despite the election result being a *fait accompli*, the competitor, Xavier, has developed a taste for the political limelight, especially given the success of his well-attended rallies, and he accuses TVTL of bias in its reporting, calling it Xanana TV. He complains about the coverage of a press conference he's given, saying he is outraged at being edited into a 3-minute story and that the whole 25-minute soliloquy should have been broadcast, uncut, into the 30-minute long news bulletin. He labels the Timorese journalists incompetent and refuses to cooperate with them until they apologise, indicating an alarming failure on his part to understand the principles and practices of an independent media.

The journalists respond by announcing that they, henceforth, refuse to cover his campaign at all, indicating an alarming failure on their part to understand the principles and practices of an independent media. They demand not one apology, but two. Thanks to the intervention of the UN, the impasse ends when the aged and ill Xavier gives an incoherent apology on air on TVTL, twice.

Xanana's campaign team complains about bias too, accusing Xavier's political party, Fretilin, of intervention, saying it is co-opting an unfair amount of airtime on Radio UNTAET, which they rename Radio Fretilin. They also point to Fretilin's attempts to intimidate the TV journalists, such as the time the head of the party stormed into the TVTL newsroom demanding a retraction for a story aired just 10 minutes before.

Regardless of the intrigue behind the scenes, the momentum of the Xanana campaign sweeps the country, culminating in a massive rally in Dili. Standing in front of the stage, I sing along with the flock to the Xanana song:

Mai hamutuk hili mak nia
Kay Rala Xanana Gusmão
Mai hamutuk tu'u ba nia
Kay Rala Xanana Gusmão
Tan nia mak manu-aman
Nia mak mata-dalan
Lori povu to'o ba naroman

Se o hili seluk, se o tu'u ba selak
O nega rasik o nia luta
Se o hili seluk, se o tu'u ba seluk
O bosok rasik o nia an
Tan uluk funu manas ita hotu hakilar
Kay Rala Xanana Gusmão . . .

I think it should replace the Our Father.

Like every capital city, Dili is more cynical and cosmopolitan than the rest of the nation, but in respect for traditions, prior to His speech, Xanana takes part in a ceremony honouring Him. Village chiefs dress Him in a fetching sarong-style ensemble, wind his waist with some old sheets and place gold horns on His head. Then He has no choice but to give His climactic rousing election speech dressed like former Australian prime minister Paul Keating at an ASEAN meeting some years ago.

Even dressed like this, He brings the devout to ecstasy, 'Viva, Xanana!' 'Viva Timor!' they chant, surging forward as

He tries to exit the stage. Bodyguards surround His Australian wife, Kirsty, and their toddler son, Alexandre, who are besieged just beside me. An eighth of the population is in rapture here today. No surprise, for He is the symbol of freedom to them. He inspired them to resist, to believe that this moment could come true, a moment when 100 000 of them could come together and celebrate freedom.

This man struggled alongside them. He didn't leave; unlike other leaders, He stayed in Timor and fought in the mountains; He speaks the languages they speak; He knows just what they have been through — illness, wounds, tyranny, fear — because He withstood it all with them, and captivity as well. I remember the first time I heard Xanana's name was when I was asked to do a story about a videotaped message He'd smuggled out of His Jakarta prison, and if the people get just one shot at voting then, God help them, they will vote for the icon who understands their lives now and the lives they've led for the past 24 years.

It's no surprise, then, that 86 per cent of the population turns out on election day in a peaceful celebration of democracy. I'm in the Popemobile in the dawn-time hours of the day, moving from polling booth to polling booth, filming an English-language round-up for broadcast on TVTL that night, including scenes of hushed, orderly queues containing the grizzled old traditional-clothed Timorese, together with youths in jeans and T-shirts. All of them are taking this voting process seriously — after all, many died for the privilege in '99. Tackling the diversity of the population, the ballot papers allow constituents to select their preferred candidate with a pen stroke for the literate or a nail punch for the rest, and so voters of every social class emerge from their ballot boxes, each with a forefinger raised high to show an ink stamp given as proof they've voted. For the Timorese, that stain is a symbol of their hard-won democracy.

And a Ministry of Foreign Affairs media release proclaims that '. . . for the first time ever in our 500 year colonial history, our people will go back to the polls . . . ' with José Ramos-Horta quoted that he 'will vote for the very best candidate, the very best son of this country, Mr Xanana Gusmão. He will be a great President.'

The UNTAET press conferences are held at intervals during the day and there is much anticipation as the international community of Dili files into the auditorium out the back of TVTL for election updates. Throughout the world, viewers are watching announcements made in front of a commanding background of the blue UN symbol, but sitting here I can't help but think back to a time, just weeks before, when this was the scene of an interrupted rained-out election debate complete with floral umbrellas. Wiser now, the organisers have fitted the burned-out building with a tarpaulin as a roof.

But there's no rain on this parade and the result leads to rejoicing in the streets, TVTL journalists dance the night away, Radio UNTAET's commiserate, and Xavier concedes his spectacular defeat with grace, accepting the will of the Faithful. Even the international media is inducted into the cult of Xanana when His Viktory speech becomes a frenzy — clamouring for His attention, yelling His name, beseeching Him to send one of those divine smiles their way all are captivated by this president né pumpkin farmer cum deity. And shaking His hand in congratulations, I may or may not have genuflected. I'll never say.

9

CODES OF MISCONDUCT

Jordanians have a particular appetite for goats. However, not only do goats make up an important part of their dietary preferences, they also hold another tasteless role. Only the pretty ones, that is.

What should be a discreet pastime is played out rather publicly at times . . . One Jordanian was sampling the delights of the local fauna when her pelvis collapsed, trapping the peacekeeper inside. With trousers around his ankles and still attached to the goat he flagged down a UN car and the startled occupants contacted the medical unit run by Australians who, as they airlifted him to hospital, were heard to say, 'Let's save the goat and put the Jordanian down.'

At that time, prior to the ratification of the International Criminal Court, UN workers were bound by the laws of their own countries. For example, in Australia there'd be some ramifications for being caught *in flagrante delicto* with a goat, but a matter of this kind doesn't concern the courts of Jordan. However, the multinational surprise at a peccadillo of that nation meant the King of Jordan travelled to Timor to explain it away, a meeting keenly anticipated by the dignitaries here, who so looked forward to hearing the King's turn of phrase when discussing the matter. Whatever was said, done, promised or paid in aid, the Jordanians have been allowed to continue their contributions to East Timor.

Certainly, above and beyond legal constraints, different nationalities have differing codes of conduct guiding the behaviour of their troops. The Australian military, for example, is constrained by guidelines and regulations prohibiting most leisure pursuits, including animal husbandry (although that particular predilection may not be specifically outlined in the rule book).

My introduction to the ways of the Australian peacekeepers here begins on this Anzac Day. I'm picked up in the darkness of a 5.30 am start and the car drives towards Christo Rei. Moving through the black night we see car lights, many of them, heading out to Christo Rei too, along the winding beach road.

Deposited at the base of the mount I start my walk up stairs illuminated by fluorescent sticks congenially placed there by First World soldiers and, in the dark, a thousand of us ascend in a solemn march, with faint whispering heard every now and then in accents clearly Australasian. I have been living and working with Timorese people for months now, eating the food, learning the local language, immersing myself in the culture, happily, but on this day I am handed a special dispensation to be Australian, to be me, and so comes a little tear of relief in the darkness.

At the platform beneath the towering statue of Jesus with his arms outreaching as he balances on an enormous globe of the world, the dawn service presides over a rising sun and, in the illumination of the new day, the uniforms and accompanying proud faces of our military (and those of the cousins) come into view. I watch the choreographed display of soldiers and twirling guns and it conveys to me the genuine duty these forces feel for Timor, a country they fought to liberate from the Japanese during World War II, then again from Indonesia in '99.

New Zealand puts its best face forward, with an eloquent commander who says it well when he describes the commitment our countries are making here. He says that the massacres of 1915 could have seen us recoil in self-preservation, but instead they reaffirmed our desire to fulfil our responsibility as free nations, that since then we have been obliged, as a result of our freedom, to sacrifice for the freedom of others.

And an enormous sacrifice it is here for the diggers. Our soldiers can only drink two or no beers a day, depending on their battalions. Some of them are not allowed to swim in this hot, hot country. But all of them, irrespective of where they are stationed in Timor, cannot fraternise. Beer rations, a swimming ban and a no-sex rule surely border on human rights violations, but these men signed up to serve.

As the day dawns I try to shoot the proceedings on a handicam for the TVTL Noticias, but I am intimidated at the thought of filming in front of an audience of men who haven't had sex for extraordinarily long periods of time. Thus, unwilling to provide a diversion from the gravitas at the podium, most of the occasion is spent by this lone civilian sheila timidly watching the ceremony.

It is a long one and I move my weight from foot to foot, slouching, standing up straight, ball of foot, toes, ball of foot, toes, and I marvel at the absolute stillness of those around me, and I am fascinated to learn how rigidly soldiers can stand for hours on end. And, even more so, I marvel at how many hours these people have, in the course of their employment, been made to stand still in order to perfect the skill.

Then the last post resounds through the air up high on the hilltop, with the sky turning from pink to blue, the plaintive sound of the bugle causing all of us to reflect on the contribution we are making, for reasons humanitarian, not of war, and I am proud . . . and pleased because it heralds the end of the ceremony and I can move legs, which have long since lost circulation and I, thus, order them to carry me towards the next event on the agenda.

Dinky-di breakfast is at the Dengue Bar in the middle of the main Dili military base, Crocodile Alley, and I could be in bloody Puckapunyal or Bandiana, mate! Bacon and eggs and a ration of one coffee, with the addition of a thimbleful of rum in tribute to those Anzacs who'd used this beverage as courage prior to heading over the trenches to face Johnny Turk in World War I. (Frankly I'd need more, and preferably something more palatable. Chardonnay?) Anyway, there's none of that trench-foot, Gallipoli gallop and bully beef business these days. The feasts provided today led my cranky Peruvian colleague to ask our military host, agog, 'Is this for your special celebration?'

'Nah, mate, the cook's been a bit slack today.'

At the traditional game of two-up the rank and file lament playing such a game with US dollars, but it doesn't diminish the enthusiasm, as they communicate in their native tongue, 'Ya galah!' 'Rightio, here she goes again!' 'Read 'em and weep!' ''Av' a go yer mug!'

In the interests of cooperating with the under-resourced local media, the army provides a car and driver (in Hawaiian shirt), so it's on to Dili Stadium to cover the dead-set sporting highlight of the year, a game of Australian Rules footy: PKF (Peacekeeping Force) v UNPOL. Driving into town, Timorese children recognise the kangaroo painted on the sides of the vehicle and they run out onto the road, yelling 'G'day mate! G'day mate!' Arriving, the arena is filled with local spectators who spend the event in stitches laughing. They mistake it for comedy, not sport. Barracking from my possie, 'Chewy on yer boot!' even I'm confused at the multi-code approach — in the fight-to-the-death melee I swear I see a few Hopoates.

To the next stop in a whirl of celebrations: an army base where the soldiers play cricket in the searing afternoon sun, dressed in sombreros, their semi-automatic guns (a phallic object they're allowed to use) lining the field, to a cacophony of 'Turn it up!' or 'Whaddaya call that, ya nong?' Et cetera. You get a four for hitting the ball past the huge military vehicles nearby, a six if it goes over the barbed-wire perimeter and (presumably) into a neighbouring rattan shack.

And a story does go to air on TVTL. I transmit a little bit of Aussie propaganda to let the local population see the essence of us. It's important to me given the Malae Syndrome and a Timorese kolega who said to me, 'Too many Australians here.' I wish my kolega had spent the day enjoying the humour, good will, massive financial commitment, elocution, sporting prowess and remarkable fashion taste of my countrypeople (and that other mob from over the Tasman), and that he could be like the cranky Peruvian, drunk at the Dengue Bar going, 'I love youse Australians,' in true honorary Australian style, while the peacekeepers watch his beer cans, longingly. And I wish I had forced my kolega to climb with me to the top of Christo Rei that morning, and I wish that he could ask himself why on earth we should give a damn about his freedom, why all these blokes should stay here for six months, why they should be crying into their softdrinks late at night at the Dengue Bar telling me they miss home dearly and they want to be somewhere where they are welcome, asking why they should forego beer and sex to distinguish themselves from the soldiers of other nationalities and to prove the fair dinkum integrity, grit and sheer strength of the Anzac character.

It's a strength of character confirmed by their restraint when it comes to the ladies. Men represent 90 per cent of the mission population and they are away from wives and girlfriends for lengthy periods, which means that the malae women here find themselves contending with astounding levels of interest from those nationalities with more flaccid codes of conduct. So much so that the saying among the girls goes, 'The odds are good but the goods are odd'. It's an imbalance that requires the imposition of standards; in the words of Zedenka — a UN serious crimes investigator and the Zsa Zsa Gabor of Timor: 'I vould never fuck anythink less than a col-on-el, darlink.'

The Australians, meanwhile, have to keep their hands to themselves, thanks to their non-fraternisation code. To lessen the burden on our troops, bromide is sympathetically added to the soldiers' drinking water to reduce sexual urge. But should the Australian defence forces prevent individuals from fulfilling natural human needs? Can't the women take care of themselves? If the defence forces allowed a bit of down-under relief, then the government wouldn't have to pay quite such a fortune on recruitment advertisements or bromide, would it? General Peter Cosgrove told me once that during Australia's first role heading a UN peacekeeping mission there was no sex safer than no sex.

Particularly as the women can't always take care of themselves. Just as the Americans did in Vietnam, the Japanese military left their mark on the lives of Timorese communities during their occupation of the island in World War II, and the inhabitants of some villages still retain those distinctive features. The effects on the lives of the local women from abandonment is catastrophic — their poverty is compounded and they are left seemingly morally soiled and certainly broken-hearted when all they wanted was a passport to a life of greater opportunity. Stories abound on the Timorese grapevine of love going horribly wrong.

Visiting Dulce in her kitchen, sweating in the heat, talking above the racket of the roosters, gossiping about malae affairs in Dili, 'Malae love crazy, hey?' I end with a dramatic roll of the eyes which says it all, I'm not like that, I condemn that sort of conduct, honest.

'But, Lynne, you know, Timorese too.'

'No!'

'One Timorese girl and Brazilian. He go home. They write and he ask her to come to him. She go there and at the airport his wife. Ay! The man say she is a new servant. She go to embassy!'

'But, that's terrible!'

'Ye-es! Terrible. You know, Lynne, there was African man with Timorese and he live with her family and they take engagement and have organise dowry and his mission end and he go.'

'But, that's terrible!'

'Ye-es!'

'Dulce, you must have heard stories of Australian soldiers.'

'You know, Lynne, many Australians here from '99 and no story.'

So one nationality within the international peacekeeping force can be seen to possess codes of conduct requiring exceptionally strong self-control. And that's got to be good for the reputation. Now, if only other countries could control their appetites, then all the females here could breathe a collective sigh of relief, including the goats. Especially the pretty ones.

10

DUELLING ECONOMIES

Driving in the Popemobile we are heading out to the township of Hera, about 15 kilometres inland from Dili, on the tail of some consequential story, meandering along the thin, winding roads dotted with banana trees. Villages are filled higgledy-piggledy with one-roomed bamboo huts, our car horn honks and honks, and children on the roadside cheer, 'Hello Missus!' when they see the malae woman whizzing by. I wave back, although I do feel rather self-conscious doing it over and over again, who do I think I am, Queen Betty acknowledging one's subjects?

Then in the middle of nowhere the car screeches to a halt and the Josés all leap out. Something has caught their eyes and they giggle as they head off to a little roadside table. I try to peer around from my front passenger seat but soon enough one of them brings me a ceremonial vessel (maybe I am Queen Elizabeth), although the dark faces peering into my open car window with enormous smiles showing off their decaying teeth make me suspicious. What are they up to, I'm thinking, as I look at the cloudy fluid in the plastic cup. It looks like phlegm. And it reeks. Even more frightening is that it came from a roadside stall and I don't think I'm being presumptuous in presuming that health inspectors are few and far between in this neck of the woods (aka: South-East Asia).

Hang on, I've heard about this stuff, 'Is this tua mutin?' They collapse in laughter. 'La diak!' I say, *so* not good! '*Tua mutin* = white wine' is made out of palm fronds and is rumoured to have an alcohol content of approximately, gee, proof. I watch as they scull theirs and mine and they clamber clumsily into the car again, roaring with laughter, 'Um, perhaps I should drive?' '*Lae* = no', apparently, while on the floor of the back seat, between the legs of my kolegas, are placed, delicately, two enormous plastic bottles filled with enough tua mutin to wipe out an oppressive army.

We drive onwards. Roads that were pleasantly snaking before, I now see as death traps. Further along and we screech to a halt again. What is it this time? A deadline looms but I am happy to be sidetracked for as long as it takes them to sober up. There is a group of market stalls here and each is selling palm frond products — weaved baskets, purses, mats — under the shade of UNHCR tarpaulins. Sitting on the tables or hanging, tied from the front of bamboo awnings are goods that vary in size and shape and colour, and some of them are very pretty. The women and children greet me, gleefully, 'Hello Missus!'

My name (or similar) is called, 'Leeen! Leeen!' and I find my kolegas at a collection of tables, behind hanging baskets, holding up sticks with char-grilled octopus threaded along each. They gesture, giggling, for me to take one and I do, to show my attempts at assimilation, and I nibble until thoughts of Dili-belly and my home discomforts fill my mind, and they collapse in laughter again.

Waving octopi skewers as orchestra batons, the drunken city folk wander along the tables, haggling with stall-holders over plaited purses in brightly painted tints. They buy one each for US$1 and I ask for one too. US$10, I'm told, 'Dollar sanulu.'

I'm surprised, perhaps I haven't understood, 'Dollar sanulu, Senhora?'

'Dollar sanulu,' she insists. One of my kolegas discusses the issue with the woman and despite his wielded stick she insists, 'Malae dollar, malae dollar,' as she points at me, 'malae dollar!' Accepting that explanation, he shrugs and walks off, chuckling.

'Hrmph,' I emit articulately, as we climb back into the car.

'No problem, Leeen. Lae problema,' I'm told.

'Sin, problema,' I say, explaining to them that I feel like a walking dollar bill. I tell them how disappointing it can be to feel that my only redeeming feature seems to be my money. I explain to them that I want to help, that I feel great sympathy for those living in poverty, that I am happy to pay more than others, but sometimes it just feels like extortion. When they say 'Hello Missus!' I suspect they actually mistranslate and what they really mean to say is 'Hello Money!' There's a two-tiered economy here, it's caused by every UN peacekeeping mission in the world, and it has disadvantages for all sides of the equation.

The Popemobile pulls onto the road just as a UN vehicle comes around the bend at tremendous speed, its horn blares, it overtakes us despite the market and the children on the side of the road, and having survived that usual occurrence we continue on in silence. Then after a while of twisting and turning through the lush tropical countryside I feel a little tap on my shoulder and, turning around to the back seat, I see a José looking at me and he extends his arm and hands me the little purse he bought a short time ago. I am so moved that I forget my Tetum and all I can say humbly is 'Thank you' to this young Timorese man with the shabby shoes and the big, genuine eyes. 'You're welcome,' he replies.

Jostled around in my seat in this particularly primitive car on the bumpy road, I look down at this generous gift in my hands, and I see that my new purse is, of course, lilac and as such it will conveniently match every item in my wardrobe, then BANG! followed soon by another, BANG! and I look on with horror as another José skids the car off the road and fights with the steering wheel in the loose dirt, lurching over rocks, until finally we slide to a standstill.

That's when I notice the stench. 'What on earth?' and I turn around to see the passengers in the back seat, all of them, covered in the phlegm-like substance. It drips from their wiry black hair as they look at me, blink, blink. Bursting out of the car door to escape the foul pong, I suspect I will never stop laughing as they swear in English, 'Sheet!' at the exploded plastic containers, wiping alcohol from their clothes and the interior of the stinking hot car.

In a change of fortunes, I'm writing the evaluation report on the communications structure established by the UN here, the OCPI and its composite parts: the TV station, Radio UNTAET and the publications unit. It is a responsible project and I am honoured, of course. Even if the idea was mine. See, I threw my hat into the ring, assuming there was one. I assumed that UN departments would be required to evaluate performance, given the billions of dollars poured into each mission. How quaint of me. Luckily, the head of OCPI, Mario Zamorano, was rather taken with this apparently innovative idea, so I get the job of reporting back on the success or otherwise of this institution to Sergio Vieira de Mello by 18 May, in time for Independence Day.

Choosing to make the evaluation report the most representative document I can, not just the mouthpiece of management, I decide to interview every staff member, local and international, in the language of their choice within the translation options of Bahasa, English, Tetum and Portuguese. A decision indicating great egalitarianism and a quest for accuracy on my part but, given the logistics, an approach that proves that: a) I am patently mad; b) this place is chaos; and c) it is all seen as a malae plot.

One barrier is the head of TVTL, who is outraged at the idea of being evaluated. She has daily outbursts at the hapless Mario, glowers at me, and confronts my assistant, the cranky Peruvian, who interrupts her tirade by saying a moth has flown into his ear and he can't hear a thing before hitting himself on the side of the head and walking off.

Despite the fact that the Timorese don't trust the process, they are prepared to overlook their concerns for a small donation to ameliorate their circumstances in the form of beer. You see, international employees have a lucky dispensation here. To counteract the high prices in the general community, our jobs entitle us to certain rewards, including cheap alcohol imported from Australia — one box of beer and a bottle of spirits a week, plus unlimited bottles of wine. This privilege certainly assists us in contending with the hardship, although there is no more mighty a contributor to the Malae Syndrome. The Timorese staff view it as plain racism and an injustice which illustrates our difference.

In the main UN base in the centre of Dili, Obrigado Barracks (which never fails to make me laugh given that '*obrigado barak* = thank you very much'), malae wander through the security gates with a flash of ID passes (blonde women need only sashay by) and inside the base is an oasis of buildings with all sorts of useful functions — the free medical centre, a complimentary dentist's surgery, gym, duty-free shop, pub, leisure centre, a supermarket selling Australian products, a food court serving pizzas, café food, roast chicken and chips, barbecue-your-own steaks, and a bottle shop where large bottles of vodka go for US$6, slabs of VB are US$12 and fridges are filled with red as well as white wine.

Additionally, for our viewing pleasure, there are TVs tuned to Australian channels that allow us to watch the news or cutting-edge programming like Russell Coight — which usually requires some translating for those other UN malae of differing nationalities watching on, baffled, in the large, landscaped, open-air eating area.

Now, I am completely aware that I am advantaged in having access to all these subsidised comforts of home but, I'm afraid, I simply can't bribe the Timorese to take part in the evaluation report. After all, there are over a hundred of them and I have needs, the UN says so.

Is alcohol a powerful means of forging multinational cooperation, I'm wondering, as I log on to minion@un.org, to find that I have NEW MAIL. I click OK.

```
— Original Message —
From: José Ramos-Horta
Subject: Re:
- Sorry that I haven't been in touch. How
are you? I have a new Mob and
- no longer have your number. Call me if
you wish to meet for a drink . . .
jrh
```

I'm stunned at the audacity, but, nevertheless, I reply:

```
Cheeky bugger.
```

And I add my mobile phone number, too, because I'm happy for him to buy me a drink — in the interests of diplomacy, of course.

11

THE FOOTLIGHTS, THE GREASEPAINT

I am writing away in the office at OCPI when I notice that all is dark around me, my blue and white screen, with its little black letters, providing the primary light source in the room. I look at the time: 8 pm. Gotta go. I have many more hours of work ahead of me tonight but I'll have to do it at home. I shouldn't take taxis in the darkness of night. Already I am testing my luck.

So I leave and catch a cab without harm, other than the booming Boney M, and I ensconce myself on my veranda under the gaze of Saint Philomena, lit brightly in her grotto, and type on my laptop.

Immersed as I am, I don't notice the Timorese inhabitants of the house calling it a night and turning off the lights; all I am aware of is the deadline looming over me. My determination to finish this report is reinforced by the staff interviews and their translations, which are providing an intimate look into the media in East Timor, with many lessons for the creation of an independent media in any new country.

Sitting here and typing away, I am convinced that democracy needs a free and questing media. It also strikes me, while reading through the testimonies of the staff here, that setting one up is more complicated than I'd imagined. In fact, it appears that we malae have taken a lot of granted. I mean, in Australia we know democracy, we grow up with it, we understand it, we expect it. We respect the range of institutions required to protect our freedom. Which is why I am engrossed by the translation of an interview on my screen. It's the comment of a local journalist who replies, when asked if he understands the principles and practices of an independent media:

> Whatever we are told to do we have to do it because we lost everything. We lost our houses, all our family are dead. We just want to work, we just do whatever we think we have to do. I'm getting very emotional. We lost everything, there's no way but just do as we are told. Even if they control now we don't mind. We are here to work.

I know that an independent media would be instrumental in preventing the horrors of '99 from occurring again; however he sees it as an indulgence right now, as he tries to rebuild his life. Yet disclosure, transparency, the check and balance provided by a worthwhile media *are* vital to him — they are not a luxury item like a television or a washing machine or a fridge. I just wish we had taught him this, yet it seems we've failed. We assumed he knew it, but how could he have?

I am contemplating that the malae have failed to understand the trauma and poverty of our kolegas when, for some reason, I turn around. Behind me I see, crouching within arm's reach, a Timorese man and he is shocked (hello? who is shocked?) that I have caught him just as he is about to pounce on me. In my surprise I calmly say 'Hey,' holding his stare. He looks at me for what seems an age, which gives me time to appreciate my circumstances and their perilous nature and, consequently, my terror grows. I keep it concealed because he is clearly unnerved, meaning that, playing chicken, our eyes remain locked until, finally, suddenly, he jumps up, spins around and runs in a direction contrary to where I sit, twisted around in my chair, far more vulnerable than he had gauged.

Leaping up, I see my would-be mugger racing into the slum behind this grand manor house, and running around to the main door I wrench with enthusiasm on the handle to find it locked. I grab my mobile phone and call for help, only to find that Telstra has, inexplicably, disconnected my phone. And so I thump and thump on the windows, waking everyone inside and they emerge, dishevelled and sleepy, to hear a tale of a blessed escape.

There's melodrama and a babble of words that I don't understand (and that's just me) but, despite the consternation from the residents here, their waving arms, the outrage in their raised voices, there is no real concrete outcome. The police are not called and my security isn't reinforced. It's a concern because my room has its own entrance made of a flimsy wood with an insubstantial lock that *I* could pick, and the bathroom window has a flywire cover most criminals wouldn't perceive as a terrible inconvenience. I feel somewhat susceptible when I adjourn to my bed, fully dressed, blood pumping in my ears in a sound like footfalls. Lying awake all night, I seek the answer to the question: It may be my dream to see Independence but how much am I prepared to risk?

The next morning I visit the main Dili police station, which is run by Australians. They don't take a statement, saying it is useless in a country with clueless law and order. Alrighty, so what do I do now? I'm advised to move house, warning that my nervous assailant is probably a rapist who will come back to finish the job. Great, that's heartening. Particularly as I am simply too busy to find a better place to live. I have no choice but to continue to contend with villains — of both insect and human variety. If I could leave, I would, but I can't. And, regardless, the dream *is* worth it, I decide, proving I have a scale of priorities that is patently unhealthy.

I go back to my first-rate, five-star accommodation and, pulling up in the taxi, I see that it really is a beautiful place. It is a large, white, stately colonial residence with established gardens. It was the home of the Governor of Timor during the Indonesian times, and it has the grand dimensions one would expect in the home of a member of an occupying elite — after all, I think it is a safe generalisation that those of a dictatorial bent are not known for living in hardship. I walk to a vast kitchen area that is far more dilapidated than it must have been in the glory days of autocracy, and doing so I cast looks left and right into the surrounding shanties and feel as though I am being watched. Ducking inside, I join my landlord, who sits at a table burdened with mie goreng, a two-foot-long whole fried fish, coagulating pork and bean stew, plain rice and ai manas (foodstuffs representing the cuisines of a couple of oppressors), within walls of peeling paint, cooling himself with a homemade electrical fan.

'I went to Dili station about last night,' I say.

'Yeah?' That got his attention away from the food. 'Why? Nothing happen, Lynne,' he says out of a mouth filled with chewed noodles.

'Of course something happened. The police need to be told about that sort of thing.'

'Why?'

'You have to use and respect the police system. You have to report crime and feel able to trust the police. That's the whole point of the system and it's an important system.'

'Oh, come on.'

'I know the police in Timor in the past couldn't be trusted but that is changing. A whole new police force is being built, and a good police force needs the population to accept it and use it as much as it requires good cops.'

'But nothing happen, Lynne, come on.' Will he just swallow, Jesus.

'Look, strictly speaking nothing's happened yet, but I spoke to some Australian police officers I know and they say there have been many violent acts against malae women and the guy from last night might come back.'

'What! Lynne, I am Timorese, I know these people. Your Australian police friends don't know the Timorese people. I tell you he won't be back.'

'How can you be sure?' I'm looking the other way.

'Sure? I know this. Come on, your friends, they like to say bad things about the Timorese, how are they sure?'

'But in the ghetto around us, these are Timorese people who don't have education, employment, a big house like you. I mean, you are not really like them. It's almost like comparing me to Rupert Murdoch, and I suspect his lifestyle and perspectives are somewhat dissimilar to mine. I wouldn't presume to know what he's going to be doing tomorrow.'

'But they are my people. I know them, I understand them. He won't be back.'

'Okay.' I drop the matter, unconvinced, and pick at a plate of rice and fish (I've been turned off my food), while my landlord eats and talks and laughs and smokes, all simultaneously. Table manners aside, he really is a very jolly bloke, and he affectionately grapples with the children who scamper in and out, throwing his burning cigarette on the kitchen floor for the maid to diligently sweep up.

And to show that the historical lack of trusty police has forced the Timorese to look for protection elsewhere: 'You know, Lynne, Saint Philomena saved you,' he says, as I look at him and try to maintain a respectful expression, free from the cynical grin it'd prefer at this moment. 'Because every night I light candles to her and I pray to her, every night, and she keep you safe.'

It is a beautiful sentiment and it could be a helpful key. Now that I know she intervenes in my life, I think I'll pray to Saint Philomena to sort out a large list of problems I've accumulated in this muddled country where nothing seems to operate, police or otherwise, including my telephonic issues. Then I'll pass her contact details around because I am not the only person in this country to have required her assistance in this regard — last year Telstra disconnected each East Timorese minister's phone after a billing hiccup. And maybe she can write a small document for Sergio for me which is threatening to bury me in the reams of paper, issues, pressures and accusations it is generating. Still, as the saying goes, if you want something done, give it to a busy woman who requires no sleep, tolerates vermin with nonchalance, has a self-washing body and can scare off an attacker with a mere word.

Just to prove I can do it all and more (or that I am a woman without boundaries), I'm summoned by the Foreign Affairs Minister and I join him for a jog — or, rather, a fast-paced stroll.

We begin at the house he is building near Arieia Branca, the main beach outside Dili. The construction is in three separate parts called a *casa separado* in Portuguese and, in deference to the environment, the windows have no glass, just wooden slats, the dining area has no walls, and each of the sections has a huge traditional-style thatched roof jutting into the air. It is due to be finished by Independence and tradesmen work in a blur as José conveys me around me the house he designed himself, a design I first saw drawn onto a serviette in a

Darlinghurst café a year ago. Then, as the temperature drops in the late day, he and I set out with some of the children from The Family and an entourage of bodyguards: 'Hello Maluco,' who clearly seethes with jealousy. So The Master and I move towards the oceanfront, perambulating briskly as a UN Land Rover drives along behind us, the driver piercing my back with his glare, another bodyguard walking alongside, a police car in front, the kids running around us in their bare feet.

'So, a big night coming up. You must be profoundly moved that Independence is almost here.'

'Yes, I am. Of course.'

'It's the culmination of your life's work, I can only begin to imagine how special it will be for you.'

'And you, Miss, you will be there, no?'

'Oh, of course. It's the reason I came to Timor. Although, I have been too busy to organise an access pass. I'd better get around to it. Anyway, I want you to admit something.'

'What is it?' and he smiles as he takes my arm to guide me over the stone wall skirting the beachfront and I am dreadfully conscious of the man who is watching from behind us at the wheel of a car.

'Tell me,' I move away from José's grip subtly, 'at the celebrations will you shed a little tear at midnight when Independence is declared?'

'No-o-o.' He breathes his laugh good-naturedly.

'But it will be such an important moment for you and your nation, how could you not?'

'Well, I will force myself to think of anything else at that moment,' he says, as he suggests a well-known technique for delaying orgasm, and I think it rather ridiculous that at the most triumphant point in his life he'd be thinking of anything else.

'José, did you always believe that Independence would come?'

'Yes, of course.'

'But in those 25 years, there must have been moments when it seemed an impossible task.'

'No, never. Sure, it was hard, depressing. But I had to remain determined. You cannot give up when it is such a cause. That is impossible.'

This road is packed with malae jogging on their pilgrimage around the point and along the cliffs, a smooth ocean to the left, then the sand again as we all approach Christo Rei. The security cars are left behind as we mount the steps and make our way up, passing as we do the Stations of the Cross — each symbolised by a concrete grotto with a bronze representation of Christ's path towards His immortality, bearing the burden of His cross.

As we sweat our way upwards in the humidity, we come across Sergio heading downwards with his companion, Carolina, who has now been elevated to a P-level position within the UN. 'Botardi!' they say as they flash past prettily. Everyone wants to be in tiptop condition for the moment when this small half an island at the bottom of Asia which was so long ignored will be immortalised by the world's cameras.

'The party will be fabulous, José. What a wonderful reward after so many years of hardship, of persistence.'

'God, sleeping on couches. Working at night to earn money, then every day at the United Nations in New York, trying to get people to listen.' As revealing as his words are, I'm beginning to think we should walk in silence because I'm worried he's going to have a heart attack as he pants away, and the timing of such an episode would be rather unfortunate.

'Should we stop? Go back?'

'No!' He's no quitter and so we ascend, the Minister determined to shift those last few kilos in time for the night of his life. How times have changed.

José was exiled when the Indonesians invaded. His wife and child fled to Mozambique. He spent most of his time in the

United States and Australia, other times in Portugal, poor, struggling. Always fighting for Independence via political means: lobbying the UN and various governments, organising First World left-wing activists who adopted his cause as theirs, and courting the media as the conduit to the mainstream populations that eventually called for intervention.

'It has been a long, long time coming, this grand finale to your life's work,' I say.

'Yes, but it became easier when I received the Nobel Peace Prize. The cause gained legitimacy, I put the money I received into my work, more people were prepared to meet with me, the media called me all the time.'

'And then it all happened. Surely you were shocked at the pace of liberation when it came?'

'God, so many people who slammed their doors in my face, now they shake my hand, they want to celebrate.'

Yes, the world now wants to celebrate alongside the Timorese. Neglected by the world for so very long, the pawns in a greater political game. But soon, on a night in May, the nations of the world will be united with them in celebrating a noble cause.

After a break to catch our breath three-quarters of the way up, we reach the platform beneath the statue of Jesus, and while His gigantic arms sweep over us and this nation soon to be free, soon to be celebrating, I turn to my left, to the man who made this dream come true, and I say, 'I still think you'll shed a tear.'

This time, as he surveys the view, he doesn't answer.

My phone rings. It is an employee of the East Timor Foreign Affairs Ministry. He says the Minister has directed him specifically to call me to invite TVTL to a media event at the Independence venue and he finished with the words 'You have powerful friends'. Actually, I have an occasionally courteous acquaintance with one powerful individual, I'm thinking, and a large complement of Timorians climb with me into the Popemobile and it heads to the outskirts of Dili, past the turn-off to the airport, rattling by countless peacekeepers painting and cleaning and carrying. How this city is being transformed! 'Konichiwa!' I yell at one battalion with my head sticking out of the window, the blonde hair flowing like a golden retriever's. Yes. The momentum is building. The countdown has begun to Independence!

Our ridiculous car is passing peacekeepers hanging a row of banners emblazoned with the logo for Independence — a design I organised in Sydney and it reminds me of how long I'd been wishing I could be here for this, to celebrate alongside the Timorese, with the rest of the world! Now the city is humming with the excitement of all of us from everywhere who have converged, as logo after logo billows softly in a humid wind created by the 20 kilometres an hour of the high-performance Popemobile clattering along Comoro Road.

Reaching Taci Tolu, we pull off onto the dry plateau and, while we are late, as habit dictates, we have arrived before the dignitaries. A Nepalese Army commander welcomes us, urging us to film his men as they work, offering refreshments, showing maps, telling us that he is proud to be preparing this location for the stages and barriers and huge television screens that will be placed here soon. See, everyone is being swept up in the tide of anticipation for the extravaganza that's going to unfold outside an immaculate Dili.

The luxury vehicles of the motorcades arrive, driving cross-country through the valley, the dust ballooning from the tyres, to our place among the bulldozers and bobcats. International and local journalists move towards the delegation, which includes two Nobel Peace Prize winners. 'Hello Miss,' says one of them to me, and I'm introduced to the other, Bishop Belo, and I shake his hand and he says it's a pleasure to meet me. (Pleasure to meet *me*!) 'Pleasure to meet you too,' (*too*!) I reply. I'm racking up the meetings with political icons and, while I realise that this is a peculiar obsession, I confess that I am a politics groupie. I couldn't care less about Mick Jagger et al; I want to meet people who are flamboyant and entertaining!

Today's get-together is designed to show the media the plans for the celebrations a short time away. Hands gesture over the landscape, indicating that the stage will go there, the VIP entrance there, the arena there, the grandstand there. But the international media needs some clarification: 'And those shacks over there? Those people will be moved and compensated?'

'Yes, they will move over to the other side of the lake and, of course, they will be compensated.'

'How much will they be compensated? There have been estimates of US$40 per family and yet some of them have been farming that land for 40 years, for generations. They're not only homes but livelihoods too.'

'God! House, crops, look at them, they're not worth much,' replies Minister Ramos-Horta.

No wonder the UN prefers to control spin. In order to prevent *faux pas* of this kind, UNTAET has embarked on a publicity campaign which suggests that Timor is a happy little Utopia filled with razzamatazz, and where the UN presents a pert, shiny image. So, as the weeks plunge on towards the Independence celebrations, journalists sit back and watch a spin that goes:

> There is no dual economy.
> There is no tension between the locals and internationals.
> There is no crime.
> This is the most successful mission in United Nations history.

It is a mantra which seeps subliminally into my thoughts; messages which are heard so many times I feel I will just repeat them in place of alternative conversation. Great thought has been put into appearances — so much so that I am convinced Sergio has a limitless supply of bright blue shirts.

Sergio is certainly a wise man — he is completely aware that, in the eyes of the world, the UN came too late to Rwanda and gathered significant criticism for Kofi Annan, who was responsible for an ill-advised memo prior to the violence there which stated that the situation wasn't as bad as other people thought; Somalia is seen as a catastrophe that led to a Hollywood blockbuster; Yugoslavia is revealed in a French/Bosnian film about the UN's incompetence, self-interest and lack of care for the local population; the collapse of many Cambodian institutions after the UN handover is outlined in a scathingly written exposé; and on and on . . . This has all left the long-term employee, Sergio, who has served with the UN in Bangladesh, Sudan, Cyprus, Mozambique, Peru, Lebanon, Kosovo, Cambodia, Yugoslavia and the Great Lakes region of Africa, with a concern for controlling the media's reporting about his organisation. Therefore, it is enough to be seen to be a success, even more than it is to be that success.

Frustrated international journalists have responded in East Timor by releasing a satirical magazine, the *Xanana Republic Gazette*, which says it quotes UN sources in articles titled 'Crime Less Than Zero', for example. Fearing reprisal, such as the loss of jobs or the removal of their media passes (further evidence of the problem), these reporters — representing some of the world's most prestigious news organisations — distribute their lampoon anonymously.

Arriving back at work, I, curious, join a crowd that is peeking into the auditorium out the back in which, amid sweltering heat created by those tarpaulins, there is a group of Timorese from a remote district dressed in their traditional get-ups dancing along to the beat of drums, all while Ignatius Jones films with a digital camera held up high in the air. 'No, no, no, no, no!' he interrupts, getting them to begin again, his way. It is a clash of civilisations that I find delightful. These people are performing steps handed down for generations with a great deal of historical significance and here's this First World creative director losing his temper under the pressure of his impossible task. 'No, no, no, no, no ' . . . It's true theatre and appropriate to these times.

But an impossible task? No, no, no, no, no. In 2001 in Sydney, when I was somewhat ignorant of the implications, the idea of this extravaganza was raised. Thinking, 'Why not? Tremendous idea,' I arranged for Ramos-Horta to attend the New Year's Eve celebrations at the Sydney Opera House organised by the only team capable of bringing to life such a vision. It was a serendipitous night and everyone agreed the idea was fabulous: a big, camp production in the middle of a dust bowl within a chaotic nation. With a flourish. Add in the funding and organisational support provided by the UN, the City of Sydney and a vault full of corporate sponsors, and these theatrical passions and flair are represented here in the auditorium out the back of TVTL.

Certainly, the flamboyant Ignatius provides for an entertaining diversion whenever he passes into frame wherever he is about town. He is a stand-out anomaly here with his scotch in hand, the effervescent style, the arms flailing, the affectionate turn of phrase, the designer combat pants, the personality which is, quite frankly, fuchsia, darling, not the requisite lilac.

Sitting in a meeting with the Independence celebration committee, UN operatives are clearly bewildered and worried by all the *Creativity* and they respond to Ignatius's requirements, describing each as impossible; pronouncing that, at best, each will be referred to those in authority for approval. They resist his pleas for them to move at pace, to be decisive, to take responsibility. The bureaucrats representing the nations of the world say they need to follow 'best practice', with a duplication appropriate to a bureaucracy like theirs, 'best practice'. Then suddenly it occurs, the fuchsia explosion, with an artiste declaring to his UN colleagues in escalating octaves, 'Right, that's it then, if best practice is taking three weeks to get this approved then we don't have a show so *we may as well all go to the pub*!'

Painting the town pink does require a massive logistical feat. It is a triumph to merely organise the transportation of dancers from the remote regions into Dili for a rehearsal in the back shed at TVTL, when they're accustomed to travelling by pony. And it all has to be done with the production team members succumbing to tropical diseases, the dreadful heat which creates a terrible thirst, the best practice of the UN's PR strategy and poor infrastructure. It's a challenge for the man who put on the Sydney Olympics Closing Ceremony in 2000 in a place with roads and electricity.

The days continue to a marching beat onwards to Independence, rrrrump pa pum pump, and I jump out of a UN vehicle, leaving Maluco waiting in the dark — it is simply inconceivable that he could come into my room — and I run inside alone, to my bathroom, stomping my feet as I shower, quickly. It is 11 pm and, despite the looming witching hour, I want to go out and enjoy the enthusiasm of this ecstatic city, and I am thankful that the electricity is on, meaning I can burst onto the social stage smelling of soap and Diorissimo, not dust and sweat. The orthodox thought here is that perfume attracts mosquitoes and increases the risk of diseases like malaria and dengue, but that is a risk I am prepared to take as I spray myself behind each ear, on my inside wrists, oh, why not? — and I send the scent down inside my shirt (you never know), lock my flimsy wooden doors behind me, rush across the garden in the dark, past Saint Philomena, and jump back into the car. 'Where shall we go?'

We discuss our options, which are many at the moment because Dili has been overrun with people and the venues are open at all hours to capture the trade during this exhilarating and lucrative time. That's when I see him. 'Shh, Maluco. Don't start the car. Look.' And in the dark I point out the small Timorese man creeping around the front of the house, hiding behind bushes, moving forward bit by bit, from one to another, towards the doors that he clearly thinks I lie behind. As he mounts the veranda steps, he's spooked by a barking dog and he runs all the way through the garden as fast as he can and into the slum behind. 'Bizarre. It was like watching a TV show except it's my life unfolding over there, or so the intruder intends. What should we do? Once again he hasn't actually committed a serious felony.'

'Oh, Lynne, I don't know.'

'Well, you're the police officer.' Just then, once more, I catch sight of movement. 'Shh, quiet, don't move, there he is again,' I whisper. And the persistent prowler is creeping, creeping. This time he decides to go around the back of the house and I watch him mount the veranda at the rear and move out of sight and he re-emerges around the side, just under the light from my bathroom window, which I realise now can be seen from the shacks out the back, and he is about to mount the veranda from the other side, just metres from my door, and I want to watch what he will do, I want him to break into my room and commit a crime so I can call the Australians at Dili police station, when suddenly some of my fellow residents burst out of a door and they chase him and I launch myself from the car and he escapes despite my very best athletic efforts.

I don't know how much longer I can rely on Saint Philomena's intervention, quite frankly. But the hotels are all filled, every available space in anyone's house has been taken by visitors, and I am so busy each day that I simply don't have the time to move house. And yet . . . I may feel happy to risk rotten mosquito-borne diseases with remarkable bravery but should I really risk rape? I hope my admirer is afraid of cockroaches the size of him. Still, I don't even bother going to the police.

I've got other matters on my mind, anyway. Work could do with some improved feng shui as well. The hostility surrounding the evaluation report has had me moved upstairs, to a desk in the head office of OCPI. Still, it's worth all the aggravation because, as one African staff member contributes in his interview,

> The media, radio and TV, are a double-edged sword. If it is given to a foolish man it will be used to destroy. If you give it to a wise man it will be used to develop.

For a document thought of as a malae plot, it gives the Timorese an opportunity to be heard. The malae are 'lazy', 'racist', 'so-called professionals', who have contributed little, apparently:

> . . . the thing that makes me really sad is that we expected to learn some skills from them. I find that from my personal experience from the last two years we haven't learned anything from them. It sounds like they came here just to earn money. If they came here just to earn money, at least teach us

> how to develop our country. Because now they're going away and we're still the same. We haven't learned anything.

Did you notice the key in there? And again:

> All I have to say to you is they can buy a car and we can't even afford to buy a bicycle.

(As I type, a sticker is placed on my computer: 'Generously donated to the Government of East Timor by the United Nations.') I'm marvelling at the irony of a station of television journalists who cannot afford to own televisions. Presenters who wear suits when their houses have dirt floors. Female reporters who work twelve-hour days then go home to tend to multiple children. All of them return home each night to shacks with little electricity and water within lives of poverty.

I remember late one night not so long ago in the Popemobile after knock-off, ten of us were negotiating our way through the dirt laneways, along the open sewer drains, in the unlit streets, scruffy children (so many of them) ran through the dark, tiny bamboo kiosks were selling identical products, and we bounced along the pockmarked surface, bounce, bounce, bums into seat alternating with heads into ceiling in a metronomic rhythm, candlelight emanating from tiny huts, until we stopped. A TVTL reporter jumped out of the car and she headed into her home. 'Bonoite,' she waved and we all waved too. 'Bonoite.'

The head of the department, Dr Zamorano, says, 'They hate us here, they hate us.' A retired veteran of three decades' worth of UN missions, he was asked to leave his native Chile again for one last job — to rescue a limping OCPI in East Timor. Yet this man is perplexed by the failure of the United Nations to unite here. 'Other missions they throw flowers as we pass, they say thank you, they bring us baskets of food they make for us. But here? Here they hate us.' And he shakes his jowls and heads off in his UN Land Rover to his oceanfront, hot-water *en-suited*, luxury accommodation behind a fence topped with barbed wire, for which he's paying a fortune in any currency.

Therefore, they want what we have. Money, emancipation, choice, opportunity, equality, the myriad benefits that the developed world has provided us, for which beer is merely the metaphor — and so is a fabulous Independence party.

Still the show must go on with that old razzle-dazzle and with the curtain set to go up, Mario Zamorano tries valiantly to secure funding for the future of the media in East Timor post-Independence. He tries to push legislation through a new parliamentary system to establish a public broadcasting authority; he works hard to ensure the journalists don't rock the boat. Yes, the hapless Mario still understands the priorities of this circus, that it must appear to be a profound success. Which leads a malae staff member to comment about the UN's editorial intervention: 'I think we all felt like marionettes. Pull here, pull there, say this, don't say that.' And: 'We're just clear about our task which is we are basically doing propaganda.'

Time moves ever closer to the show and the planes start coming in at all hours of the day and night, dropping off those who wouldn't miss this event for the world, and my fingers are still a blur on the keyboard when a rock is thrown through a window of my landlord's car, and a cousin whispers that the people in the slum are threatening to overrun the house on Independence eve and she is terrified. But I can't put my thoughts in that direction, I have to keep going, to the beat of the marching band, in the direction of Taci Tolu, assuming that this build-up of tensions is Timor's equivalent to the millennium bug.

Heightened emotions must also be responsible for the now customary catchphrase, 'Malae go home', which the Timorese articulate gleefully. 'Gee, ta. No worries. You're welcome.' At a meeting at OCPI with members of the Timorese leadership, including the nation's leader, Dr Alkatiri, the media sector, it is said, will no longer be subjected to any malae interference. But there is a problem: the OCPI is not able to survive without malae assistance. These Timorians say they want to be left with a fully functioning media sector which will be all theirs, but they haven't worked out answers to some pretty fundamental questions, such as who will fix the equipment without technical know-how or parts.

I sit and ponder whether it was sensible of the UN to have ever spent all those millions of dollars setting up a TV station in a Third World nation where the second largest city, Baucau, hasn't had electricity for the last two months? Given that a TV can cost twice the average monthly wage of a Timorese police officer, how many locals have access to the medium?

But then, in an egalitarian world, shouldn't every effort be made to provide everyone with all avenues of communication, to give people the information they need to promote a stable, useful democracy in their country? If they do not have access to electronic media will they be condemned in an ever-widening gulf between the Third and First Worlds? Does television provide a worldview of tolerance and ideas that other methods of communication cannot? Does it lead to aspirational development because those in the developing world can see lifestyles they may covet — with Art Deco apartments, colour-coordinated fridges, Hermès Kelly bags, lip gloss, flared hipsters, *Big Brother* and educated women, well-fed children, effective healthcare systems, law and order, freedom of speech, truthful and transparent government? Is it essential, therefore, that the United Nations establish a television station before it provides a more tangible, immediate, concrete alleviation of poverty? It's a debate that seems kinda moot, I'm thinking, while I paste in a quote by one Timorese employee who says: 'I always compare with previously and the present. So the present is not as good as with the past.'

Whatever, they get to celebrate at The Greatest Show on Earth! And as the caravans pour into town and the Big Top takes over a field in Taci Tolu I press PRINT on the evaluation report and a sick feeling rises in my guts as I realise, *oh no*, it's true, I don't have a pass to the main event! I mean, it's the reason I came to this place. Cockroaches, a monochromatic wardrobe, cold-water showers, a non-flushing toilet, dust, sweat, pigs, Dili-belly, a Timorese stalker, theft, homesickness, rotting Scanlan & Theodores, a haircut that is two inches too short on one side from the salon in the Thai restaurant, all that bloody suffering and sacrifice ... and it was all for nought. Because I'll be watching it on television after all.

12

ROLL UP, ROLL UP

I may as well be in Sydney for God's sake. It's a catastrophe. Who do I know with a television here anyway? Thank God for the UN alcohol rations because I'll need to drown my sorrows, but then again I'm not really supposed to drink in front of the Timorese so I'll have to do it in a cupboard somewhere, secretly like an old wino, which may or may not be particularly far from the case.

I'm beginning to manifest genuine hatred towards the people around town who are already wearing their access passes around their necks, dickheads, but maybe there is someone else I know who isn't going and we can make a miserable night of it. You probably can't even buy cocktail umbrellas in this joint, just to compound the pain, I'm thinking, as I lie on my bed, throwing paper planes at the cockroaches that scuttle along the floor.

I've sent messages to everybody I know in this city and they all seem to have glamorous and consequential jobs right in the middle of the action. Beep, beep. Beep, beep. My phone. **1 new message. Can you help with hosting international guests?** says the Foreign Affairs Minister. I read the screen on my phone and my mouth falls open. **Can I? I'll wear a lilac clown suit while doing it, if required!**

Everyone wants to be a part of the circus. Even some rather large and uninvited guests have gatecrashed Dili. Enormous warships are in the harbour, and one of them is docked with a very bold and bright insignia surveying the town and its people. Surely not. It makes no sense as well as contravening a number of international conventions. Yes, they are all Indonesian. How utterly extraordinary that the military of the recent oppressors would send its warships into UN territory, waters that will be East Timorese come tomorrow night. It's a provocative act and it only serves to make that government look petty and foolish. To counter such an impression, the Indonesian Government publicly states that it didn't order this influx of six warships, that it's the military's fault, which is a suggestion that doesn't fill many with an enormous amount of confidence in the cohesiveness of a neighbouring nation that lies within sight, just past the fleet of battleships, especially given the events of '99.

Regardless, international relations are going very well for me. Maluco and I drive around, soaking in the carnival air. The suburb of Bidau Lecidere, where I live, is the hotspot, with people swarming over the streets and UN and diplomatic vehicles among the cafés along the main strip. A motorcade passes us, the Prado in the centre has the numberplate '2' and my mobile sounds: Beep, beep. Beep, beep. I press the MENU button. **1 new message. God, you have no taste.** It's José in diplomatic form, and I laugh. He'll never be able to provoke me again after giving me a role during Independence. He's a hero to me, and his off-duty bodyguard negotiates the traffic carefully from the driver's seat beside me.

'It's all very exciting,' I say.

'Yes, kitten.' Maluco smiles then moves the car towards the waterfront, Indonesian warships float in the distance now while the GNR patrols by in the setting sun and we stop at the Sea View Restaurant. This place is a maze of tables under canopies of palm fronds behind a fence, with a TV showing BBC World; enterprising street kids sell Independence souvenirs for entrepreneurial price tags (which I nevertheless pay); glasses are raised to toast this occasion; I raise my glass too.

'Congratulations,' says Maluco.

'Yes, it is a big moment, my friend, the report's finished and I imagine it's being presented to Sergio as we toast.' Savouring the Australian white, I watch the stream of cars and the Indonesian-style food stalls on tiny trailers being wheeled on foot along on the road between me and the ocean, and sheer delight courses through a body filled with adrenalin. The buzz in the city has filled me with buzz too. I'm going to burst with it all!

'Yes, Lynne. That's good.'

'It's more than good, it's immense! Maluco, everything is so great. Feel this city!'

He laughs. He too is filled with the ecstasy of this event. 'So, you are happy with your work? It was interesting?' he says, his ecstasy leading him to feel my leg too.

'It was fascinating. I tell you what, the Malae Syndrome, it's such a deep scar,' I reply, removing his hand and placing it on a leg that is not mine.

'Yes. You know, I looked for a Timorese on my team.' He puts his hand on my hand.

'The Tiger team,' I proffer, holding his hand merely to put it back over onto the table in front of him.

'Yes, kitten,' he smiles, 'and I go out to the car and there he is, lying on the driver's seat and it's all the way back, his trousers open, his gun on the passenger seat beside him and he is asleep!'

'That'd have to make The Master feel safe.'

'Yes, I told the guy that anyone who want-ed to get to The Master would kill the protection officer first and it would be easy.' He puts his hand back on my leg.

'Absolutely. And the assassin could use the protection officer's gun if he hadn't self-catered. So what did your bloke say?'

'He swore at me, laugh-ed, roll-ed over to get back to sleep.'

'He's scaling the heights of professional conduct. And tomorrow they will be in control. They will be our bosses and, saying that, you know you can't be affectionate in public here, it's not acceptable.' He takes back possession of his hand, unwillingly, as our dinner (together with the requisite hair as garnish) arrives. 'Hey, aren't the celebrations having a rehearsal tonight?'

'Yes.'

'You have an all access pass on your car, don't you?'

'Oh, yes, Lynne, we can go anywhere you want, you'd like?'

'I'd like.'

We leave and I'm walking to the car, chatting with a friend who's joined us. We cross the little laneway just beside the restaurant, deep in happy conversation until, looking to my left, I see a Timor taxi heading straight for me and the driver doesn't slow down; in fact, he deliberately swerves in my direction and I jump away just in time to prevent contact between my body and the metal panels. I swear at the driver and, regaining my composure, walk onwards, relieved, to our UN car, when a yell from behind makes me turn around.

Maluco is running, he is drawing his gun and he sticks it in through the window of the now stationary taxi and he rams it against the driver's head, at point blank range.

I am horrified and I watch as Maluco screams in Portuguese, bouncing in fury from foot to foot.

'Maluco, put down the gun. It's okay. Just put down the gun.'

All those months ago he did tell me that he'd take care of me and be my close personal protection, and I have felt his deep displeasure when I have been near his Master, but on this night I am witnessing the most horrifying act I have ever seen in my life and I don't know if he is going to pull the trigger, and I can see the face of the driver who has a loaded, cocked gun jammed up against his head, eyes open wide, and I see the passenger too, looking at me in terror, while Maluco's entire body remains contorted with his rage.

'Maluco, please, just put it down, it's okay, everything is okay.'

Driver, passenger, me, none of us knows if the trigger will be pulled. Finally we do and Maluco lowers the gun. He does. Thank God. He does. I move to him and spirit him to his car. He is shaking, realisation, guilt perhaps, is starting to filter into his system and he gets behind the wheel and reverses out of the park quickly and we drive along the oceanfront, past the Australian Embassy residential compound, the Brazilian Embassy, away from Dili, when suddenly there is a car beside us. It is the taxi. 'Everyone, down!' Are they armed? Luckily their weapon is their car and it's a lot smaller than ours. They try to run us off the road for the duration of the busy way to the airport, yelling obscenities, while Maluco manoeuvres a car and furious people below his window gesticulate with their hands, trying to ram us with the dilapidated taxi, until finally we turn sharply into safety through the security cordon at Taci Tolu where they can't follow us because they are Timorese, and we are in the venue for their Independence celebrations and safe in the Cirque de Josés.

In the dawn, I'm waiting at the Protocol Office to perform the most important task of the day — arranging my backstage pass to the party tonight. It's the day a nation has prayed for through the violence of decades, it's also the lure that brought me to a place filled with nutcases and guns (even worse: nutcases with guns), a place that's overflowing with adrenalin and emotion. It's the pinnacle of the lives of those here today.

The New York people who have flown in to work on the celebrations appreciate my help with the bilateral meetings and they promise that for my effort I will not only get a pass to the circus, I'll also get to meet Bill Clinton. This place has gone Clinton mad. He's not even the leader of his nation any more, and he is yet to fly in, but Clinton Fever is gripping Dili with a passion quite like Beatlemania.

Many delegations representing various nations will be having meetings with the Timorese leadership to discuss all sorts of foreign policy issues, primarily the continued support by the international community for the rebuilding of this nation. All of them are of vital importance to Timor, but Bill Clinton is the leader of the pack, the pop president, the guy who cemented this cult of celebrity in international politics. What a remarkable legacy he's left, this man has star power! He's made affairs of state the fascination of voters from every constituency.

Heading into the big white UNTAET building, I am excited! To the meeting room I bound! And in I go to find it filthy and in disarray. I can't imagine Bill and I making ourselves acquainted here; it seems contrary to the scene as I'd imagined it (a thousand times) and a New Yorker is aghast at what is far from best practice: 'Oh no! This is, like, *wrong*!' He approaches every Timorese woman he sees and asks them if they can mop the floor. No, no, no, no, no. With increased hysteria he gives it another try, approaching a dark-skinned woman and beginning with his request, 'Excuse me, could I ask you to . . .' I grab him by the scruff of the neck just before he enunciates the word 'mop' and, yanking him away, I explain a near bilateral disaster; 'Ana Pessoa, Timor's Minister for Justice, ex-wife of the Foreign Affairs Minister, member of the Prime

Minister's faction, with a personality *so* not likely to respond well to a request to *mop the floor*!' Actually, no Timorian will allow herself to be told to mop a floor on this of all days, so I mop it instead, thinking how remiss of me it was to forget to wear my French maid's uniform. Bill might have liked it.

Beep, beep. Beep, beep. My phone. **1 new message. Good to hear you are working hard. If you go missing we'll know you're with Clinton.** It's Ramos-Horta. Yes, Clinton Fever has hit town and his fans include his political colleagues. I lean on my mop and watch the planes in the sky, so many of them arriving from around the world. I'm on the first floor, looking out of the windows and contemplating the people and cars and boats below me. What a remarkable undertaking this has been. Who would ever have imagined that the world would be celebrating here today?

Carloads of delegations and security officers are snaking their way to this room now . . . Norway, Britain, Malaysia, Angola . . . the running sheet has a sequence of audiences with various Timorese leaders, but, as they arrive, everyone announces their desire to meet the charismatic Timorese hero, the non-executive figurehead, Xanana, followed by the world-famous Nobel Peace Laureate Ramos-Horta. Most seem visibly disappointed to hear they have been scheduled to meet Alkatiri, the executive leader of East Timor, the man who will be Prime Minister in a matter of hours, when Independence is declared at midnight, the statesman without the power of celebrity that leaders require these days. 'Who's he?' they ask me.

'Er, the leader of East Timor,' I reply. Britain simply won't leave the meeting room, despite appeals for them to join my coalition of the willing, until they chat with Xanana and his wife, which throws the timetable into chaos. I go and seek out Kirsty in her offices. 'Hello?' I'm knocking on the door and letting myself in.

'Hello,' comes a voice from another room.

I follow it. 'Hi, Kirsty, I'm Lynne. Um, the British delegation would love to meet you. In fact, they won't go until they do and I was wondering if you could see them, like, really quickly, because we have a bit of heavy multinational traffic.' The pregnant first lady tells me that she has significant bladder issues, the baby's foot, you know how it is (I have no idea), and she just needs to pop to the loo, again, it's never-ending, apparently. Okay. That's an unusual introduction to a woman of her status but I guess there's a lady in every First Lady.

In the corridor I'm confronted by a Timorese Foreign Affairs employee who is apoplectic. Brunei has arrived. Is there anywhere for them to wait? I enter a space not designed to house someone who is accustomed to eunuchs waving palm fronds. The Timorese employee looks around at a clearly inadequate area and his eyes take on an expression of fright. He is certain now that he will be sacked. 'Don't worry,' I tell him. 'I'll look after Brunei.' I've followed international relations closely and I'll provide a diversion by testing my skills in diplomacy.

Meeting the Foreign Minister of Brunei (His Royal Highness Prince Mohamed Bolkiah; otherwise known as Duli Yang Teramat Mulia Paduka Seri Pengiran Perdana Wazir Sahibul Himmah Wal-Waqar Pengiran Muda) on the staircase, I introduce myself. He doesn't reciprocate (I guess it would be time-consuming) so I follow with, 'Ahem, er, well then, how long have you been in Timor?' while smiling agreeably and guiding him into the waiting area, such as it is.

'One hour.'

'Welcome,' I offer graciously.

Silence.

Okay, this politics caper is not as easy as first thought. 'So, first time?' He's hardly in my thrall.

'Of course.' I'm running out of techniques for appeasement. Still, this is important work. After all, Brunei is an extraordinarily rich country and it is essential that this individual from an oil-rich nation gains a fine impression of Timor.

'Well, I am sure you will enjoy seeing this beautiful country.'

'We leave in three hours.'

Right. 'Ahem, please excuse me for a moment.' The Timorese Foreign Affairs employee is waiting, wringing his hands in despair, appealing to me to save his job. 'Don't worry, piece of cake. It's all under control,' I assure him, then race, desperately, towards Kirsty's offices again.

Politics is being demystified in my mind, frankly. I am starting to see that behind the scenes it's populated by people with all the moods, urges, frailties and peccadilloes of humans. I guess I'd always thought that leaders, given their consequential jobs, had to be magnificent and superhuman. I feel somewhat deflated. Which is why I don't mind so much when I'm told that Bill Clinton's plane is late and he and I won't be having a bilateral meeting of our own after all, because when I think of it, he's the most visceral of them all, a man before a statesman.

So I head off to the planned champagne events, beginning down on the waterfront with Kofi Annan inaugurating a park. We stand side by side and he would have a yack with me, I'm sure, if he'd notice me at all (if only to ask why I am at this important function wearing clothes covered with the evidence of mop water). Then we adjourn to a marquee and take glasses from passing trays. There's Bill, I note disinterestedly, he's towering over the people who surround him wearing their ceremonial best. The sunset shines through the coconut trees and the colossal headdresses of a collection of foreign leaders. Funny thing is, despite the dark skins of some of the visitors, the host country has very few of its own in attendance, other than those who carry the trays (popular as they are).

Drinking the imported wines and dining on catered food provided on massive platters covering trestle tables which stretch in an arch for 100 metres or more, I'm observing the mingling luminaries who represent countries from all over the various worlds and I realise that the collective power of these individual humans controls the lives of so many of us. As they quaff I find the thought a little unsettling really. In fact, I find that I'm developing some cynicism. I don't think I want to be a politics groupie any more.

As night falls, guests hop into motorcades or Sydney buses that say 'City-QVB' on their destination boards. I'm surprised to see one of the significant contributors to this event standing patiently *sans* a protocol host. It's the Lord Mayor of Sydney, Frank Sartor, the man who provided the flamboyant creatives behind the fabulous party to come, but he's not a world leader and the New York protocol officers have left him to his own devices, so he stands, patiently.

We board a minivan heading out to Taci Tolu and I am thrilled to be slowly snaking along in the long line of transport that finally arrives at the VIP entrance. Disembarking from the bus and moving along a concrete path, I find José at the end, welcoming arrivals on his own. He takes my elbow and positions me beside him, introducing world-renowned individuals to a woman who is filthy. No fetching designer dacks on me, no lovely fragrant scent, no shiny coiffure, just grime and sweat. 'I hear the Saudi delegation needs assistance,' I say, trying to flee.

'No, Miss, they'll be fine. There's no need to go.' He grabs my elbow again and I look up at the next wave of immaculate international visitors. When did everyone else get the chance to toilet? The delegations continue to step up and I continue to extend my dirty hand in welcome. I discreetly lick my palm and try to pat down my hair, wipe under my eyes and brush away some of the accumulated dirt from my business apparel, as beautiful envoys take my hand (do they follow by wiping their hands on their thighs?), until José is called to the world's stage. 'Congratulations, Minister.' The moment has come. Timor's moment. His moment. I look at the man who has contributed so much of his life to his nation's Independence and I kiss him on either cheek then he heads up the stairs and onto the VVIP podium, thinking, I imagine, of anything but this occasion right now for fear the tears will fall. They fill my eyes already.

I am relegated to the VIP area and, choosing to sit in the dust at the edge of the field where the show starts to unfold, I am mesmerised by the cultural performance, some the rehearsals for which I'd seen in that building in the back yard of TVTL. Here they are, groups of Timorese men and women, thousands of them, representing all the districts, each in their traditional dress with variations in the tais wrapped around their bodies, feather crowns or bull's horns on their heads, bells clinking around their ankles, troupes moving around the arena to take their turn to dance for the VVIPs and the cameras, the women still clutching their handbags.

Enormous TV screens surround the field and they're transmitting the images I can see in front of me which are being seen around the world: there is the requisite segment with children holding candles, an ode to the heroes of the resistance, an enormous construction of a crocodile floating while the banks of lights illuminate the field of dreams come true, and 200 000 Timorese people (a quarter of the population) watch on in the dirt of the valley around us.

The speeches begin and an announcement is made. President Megawati Sukarnoputri of Indonesia has arrived and she joins the VVIPs to the sound of the audience erupting in foot-stomping, hand-clapping cheers for her, which makes absolutely no sense to me.

Standing just in front of the stage now I can see Bill Clinton and Sergio Vieira de Mello on the same stand. There's my Prime Minister, John Howard. Helen Clark from New Zealand is seated off to the side, having to crane her neck to the left to see the stage, her view obscured by a couple of egos, a grey bouffant or two, and some African headdresses representing GDPs less than hers. Kofi Annan rises up and says some words just before midnight, and the emotion is starting to peak as he proclaims to the Timorese that he is:

> . . . deeply proud of the partnership between you, the people of East Timor, and us, the United Nations. Together we have laid the foundations for a prosperous and democratic future. While your determination assured the success of your cause, you have also been helped by friends from all over the world. For the past two and a half years, a global alliance of nations have come together to make this day possible.

Pity the Timorese couldn't understand an English word he just said, but I thought it was a cracker. And the clock strikes twelve and hundreds of years of domination end as freedom is proclaimed and the flag of the United Nations is lowered and the new flag of the First Nation of the New Millennium is raised. Surely there's not a dry eye in the house, as Xanana Gusmão is sworn in as the first President of the Republica Democratica de Timor-Leste. At the beginning of liberty, I look up at José and he does indeed manage to stifle that tear.

So history occurs and the sky explodes with two fireworks displays — generously donated by the countries of China and Thailand, the magnificent glitter reflecting on a lake which was a favoured place for the Indonesians to hover over in helicopters and throw people to their deaths during the occupation. And now, on 20 May 2002, the red, green, white lights twinkle benignly alongside the stars — lunar and political — and the banging sound is no longer gunfire, it is the happy burst of sparkles lighting up the sky. Yes, it's been a fabulous party.

At 1 am the VVIPs and VIPs all start to leave in their motorised convoys. Meanwhile, the Timorese, who were made to walk, are given a concert to keep them occupied at Taci Tolu for another three hours to allow a clear and convenient run back for the international visitors. I decide to stay and I can hear the melodies in Tetum start up as I head backstage, where the production team are all surprisingly subdued. After bringing this impossible spectacular to life, they aren't celebrating, they seem stunned, exhausted, relieved. Ignatius and his company have toiled for three months, earning UNV wages, defeating peculiar Third World obstacles, and UN ones too, putting on a breathtaking party; and now all they want to do is have a quiet VB to satisfy their hard months' thirst.

Frank Sartor, however, is buoyed by this triumph and he tells me he's heading for parliament. He's been offered a blue-ribbon seat to contest in the 2003 NSW election with a guaranteed ministerial portfolio and I think about First World politics and I can see that Frank has it all worked out — that it is about parties, fabulous ones. It's all pop-culture-popularity-policy. And somehow it seems so inconsequential in comparison to the work that has to be done here. Here they need what we have, and I want them to learn from those of us who come from a robust democracy, a place where we know how to be free, where democracy has allowed us to become rich, a place where we put on fabulous parties — because we can afford to.

But here the democracy needs to come first and, upon reflection, I can see that this is not New York and this is not the First World; somebody's geography is on the fritz if they think that millions of dollars' worth of pomp is best practice for the use of money in East Timor.

I walk up onto the stage area where Timorese pop stars are belting out tunes in their language. The crowd has spilled into the arena and there is the biggest dance floor I have ever seen in my life as the joyous people scream 'Viva Timor!', feathers bouncing up and down on the heads of those in the middle of the mass who performed for the world just an hour before, and I sit in the seat recently occupied by Bill Clinton and watch with my chin on my hand as it all culminates, with a flourish, this time for the people who are the true VVIPs, the Timorese. Finally they are celebrating on their own, in their style. No champagne, no liveried waiters, no international broadcast, no speeches in languages they can't understand.

Sitting amongst the empty seats reserved for the world's elite, their name cards scattered around me, it occurs to me that the Timorese now govern their country, independently, and it is desperately poor. With that thought, I wish now that the party for international palates, as fabulous as it was, hadn't occurred at all. I wish we'd had the sort of celebration the Timorese deserved, that we'd flicked the switch on a dependable electricity station or inaugurated a filtered water system, and let them dance all night.

Instead, in the eyes of the world this UN mission has been a tremendous success, celebrated with a popularly acclaimed closing-night performance of UNTAET.

13

A NEW CHAPTER

Lying on the beach, sand in my hair and down my pants, holding a glass of duty-free scotch and feeling its lovely warmth in my throat, there's the sound of water lapping nearby and I'm looking up at the constellation of stars directly above me. 'Did you see that? Quick, make a wish!' And in the darkness, lying with two Australian women I've just met and the cranky Peruvian, I make my wish on a mystical shooting star: I wish that I would fall in love in one month, then promptly burst into peals of giggles at the stupidity of my request to the galaxy but, nonetheless, we debate whether we'll have to split the proceeds into four.

With Independence comes international responsibilities, including the singing of treaties. There are various agreements which protect certain lovely, thoughtful, philosophical ideals, such as eradication of poverty, equality for women and a peaceful interaction within one's worldwide family of states. Yes, all very idealistic but, let's be honest, the treaty causing the most interest today is that relating to the profits from the Timor Gap.

The oil- and gas-rich underwater paradise of the Timor Sea has been the cause of Timor's suffering for 25 years, and now the Timorese leaders think it would be a tidy piece of karma for them to use the proceeds to pay for the creation of an Asian state the likes of Singapore.

However, international politics doesn't work quite that simply. A country doesn't always get what it wants or deserves. The world is, after all, just like a school yard with the tough kids and the cool ones, a bully or two, the conscientious few, and a few scrawny nerds. (Put a country to each description. Play the quiz and win.)

Australia was the previous recipient of a significant proportion of the oil and gas deal in the treaty (now void) it signed with Indonesia, and it wants a cut now too. Australia reckons it deserves it because . . . um, we're neighbours . . . and, um, we led the peacekeeping force into Timor in '99 . . . and, ah, because we fucken say so, ORRIGHT! And, as is the case when faced with a bully in any playground, big or small, the Timorese really can't say no, given that Australian aid is rebuilding a significant proportion of the country's infrastructure and aid is not a gift, it is a transaction; that Australia will be a significant economic partner in the future; that the petroleum companies want Australia involved to provide necessary utilities such as a working tax system, law and order, a highly trained workforce, and a generally corruption-free government and economy; and that Nigeria showed how a poor country can fall victim to mining interests with profit as the priority. Therefore, irrespective of its need or peeve, Timor can't put its foot down when it's not yet standing on its own two feet.

Back in the room I so diligently mopped, now milling around on my clean floorboards is a motley crew: (in ascending scale of height) the Prime Minister of East Timor,

Dr Mari Alkatiri; their Foreign Affairs Minister, Dr José Ramos-Horta ('Hello Miss'); my Prime Minister, Mr John Howard; and, towering above them all, Australia's Foreign Affairs Minister, Mr Alexander Hagrid Downer, *sans* fishnet stockings.

The Australians beam for the cameras, while Dr Mari Alkatiri's grimace suggests that he's been required to sign the treaty in his own blood or, more so, the blood of his people. Then Mr Howard presents a tribute in English to his country's neighbour, reiterating Australia's contribution to Timor's phoenix-like rise from its ashes. And there is truth to this: Australia has made contributions from 1999 to 2001 of around A$81 million in humanitarian assistance and near A$1.4 billion to peacekeeping, plus there was the pledge of A$150 million over the following four years in bilateral aid.

So, with the charitable credentials of Australia reinforced, there is a bottle of champagne to open, of course. This is politics, after all, plus it is a tradition established in 1989 by Gareth Gareth Evans, then Foreign Affairs Minister of Australia, when he toasted Indonesia's equivalent, Ali Alatas, as they flew over the Timor Sea, celebrating their version of the treaty — the signing of which made Australia the only country in the world to legally recognise the Indonesian occupation of East Timor. So these *bon vivants*, today, are raising their glasses and following the lead set by Gareth Gareth, the man who would-be-if-he-could-be head of UNESCO, who dreamed of being the world's next Secretary General of the UN after Boutros-Boutros Ghali, the accomplished inter-party liaison, the original *bon vivant*.

Watching the infant Timor take its first toddling steps, while it holds onto Australia's hand, I can see that this new nation needs to learn how to be independent in capability as well as in name. It's lucky, then, that after these generous international guests have departed, the UN will remain, no longer as the nation's de facto government, but as mentor to the Timorese one.

The United Nations Mission of Support for East Timor (UNMISET) is tiny compared to its precursor, UNTAET, and the mad scramble for the few P-level jobs is a fantastic experiment in game theory for any student of international relations. After all, if you were a malae in a comfy position of authority, you would hardly choose to end the sequence of colossal pay cheques would you? In line with the component of human nature that promotes self-interest, the people who hold the lucrative UN positions hang onto them for dear life, creating an environment of nepotism and cronyism. Many want to secure one of the posts on offer here or, even better, a promotion to Geneva or, the Holy Grail, a posting to New York. Afghanistan, anyone? Bugger off!

Australians are disadvantaged because, despite being well educated and capable, we are specifically crossed off the lists for positions due to a UN policy called National Balance. It is an affirmative action policy that requires people to be hired from all over the world. Fantastic idea, in theory. In practice it's not the best. According to the policy, the balance of nationalities working in the UN must be proportionate to each country's financial contribution to the UN. In other words, each member country pays money each year to the operating costs of the UN, an amount calculated relative to a country's gross domestic product (GDP). Australia, with its population of only around 20 million, has a financial contribution that is relatively small so only a relatively small number of UN personnel can be Australian and we have reached our quota. This means that incompetent candidates from developing nations with low literacy levels and professional standards but higher GDPs are chosen to meet those quotas.

Idealism is a wonderful quality, but it has disadvantages if it actually precludes merit — specifically in a new and unstable nation which requires a peacekeeping mission. Thus, self-interest and National Balance combine to create a bittersweet soup of culturally proportionate, interrelated idiots.

Upon the conclusion of my contract, Dr Zamorano says he'd be happy to recommend me for a position with the successor mission, UNMISET, but National Balance precludes it. 'Australia,' he says, 'is a migrant nation. What is your cultural background?'

'Ukrainian,' I reply.

'Can you get a Ukrainian passport?'

Sure. And wear ribbons in my hair, red knee-high boots and cross-stitched peasant shirts, all for a job. (Generally, only those who aren't Ukrainian will go to these lengths.) Still, in the interests of sheer self-interest I phone my mum.

'Mum, could you find out if I can get Ukrainian citizenship?'

'Why on earth would I do that?'

'Well, ignoring that you struggled to raise me in the developing world in which I'd have opportunity, I'd like a job with the UN and I need to appear poor and disadvantaged.'

'And just how would I find out about Ukrainian immigration practices, Lynne?'

'There must be a Ukrainian consul in North Melbourne.'

'I doubt you'd be able to, Lynne.'

'Somehow, Olga, I don't think they turn down many people who want to migrate from the First to the Third World.' (Message to self: don't arrive by boat.)

I decide to take matters into my own hands.

'Ring ring.'

'Zshch dobrrrraaaaa rrrrrovnik . . . blah, blah, blah.' Stuff I don't understand.

'Hello, I was wondering if you could help me. I'm from a family that arrived post-war in Australia and I would like to get Ukrainian citizenship. Do I qualify?'

'Vun moment.' A hand is placed over the phone and I can hear the blah, blah, blah with the addition of another sound . . . is that laughter?

'Ve vill gif yoo citizenship but . . . ' she *is* laughing '. . . zere iss a prrrrroblem. Yoo cannot haf dyool passporrrrrrrrrrrrt.'

'That'd be right! The Australian government *would* make this impossible.'

'No, ve vill not allow it.' Then rather ominously, 'Ve vant ourrrrrrrrr people to go back.'

'Oh.'

So I need to choose — Australian citizenship and no UN job, or Ukrainian citizenship and up to the dizzying heights of the UN (then back to the Mother Country apparently). What should I do? In the short term I go to the beach. The car heads out towards Arieia Branca then turns right, past José's house with the enormous thatched roofs which was completed just in time for Independence, then over the hill and a turn to the left and bumping along a cross-country track. On the right, at a little secluded beach, I notice the ringmaster, Sergio, and his companion, Carolina, entwined, she's stroking his hair, on their very last day in Timor before they head towards their promotions — he to a rumoured post as head of UNHCR and she to a posting in UN New York headquarters. It's a beautiful scene of two people in love.

As eve falls it's time for the last party on the Independence celebrations social calendar for those of us who worked here as UNVs. A special function in honour of the plain label UN workers — and at this no-frills do we have to pay for our own drinks. Back on the harbour foreshore, the marquee is long gone and we sit on plastic chairs in the encroaching darkness and say our farewells. The time has come for most of these people to go home. The head of UNVs worldwide, Sharon Capeling-Alakija, a Canadian, is in town. She is a delightful woman who cares very deeply for her protégés and the work they do. Sharon, with her representative in Timor, Kevin Gilroy, asks me about my time here. 'Oh, I love it. It has been a time of celebration but also of good work.'

'What work?'

I tell them about the evaluation report and Kevin comments, 'I heard about that project but I didn't realise a UNV was doing it.' An elephant stamp? Another contract? Strings pulled? Anyone for a blow job? They are swamped by others with the very same questions. Maybe this is my farewell too, I'm speculating, as I raise my beer sadly to my mouth.

'Hey Lynne! You're not going to believe it but I've got a job!'

It's a colleague from OCPI. 'Where?'

'Here!'

'Here?'

'Yes! I found out about it today! Do you remember I told you that I knew someone who worked in the Timor Sea Office, someone who used to work for my father?'

'Sure, I remember.'

'Well, she told me today the office wants a media adviser and she says I can have the job if I want it.'

'But you've never expressed an interest in staying on in Timor to me.'

'I didn't want to, but this is too big an opportunity for me to turn down! It's huge! They want me to provide my CV but that's just a formality.'

'Well, gee, congratulations.'

'I know! The government here wants to target the Australian voters and turn them against their government, so it's huge! Anyway, I was wondering if I could ask you a favour? As you know, I haven't ever worked as a journalist and I've never been a media adviser before and I know nothing about the Timor Gap treaty so I was wondering if I could maybe meet with you for a couple of hours and you could teach me everything there is to know?'

'Yeah, sure, that should just about do it.'

On Comoro Road there is a remarkable stream of traffic heading to the airport. UN contracts are ending, aid organisations are pulling out, businesses that made a fortune during the party period are leaving. The building that was previously known as the Australian Consulate is replacing a sign with the new shiny words proclaiming that it is now an embassy.

At the City Café on the main drag it is clear to see that, with so many catching their one-way flights out of Timor, the city is now a ghost town. I expect to see tumbleweed as I sit and drink my long black, and stare out onto the road. Where are the traffic jams of UN Land Rovers, the horns honking, the multilingual chatter, the energy? I'm shocked to realise that East Timor may even become tranquil. Who would have thought? The peacefulness is interrupted by a UN helicopter at low height flying overhead, whump, whump, whump. Then the GNR drive slowly by — thank goodness some things remain the same, the view would be awfully barren without them.

I'll be pleased when the goodbyes are over, they can be awfully depressing, especially when they seem a portent of mine. Tonight's is a farewell at the Australian Embassy residential compound. The long-time consul and newly promoted ambassador, James Batley, is throwing his with chardonnay and gourmet finger food on trays carried by Timorians.

I'm here today with the remnants of the chattering classes in Dili and I recognise many of the faces — great, right before I have to leave Timor and go home. But at least in this cultural context I feel it allowable to wear a short, tight skirt and some stilettos. 'Hello, Miss,' says a sometime Australian resident. Oh, fuck, now I'm in trouble. 'Hello, José,' and I stamp out my cigarette and try to tug the skirt down below my knees. 'You look beautiful, did you dress up for me?' causing me to decide that I will *never* understand that man. Otherwise, it's all 'G'day', 'G'day', 'G'day', from the assembled faces until, 'G'day,' says a bloke I don't recognise at all, 'how ya g'arn?'

'Fine, thank you. And you?'

'Fine, yeah. So, what brings you to Timor?'

'Well, I'm coming to the end of my UN contract, but I hope to get another one and stay.'

'Yeah? Geez, why?'

'I like it here. For me it satisfies the combination of my principles and professional skills.'

'Yeah? Never heard it described like that before.'

'You're an Australian police officer, right?'

'Yeah.'

'Well, I love East Timor, I just have an ongoing issue with a certain Timorese admirer I've attracted who likes to stalk me at my house.' I tell him the tale and he is concerned, and I am pleased to have my anxiety validated by a professional security enforcer who assures me that Australians always take care of their own, that it's a responsibility under an international treaty of some kind.

Beep, beep. Beep, beep. My phone. **1 new message. Call José Guterres at the Prime Minister's office now.** It's José Ramos-Horta. I make the call as instructed. I reach the voicemail. I send a message saying just that to the Foreign Affairs Minister, who calls me immediately from the top of Christo Rei. '[Huff, puff] I told you to call him straightaway.'

'I did but I can't get through.'

'God, if you want a job I suggest you keep trying *until* you get through. If this is so important to you, continue calling.'

Which is why I try and try and try and it really is a trying exercise as days pass by. Finally, I am summoned to a meeting with the leader of East Timor, the Prime Minister, and I wear my very most conservative outfit and arrive at his offices in the big white building that is occupied by the government now to be ushered inside a room which is very plush and I sit with him on a big new cream-coloured couch.

I interviewed Mari Alkatiri from Australia in 2001 when I broke a story on a 30-year-old mining concession for the Timor Gap owned by a US company called PetroTimor. But the last time the Prime Minister and I spoke was when we sat together in a café in a remote, mountainous region of Timor, and I was swaying under the effects of car sickness and he told me that he's been known to suffer from the illness too, that on one occasion the entire Timorese Council of Ministers was afflicted when they'd travelled to an outlying area. So he and I greet each other genially and I begin by wishing him parabens on the Independence of his nation. They are congratulations he accepts, happily, before pointing out that his nation celebrated its Independence at a succession of champagne events at which Timorese people stood beyond the gates. Then, back to the matter at hand, he says to me, 'Lynne,' he says, 'I know I am not an enigmatic man' — he means to say charismatic — 'and so I think this will be a wonderful collaboration.' He is known for his lack of cooperation with the media here so he needs advice, which suits me fine when he offers me a job as his adviser. HA HA!

I return to my room with its flimsy doors and cat-sized cockroaches and I pack to fly out to Bali for a well-deserved R and R with hot-water showers before the work begins again in earnest. And, as I wait to board my plane, the police officer from the embassy party comes up to me, saying he'll find accommodation while I'm gone, that it's not safe for me to stay where I live, and he'll pick me up from Dili airport when I return. Ah yes, I'm starting to learn that in this playground, as with others, you need alliances. It's not about what you deserve, it's about the relationships you build.

14

MATE'S RATES

I am back at the airport but this time my arrival is somewhat more auspicious and far less traumatic. In fact, I am a model of composure, given that I have flown in with a job to come to, accommodation arranged, a lift awaiting, a suitcase of new ensembles from a meander through Ubud, refreshed from hours under a high-pressure, clean, rodent-free shower, and a manicure, pedicure and full day at a spa behind me. And, thus, I float into the arrivals area with all the sparkle of Doris Day.

'G'day,' says BH1.*

'Oh hello, dear fellow,' (or similar) I reply.

My bag is taken from my hand by the chivalrous gent and we skip throo the forecourt . . . to be swamped by the dirty throngs of poor Timorian teenagers, 'Taxi Missus? Hello Missus. Dollar Missus?' That's enough to drop me down to the grotty earth with a thud, and we hop into a UN Land Rover, taking off to pick up my personal effects (twinsets,

*Police-style pseudonyms have been used in the place of the protagonists' real names. Any of the many Australian police serving in East Timor (resident of the compound or in private accommodation) who have been omitted from these descriptions were incidental to these events.

pillbox hats, corsets? No, insect repellent, frayed G-strings, hermetically sealed stilettos, and clothing no longer in the perky shade of lilac but mimicking Timor's water in a shade of pale brown instead). Welcome back Missus Leeen.

'There is a room in the police compound. You're not really supposed to stay there but one bloke is in Australia so you can have his room for free for three weeks until he comes back. I've spoken to him and he says it's fine.'

'Really? The Australian police compound?'

'Yeah. You are at risk and policing isn't only about catching crims after they've committed a crime. Responsible policing is about prevention too.'

'Oh, thank you. I think that's a great perspective on policing.'

'Well, you're one of us and, even overseas, Australians have a responsibility to take care of their own.'

I am moved by this nationalism. I am so happy to know that I am part of a caring, selfless community. How moving it is to feel safe and protected within a society, wherever we may find ourselves in the world.

'Thank you, really. How can I ever thank you enough?'

'Don't worry about it.'

With my assets on board we travel along the oceanfront in the stark daylight, continuing onto a road in Dili that is truly a filthy eyesore. Debris lines the uneven bitumen — rubbish, vermin, dilapidated shacks, vandalised burned-out buildings with 'For Rent' signs placed in front by wishful locals. But even worse than the aesthetics is the dust. You see, it's the dry season and while it provides a respite from the humidity, it comes at a price. Everything is dirty, cars inside and out, clothes, air, skin, mouth ... simply everything contains ground-in dirt and dust. And Comoro Road, with its heavy traffic and bleak streetscape, is the dustbin. To think I arrived just a short time ago with the fragrance of a flower petal bath still wafting from me and already I feel covered in a brown grime.

Approaching the Australian Embassy we turn right just before it and, 200 metres down another dusty road, we stop outside a big white fence with barbed wire on the top and a gate on one side.

We walk inside the gate, past a small blue car in the driveway and through another gate is a large common area with a long black table surrounded by the ubiquitous plastic chairs of Timor, a fridge and chest freezer filled with the food and beverages of this bunch of cultural gourmands, and it is surrounded by a kitchen container, accommodation containers and a toilet and shower container.

I am directed to my temporary digs and inside I find a queen-sized bed, a police-issue chest, uniforms in the wardrobe, family photos on the table, and a . . . can it be true? . . . stereo. Turning on Triple J, I jump on the bed and go 'Yippee!' at my clean, cool, white, private, comfortable, serendipitous circumstances. All is right in the world, I know at this moment. All is right in the world.

That evening the other residents arrive home one by one. It's a motley crew. But the common thread of compatibility that runs between them, other than their chosen profession, is that all of them insist: 'It'll all go to shit when we leave.'

They are a mob of caricatures and, for the first time since I came to East Timor, there is no need for me to be lonely. I have company whenever I want. I have friends to talk to. My homesickness is lessened as I am shown a vibrant underbelly of Dili that is colourful and fun and mad. I am having a ball as I am launched onto society's circuit. Ta-da!

There are platters of prawns and lobsters at a restaurant hidden behind a bamboo wall, the plastic furniture placed on an uneven concrete floor, foodstuffs covered in the oil so beloved of any cook influenced by the Portuguese style of cholesterol augmentation, toilets that leave one terribly concerned about the conditions in the kitchen, loud laughter and booming obscenities, 'Ya fucken cunt!' created by the combination of environment and food — and the beer we've brought with us in true Aussie BYO style.

And there is the karaoke bar in the late hours of the morning where our nation's finest belt out 'East Timor, East Timor . . . If I can make it here, I'll make it anywhere . . .' as I go through the crowd, picking up mislaid weapons — tap, tap, tap on a shoulder — 'Not now, Lynnie . . . I want to wake up in a city that's full of pigs . . .' — tap, tap, tap on a shoulder — 'Lynnie, Jesus, can't you see this is important . . . Top of the shit-heap, a . . . pain . . . in . . . the . . . bum . . .' — tap, tap, tap. 'For fuck's sake, Lynnie, what?'

'Um, aren't you missing something?' I say, as I point to the three gun-belts around my waist.

'Ah, good on ya, Lynnie. Look after 'em for us, would ya? . . . I'll make youse make a brand new start of it . . .' Tap, tap, tap. 'What now?'

'The only reason you can assume these guns are safe is because I couldn't shoot them if I wanted to, I don't know how.'

'Good enough for me, now rack off . . . If I can make it here . . . I'll make it fucken anywhere. It's up to you, East Timor, East TIMORRRR . . .'

Then there are the evening hours when we sit back with beers in hands and these men tell me of the frustrations of capacity-building a competent Timorese force to assume the mantle once the UNPOL leaves, as it will in two years or so. The problem is in attitude, apparently. According to the Australian police officers, the locals have adapted to receiving assistance from the Portuguese, then the Indonesians, then the United Nations and, as a result, they simply don't have the work ethic or ambition to have their capacity built. The coppers say they are taken for granted and, thus, with a nod to Monty Python, my new social circle parodies the Timorese:

> 'What have the Indonesians ever done for us?'
>
> 'Well, they built the water system, the telecommunications infrastructure, the electricity station . . .'
>
> 'Yes, but other than the water system, the telecommunications infrastructure, the electricity station, what have the Indonesians ever done for us?'
>
> 'Well, they provided the education system, the health system, the clam-shell shelters on the beach, the statue of Jesus . . .'
>
> 'Yes, yes, yes, but other than the water system, the telecommunications infrastructure, the electricity station, the education system, the health system, the clam-shell shelters on the beach, the statue of Jesus, what have the Indonesians ever done for us?'

Killed one-third of the population? So while it is terribly politically incorrect, I belly-laugh along to this expression of the irritation the Australians feel at the Malae Syndrome they encounter every day in the course of their work, and I suspect my eagerness to join in comes from my own irritation, which is outgrowing theirs. I've had no word from Prime Minister Alkatiri's office and I sit in the compound every day, leaving messages with his office, stressed about my peculiar situation. I mean, I am in an expensive country, with no money coming into my bank account, worried about a job that seemed so certain and appropriate given that it came with a PM's handshake. Surely that has a certain clout? Still, all I can do is exercise patience and presume that the combination of the UN's bureaucracy and the training wheels on the East

Timorese Government has created the delay. Thank God I have sanctuary here.

It's a sweltering afternoon. One of those times when everything moves in slow motion. Conserving energy, unable to push through the wall of heat with ease, I've just emerged from a shower and I'm languishing in a towel in an air-conditioned container-room when the phone rings, 'Hello.'

It's BH1. 'He's struck again. Last night. It was a woman sitting on her veranda working on her laptop. She was hit in the head with a machete by the bastard sneaking up from behind her.'

'Oh my God. Is she all right?'

'She's in hospital. Pretty cut up. Two machete strikes to the head, one went through her hand when she lifted her arms to protect herself from a blow.'

'Where did it happen?'

'Two blocks from your old house.'

'Oh.'

'So we were right to err on the side of caution in your case, Lynnie.'

'Yep, seems so.'

It's hard for me to fully comprehend the enormity of this. I feel no relief that it was her, not me. I just feel lucky to be here, safe. Two machete strikes to the head. One through her hand. How blessed I am. How can I ever thank these Australian police officers enough?

The ongoing safety issue, my financial situation, the rising hysteria I feel about the elusive job contract and the boredom of my days has made me even more dependent on these angels in the guise of big boofy coppers. As each of them leaves for and returns from a CTO (cumulated time off holiday period), I move from room to room. I lay my head where I can, gratefully, emerging in the hot mornings to eat Vegemite on toast and drink cups of tea, listening to the chatter of Francis Leach from the radio, watching pirate DVDs in the afternoons (war movies, mostly — the men seem to have interests contrary to their role in a mission for peace) and waiting until 5 pm when, one by one, I hear the UN cars pull up out the front and in come my mates in their blue combat pants, black boots, gun-belts, short-sleeved blue shirts with the Australian flag badge and the UN one too.

As a tiny token, I try to repay my benefactors in a style I know that men of their sort will appreciate — a barbecue . . . with a twist. And so it is that on one moonlit evening my friends behold a sight previously unknown in this environment. Scented candles burn and tropical flowers (picked from neighbourhood trees) adorn the table centre. The dress code, I've told the boys, is black tie — they come close with their shorts and thongs. While the hostess is resplendent in her tiara, 'Good evening, gentlemen,' I greet them.

'Geez,' they all say. 'Princess, you didn't have to do this.'

'It's the least I could do.' Once the table is cluttered with empty plates, we turn to conversation. 'A few of you have served on more than this mission, haven't you?' I ask.

'Yep, me.'

'I have.'

'Me too.'

'How many missions have you done?'

'Four.'

'I've done five.'

'Two.'

'You're all pups, I'm on number six.'

Australian police have contributed to missions in Cyprus, Cambodia, Mozambique, Haiti, Somalia, Bougainville, Solomon Islands, East Timor and our external territories:

Christmas, Cocos and Norfolk Islands. Cyprus alone has been availing itself of our resources since May 1964 and it continues to do so. I wonder about the strategic interest for us in that place or the international brownie points achieved, and I also wonder why on earth the place hasn't been stabilised by now. Either the coppers haven't done a very good job or the island is beyond redemption. Still, these overseas jaunts require a never-ending revolving parade of armed and uniformed representatives of Austra-ya (as they say on Triple J).

'A mission length is six months, right?'

'Yep. Sometimes you can get an extension to nine months if you want.'

'God, well, how do your families cope?'

'You all have to adjust.'

'But it must be agony. How much of your children's development have you missed? Actaully, how many of your children's births have you missed?' There are nods from a few faces around the table and a couple of raised hands in the flickering light. 'So why do you do it?'

'The money!' They chorus and high-five.

'What price a family though?'

'Princess, you do one of these missions and you can pay off your fucken house.'

'That's great, but how many of those houses will still have a wife inside them?'

'I tell you what, the missus is pretty happy to own the house and have the money to spend on clothes and rubbish.'

'Clothes and rubbish, every woman's dream.'

'Well, if you do two missions you can have the car, the pool, the Great Australian Dream.'

'We can set ourselves up for life doing these jobs.'

'Yeah, I can see that, but it depends on your priorities. You can set yourself up for life *financially* but the strain on your families must be enormous.'

'None of that sentimental bullshit, the opportunity's too good.'

'You've explained why you do one or two missions, but why would you need to do six?'

'We do 'em because we can. Missions are handled by the Australian Federal Police.'

'Although some are here from the NSW and Victorian police forces.'

'Because they need the numbers. The AFP had to allow the other forces to contribute.'

'If you choose?'

'Oh yeah, if I choose and I do. But for some blokes the missus puts her foot down.'

'Mustn't be swimmers. Talking about rubbish, when one of you is going to the tip next can I come too?'

'Why the fuck would you want to go to the tip? That's no place for a princess.'

'I hear it's a real example of the struggle of the Timorese. I hear it's painful and profound.'

'The tip? You're bonkers. You'll just see filthy kids scavenging.'

'Yeah, that's the point . . .'

Certainly, tonight seems to be proving that friends don't have to share political convictions, outlooks or turns of phrase. Still, they are taking care of me and I am beginning to feel some affection for each of them, caricatures as they are.

15

ONE MAN'S TREASURE

Thus it is that I find myself in a UN police car laden with a week's accumulated First World refuse, bumping along a Third World road. Down towards the town of Liquica we go.

'Any word from the Prime Minister?' asks BH1.

'Nope. That's such a funny question to ask nonchalantly: "Any word from the Prime Minister?" It's like: "Any word from Brad Pitt or Karl Lagerfeld?"', I say.

'I'm worried about you, Lynnie. Now, you know you are welcome to stay as long as you like in the compound, don't you.'

'Thank you, that's great.'

'It's true. Do you need money? How are you living?' he asks as he scours the roadside for signs of debris beyond the normal level in Timor. 'Can you see any signs to this tip? We were supposed to go out on the Liquica road then continue straight on past the turn-off and there's supposed to be a sign that points to the tip.'

'I haven't seen a sign. What language would it be in anyway? Look, I'm fine with money. I can make do on what I have for a while, especially with the accommodation in the compound. It really is giving me more time and less stress.'

'Do you want to borrow my phone to call your family?'

'Oh, no thanks. I talk to them. They're not worried. I've been putting them through this sort of thing for years. They're used to me being away, they know I can look after myself.'

It really is beautiful countryside up here. At this point we are a little elevated, and down below the car I can see undulating hills disappearing into a faraway basin and trees fading in colour from vibrant green beside me through to translucent grey in the distance.

'I'm gunna do a U-ie, I think we've gone too far.' BH1 concentrates on the rocky road. 'The delay with the job must be getting you down, though. I mean, before, whenever I saw you, it was when you were working or at a function, so this change in your situation must be pretty hard to handle. You don't have to put on a brave face for me, I'm here, I care. You're allowed to be scared.'

'I'm fine. Really. Yeah, it's frustrating but it's fine. It'll all work out. But hang on a minute, just to backtrack, when did we meet before? I feel awful, I can't remember.'

'I saw you when you were on a helicopter and I was looking after a delegation of police officers. We were looking at the borders with West Timor. It was in the run-up to the presidential election, before Independence . . . Where is this place? Right, I'm going to turn around one more time and that's it. It's getting dark.'

'Oh no, we can't give up, I've been looking forward to this!' The car bumps around and changes direction.

'All right.' He looks at me and smiles, 'Yeah, and I saw you at another embassy function and at the footy game on Anzac Day.'

'Oh, okay. But we didn't actually talk on any of these occasions, did we?'

'No, we didn't really.'

'For a minute there I was worried I'd offended you.'

'No, of course not. And, look, it's the sign!' I am deep in thought as we drive into the dump.

The UN police vehicle pulls to a stop on the dirt track among hills of debris and suddenly they appear. The children of the tip. They run to us and dexterously leap onto the back of the ute and with great strength they quickly, desperately, unload the bins to the ground then begin their excited search for treasure. It's enough to break your heart. These kids live here and they exist by trawling through our rubbish, our discarded objects, looking for something to eat, to sell, to use. They are filthy, of course. They're throwing themselves into the bins, scrambling in, reaching into the depths, into the smelly, rotting contents. (This is why the military flies its refuse to Darwin to protect confidentiality.)

The bins emptied now, we tie them back onto the tray of the car and I hand these pathetic urchins one dollar each in pity and a Timorese adult approaches. I watch to see if the man removes their money but he walks over and tells them they are bad children. No they're not. *Sin. Lae.* He clips one of them over the head and points at me. They follow his instruction and say, 'Thank you.' And, with tears in my eyes, I tell them '*Nada* = you're welcome' in reply when really I should be thanking them for the grace they've shown despite their poverty, I'm thinking as I turn away and, reaching for the car door, I see BH1 watching on, and he has tears in his eyes as well.

Under the shade of a tree I lie in my bikini, propped up on my elbows, looking after the gun-belts while the boys play football along the waterline. Up there Cazaly — well it would be but for the considerable bulk these players are carrying which weighs down their efforts to launch themselves from the ground. I am in stitches laughing at the antics. There goes BH6, he bounces, in control, as he heads down towards the goalposts (two sticks). Oh wait, a threat comes in the guise of BH8, hang on, that's not strictly in keeping with the rules, is it? Now here's the relatively sprite BH7 lunging for the ball, and it's snatched and, oh! Who would have thought BH6 could be so nimble and he's streaking ahead, he prepares his position for the winning kick and the others are nearing on him, then, all of a sudden, oh my God, there go his dacks!

The beach has erupted in laughter and I'm clapping, proudly, when BH1 arrives and sits down beside me, in full uniform. 'There's a riot at Becora Jail,' he says.

Ah, Becora Jail. Legend has it that the rebel elements in Timor are all accommodated in this place. When the New Zealanders ran it, the food and conditions were better than those back in the villages of home. Now, however, with the Pakistanis in charge, the establishment has lost a couple of stars from its rating. No longer is it the preferred accommodation of the bandana-wearing Timorese residents and, hence, the disgruntled tenants, angered by a clear drop in standards, are summarily ripping up the lovely rock gardens for ammunition as they congregate in the jail yard. That's the way to get the management's attention.

'They're no match for an international police force, surely.'

'We don't know whether to send the riot police in. We've been meeting all day in headquarters deciding how we react to this.'

'I'm guessing negotiation isn't an answer?'

'They need to be disarmed and put back into their cells. They've gone mad. The aggression and the hatred. You can see they want to kill us. They will if they can.'

'That's a compelling reason to disarm them.'

'Sure, if no one's killed doing it.'

'What about the GNR and the Timorese riot police?'

'Yeah, they are awaiting instruction, that's the decision we've got to make, and there are other teams of riot police waiting as well.'

'Ah, yes, the Brazilians. They should be experts, prison rioting is a sport in their country.'

'Lynnie, the people in there are crazy and the thing that's important to understand is that they are filled with hatred. This is something we don't see a lot of in Australia. What is a group of people motivated by deep-seated hatred capable of doing?'

'That's why you send in the experts. The GNR are in this country for this very reason. Surely it's time to see if they're more than pretty faces?' Here I am, involved in policing strategy in a pressure-cooker moment with a great deal at stake and I'm resplendent in my camouflage outfit. A green bikini.

I'm shaken out of my thoughts on essential policing matters when his phone rings. He answers, 'Yep, ah-ha, right.' He hangs up. 'It's on,' he says to me, 'we're going in. I've got to go.' He gets up from the sand. 'We're still on for dinner though, right?' he says as he goes.

I resume my position reclining in the sand and marvel at the dichotomy of Timor — that a peacekeeping mission is under way around us, with armed riot police engaged in securing safety, risking danger, quelling the continual threats to the stability of this country, while, at the very same time, others can be enjoying a day at the beach, me in my cossie, BH6 and BH8 holding BH7 upside down, off-duty professionals from all over the world watching on from their towels, Timorese men lined up along the fence for their day out perving at the white-skinned female bodies, local children moving through the crowd selling cigarettes, Latino music booming from the Caz Bar where malae go to buy beer or chilled coconuts to drink looking out at the sea.

The now sunburned policemen thud themselves down nearby to me. 'Pass us a tinny, would ya Lynnie,' says BH6, laughing at his poetry.

'Look at those fucken slimy cunts,' says BH7, pointing over to the Portuguese men playing soccer with Timorese children.

Up he jumps and he postures, mincing in front of us with his biceps clenched, stomach pulled in, sunglasses on, and a swarthy, cocky tilt to the head, 'Ola, you beautiful lady want make salsa with me big Latino stud?' he says in a faux Portuguese accent that doesn't in any way replicate the original. Laughter roars at the wickedness.

Meanwhile, at Becora, teams of police are swarming in behind their shields, with batons raised, in waves, while rocks rain down on them.

That night I wait until the late hours. Eventually BH1 walks in, dishevelled, exhausted, perturbed. He has a couple of small facial wounds but otherwise the damage isn't of a physical nature. 'I cannot explain to you what today was like. I have never, in all my years of policing, seen anything like that. It was raining rocks. So many. Like hail.' He is clearly shaken.

'Are you okay?'

'Oh, well, you have to be. God, Lynnie, their eyes. It is so difficult to explain what it looks like to see a mob of people all of them with eyes looking at us as though we should die. Pure hatred. These are battle-scarred people, Lynnie.'

'That's what they've been raised with, I guess. They're socialised with violence.'

'Yeah, they have a capacity for it, all right. The lot of them. In Australia you get an individual like this every now and then who is pretty rotten but it is beyond comprehension that you could have an entire group of people that is capable of terrible violence.'

'What about the other international police?'

'The Brazilians thought it was a walk in the park.'

'Ah, practice makes perfect. How did the GNR conduct themselves? They didn't damage any faces, did they?'

'They went in and got the prisoners into their cells and seized their weapons. They broke a few local bones doing it but it was never going to be a waltz.'

'Broken bones?'

'Yes. The real damage was done once the prisoners were back in their cells and the Timorese riot police set upon them. By this stage, Lynne, the prisoners were unarmed and yet their bloody countrymen started beating the shit out of them.'

'That's a human rights violation.'

'Absolutely. As well as being a fucken ugly thing to do, to be capable of. See what I mean about these people?'

'What did you do?'

'We had to dismiss the Timorese riot police, tell them to go home, which is the biggest insult we could give them.'

'Oh, gee, that'll learn 'em.'

'You should have seen Viktor, the GNR commander, he came into the office and he threw down his helmet in fury saying he'd never seen anything like it in his life, that these people weren't police officers.'

'And this is the man who'd just overseen the breaking of bones himself.'

'Yeah, but he did his job with minimal force, only as much as was required. The Timorese, though, they'd been terrified and cowering out the front, they'd refused to go in while the whole riot was going on, but once the prisoners were in their cells, unarmed, sitting ducks, they laid into them. Amazing.'

'They clearly haven't been capacity-built in human rights and self-control.'

'Exactly. Police officers have to understand the power they have and how important it is not to abuse it. It doesn't matter how pissed off the Timorese were, you just can't resort to brutal behaviour. Policing isn't about brute strength, it's about intelligence and humanity. That's where you can see the difference between dickheads in uniforms and highly trained police. I was impressed with Viktor and his team. You know, he was genuinely upset to see the prisoners being abused. He's a good man. As much as we like to make fun of them because of the way they look, you've got to be impressed with the Portuguese when they actually do some work.'

'Hey, I don't make fun of the way they look!'

Finally, a smile. 'I'm going to have a shower.' He ups to leave, then he stops, remembering that he's actually failed to fulfil his most important responsibility of the day, 'Hey, I'm sorry about dinner.'

'No worries. I'm just glad you're all right.'

'Thanks, that means a lot.' I can tell he means it and I guess I'd need someone to care if I'd had rocks thrown at my head today.

But that's enough emotion, this is a police compound! 'I'm sure the shield helped,' I joke.

'I didn't have a shield.'

It's late morning and I'm entertaining myself with a copy of the police newsletter, riveting though some may find it, when there's an entrance.

'I tell you what, Lynnie, you are right when you talk about the locals and their fascination with the international women. The prisoners' cells were just plastered with pornographic pictures of white women.' BH1 joins me at the table in the common area of the compound. It's a little early for lunchtime but I am pleased to have the company.

'I wish I could say that surprises me.'

'It's made me worried about you, actually. They were pretty disturbing images. Nothing romantic, pretty awful.'

'You're not telling me anything I don't already know. They literally think we are all porn stars, culturally predisposed to feats of extraordinary contortion and, of course, moral-free.'

'You've got to be careful, Lynnie. Really careful. I'm serious.'

'Yeah, I know, that's why I'm not flaunting my shoulders in the streets.'

'They're fascinated by more than your shoulders, I can tell you that.' I shouldn't be flippant, BH1 does genuinely look out for me.

'Why do you worry about me so much?'

'I like to think that if I had a daughter overseas on her own that she'd be safe, that people would take care of her.'

'I'm not as fragile as you think.'

'No, I know, but everyone can do with a hand every now and then. It's no big deal, it's nothing.' Bless him. 'Anyway, I've got something to show you.' He gets up and opens the padlocked doors of the entertainment unit. 'I thought you'd like it. Don't tell anyone you've seen this.' He gets me to move to a chair in front of the TV, puts a video into the player and presses PLAY.

The images show a dirt road outside a chicken-wire enclosure from where some rocks are falling among a lot of terrified-looking police officers of all nationalities. We see the damaged offices of Becora Jail, the taunting mob in the yard, and we see the GNR putting on their helmets, shields in hands, batons erect, ready for their gladiatorial conquest. It's like watching a movie and knowing the ending. But where is the hero? 'Which one is Viktor?'

'That one. The one without the shield.' Ah, yes, right answer.

The gate squeaks, 'Oh shit', BH1 fumbles for the remote control and turns off the video as someone walks into the common area and gives us a very curious look as we sit up close to a blank screen.

'Why did you do that? What does it matter if I see this video?' I hiss at him as the intruder keeps on walking and goes to his container-room. And looking around, apparently guilty now, I notice the Timorese security guard craning his neck, paying keen attention to us.

'You're not supposed to see it.'

'Shouldn't it be publicly available? Don't tell me it's being suppressed? What, we wouldn't want the international public to see the way the UN interacts with the local population?'

'It's an internal UN video.'

'Yeah, but I can't see the reason for the secrecy. You're not a secret police force, are you? The police should be accountable for their conduct on that day and, anyway, from what I hear the conduct was pretty good, except for that of the Timorese. And now everyone here will all think we were watching jiggy jigs!' We burst out laughing. 'It's good to see you laughing,' I say.

'It's good to laugh. Thank you.'

'God, you don't have to thank me for making you laugh. Consider it my job around this joint!'

'And you do it very well. Really, you've made me the happiest I've been here, which is no mean feat when I've been finding it pretty hard.'

Blush. 'No worries. Although, I have a bone to pick with you, I hear the GNR have a compound which is like a Club Med with its own bakery and gym and telecommunications and a bar. How can they have a bar when the Australian police compound doesn't? That's a national disgrace!'

'You know, they're having a party there soon. Do you want to go and have a look?'

Ah, hello! Person with double-X chromosomes at twelve o'clock. What woman wouldn't want to go to the GNR compound for a look at the facilities? Not wanting to exacerbate the rivalry between the two police forces, however, I say, 'I guess I could don a frock and bother myself to go along. Only to give you company, of course.'

'I'll see what I can do. I hear tickets are hot property but I'll talk to Viktor and see if I can add one more person to the list.'

'Yep, whatever, no big deal, don't go to any trouble,' I say with studied indifference. But I'm planning, already, to have my shoulders on display.

16

THE STARS ALIGN

I'm getting ready for the event of the season and wouldn't you know it but the water is off. It requires ingenious problem-solving techniques to ingratiate oneself into the Australian Embassy residential compound to ensure that all sweat and dust is removed and that one smells of something floral with a subtle spice undertone.

So dusk sees me in a car that is parking in the area surrounding the Portuguese special police forces installation and we disembark, making our way towards the entry gates at which stand a few taut GNR in civilian clothes. It's a strong early showing. As we announce ourselves, another fine example of the Portuguese gene pool joins us and there are introductions around the group, 'Viktor, this is Lynne.' I shake the hand of the famous commander.

Having been touched by royalty we walk on, down a paved path, past a large communications structure, through accommodation containers, then offices, a large lawn dotted with tables and chairs, followed by vast grass-roofed dance, dining and bar areas, where we find many, many men in particularly tight muscle shirts and jeans. It's all very impressive. (Although it does have an unsettling similarity to Darlinghurst, in spite of the tropical setting.)

Latino music plays and I nurse a beer surveying the scene, before I realise that for the hundreds of men in attendance I am a scene being surveyed too. I feel naked and yet I could have sworn I was wearing a black skirt and dark red Asian-collared top. Anyway, it seems I could be wearing a muu-muu and still seem ravishing. (And thus any comparison with Darlinghurst ends.)

The Australians group together with the addition of the Canadian commander, who is shaped like a barrel of beer and can consume similar liquid weight in a single sitting, and proceed to get really drunk and smoke far too much while talking utter crap. That's multitasking. Whoever said men can only do one thing at a time has never been to a licensed establishment. Ah, yes, cheers! We are enjoying all of this slap-up hospitality. We don't even bother to mingle, why would we, fucken wogs, until proceedings are interrupted by a cultural performance that attracts everyone's attention. A sudden silence falls over the arena and through the entranceway from where three individuals stride triumphantly into the event. Legs in sync and arms swinging with determination, all of their curves snug in extremely tight jumpsuits (excuse me?) in primary colours, all of them women with make-up brightly highlighting their features (how do they do this in the humidity?), all of them with manes flowing wildly (I'm not the only one to have packed hair product). My goodness, those Latino women know how to do sexy (once one gets over the Teletubbies likeness). I anticipate that they'll get to the front of the audience, stage lights will shine from nowhere, a backing track will strike up and they'll burst into song and tightly choreographed dance moves.

Feeling somewhat androgynous in comparison, I . . . wish I hadn't worn flat shoes, damn it. Sure, I had thought it best not to tower over one's hosts, to accept their shortcomings, but now I desperately want elongated calves. I plonk down into my seat, cursing my chin-length hair, square frame and complete absence of sensuality. I neglected along my way in life to accomplish the flounce and I'm yet to learn how to release the inner siren.

I need not be too concerned, though, these vixens haven't captured all of the male attention. Looking at my companions, I note that they're watching the scene with expressions of aghast bemusement on their faces. At this moment, I feel real affection for my countrymen. They clearly believe they would be eaten alive by Latino women, and I am relieved that I may actually fulfil requirements for some of the world's men. Then I take a really good look at them — yep, even through my beer goggles I'm staring straight at a mob of tall, fat, bald blokes.

Although nutcases with anger management issues appear to find me appealing too, and so I hear, 'Lynnie.' I'm nudged by one of the blokes and look over in the direction he indicates to see Maluco staring at me with disconcerting menace.

'Yeah, yeah, I'm onto it. He's been there all night.'

'Lynnie, it's fucking spooky.'

'Okay, okay. And you only know the half of it.' But, saying that, I feel it best to defuse any problem and extend the hand of friendship. I go over, 'Hey.' He ignores me which, hello, makes no sense. 'Great party, hey?' I try again. He stares ahead of him. 'Oh, look, why don't you come and join us?'

'No, Lynne, why don't you go back to your boyfriend. Just go on ignoring me.'

'Actually, I'm not ignoring you. I've come to talk to you and, if we're to be sticklers for accuracy, I could point out that you're ignoring me.'

'Just go back to your boyfriend.'

'What boyfriend? They are all friends.'

'Sure, Lynne. You can tell me that you are friends but I can see.'

'Nothing is happening with any of them! That is the God honest truth!'

'Oh, Lynne, I am a man and I can see.'

'See what? I am struggling to understand what you mean.'

'I can see one of them doesn't think this.'

'Look, I've told you before that in Australia it is completely normal for men and women to have friendships.'

'Friendship? You are so stupid.'

Right. 'That's enough. Come and join us, there is nothing going on.' He ignores me. I stand to go. 'Okay, I have extended a hand but if you don't want it fine, I won't beg you.' I move to go, calling his bluff and, wouldn't ya know it, but finally he rises.

We sit at a table littered with the evidence of our debauchery and BH1 makes his excuses and leaves and the carousing overcomes the Brazilian too and soon the behaviour of those who are left has degenerated so much that we take a turn on the packed dance floor, with the Australians (God, they must be pissed) and a Brazilian, each with two left feet, twirling me around this way and that, under the surveillance of the frighteningly large number of small Portuguese men who've resorted to dancing with each other while awaiting their turns with the three wild strumpets in the inexplicable technicolour jumpsuits.

My feet are black and blue, I have a dizzy head (although that could be due to a number of factors), then the night meets with disaster when we run out of smokes at a time when they seem essential. See, nothing good can come from a smoking dependency. Pondering potential solutions, none of which is to quit, I look over to see someone I know lighting a cigarette about 20 metres away. 'My friend Viktor has cigarettes,' I pronounce as I point in the direction of the commander of the GNR, whom I met for a moment at the gate. Intending to ingratiate himself with me, the non-smoker Maluco heads that way and after a short discussion, during which a finger is pointed over here, he is back clutching a small handful of L&Ms. I distribute them, generously, like lollies and faces light up. 'Now, savour them, kids, that's the lot,' and we begin where we left off — there seems to be an inexhaustible supply of absurd subject matters that we need to traverse tonight — until we are interrupted.

A figure appears behind me. 'Hello. I apologise for my gap in the hospitality. This is my gift to you.' Looking up, exhaling, I see Viktor looking down at me and in his extended hand are two packets of cigarettes.

'Thank you.' And his eyes stare into mine in a direct gaze which is held for a significant length of time, significant to me, anyway, for it is the precise amount of time required for me to fall head over heels in infatuation with a man.

Feigning composure, 'Would you like to join us, captain?' I say.

'Of course,' he replies, as the obliging Maluco vacates his seat beside me and instantly realises what he's done (and then he does or does not hang around for a while, I couldn't say, before apparently storming off).

Meanwhile, my attention is engaged by the man who is seated beside me now and I'm wondering why his presence feels so completely comfortable, his knee sitting just a few centimetres from mine.

I am perplexed and overwhelmed by my body, which is alive right now and feeling drawn to a stranger's. I look at him for the physical signs of the animal magnetism he clearly possesses. There is the dark olive skin. The intelligent eyes. The wide forehead crowned by closely cropped brown hair with a cowlick at the fringe. The pert, chiselled nose, strong chin, his lips turning up at the corners of his mouth in a cheeky smile, all atop a fit body and honed biceps (of course) peeking from the sleeves of his shirt, and it's carried with a self-assurance that comes from success. His is the perfect package.

Despite the all-consuming chemistry, there is one thing that needs to be established before we proceed. 'So, let me guess, married?'

'No, divorced.' That was rather quick and definitive. Suddenly he's even more attractive.

'Great party. Thank you for letting me invite myself.'

He laughs. His English skills are advanced enough for him to understand my humour and, even better, he seems to share it. 'If I know you are in Dili I would invite you. I am surprised we haven't met. But I work so much I don't get out so much. My guys, I know, they are out every night at the City Café and the nightclubs but I don't go.'

'That goes against the stereotype of the GNR.'

He laughs. Yes! 'I have to stay here and work, it has to be this way, I'm always so busy but I am happy my guys go out and enjoy.'

'Oh, don't worry, they do.'

'How do you know this?'

'Not from experience! From observation.'

'So, you are here with many Australian police?'

'Yes, I live in the Australian police compound.'

'But you're not police?'

'No! I'm their mascot. I had a Timorese stalker and so I'm in police protection of sorts. They call themselves my brothers.'

'I should be careful.' He smiles.

'You don't need to worry. They're Australian police, probably more harmless than most. More rhetoric than threat, really.'

After an amount of time which seems impossible to count in mere conventional increments (one hour? two hours? more? less? I don't know, who cares?), all of it filled with intense and uninterrupted words, I am so shocked to be talking to this man in this way. He seems so sincere, thought-provoking, culturally tolerant, kind, philosophical. Too good to be true? But he is true and he's sitting beside me, at his party, ignoring everyone but me.

Latino grooves are filtering over us. 'You want to dance?' he asks.

'Yes, I do.'

Finding ourselves in the middle of the gyrating mass, him and me, my right hand in his left, my other hand on his shoulder, I follow his lead in a salsa, the sensual movement, our bodies so very close, our eyes still locked. With the music's tempo as his guide, he throws me under his arm, a swirl in a circle then back to face him, my left leg pressed back by his right, his groin swaying to the beat, my right leg taking direction and my hips giving a swivel as instructed by his right hand in the small of my back. He flings me around and his arms are crossed over to the front of my body, clasping my hands at the waist. I am enveloped in his embrace now and, looking to my right, to his face over my shoulder, I feel his breath on my neck.

'My guys are surprised,' he croons. 'They never see me dance.' And I am convinced at this moment that I have never danced before, what has come before has merely been an imitation. For me, the world no longer exists beyond this dance floor, was there a past life lived? There seems to be only a present. I am completely possessed by him and the rhythm of us, right here, right now.

The only intrusions by reality come from the Australians who take turns to sidle up to me, tap me on the shoulder and ask if I'm all right. One tries to steer me away, 'I think we should go'.

I resist, 'I'm fine, really, I'm fine.'

'Lynnie, do you know what you're doing?'

'I'm utterly sure, not a doubt.' There is no doubt in my mind that I am having the time of my life with a wonderful man. And, hey, they don't know him like I do and I'm not going to let this become part of a competition between the cultures. So I turn back to Viktor with a smile on my face and my body ready yet again to follow his orders and move into the night as a new song begins. I don't even understand the Portuguese words but a woman is singing about what can only be new love and her voice carries me away with her and him.

'I want to show you something,' he says into my ear. Leading me away from the throng, the music fading into the tropical night, he takes my hand. The temperature seems awfully hot and I can't really breathe, still I manage to follow him through a door. 'Here, this is my office. Can you see what it is I've done?'

'No. Not really.'

'Look.'

'Um, I'm not sure what I am looking for?' (but I think I've found him).

'The shape. Is a pentagon,' he beams. 'I made my guys build an office out of five containers like a pentagon.'

'Oh, I get it. That's very cute.'

'Cute, huh?' he shakes his head, smiling. 'And here,' he says, 'here is a book on the GNR, the history, the work we do.'

'You love your job, don't you?'

'Yes, of course.' How soft his voice is in spite of his line of work.

As we leave his work space and move once more into the heat of the outside, just beyond the door, he draws me to him and, taking a look around, checking for discretion, we move behind a tropical tree and his face edges towards mine, Oh

God, can it be true? and, yes, it's true because our lips meet in a kiss, a sweet kiss, a delicate kiss, a respectful kiss, a rare kiss.

For the sake of propriety it's essential to disengage, but how I wish it wasn't. I could stay in this spot in my life forever. Just here. Behind a frangipani tree, kissing this boy for the very first time.

Resuming the tour of his huge compound, hand in hand, we steal a kiss every now and then — in front of a plaque, behind a hibiscus, there's the accommodation section — jumping apart, giggling, whenever one of his GNR or, heaven forbid, an Australian walks nearby.

We have to return though, reluctantly, so we make our way back to the bar and an enormous creamy cocktail in a glass adorned with a melodramatic display of fruit is pushed my way. As I sip at the elixir of love, I observe a conversation beside me: one of the three Teletubbies, who, up close, looks frankly like a drag queen, begins a dialogue with the captain in Portuguese. Even though I can't understand a word it seems unpleasant. Taking another sip I hear an outburst in English as she announces, 'Congratulations, commander,' and struts away, mane flowing, bright red rounded bottom jiggling in time with the techno beat. 'What is going on, Viktor?' I ask.

One of his men whispers in his ear. 'I think you like this,' he says. 'My guys, they ask if we like the dance floor empty so we can dance alone.'

'Oh, how wonderful but, really, that's not necessary.'

'My guys, they never saw me dance and they would like for us to have privacy if you like.'

'Thank them but no. I couldn't possibly end the party for everyone here. A dance floor is supposed to be filled with lots of people having fun.' He speaks to his GNR who leaves.

'Viktor, what were you talking to that woman about?'

'Who? Oh, is nothing.'

'It didn't sound like nothing, it seemed rather angry.' He lights a cigarette and hands it to me then lights one for himself.

'Well, she likes me, she came here tonight thinking I spend some time with her and she is jealous, that's all.' That makes sense to me, still . . .

'Why did she feel she had ownership over you?'

'Because she has known me and my guys for a long time. And because you are Australian.'

Cross-cultural relationship-building isn't popular here. Regardless, we dance, free of doubts and consumed by a surprisingly believable passion. Music, bodies, sweat, and another bloody tap on my shoulder. It's one of the Australians: 'Lynne, I'm going now. I think you should come with me.'

'No, thanks, I'm fine.'

'Are you sure? How will you get back?'

'I'm sure I can get a lift, don't worry about me, I'm fine.'

'Are you sure?' I'm more than sure and better than fine. In fact, I am the happiest girl in the world and everything will work out just right, including a lift home, all of it, on a night that is simply everything I'd ever imagined but never dared hope for. A princess with her prince, finally.

'So this is what we do,' says Viktor, now that my attention is back on him. 'Tomorrow I pick you up at ten in the morning and we go scuba diving then we have . . .'

'Um, look, at the risk of sounding . . .' completely boring and unappealing and . . . 'a tad inflexible, it's just that I don't scuba dive, and it's not that I have any fundamental philosophical problem with the pursuit or those who pursue it, and I will just note that I am an extremely active person in any number of similarly trendy and daring . . .'

'No problem. So what we do is I pick you up in the morning at ten and we go to the beach for some hours then we take lunch.'

That's a relief. Easily resolved. 'Great,' I say and I smile at him, peering deep into his eyes, luxuriating in their clear intelligence and humour, that combination I've been searching for all my life, swimming in their gaze . . . swimming . . . hang on . . . and I realise . . . with a sense of rising horror . . . that I have just made a first date with a GNR . . . and not just any GNR . . . the commander, the leader, the Type A, top-dog, naturally selected superior model GNR . . . *at the beach!*

Words are simply too inadequate to express the dismay I feel when I realise I have agreed to imminent humiliation. How on earth was this allowed to happen? It's a cruel act of fate, karma and God's wrath all wrapped into one cleanly delivered payback that will have me shortly parading before this man in a bikini — a bikini that is now out of season, I might add. What did I do to deserve this? Oh, man, this has to be some crazy carry-over from a previous life.

I put down my drink, having decided that I will be on a complete zero consumption diet in the how many? in the seven (shit!) seven hours left . . . Oh fuck, I'm thinking, as I pick up my drink again, realising it's the only thing that will get me through. 'I'll have another one,' I say to the barman as I drain my glass.

At 4 am I tell Viktor that I have to go home. I need my beauty sleep and, to be honest, I am very drunk now and I suspect that slurred words aren't terribly attractive, even to a man who speaks English as a second language. So he says he will take me in one of those big vehicles, the one with the numberplate 'GNR 1', me in the right-hand seat of the left-hand drive, and the streets are empty but for an errant pig and he holds my hand in his, smiling at me and he shakes his head. Yes, who would have imagined that Cupid could strike his arrow with such forceful accuracy that two individuals could find themselves combined as one in a night?

He stops on the street in front of the Australian police compound and in the dark, without a care for the Timorese who might observe an inappropriate display, we kiss. We dissolve into a kiss.

Reluctantly dismounting from the car, I walk to the gates, turning for one last glimpse just to make sure it really is true and, determining that it is when he waves, I enter my sanctuary, creeping across the common area and into my room. Then, clutching my singing heart, I fall onto my bed, wide awake, with the images of a wonderful night continuing to play on repeat inside a head filled with uncommon notions of romance and hope.

17

RULES OF ENGAGEMENT

My alarm gives off its horrid scream and I wake up giggling — a sure sign that I'm still pissed. Good, that'll be helpful today, I'm thinking, as I make my way up to vertical and, with a wobble, stand in front of my clothes. Hmm. Discarding items and flinging more of them out from under the bunk bed, I am creating a mountain behind me. Red togs? Green. Casual khaki cargo pants with a little tight T? Nuh. Funky Mooks knee-length shorts and a feminine cotton peasant shirt that subtly highlights the cleavage? No, I'd need cleavage to have it highlighted. Slightly see-through white sundress? See-through? Jesus, remember, Lynne, he's a GNR, so we can predict with some accuracy that he has the body of Adonis and, meanwhile, yours requires airbrushing, the Zone diet, antioxidation, clever lighting, and an all-body black ensemble. Hello, moron, who should've gone scuba diving. Ha ha ha ha!

I boldly decide on the dress. You see, with the help of many scrummy cocktails which are swimming, *swimming, ha ha!*, around in my system I shall live in denial and believe that my figure is truly covetable, even in a green cossie and see-through white frock! Good then. Now that my selection's made I turn to go out to the shower but I'm ambushed by the monster load of discarded ensembles and free fall down with a ku-thud. Ha ha ha ha ha ha! But don't worry! I feel no pain.

Getting up requires three absolutely hilarious attempts and, when I'm finally relatively vertical, I reach out towards the door handle and that's when I spot my reflection in the mirror and quite frankly that's the funniest thing of the day. Ha ha ha ha ha ha!

I weave my way via the empty (thank God for that) common area and negotiate the four steps, bounce through the doorway, lock the bathroom container door behind me, turn on the shower, throw off the clothes of last night and hop under the sprinkling warm water and straightaway become conscious of the fact that I've made a terrible mistake — oh, no — and I promptly sober up, which is not nearly as fun as the state I've just left behind.

Looking in the mirror again, the image staring back at me isn't nearly as amusing as it was a short time before. It's as hideous as the picture of Dorian Gray except that in this instance I know it is, in fact, in direct correlation with my visage. Is it too late to do a pact with any supernatural fiend?

There is simply nothing I can do about the dark bags under my eyes, a cosmetic hasn't been invented with the power to overcome my excesses, and I am condemned to be seen in the harsh rays of daylight while in this condition. Mind you, realistically, at my advanced age, harsh sunlight isn't a great idea in general, even if I had the benefit of two days of continuous sleep, a macrobiotic diet and Botox.

Just last night the captain met me in a darkened environment when he was drunk and in the context of a testosterone explosion. Appreciating this, I sit at the big table and await his arrival, plopping my head onto my hand, the maid moving around in her slow, loping way from room to room, giving each a perfunctory once-over, while I feel increasingly tired, ugly, fat and nervous — I'm going to knock his socks off with my sexy confidence, aren't I? Will he see the crow's feet and broken capillaries? Man, I could do with a cocktail.

And so, I wait. 10 am comes. It goes. And I wait. The maid lopes by me. 'Bondia,' she says with the same lethargy as her movements, bon . . . dee . . . ya. I watch the fireants marching over a jar of peanut butter, all of them following the same mesmerising patterns. The Timorese security guard sleeps over in the barbecue area, where there is some respite from the heat. The ceiling fans above me make their revolutions, around and around, with no real benefit to the woman sitting below them, sweat developing over her entire body surface (a significant water table).

10.15 am comes. It goes. Well, what was I thinking, anyway? As if the commander of the GNR would want to go out with me. Tick tock, tick tock. I wish he would come though. My self-esteem which had peaked at a dangerously high level last night is nosediving terrifyingly.

10.25 am comes. All right, all right, it goes. Dejected, I rise to go back to bed, undoing the bow on my dress at the front as I do. Nothing's very bloody funny any more, is it, Lynne? I'm thinking, as I adopt the slow, loping walk of the Timorese maid which, in my case, results from a hangover coupled with powerful despondency. What *was* I thinking? At which point of last night did I cease to be a realist and allow the vain hope of fairytales to infiltrate a normally rational mind?

My phone rings, 'Hello.'

'Hello, Lynne. It's Viktor.' It's Viktor! Relief and infatuation wash over me. It's Viktor, sigh. With his caramel voice suggesting his caramel hair, caramel eyes, caramel skin. He apologises for his lateness, I didn't even notice, asks if I still want to go out with him, oh, all right, and tells me he'll be in front of my compound in ten minutes, woof!

Ten minutes sees me, with a frighteningly re-energised self-esteem, walking out into the bright sunlight towards his enormous car with the 'GNR 1' numberplate. There is no hiding behind a cloak of darkness now, but I happily go to the left-hand side of the car where our faces come together through the window and we kiss on each cheek, lips very nearly touching lips, so very close.

'Hello.'

'Hello.'

Standing there, me looking deep into him, him looking deep into me, are we the people of the night before? Is he the man I met and instantly loved? Is she the girl who stole my heart away? (Okay, I'm speculating on his thoughts, but my inflated self-esteem's doing the talking.)

The chemistry of the night before was not a construct of alcohol, I can see, for right here, right now, in the middle of a dirt street in the middle of Dili, East Timor, in the bright light of day, I know, without a shadow of doubt, that he and I are at the very centre of the universe, where nothing else exists but this point here. The rest of the world is dark with a spotlight shining only on us, all efforts of the gods are currently focused on this union; and they must be because the power of this moment is simply too great for him or me to have created with our mere human means. (Is that choirsong?)

'What we do,' he says, 'you drive to the beach in the little car and I follow you.'

'Oh. Well. That seems a bit odd, really, when you've got a perfectly good car, and this car in the driveway isn't mine.'

'But women cannot come in GNR cars.' Silence. 'What, you want to come with me?'

'Absolutely.' And I move to the other side, him unwilling to protest and, hopping in, I see him shaking his head, the smile reappearing and we take off in a straight line towards a certain destiny . . .

First stop: Arieia Branca, where I note his ensemble. It's a nervous moment because, let's face it girls, we want a man with panache — and I've found him. Navy blue shorts, a casually untucked short-sleeved navy blue and red checked shirt with Havaianas thongs (not a Speedo or Hawaiian print shirt in sight). And, my God, I approve.

Meanwhile I have an issue with my carefully contrived outfit as we sit on the beach, and I am loath to take off my white sundress to reveal the multitude of sins encapsulated within approximately 10 square centimetres of total bikini fabric.

So, remaining fully clothed, we talk, drawing in the sand with sticks as we do. 'I call my deputy today and he comes to my container. When he arrive, I open the door and he sees me and I'm dressed like this and he says to me "Is everything all right?" and I say, "Of course," and he says, "Are you sure everything is all right?" and I say, "Yes," and I tell him that he is in charge and I am going to the beach. He is shocked. But, you know, my guys, they are very good guys, they care about what I do and they had never see me take a day off to go away from my compound to the . . .' He stops and tells me to turn around, saying quietly, 'Look.' And together we watch a mother dog suckling her puppies.

'Oh, how beautiful.'

'Yeah.' And we watch the scene, enthralled, until we exchange glances that seem loaded with a certain profundity.

'I'd love a puppy,' I say. 'Timor dogs are so cute, if you overlook the festering sores and exposed ribcages. If I had one, I'd be really innovative and feed it and worm it and I think it would be gorgeous.' Excited, happy pups help themselves to a teat each. They are yet to succumb to the diseases that inevitably await them. Right now they have short fluffy fur, small erect ears, and black, white and tan blotches of colour.

It's all contributing to a perfect scene: playful puppies, tropical scene of palm trees, coconuts dotting the sand, mountains shooting up into the sky in a U around us and the expanse of green sea spreading out to Thailand, Singapore, China, America. I could be in a Fijian resort, not a peacekeeping mission.

Continuing to be dressed seems rather ridiculous and it is, therefore, with great aplomb that I disrobe — I'll bet he didn't even notice that pull-in of the tummy (with dubious effect but I'm a creature of habit). And I stand and walk with my paramour, the man who makes this place a paradise, into the water ... albeit using a peculiarly crab-like movement designed to keep my bottom facing away from him.

We don't swim, we sit in the shallow water and continue to talk, both of us deeply moved to discover that we share so much in common (apart from our genders, diametrically opposed careers, nationalities separated by a whole wide world, star signs, heights, backgrounds, ambitions ...) I mean, we both have a master's degree in similar disciplines — his war, mine peace. We're both in East Timor. We both live within a 1-kilometre radius in vaguely similar police compounds. We are both so utterly and ridiculously besotted with each other to the point where we are grasping any sign of connection.

Cold at the very same time, both of us leave the water and the talk continues ('No? Me too!') while I skip stones across the still ocean water, no longer uncomfortable; in fact, feeling surprisingly desirable and sharing views ('I was going to say that!') on everything in an easy dialogue that convinces me we are made from the very same cloth.

By three o'clock, it's time to go driving to Diana's Restaurant, which lies a couple of kilometres back towards Dili, where tables front the pebbly beach and large whole barbecued fish come accompanied by plates of salad and fried potato chunks, all of it washed down with Portuguese wine under a palm-frond thatched awning.

'Can I ask you a question?' I say.

'Yes.'

'What is your name?'

'My name? You want to know my name?'

'Well, I know your first name, of course, Viktor . . .' he laughs with relief at that '. . . but it's all I know, so you are rather mysterious to me.'

He smiles. Taking a paper serviette and a pen he writes: 'Vitor Carlos Mesquita Fernandes' and around such a name he draws for me coconut trees and an ocean scene just like the one before me. 'There. That's my business card.'

This restaurant is extremely public and, given that it is on the way to the beach and that civilians are knocking off at this time, it is a common route for GNR patrols which drive by on their way to stare at any girls on the beach and, recognising their commander's car, they all make sure to wave. He smiles and shakes his head at each intrusion. He no longer seems to mind that he is breaking every rule he has ever set for his police contingent. And I'm sure they don't mind that he's breaking them either and is, instead, living up to the GNR reputation with the added advantage of diminishing his ability to discipline for comparable conduct.

Surveying the view to check his artistic representation of it, I spot a figure approaching along the roadway. Oh dear. Here comes Maluco jogging towards us. Sure enough, he sees the car, he looks to the right to where I sit with the man he brought to my table the night before and he visibly baulks. I'm surprised he doesn't topple over. And, as his momentum carries him by, I wonder how he is able to keep running when his head is swivelled around now and appears back-to-front on his shoulders.

'The Brazilian,' Viktor says, with the clear pleasure of the triumphant male, nodding in Maluco's receding direction.

'Ahem, er, you certainly are given a lot of names in Portugal. I'm afraid I only have three.'

'Yeah?' His interest is on me again.

'Lynne Maree Minion.'

'Lynne Maree.'

'Yes, the Maree is my mother's second name. It's Anglicised from my grandmother's name, Maria.'

'Maria, it's a very Portuguese name, it is a beautiful name.'

'Well, it's also a beautiful Ukrainian name.'

'Ukrainian, of course, I can see. In Portugal we have the first name, so Vitor, or Viktor as you say. Then a second name, for me, Carlos. A surname from the mother's side, Mesquita. And the last name is my father's, Fernandes.'

And here comes Maluco again. Run Maluco, run. He's clearly consumed by what he sees. As reluctant as I am to end proceedings, I feel we've become a spectacle and Maluco's developing habit of watching me is becoming alarming, particularly given the gun he carries and his willingness to wield it in his personal dealings. 'Viktor, maybe we should go,' damn it, 'because, um, I don't want to get cold.' Actually, I would happily stay here if a cold was the only malady on offer, but we are risking something far more significant than that, obviously.

Viktor is watching Maluco jogging by on this second sweep and his earlier pleasure seems to be replaced by intrigue. 'Okay,' he says and turns to face me. 'Yeah, you're right. So, what we do, if you like, is I take you back to your place, you shower, I go back and see my guys and how is everything and then I shower and I pick you up an hour later, maybe 45 minutes, so we go to dinner. Yeah?'

'Oh.' Oh my God. 'Okay.' Can it be that the curse on my romantic life has lifted, finally, at my age, when I'd almost given up hope of ever finding a man just like this one and here he is and, even more shocking to me is that he likes me? 'I think that is a good plan. I'd like that.' This man likes me! All the foreboding today and all my life was a waste of time because, it appears right now, that wishes do come true. 'Yes, I'd like that very much.' And with that my self-esteem skyrockets and heads off on its way over the moon.

18

EXCESS BAGGAGE

On this night we are driving to a restaurant called '*Uma Mutuk* = Burned-out House', a name which could be either a brave show of defiance or a literal reference to the tables set in the rooms of a burned-out house. The roof is missing, the walls retain the scars of fire, it bears the eerie hallmarks of the devastation of '99. The lighting is provided by candles, lending a surreal and profound atmosphere that is arresting in its beauty. It is breathtaking. And in these damaged, dilapidated and candlelit surroundings, a girl possibly looks her very best and, for that alone, the place deserves quite a few Michelin stars.

The menu, which is incidental to the success or otherwise of these proceedings, is said by the waiter to be chicken or meat, that's it. There is no further description, it is a lucky dip. Far from ostentatious, in this establishment there are no printed pages filled with flowery prose. Heaven forbid any allergies, intolerances or dietary preferences. Vegetarian? Impossible. Vegan? Fuck off. Mind you, being a committed omnivore, as I am, is not as useful as one would think right now, because I cannot eat, and this, if anything, is a momentous sign that I am falling . . . I'm oblivious to mere bodily needs. Food, sleep, water, air. I can survive without them. I am no longer mortal. I don't need to bother myself with corporeal pursuits, I've transcended earthly needs.

Thus, I nod as he speaks, transfixed, ignoring the plate in front of me: 'My guys, they have never seen me like this,' he says. 'Every day of the mission, every night, I am there working but now they never see me like this.'

'You haven't dated anyone in Timor?'

'No! A couple times I go out with some of my guys and they are always bringing some woman to me, they want me to have a date. But they are bringing the dark girls with the big black hair and it is embarrassing because I have to talk to these girls. I don't want to offend them and that is all I feel. I tell my guys but still they bring them to me.'

'But those Latino women are very sexy, aren't they? I thought Portuguese men saw them as a vision of physical perfection.'

'Some, sure. But I always like blondie girls, like you.' Viktor pronounces the 'e' in 'blonde' as 'ie'. It is a cute idiosyncrasy that adds to his exotic accent.

'You haven't been with even one woman here?'

'No, why? You hear something?'

'No, I just wondered. I mean, you are a GNR.'

He laughs. 'Yeah, we have a reputation. My guys, they like the women and I hear the women like them. But for me I don't meet nobody special before you. I feel very well with you.'

'So you've worked pretty much all day and night ever since you came to East Timor?'

'Yes. Sometimes I need to take a break. I need to get privacy and I go to the Ocean View Restaurant.'

'And eat on your own?'

'Sure, why not? I like the good wine there and the food is good, many of it Australian, and I have some time on my own.'

'I imagine it is hard to live in a compound all the time and always be available to your men. I tell you what, the short amount of time I have spent in the Australian police compound has provided me with a real understanding of how the lack of privacy makes you feel.'

'Yeah?'

Beep, beep. Beep, beep. My phone. **1 new message.** It's BH1.

Every night, after spending hours with me, Viktor returns to his compound and works. He works until he falls asleep. Then he wakes at dawn and presides over the GNR parade, before handing responsibility to his deputy as soon as he can and driving to me to begin the routine all over again. Any absence from my side is compensated with phone calls and text messages.

Me? I'm somewhat more circumspect. 'Before we go any further, Viktor, I have to tell you something. I need to tell you that you have a duty of care. I have not been in love since my marriage ended. My ex betrayed me and I haven't been able to trust a man since.' I have looked a lot but no one's touched my heart.

'When was that?'

'1998.' Since then I've thought it best to err on the side of caution.

'What! Four years?'

Okay, okay, for an unhealthy amount of time. 'Give or take a month. He was drawn to a French woman whom I've subsequently referred to as Le Gâteau, The French Tart. So you can see the significance to me of getting into a relationship with you. That's why you have to tell me now if you are available — or not.'

I look into his eyes to make sure I note every nuance of expression while he answers me. 'Lynne Maree, you know this, I tell you before but, if I must, I tell you again: I am available.'

I can see no trace of guilt, no evasiveness of gaze, not even a hint of awkwardness as he answers me, clearly, confidently. How relieved I am. How very deeply happy I am. Yet how embarrassed I am that my naked vulnerability is on display right at this minute. 'I care for you so much that I want to share the most important thing with you. This is the biggest honour I can give. I don't give this to no one else, it is so private, so beautiful, you understand?'

'I guess.'

'I want to show you photos of my daughters, both of them. I love these girls more than you can imagine, you are the only one in my life who can come close to them in the way I feel. These photos, they are a gift to you. I want you to understand this.'

In the flickering of candlelight bouncing off the charred walls I see images of two young girls looking out at me. They look a bit like him, staring out from the swirl of the patterned plastic tablecloth. One of the shots shows him with them and his love is captured for anyone to see. It makes me find him even more attractive, a man who can feel such emotion for his family is a remarkable man indeed.

'They're beautiful, Viktor.'

'Yeah.' I'm speaking to the converted; he clearly agrees. 'Yeah, they are beautiful. I give them boys' names because I want a son. But I have no son and I have sisters so my name will stop here, with me.' It's a difference between our cultures and, like everything else about him, it fascinates me.

Likewise, I imagine Portugal is more conservative when it comes to divorce. 'Why did your marriage end, Viktor?'

'My work. Too many mission. She tells me the distance and time away is too much, too much, but I don't hear. So one day, when I arrive in Lisbon from my second mission, I arrive at the airport and she is there to meet me and I know. I can see in her eyes. The love is gone. There is nothing.'

To me such a scene is unimaginable. But, looking at him now, I am thankful that he continued to do missions. I'm thankful, even, that his wife's love died. I'm thankful for this man in my life because he, unlike me, is not afraid to love. He remains bold and brave. I want to learn from him that the past has its place — consigned squarely there, in the past.

'G'day,' I say, as I run to the shower container and lock myself in. These days I am keeping a wide berth of the coppers. I can't tell a soul about my days and nights, and so I'm always darting into the compound in the evenings, showering, then darting back out again, 'See ya.'

'Where are you going?'

'Out!'

Except on this day. I've promised to have lunch with BH1 and so we are sitting at the Purple Cow which is a new restaurant and nightclub on the waterfront.

'I never came to the beach in Timor before you came along,' he says.

'That's such a shame. This place can be a tropical paradise if you choose to experience that side of it.'

'Yeah, I can see that now.'

'So how's work?'

'We had a microlet drive over a cliff. Fifteen dead. It's so ridiculous. They overload those things and people sit on the roofs. We've tried to stop the practice but they still do it. The problem is the drivers don't have licences so they go around these mountainous roads and, of course, they lose control. And when they do, they kill more than they need to.'

'Maybe the roof is the safest place to be because you can jump off?'

'I don't know about that. We've got to do something about the driving practices here. Too many people are dying.'

'You care about them, don't you?'

'More importantly, I'm worried about you. How are you?'

'I'm fine, really.'

'It's just that I haven't seen much of you and I know you are going through a stressful time.'

If only he knew I am having the time of my life. 'I'm fine, great. No need to worry. I can take care of myself.'

'No, there's no need to do that. We're all here for you.'

'Thanks.'

It's awkward being here with him. I don't know why. Regardless, I practice avoidance techniques, talking about anything other than me and soon he is dropping me off at the beach with the book he has provided for company, *A Dirty Little War* by John Martinkus, the seminal book on East Timor.

I am relieved. Settling in for a relaxed afternoon alone, my phone rings. 'She's conscious, she's given an ID from her hospital bed. I need to see if you identify the same fucken bloke.' He's on his way and soon BH7 crunches to a halt at the beach and I hop inside his UN police car.

I'm happy to assist investigations but this is pretty nerve-wracking for me. We drive into town. Arriving at the Dili police station I follow him upstairs and I'm surprised to see the condition of the place. The rooms are half-burned in a building that has never been properly rebuilt.

'Now, Lynnie, you know I can't give you any indication of who she identified and I can't tell you if you have chosen the same bloke as her. I'm going to show you some photos of people of interest and I want you to tell me if any of them is the fuckhead who tried to attack you. If you don't see anyone here who is familiar, that's okay. Okay?'

'Okay.'

Turning over pages of black and white images, pretty soon I see him. 'That's him.'

'Are you fucken sure?'

'Yeah, I'm sure. I got a good look at him when he was creeping around, trying to get into my room. I deliberately tried to remember every feature of his face. So I'm sure.'

That afternoon, I'm yet to leave for my date with Viktor when the cops come in from work. BH7 wasn't allowed to tell me who I'd identified, but he was able to tell his colleagues, which is why they are treating me like a delicate princess as they arrive one by one. So I was lucky. These people really did provide me with protective custody. Because I identified the very same person who, only weeks after he had targeted me, would machete a woman in the head twice, and once through her hand.

Viktor phones from down the street to say he's arrived to pick me up and I run out to encounter a UN police car coming towards me. Oh great, caught. The Australians have been at a barbecue on the oceanfront and it must have ended early. 'G'day,' I say as the car pulls up nearby.

'Whoshat? Lynnneee! How ya gaarn? Where'sha been? Why didnya come to Dili Rock, fucken graaate do, the besht!' BH9 fumbles with the handle, the door opens and he falls out.

'Yeah, I can see. Look, must go' (before the others arrive), so I walk swiftly to Viktor's car and jump inside. 'Quick, go.'

'Everything is all right?'

'Don't worry, there is no way he could possibly have recognised you, much less remember to tell anyone. He is completely drunk.' BH9 has recently returned from cumulated time off. Another brother. When he's on-duty, he trains the Timorese in riot control and decorates his uniform with knives, spray, baton and guns strapped around his waist and legs; today he's legless.

Viktor and I dart past, as BH9 struggles to unload a barbecue from the back of his police car, and we head to the Turismo. It is a famous hotel that survived the various struggles and invasions in East Timor, housed the international media during the most fractious times, and now accommodates aid workers in what is probably its most lucrative period. It lies on the waterfront near the centre of town, close to Bishop Belo's rebuilt, pink-painted residence and the World Bank building. Inside the cocoon of rooms-for-hire is a lush garden with tables under canopies of tropical greenery.

Illuminated by fairy lights, we throw food to cats that meow at us, laugh without restraint and talk for hours on end without pause. I look around at those on other tables and I can see that none is as happy as me. I am content. Well, almost.

He takes my hand over the table boldly and smiles at me. I smile too and look deep into his eyes, looking, looking. I feel the need to be safe — there's no harm in that, is there? My intuition is telling me to be certain.

'Viktor, I'm sorry to raise it again. I'm sure you won't mind. Something's bothering me and I just have to ask you again.'

'What?' I sense his hackles rising.

'Well, um, I just need to ask you: are you really available?'

He takes his hand away. 'Lynne Maree,' his voice has hardened, 'we have discuss this, I told you.'

'Well, humour me and tell me again.'

'Okay, it's the last time. Yes. I am available.'

'Wait, hang on, just so I can be clear, are you *completely* available.'

'What is this *completely* available? What is this all the time, these questions? I tell you, yes, yes, I answer you each time but stop, it is enough, I don't want this any more. What can I do? Nothing. So it is enough!'

Viktor is furious. I've never seen him like this. 'I just wanted to be sure, Viktor. Don't be angry.'

'But every time, every day. I don't know what I can do? When do you believe me? How can I make you believe me?'

'I'm sorry, you're right, I am paranoid. I have to trust you.'

'Enough, we go.'

In the car, along the seafront in the dark night-time, and I am devastated. He is right. I cannot judge him by what has come before. He has every right to be liked, trusted, believed. Am I really so desperately scarred that I can never trust again? I know I came to Timor with a mountain of luggage but I didn't realise I'd brought along *my* baggage too. Oh God, no, I've fucked it, I've fucked it, I'm thinking, as I cry quietly and look at Viktor.

'I'm sorry', I say when we reach my street. It's all I can say, as I leave the car. And I just have to pray that the damage doesn't run too deep, that it can be repaired and that, once again, my perfect man can be completely available to me.

19

LOOKING FOR LOVE IN ALL THE WRONG PLACES

I am starting to believe that my life is a series of restaurants. Although, that's not in any way a complaint since it means that my life is also a series of moments filled with laughter and affection. Things I certainly didn't come to Dili expecting to find. On the contrary, I didn't assume these things would be waiting here for me, among the pigs and poverty of East Timor.

But they are. And so here I am with my remarkable man, sitting at our favourite restaurant, taking the cigarettes he lights for me, holding his hand, both of us always ordering the very same thing. Yes, we suit each other perfectly, he and I. Together we are the yin and the yang, the bird and the bee, the H two and the O. A man so rare he can even forgive, which he has done — without reproach, silence or blame, with discussion and reassurance instead. And as a result, he seems to have cured me of years of bitterness and suspicion. I have no reason to doubt him. Which is why I smile at him now with a sense of lightness, in this place.

The Ocean View Restaurant lies a fair way down a dirt road and it's worth an increment of inconvenience because it presides over a lonely segment of sleepy beach. We like it here for the prawn salad and white wine that complement, nicely, the laughter and affection which flow so freely they should be on the menu. Viktor and I come here, too, because our passion can play out in a privacy of sorts, a privacy supervised by the manager, who allows us minimal interruption by his staff, who seats any other customers away from us, who smiles when Viktor walks behind me, leans over the back of my chair and, as I lift my head towards him, kisses me softly on my mouth. Therefore, at the Ocean View, we can while away the hours enjoying our ardour.

On this day we leave our table, walk out the gate and head along the beach, walking for miles, all the way to a pier that juts out towards Indonesia. Timorese fishermen bob in their handmade kayaks on the sea, menacing teenagers in bandanas scowl as we pass, children build shacks in the sand, 'Hello Missus!' 'Hello Mister!' they greet us, giggling at the malae couple, he carrying her sandals, she playing in the water, her jeans wet up to her knees.

Then they merge and he holds her hand and she couldn't care if it is culturally inappropriate, for right now there are no rules and mores in the world that could possibly, in any fairness, condemn their actions, surely.

Stopping for a moment, the sweethearts sit down and gaze — an audience watching an audience watching it. We are intruders upon a scene creating a scene. So, under attentive eyes, we court.

'Lynne Maree, you are a writer, you should write about this.'

'About what precisely?'

'About this, about us, about a love story so special. I want you to remember it all. Please say you write about it.'

'Oh, well, I don't know if I'll have an opportunity.'

'Say you will, say you write it, it needs to be known that this love happen, that it is true.'

'I'll see what I can do but I speculate that the story, as special as it is, will get no further than my diary.'

'Lynne Maree, I ask you a question.'

'Okay.'

'What would you name your son?'

'God, I have no idea!'

'Do you know any names from Portugal you could call your son?'

'Oh sure.'

'What are they?'

Excuse me? Are we really having this discussion? 'Ah, I can't really remember but, God, under pressure, um, maybe Luis?'

'Why? Who was he?'

'No one!' Well, that was a *faux pas* apparently. 'Do names in Portugal have to relate to a specific person? It's just that in Australia we don't have to do that, we choose names because we like them.'

He seems vaguely satisfied with that explanation. 'Any more names you like?'

'I can't think, really.' There is clearly a right and wrong answer here.

'What about . . . ' he shrugs '. . . you know someone with a name Viktor. What you think? Would you call your child Viktor?

'Oh! Of course! Yes, Viktor is a lovely Portuguese name, the very most lovely, strong, distinguished, manly name and, yes, of course, ahem, I mean, it's also a Ukrainian name!' I so doth protest too much.

'Lynne Maree, I don't know. I don't know what's going to happen?'

'What do you mean?'

'I mean, what's going to happen to me?'

'I don't understand.'

'Lynne Maree, what do you want?'

'What do I want?'

'Yes, what do you want?'

A deep breath, 'I want a worthwhile life. I want certain things in my life to make it worthwhile.'

'What is that, what is worthwhile?'

'Well,' here goes, 'my mother always says that the true measure of success in life is your relationship. She would say that when you are on your deathbed you wouldn't say I love you to the GNR or to the UN, you'd say I love you to your partner in life, even before your children.'

With that said we sit in silence, on the sand, the bobbing fishermen, the posturing youths, the happy children around us, the sea and the sky a mirror of the other, the salty wind playing gently with my hair, and then he turns to me and says, 'Lynne Maree, tell your mother I love you.'

20

FOLLOWING ORDERS

Beep, beep. Beep, beep. My phone. **1 new message. Where are you?** It's 7.30 pm and I am with my man and we are holding hands while we wait for a main course of seared Australian sirloin steak (rare) to come our way, sipping gin and tonic as we do. It's all a bit much to place in a text message.

The phone rings; I screen it.

Beep, beep. Beep, beep. My phone. **1 new message. I need to speak to you.** It's BH1 again. I ignore that too.

'Why don't you reply?'

'Because he's driving me insane. I've told him my phone is faulty and it doesn't always get text messages, that it's a random problem.' The phone rings.

'Answer him.'

'No, the food is coming. We're at dinner.'

'Answer it, talk to him.'

'Oh God, all right . . . Hello . . . I can't, I'm at dinner . . . no, literally, the food is on the table . . . no, I can't leave a dinner, that would be extremely rude . . . can't it wait? . . . what's it about? . . . what about tomorrow? . . . I won't be back till very late . . . well, at least midnight . . . (sigh) okay, all right.'

'What does he want?'

'He says he needs to talk to me. He says it's urgent.'

'Why?'

'He wouldn't tell me, I'm sure it's nothing at all, just a ruse to get me to talk to him. He wants me to knock on his door when I get back to the compound tonight and I think that's patently inappropriate.'

'Yeah? Tonight? The door to his room?'

'I told you, he's getting out of hand. You've seen all the calls and messages. It's not normal. I've been looking for somewhere else to live but it's hard to get good accommodation in this place. And the fact that my job hasn't come through yet is putting me in a terrible situation. It is financially safer for me to stay in the compound and I am supposed to be living there for my own personal safety. But I've got to find somewhere else.'

'Yeah?'

'I am sure it will all be fine. I have never indicated that I think of him in any way other than my benefactor. I owe him a lot but that is all I feel for him, grateful, and if he thinks I reciprocate his feelings for me then he is dreaming.'

'Why is he desperate? It's not normal. It's too much.'

'It is *so* not normal but he seems to have lost all rational idea of how to behave in a friendship. I think it's because his marriage is ending. That's the pressure of the mission on so many couples, as you know. It's almost like he wants me to just pop myself into her shoes and that I will fill the void of loneliness and pain. Problem is, he is a depressed, alcoholic, insomniac who is old enough to be my, well, uncle.'

'You have no idea what he will talk with you about tonight?'

'No. It's almost as though the closer you and I have become the more desperate he has become.'

'He knows about us?'

'God, no. I have been extremely discreet about you but he

must be able to tell that I am never at the compound. And he can probably tell that I am falling in love.' At this, I blush and suddenly I don't give a shit about any pending discussion with BH1. I have until midnight to continue falling in love.

And I need to savour every moment because Viktor is here for only a few more days. That's right, Viktor's mission is coming to an end. 'I wanted to go and now I want to stay,' he says.

'I wish you would stay.' But, instead, the GNR is leaving, taking with it this man, returning him to Portugal.

Frustratingly, it was Viktor's decision to pull out of Timor, made before we met. He was devastated by the machete attack on his contingent member, the one who was with the Australian woman all those many months ago, in a car nearby. When the alarm was raised during that night months ago, Viktor rushed to the ambush site and, as we drive past it now, I see the piece of road and imagine him on his knees, in the blood-stained dirt. That was when he'd decided to leave Timor and that exit looms over us.

Sure, I can curse my luck but that would be pointless — because one thing is assured here: tours of duty come to an end. I knew this when I met him. And the same can be said of every man and woman who weeps at the airport when it's time to say goodbye. People are thrown together here, but they're also wrenched apart. It's a feature of peacekeeping missions, whether I like it or not.

So I choose to celebrate every remaining minute I have with him. The inevitable pain? I'll face that later. Right now I am happier than I have ever been and I choose to feel this joy for a moment in time, however short.

That's why I don't want any evening to end but each must; each one moving us closer to his departure, this one too, but finally I have to walk away from Viktor's car. Turning, I see his smile and I wave. Then, moving inside the gate, I head straight to my room. I don't knock on the door of any room. It is late and I want to lie on my bed and think of the man who is stealing my heart and taking it away to another country where I have never been.

My phone rings. I read the name illuminated on the screen. Oh for fuck's sake. I answer, 'Hello . . . I am very tired . . . surely it can wait until tomorrow . . . okay, the common area . . . who will overhear us? . . . everyone is asleep . . . we'll talk quietly . . . what on earth is so private? . . . I don't think it is necessary to go to your room . . . I don't think it is appropriate . . . okay, okay, I'll meet you outside.'

BH1 and I converge at the common area, the medium point between our two rooms, where the debate resumes . . . 'It's perfectly private here.'

'No, it's not, we'll be overheard.'

'Who on earth would listen?'

'It echoes in here.'

'What could we possibly need to talk about that is so secret anyway?'

'It's important, very important, we need to discuss this now.'

Sigh. 'Okay, okay.'

Before I mount the steps to his doorway, I kick off my little mother-of-pearl shoes in line with custom and, walking inside followed by him, I turn around as the door closes behind us and I notice his hand reach for the key and I hear the sound it creates: click.

21

POLICE POWERS

He has me down on his bed. He's on top of me. His mouth is on mine. I'm trying to move away, carefully. I don't want to enrage an unstable man. 'I love you, Lynnie, I love you.' I am dying inside, I can't get away. How desperately I want to get away. I inch away, bit by bit, I try to move away from his urgent erect cock. He is above me, I am so small beneath him. His weight is pressing down on me, I am moving my pelvis to the left, I am trying, subtly, to move away from his groin. I am sobbing. He is heavy. He is so heavy on me. His mouth, the kissing, and the words: 'Lynnie, she doesn't understand me, you understand me, you do, don't you? I know you do.' I don't.

I can't stop the tears washing my face, running down my cheeks, into my ears, how I wish they would wash these sheets away, this bed away, me away to safety in a tide. 'No,' I say. 'No.' Clearly. There is no cause for confusion. I want to be anywhere other than here. His weight. He is reaching down to my trousers, to open them. I move discreetly to increase the degree of difficulty, 'Talk, tell me how you feel about your family, tell me about your wife,' I say.

'She is leaving, we can't talk any more, the fighting,' and his anger rises.

Okay, try again, Lynne, quick, divert his thoughts, something, anything, quickly, 'Tell me about your children, what are their names again?'

Hours have passed now, hours in this perverse, macabre dance. He is reaching up inside my top, trying to reach my breasts, I am moving my arm to prevent his access, 'No.'

'You can't leave, even if I fall asleep, you can't leave.'

Should I scream? I am in a police compound. How would they react? His friends, his colleagues. I am humiliated. I am sobbing. I am heaving with my sobs. Oh God, I don't want to provoke him, I need to endure till morning, I need to manipulate him, emotionally, psychologically, 'You must miss your children very much.' I pretend concern for him when I feel none.

'I love you, Lynnie.'

'How long is it until you see your children?'

'Days until I go home and see her and I dread it. Only you understand the pain.' Oh shit, again.

'But it'll be great to take the kids to the footy, yeah?' I say as he pushes himself into my crotch through the layers of fabric, which form my coat of armour.

'I can't sleep on my own. Night after night. I need to have you here, with me. You can't leave.'

'I need to leave.'

'NO! You won't leave! If I fall asleep you are not to leave,' there is a menace that alarms me.

'Your children must miss you. How wonderful to be a father, it must be wonderful to be a dad.' And he is sobbing now, too, which disarms him.

We lie in spoons with my back to him, my hands cover my breasts, and I watch the lights from outside illuminating patterns on the wall and he sleeps. I lie awake, wide awake. I try to move, bit by bit, extricating myself from his arms, he wakes. 'Lynnie,' and his hands move tighter around me, they reach into my pants, 'You can't sleep in these, take them off.'

'No.' He presses up against me. He falls asleep again and I notice, thankfully, that as he lapses into slumber his hard-on softens gradually too.

Lying there, imprisoned by the limbs of this man who was meant to protect me from harm, the man I trusted, and I am aware of the door behind me, beside the bed. I wish dearly that I could leave through that door. Instead I have to lie here, as still as can be. Too still to breathe. Or the dance will begin again.

The patterns change on the wall, as eventually the dawn starts to break. I hear movement as the other occupants of this place begin their readying for the day, walking by from their rooms to the communal bathroom which lies just adjacent to the room I'm trapped within. And, suddenly, I am mortified to remember that my little pair of mother-of-pearl shoes are sitting neatly aligned outside the door, and I know that his colleagues will believe that I am in here by my own volition, having an affair with a married man. But those shoes are so pretty — can't you see that only a *girl* could wear those shoes? A vulnerable girl? Not the temptress you presume, but a girl who can't fight a man a foot taller than her? Why can't any of you people see? Why can't trained police officers see the signs of rape? Why didn't you see his developing obsession? Why don't you save me as I lie here, wrapped up in him? Help me, please.

So I have no choice but to continue, desperately, to try to save myself. I know he is about to wake up. I am terrified. If he penetrates me I will kill him. I will scream and scream, and I'll kill him dead. But clearly that isn't the best outcome for him or me, and so it is up to me to ensure that we survive this, both.

He wakes. He is on top of me. Kissing me. 'Lynnie.' Jesus Christ, how can a man of his age and poor health find desire after two hours' sleep? Still, I know that time is on my side now and he will have to leave in one interminable hour. His hands move inside my shirt, my tears well up, looking him in the eyes, eyes that are 10 centimetres away from mine, and I am searching for signs of conscience. Can't he see, now in the daylight that is washing in from behind the curtains, can't he see what he is doing to me? I gently shift his hands away from my chest, yet again. Then he says, 'I have to shower, you can't leave when I'm in there. Okay? Okay?'

'Okay.' At least he'll be in there and not in here. He showers with the door open and I know he can see the exit from his spot beneath the jets of water and I lie curled up in the foetal position under the covers and wait. 'It's almost over, Lynnie,' I whisper aloud to myself, over and over again. 'It's almost over.' The water turns off and he comes into the room. I am facing the wall. I pretend to sleep.

He dresses, slowly. He moves around, performing the rituals of the working man, an officer of the Australian police contingent in East Timor.

I bristle with an overwhelming feeling of revulsion when I sense him moving near me. He sits on the bed and drapes an arm over my body: 'Wait until 8.15 to leave the room. By then everyone should have left for work. Don't let anyone see you. Right? Right?'

'Right, ' I say, turning to look up at him with hatred.

'Lynnie, it was wonderful waking up beside you. It made me the happiest I have been in this place.' He strokes my tear-stained, puffy face.

And so he goes. This man in his uniform with the flag of my country on his shoulder finally leaves. Oh Lord, thank you, and I weep as I watch the hands of the clock and I sob with pure relief and the second hand moves with lethargy.

I arrange the doona to look as though one person was in this bed and, quietly, I pull open the door of the container just a wafer-thin crack and peak outside into the common area, making sure no one can see me emerging. No one is in sight, it is empty, everything is still, all is quiet but for the roosters next door, and in the new-day sunshine, through the potted palms, past the barbecue, faster than I've ever run before, wearing a pretty pair of mother-of-pearl sandals, I sprint to my room and burst through the door to my room.

Slamming it behind me, turning the key and locking it tight to protect me, I hear it go click and I see my wet, grotesque, swollen face reflecting back from the mirror behind the door and, looking at it, at a new me, I can see that a piece inside of me *has* died. But, fuck him, I got away.

22

IN THE EYE OF THE BEHOLDER

Why am I crying now, I'm safe for goodness' sake? Yet the floodgates have opened. I guess I'm crying with the relief and anguish, all wrapped up with a good dose of anger. I'm balling my eyes out without restraint because I can, now that I am behind a locked door — a door I have locked myself.

Alone. Now I am alone. Completely alone. But am I? Picking up my phone from the place where I'd left it on the bed late yesterday, I can see the missed calls and SMSs left by the man who was thinking about me all night too.

Tracking Viktor's attempts to contact me throughout the night, I can see his concern is growing as the hours go by without reply and he varies between fearing that I have been harmed to being convinced that I have run off with another man. Composing myself I dial . . . his phone's off . . . I'm diverted . . . I leave a message: 'Hey, it's Lynne. Sorry you haven't been able to get on to me for a while. Give me a call when you can and I'll fill you in . . . Oh, and, um, don't worry, everything's fine, now.'

Now. How could the events of last night have occurred? Here? In my sanctuary? How can a police officer have done this? At what point in his life and career did he lose sight of normal interactions between a man and a woman? Can't he see that he can't force a relationship, that it has to be consenting . . . and beautiful?

Argh! I'm going to drive myself mad unless I stop these questions. And I *will* stop them. I won't have my last days with Viktor ruined. I'll suppress every memory of last night and deal with them later. It is a question of will. Mind over mind. Life is a matter of perspective, after all, and I am focused on Viktor right now and the last snatched periods of happiness I have left with him. My phones rings. 'Hello.'

'Hello. Thank God. What happen?'

'Oh, look, I'll tell you when I see you. When will I see you? What are you doing?' I am trying to sound cheerful.

'I am at headquarters. I just have a morning meeting with everybody.'

'Including . . . ?'

'Yeah and I hadn't heard from you so I was looking at him thinking what happen.'

'Did he look unusual in any way? Tired, perhaps? Guilty? Evil?'

'No, we have a meeting and he talk, I watch him, I look for strange behaviour . . .'

'Strange, that's a word to describe him.'

'No, I see nothing so I don't know what happen and I'm worried.'

'I'm sure you must have been worried. Don't. Everything's fine now.'

'I pick you up soon, when I get there. I must go back to my compound, speak with my deputy. I am there soon.'

I want to get out of the compound before BH1 comes back for lunch and, to this end, I run across the common area and leap up the stairs of the bathroom container, lock the door behind me, undress, step under hot water and shower with a curious aggression, washing away his saliva and my tears. I want to be fresh and new. Scrubbing my skin, rubbing it raw, I try to exfoliate back to a fresh layer of thick skin. Can I remove the night before?

I turn off the tap, but I can't bring myself to leave the cubicle naked. With the curtain around me, I reach for my clothes and snatching them to me I dress. Then, emerging, I walk to the mirror and see my distended eyes and they fill with tears again. Lynne, they'll never go down if you don't stop crying! An hour after being liberated from that room, I'm trying hard to stifle the feelings but my appearance tells of the trauma.

I'm drying my face when my phone rings and Viktor says he's out the front. I look left and right out the door of the shower-block container and with the coast clear I run to my little bedroom container, grab my handbag and rush outside. 'Hey,' I say as I jump into the passenger seat, 'how are you?' I smile at my caramel man, safe, while he looks at me, troubled.

'My green eyes, they've been crying,' he says.

'Yes, they have been but it's okay now. Still, let's go, quickly. I don't want to bump into anyone right now.'

'But what happen?' He's shaken.

'No, really, Viktor, foot on accelerator, quickly . . . please.' I really don't want to be seen leaving with him, that would do me no favours.

'Tell me,' he says as the car pulls out onto the dirt road.

'Oh God, what happened? Well, last night I went into the compound and even though I tried to be ever so quiet I was heard arriving. He said he needed to talk to me and that the talk had to occur in his room.'

'What?'

'Yeah. I tried to resist but I had no choice.'

'What? Why?'

'Well, it's difficult to explain. But, really, Viktor, trust me, I would not have gone in there if I hadn't felt enormous pressure. I'm sure you've never been subjected to that but it is hard to stand up to a man who is a foot taller, stronger, drunker, more desperate and my kind benefactor. Anyway, he locked me in and I wasn't allowed out until the morning.'

'What! That's not possible.'

'Don't worry, nothing happened. Not for lack of trying, his that is.'

'But what happen?'

'Nothing!' I really don't need male jealousy on top of everything right now. 'He tried hard to make me have sex with him but I resisted. Of course. You're the only man for me, Viktor. Don't worry about that.'

'But you spend the night with him?'

Oh God. 'Not through choice.'

'In the bed?'

Jesus Christ! 'Yes. It's not what you think. I did not in any way want to be there and it was horrible. It was force, Viktor. I was lucky to get away relatively unscathed. Really, don't worry. I don't want to talk about it any more. I don't want either of us to let last night affect our time together. Please.'

'You think it was anything to do with me?'

'No. Well, I suspect that he suspects something is going on. I think he can tell I am seeing someone. I doubt he knows who that someone is.'

'I see him every morning at the meeting at headquarters and I feel a change. We had very friendly time before but now he doesn't speak to me. It's okay for me, I don't care, but I thought it could be bad for you in where you live.'

'Viktor, you have to remain silent for me. You can't do anything. Look, I hate that he will get away scot-free, obviously, but I don't want to think about it now. I'll work out what to do after you've gone. But for now, I want to spend an idyllic time with the man of my dreams — you — no one else!' My puffy face beams at him. To be honest, I'd love this commander to confront him. Of course I would. Still, there is no time for that. So we drive along, dodging wildlife, my hand on Viktor's thigh, him leaning over to me, planting kisses on my cheek.

'I give my guys a surprise today.'

'Yeah?'

'Yeah, and they thank you for it.'

'What on earth did you give them?'

'Today at the parade in the morning I tell them all that I am taking away the curfew from now until we leave the mission.'

'What? That's amazing!'

'Yeah. But I want this thing and so I give it to all of them too.'

'Leading by example.'

'Of course.'

The GNR have a reputation for populating the bars and nightclubs of Dili each night but a curfew had them all back on base by the early hours of the morning. Until now. 'So how did they react?'

'They cheered, of course. And they chant your name.'

'They did not!' I squeal and hit his arm playfully, while secretly hoping it's all completely true. Certainly, it is true that the curfew has been lifted because Viktor and I are on our way to the town of Maubisse in the mountains of Timor. For one night, alone.

It is a poignant occasion because this will be our first night together. And I mean it. We have never slept together. He and I have never been, um, intimate. Okay, you want me to be clear? In other words, Viktor and I have never made love until this point and I think I can speculate that we may very well find ourselves engaged in such a pursuit upon arrival at our idyll on the mount.

So I am quite nervous, really, as the car is directed out of

Dili (after a few wrong turns which are rectified by calls to his multiskilled deputy for directions) and we head upwards and away. The road curves through pockets of forest with coverings of dark green foliage. Knotted trees preside over us just as they've presided over decades of political change. Bamboo huts with palm-frond thatched roofs dot the roadside every now and then, sometimes in clusters, sometimes in isolated and lonely spots. Every so many miles their design changes — for a short while they have pointy roofs, then they have a little kitchen hut out the back, or they may very well be made of wood with a pretty painted detail around the windows or doors.

Emerging from beneath a crown of *verde*, we drive onto a plateau with an unobscured view to Dili below us by miles, the cloud of pollution floating over it, the expanse of blue water beyond, and the island of Atauro peaking over the sea level. Then we dash back under the awnings of tropical leaves and turn around obediently, following the precarious cliff-side twists in the road. This way and that we go. It's very difficult to hold hands on roads like this, especially when the car is a manual. But there is no underestimating the doggedness of new love, which sees us repositioning our hands after each of the hundreds of gear changes, and the royal waves to the Timorese children. 'Hello Missus!' they yell as we pass by.

'Where is this place?' asks Viktor. We've been driving for hours now and the town must be around here somewhere. Certainly we are up very high. I have put on a cardigan to keep me warm in the mountain air. Then we drive by a cathedral, all pretty and pink, and on the left there is a sign indicating that the Maubisse Pousada is just up this track, under a concrete arch. We drive past tiny houses and overstuffed kiosks, coffee beans drying in the dwindling sunlight, people waving us welcome. Up the hill and around to the right and we stop at a set of stairs leading to a landscaped garden of roses, gladioli and daisies, and a grand manor house.

Ascending a further set of stairs, hand in hand, we walk over a veranda in the crisp, cool of the day and, turning around, observe a breathtaking scene of mountains and valleys. Bells chime from the cathedral tower and a Timorese man comes and takes us through the old Portuguese mansion to our room at the very rear. Our room. The view from the windows captures the magnificence of the location and a wind blows the curtains a little, relieving the smell from the bathroom which reminds us that we've not left Timor after all.

We lie on the bed and I am taking instruction. I don't know what to do. What should I do? He comes towards me and we kiss, languidly, ah, I can follow instruction well because I fall into his arms and his mouth. Can I stay here forever? I find my hand on the back of his head, my fingers in his hair, softly drawing him to me (that was my independent contribution), his strong limbs wrap around me, our eyes are open, allowing us to share our thoughts and feelings and then knock, knock. He bites my lips, opens his mouth wide over mine, knock, knock. Oh, okay, what? Smoothing down his dishevelment, he reluctantly leaves the bed, opens the door, has a discussion in Portuguese and, turning, says, 'Where were we?' and, as he jumps on the bed, we giggle and resume proceedings. He lifts my T-shirt a little, looks at me, smiles naughtily, then bites my waist, 'Ha ha!' and we are wrestling and laughing until the peals are stifled as our open mouths plunge together. Knock, knock, and his head collapses onto my chest and he looks up to my face, saying, 'We go to the restaurant.'

'We what?'

'Our friend, he says the dinner is served now. Only now. We must go.'

He grabs my hand and pulls me up. I place my clothing

where it was designed to be, give my hair a pat down with the palm of my hand and eradicate any amorous thoughts with a shake of my head and enormous restraint, as he opens the door and directs me out.

He pulls back a chair in the restaurant. I sit down daintily, 'Obrigado, Senhor.'

'De nada, Senhora.'

He sits beside me and we are told the menu is chicken or beef. Who cares what we choose? We drink Portuguese wine. Who cares which one we've chosen? Although, I'm sure it fuels a meal that sees us enchanting each other with remarkable wit.

The other diners total two women, Australians, I gather from their conversation, which I catch in between the few silences at my table (simultaneous drawing of breath is the explanation). They must think we are mad as we continue to erupt with mirth. Certainly we are indicating to a public audience that we have a mean age of, oh, maybe sixteen? We are precisely like teenagers. Silly, indulgent, inane . . .

Let's face it, as a rule of thumb, the period during which one is falling in love precludes:

Maturity
Intelligence
Rational thought
Sensible decision-making
Any responsibilities one might have.

We pass a serviette between us, adding love messages, gleefully. They're ridiculous, such as my contribution: 'You are my shooting star,' for which I blame the intoxicating effects of the Portuguese wine coupled with lust. Although, by way of forgiving my failure as a poet, take Viktor's reply: 'I would like to shine in all your life.'

Sure, it's a bit early. We've known each other for so little time. But I don't see a problem with Viktor's zealous interest in me because I feel his intensity in kind. Therefore, after a meal we barely touch, I take his hand and say, 'I have something to show you,' and I lead him outside, through the manicured garden, to an item I noticed amongst the flowerbeds. It's a children's boat swing, very quaint and rusted and I hop on board and pat the other seat. 'Come on.' He does, facing me and we swing higher and higher, and with us rising and falling, up and down, in the night air, I find the courage to say the words I feel I have to release from a bursting heart. It's then that I say, as we swing, 'I love you.'

Was it love at first sight? For the first time in my life I believe it was, that this does indeed occur. And I am so content because I do love him. So we kiss on that swing. In the moonlight. And we kiss with the mountains and the roses and the valleys, the cold air and the dark sky around us, all of them contributing to this moment, as we kiss. And it is clearly beautiful.

23

ETHNIC CLEANSING

I'm flying, I'm flying around the sky, until my mind leaves the world of clouds, the brain switches on, I discern an unfamiliar sense of being wrapped up in a warm, affectionate, breathing cocoon, and my eyes open to see that the dream continues. 'Good morning, sweetheart,' I whisper.

It's inconceivable that he should be able to continue in a state of slumber when there are more memories to generate — for soon they will be all he and I have — which is why I poke him. An inhalation of breath precedes the opening of his eyes, their focusing, and the simultaneous, involuntary smile, which takes over his gentle caramel face, inhabiting those eyes, 'Good morning, my Lynne Maree.'

It's fair to say that at this moment I'm happy, perhaps blissful. You can't complain about this caper called life when it hands you everything you've wished for, I'm thinking, as his body provides cosy insulation from the cold mountain air which has seeped its way into our room overnight.

Still, we have to leave, our time is finite. Viktor is supposed to be overseeing the dismantling of his GNR camp in preparation for repatriation, and delegating to his deputy can only give us stolen time. Moving into the malodorous bathroom, we transform it with steam and water rivulets down torsos. He washes me, my arms, my neck, my hands, I caress the muscles of chest, his waist and he says into my ear, under the jets of water, in Portuguese, that I'm beautiful. I want to stay here forever.

We are collecting our intermingled possessions when I note the sheets, 'What on earth . . . ?' then I realise, 'Oh God, they're going to think we were involved in some sort of sacrificial ritual last night.'

'What?'

'Look . . . at . . . that!' I'm pointing to a sheet covered in stains . . . from the cumulative blend of passion and the rose petals I'd scattered there the previous night. 'By the time they notice we'll be gone!'

Checking out, I stand and listen as he speaks in Portuguese, a language of romance. Even though Portuguese is the official language in Timor, a small proportion of the people speak it. This hotel, however, is run by a Portuguese company and so he talks in his language while I go weak at the knees in the background and he pays the bill. Now, this is another point of distinction. In addition to language skills that fill the air with syrup, he pays. He always does and, at the risk of losing my feminist credentials, I will boldly declare: I like it. I also like that he carries my bags, that he opens my car door, that he is a chivalrous man who knows how to treat a woman well.

It's an unusual package for me; I'm from a country where many men have selectively adopted feminism — it's cheaper and less labour-intensive for them to be egalitarian yet, as a curiosity of our nation, they can still prefer a woman's body over her brain. In contrast, despite assumptions, the conservative Catholic Portuguese model seems surprisingly liberating — I can have my doors opened and meals bought for me and simultaneously be respected and respectable. Ah yes, it's lovely being a woman in their language.

Before we leave, we take one more look at the vast expanse of natural wonder from our mount. Viktor needs to capture this time and he hands the bellhop his camera. This man is the anti-commitment-phobe — he wants to say the L word, he wants to immortalise me in his life, he wants the world to know! So, against a backdrop of exceptional splendour, the shutters turn over and we kiss, we gaze, we embrace, there's a swing in the background, she appears laughing, he's wrapped her in his arms, he's nibbling her neck, the digital images from his camera available immediately to captivate them as they head off through the town of Maubisse and downwards towards Dili again, 'Look, how lovely!' and this time they're not talking about the scenery, they're talking about themselves, static and permanent in their love.

If only that were true. Viktor has told a progression of waiters at a parade of restaurants that we are on our honeymoon. Each time he does it, followed by a wink at me, I am moved by his telling of an impossible dream. And it is impossible. I am here, following a different dream. Love wasn't part of the plan and I wonder if it can be altered because a man has come along, even a wonderful man. This is the time in my life, perhaps the last time, when I can achieve this dream of working to rebuild a nation. And it doesn't preclude love, but it does preclude committing to a man who comes from the other side of the planet, doesn't it?

'You know, I work in other countries sometimes, for months sometimes. We do this exchange with other police in France and I do it in London. Maybe I could organise to go to Australia?'

'Um, goodness, maybe? I don't know. Isn't it odd that it's always the women you see working in the rice fields? It's such a beautiful image, can we stop and take a photo?'

'Of course.' That's good, change the subject. I just want to focus on enjoying it for what it is, for now.

In addition to his commitment to me, Viktor also has professional ones. So during his absences I wait in the Australian police compound. The UN classifies East Timor as a hardship mission, and it's true that it has its hardships — machetes, pigs, filth, rabies, malaria, dengue, tuberculosis, showering with your mouth closed, no effective infrastructure, erratic power and substandard housing — none of which would be tolerated in Australia. But another cause of hardship is the lack of diversions — no cinemas, theatres, music performances, magazines, books, quality newspapers, shopping, consistent television. Imagine eradicating all those things from your life! What would you do with your time?

In Timor, probably due to the vast proportion of men, the cultural life revolves around drinking and eating. Another idle pursuit is watching the pirate DVDs that are plentiful in South-East Asia. That's what I do.

I avoid BH1 all I can. I don't feel I can face him about his behaviour yet. I am confused. Evasive tactics are my preferred strategy.

Meanwhile, the alleged Timorese machete stalker was captured at Comoro market, the culmination of a dedicated international police strike force, but, when he was bundled into the back of the police car, the African officers forgot to secure him in the back. So, as they got into their seats in the front, waving to the Timorese audience watching on, the alleged perpetrator opened the window, hopped out and ran off again.

It is a setback for the investigation and it's a setback for me, too. Is it safe for me to leave? There are further complications: Timor doesn't have real-estate agents or newspapers with a For Rent section, both of which I've come to see as First World luxuries, and my job is yet to come through. But I can't be concerned with all that now. Instead I watch DVDs, waiting for Viktor's phone calls, telling me he's on his way.

It's the night of a party by the Australian police, one I have to attend. Viktor has convened the last supper with his senior officers to coincide. There's no need, he says, to lose any more time together than necessary and in a show of cultural magnanimity he says he'll contribute some bread freshly baked from his bakery. He phones upon approach and I go out to meet him in the street in front of the compound to find he is in a GNR car with three of his guys, their biceps pressed against the car doors for maximum effect and Viktor is in . . . his . . . uniform. I've never seen him in his uniform in person, which was quite an oversight of mine. Navy blue combat pants, navy blue shirt with assorted patches, symbols and flags, black boots, beret. I have some strange biophysical reaction to this sight. Captain, my captain. I want to salute and follow his orders but I compose myself and say, 'Come in, you can put it on the table.'

'In there? I cannot go in there. Is impossible.'

'Don't worry, no one's here.'

He is uncertain and fast. The rivalry between the police forces has him behaving as though he's entering enemy territory. 'Call me as soon as your party finish, yeah? I love you.'

'Absolutely. Me too,' I say as he retreats.

Inside the bathroom container I shower with him, well, the memory, so fresh, of my hands and a bar of soap mingling with the water running down his body, and the sensation of the water on my face reminding me of kissing him, deeply, in a similar environment. I shake my head to bring me back into the present surroundings: the second cubicle of six, four of them toilets.

In this prosaic place, with the door locked, I finish. Viktor was nervous walking in here? God I'm about to see all of the blokes, many of whom I haven't encountered for some time thanks to my recent elusiveness. I dry myself and dress behind the plastic curtain, open the door and run across to my room, lock the door and turn on my hair dryer. By the time I've summoned all my courage, and my hair has a style quite like Einstein's, the common area resounds with male voices. I take a deep breath, leave my room and immediately lock eyes with BH1, who is sitting in a plastic chair, facing my door. Fuck, fuck, fuck.

Immediately he rises and makes his way over the couple of metres to me. 'I want to talk to you,' he says quietly and we both look nervously to the others. 'Do you have some concerns, you know, a problem with what happened between us the other night?'

With what happened between us? Between us! The terminology is fascinating. It's an outrage but it's also an indicator that the man is insane. Between us! 'I really don't want to talk about it right now,' I reply in measured tones.

'Lynnie, I want to know. You seem distant, you're pulling away from me. Tell me.'

'Look, I don't think this is the place.'

'All right. How about dinner?'

'I'm not free until next week.'

'Oh, what night then?'

'Monday at the earliest.'

'Monday it is. But everything's all right, we're all right?'

Suddenly, while I'm contemplating the appropriate response (violent or verbal, I can't decide which), a noise thankfully interrupts and instead I say, 'What on earth was that?' Again it sounds. It's not a peculiar sound in Timor, in fact it's unremitting, it's rooster crowing, but this one has come from a very close quarter.

BH5 wanders behind a container and emerges, looking perturbed. 'There's about six bloody roosters back there.'

'Inside our fence?'

'Too right they are.'

'Where did they come from?'

BH9 walks past carrying barbecue utensils to a car and reports in passing that the resident landlord, a Timorese-Portuguese man raised in Australia, has brought the roosters here for a couple of days, then he's going to take them somewhere else.

'He's not bloody leaving them here,' agree all other residents.

'I'll tie 'em to his bloody door and see how well he sleeps. They won't be here for long,' says BH5. Laughter crows all round as we all jump into police cars and a convoy starts off into the Dili night to the chosen venue — a mechanics' shop on the main café strip.

At the party, chickens roast over coals in among cars up on jacks and dismantled engines while music plays and VBs swing back and forth from hands to mouths. 'Can I get you a beer?' asks BH1.

'Sure.' I could do with a keg of the stuff, actually.

Standing in the middle of the group, the blokes towering over me, I nibble on bread, swap jokes and try not to touch any surface covered in sump oil, all while dressed down in jeans and a shirt — I don't want to show too much flesh in this company — there seem to be so many reasons to cover up in this country.

Even after a couple of beers I feel uneasy. I've been faultlessly genial but maintaining this act and BH1's proximity are wearing on me. I need a break, which is why I put my bottle on a car boot and go out the front, onto the street. Standing in the dark night-time air, listening to the laughter coming from the party behind me mingling with chatter from the City Café nearby, and I'm trying to work out how I got myself into this situation. I'd give anything for it all to go away. And maybe that's exactly what will happen? After Viktor's gone, maybe everything will be as it was? I don't know. All I do know is that right now I'm mobbed by homeless Timorese children, who shake me from my worries. 'Hey, alin. Bonoite,' I say in a Tetum-English patois which doesn't showcase the daily US$8 language lessons I was having for months. These kids understand, nonetheless, thanks to their exposure to the Australians who've done their tours of duty in Timor over the years — around 20 000 peacekeepers, police and aid workers.

Music floats over us, it's a salsa and I dance with these children who show real talent. We're laughing as they take turns to partner me back and forth along the broken footpath. The things they learn living out here on the streets! Then one of them interrupts and asks me, of course, for a 'Dollar Missus?' I bend down, our faces level, and tell him no, that he shouldn't beg, that he should go to school, and I ask him why he wants the money. 'Hungry Missus.'

Telling them to follow me, three of us enter the gate to encounter men, Timorese and Australian, trying to chase them away and back out onto the street again but they cry that they're with me! I take their hands and lead them to the barbecue. Their eyes are wide as they're handed plates of food, chicken and bread, even wider when they're given cans of Cokes, the biggest treat of them all. 'Obrigada Missus!'

'Nada.' You're welcome but you're not to touch any beer, okay, it's bad, and they nod with saucer eyes looking around at the big white men and they move their hips to the grooves as they fill their mouths. Some of the Australians come up to me, 'Do you know what you're doing?'

'Sure, they're hungry and I can't see any reason why we wouldn't offer children some food. I'm sure you don't mind.'

The police officers look at the children and their stares soften. 'Why are they on the streets?'

I ask them, with the help of a Timorese interpreter where my Tetum fails me. 'This one, his parents where killed in '99. The other one, his father died and his mother has a new man and they say they can't afford him any more. They hang out on the streets around here during the day and sleep at the Comoro markets.'

'How old are they?'

I ask the boys. 'This one's seven. He's eleven.' They are tiny. 'You know, in three years they could be gang members. They could be doomed to be machete stalkers. But maybe they could grow up to think that the malae are okay if they're not made to stand behind the fence.'

They've finished their meal and chicken grease covers their skin. I tell them to wash their hands. Their eyes open wider. Come on, this way, you have to wash the chicken off your hands, hygiene is good. They follow me to a tap on the edge of the concrete slab and I turn it on. 'Mai, come on.' They plunge their hands in. I tell them to wash their feet too, while they're at it. Their eyes are now so very wide and they stick their feet into the water and the filth rinses off. I'm surprised by the enthusiasm. I ask them if they want to wash their whole bodies and they nod, excitedly. They can't believe their luck! And I walk away, to give them privacy.

When they are clean, their hair wet, skin glistening dark brown, they come to my side again, one of them taking my hand in his, the other holding my arm. Okay, little ones, you can stay and dance but no beer, okay?

They ask my name. 'Lynne.' Here we go.

'Line?'

'No, Lynne.'

'Leeen.' Okay, I concede.

They dance and I take the opportunity to check my phone for news of Viktor. It's a difficult time for him. Not only is he working through most nights and trying to supervise the packing up of his compound, but he has to pay tribute to the senior officers who have served him loyally with their restaurant reviews and resort bookings. Tonight's farewell dinner on the Central ship is an important occasion, yet it appears that he's also had the time to leave a sequence of messages on my phone. I'd better reply promptly . . . I dial . . . he answers, 'Tor.'

'Hello.'

'Where have you been? I call you many times and I hear nothing. Now I come back to my camp, I just arrive.'

'Oh, okay. Sorry.'

'I sit now in my car out the front of my camp but I leave again and come back to you. Where can I meet you?'

'I'll wait for you at the Metro Café.'

'Ten minutes.'

'Okay, ten minutes.'

I bid my very awkward goodbyes to the pack, 'See yas all later, ripper party, ta for that,' as I go for the gate. But it's not going to be that easy, is it?

'Where ya garn?'

'Oh, you know, it's time to pull up stumps for me, I'm afraid. It's been a beauty but. Thanks.'

'How ya gettin' back to the compound?'

'Well, I'm just going to meet a friend and . . .'

'What? At this time of night?'

The scrutiny I find myself under in Timor from almost every man I encounter requires quite a significant attitudinal adjustment on my part. Who would ever imagine that I am an independent woman who makes her own choices when she is in her country of origin? I wasn't aware, when I flew to this country, that passing a certain degree of latitude resulted in the simultaneous loss of my ability to self-determine. 'Yep, at this time of night. But I don't actually think all carriages turn into pumpkins at midnight, that's my suspicion anyway. So I'm sure I'll be fine. Thanks for the concern.'

A few doors up, I sit myself down at an outside table in the hot night air, a couple of metres away from the crumbling gutter, with a clear view of the late-night traffic on a thin road that's chaotic even at this outlandish time of night. The children have followed me and they watch from the street. There are three free seats at my table, come on, sit down. 'Do you want a Coke?' They hesitate. They can't sit there. That's where the malae sit, not the Timorese, especially not them.

They look at each other, at their feet which are bare. I kick off my shoes. 'Come on, kids, sit down.' They look at each other again, they can't resist. And this time their Cokes come with chilled glasses, '*obrigado loos* = thank you so very, very much'. The waiter places mine down and the kids rush to pour it. They delicately close the lid on my lovely Balinese handbag, pronouncing it '*kapas* = cute'.

Their co-residents on the streets of the city wander by plying whatever trade they're peddling tonight. After consultation with my tiny and exceptionally clean kolegas, I beckon a CD seller to our table. The children have the power of veto. This one? No, apparently not. This one? No, my advisers have spoken. This one? A moment please while one of the selection committee tops up my glass before nodding his consent. Thanks to my associates, the collection grows until I become aware, mid-transaction, of a sense that I'm being watched and, turning, I see that I am indeed, by a man moving towards me, smiling and shaking his head. Suspend trading. He is introduced to my consultants who shake his hand (how did they get dirty so quickly?).

He kisses mine, smiles and shakes his head. 'You enjoy your party, Maria?'

'Why did you just call me Maria?' I turn to him.

'Maria!' the children yell.

'Well, your name is Lynne Maree and in Portugal this is Maria and it is a beautiful Portuguese name.'

'Oh, that's so lovely . . . and they get it!' I say pointing to the children.

'Maria!' they shout, proudly.

So we buy CDs, Viktor pays the tab and the meeting is adjourned. But not before the enterprising audiovisual merchant whispers, indicating a natural talent for tailored marketing, that maybe Missus Maria might like a jiggy jig too.

24

SANTA MARIA!

Peering indolently out of new-day eyes right now, I wonder what country I am in. Adjusting my sight to an influx of muted light, I survey a sumptuous interior of new beige carpeting, tasteful wood furniture and a large-screen television with a remote control that I lazily press to view a variety of Portuguese game shows beamed via satellite. On the bedside table sits a pile of CDs. Still sleepy, I flick through my purchases from last night: high-energy Indonesian dance compilations. My consultants, it seems, weren't worth their fee — two cans of Coca-Cola.

Viktor is already awake. He needs to get back to his camp he says, and with a sense of urgency he kisses me on the cheek and reminds me that we promised to buy the street children bikes today.

'We did? Perhaps that seemed wise at the time.'

'We said we'd meet them at 9 am.'

'Did we? Perhaps they wouldn't notice if we didn't turn up.'

'But we promised. They will be there.'

'Did we? Will they? But I warned them that liquor does terrible things to people.'

'I can't come with you. I feel bad if we disappoint them.'

'You will? But they've been let down all their young lives so they'll be accustomed to it. Okay, okay, I'll be there.' I rise onto an elbow, I'm part way there, I'm doing this in stages, any faster and my head produces a splitting twinge in retribution for my disrespect of it. I'm trying to motivate myself with selfless thoughts of those younger, cuter, poorer than me but, despite my charitable impulses, they are not a priority now that my body has embarked on a protest campaign. It's demanding regime change.

The spritely Viktor, on the other hand, points to the other side of the bed, requiring me to turn my neck, contract my shoulders, swivel my waist and follow his gaze. I feel terrible, he says, pointing to US$100 dollars on the bedside table. I feel that I'm paying for services rendered, he says. Oh, darling, I say, indeed you should feel terrible, is that your idea of a good service tax — GST? and then I find the energy to burst into peals of laughter and that in turn sparks a revolt in my brain and I fall back onto the bed, horizontal.

No, I haven't diversified my career, despite my job situation. The money is actually to pay for the bicycles for the boys. Clothed now, Viktor picks up his phone, keys, wallet and prepares to leave. Kiss, do you have to go? Kiss, I must, Lynne Maria, but I don't want to go.

'You know, in Australia we have this great tradition. It's called a sickie. In your job you accumulate sick days, yeah?'

'Yeah.'

'And you probably use them when you get sick, right?'

'Yeah.'

'Well, in my country you never use them when you're sick. You use your sick days for times like when you're falling in love. It's a national institution, the sickie.'

'It sounds like a good idea, but . . .' he reaches under my back and draws me to him, looking straight into my eyes, 'I have been doing this since I meet you. Today I must go to my camp.'

'It was worth a try. You're clearly not an Australian, mate.'

'That's right, mate.' And in the customary and rather annoying way of the newly in love, we tickle each other and burst into laughter before he stands and takes himself away, 'Now go to the children.'

'Yes, sir!' I salute him as he leaves, shaking his caramel head.

I know I have to go to the children, but look at this room! I reach for the remote control and have a flick again through the Portuguese programs, all glamour, glitz and big tits. It reminds me of the First World. Sometimes it's easy to forget just how opulent it is in other countries. Over time, anyone, even me, can adapt to the Third. But it doesn't mean you always like it; and it is wonderful to find a balance between the here and there I'm thinking, as I go into the clean, marble environment of the bathroom. A gleaming bath, a sink set into an unstained, pubic hair-free cabinet decorated with sample-sized beauty products, a Western-style toilet able to be sat upon and flushed. Funny how something as routine as toileting was always something I took for granted, but in East Timor it has become a high priority in my life.

If I were asked, before I came here, what I thought the most important public utility was, I'd have said electricity. It powers most of what I viewed as essentials in life — hair dryer, microwave, stereo, television, and even the more incidental items like laptop, colour printer, dishwasher, track lighting. But, being here in a place with unreliable electricity and few of these goods, I can still get by. Water, however, is essential to life. And the ramifications are of greater consequence than one's access to hot showers and the ruination of a wardrobe (although these can piss me off).

I have come to realise that water allows for hygiene, is essential for producing, cleaning and cooking food, and even a girl who takes a lackadaisical approach to hydration, and prefers to drink substances deriving from grapes, needs to drink water to survive. At least I can afford to use bottled water for all of these things, even though it can be tiresome when you're brushing your teeth, but how do people survive in this country when they don't have the money for bottled water, when they need to cook for ten children, when they simply do not have access to showers — hot or cold, and when they will never find themselves in a suite at the Hotel Timor? I have adapted profoundly to the circumstances I find myself in each day in East Timor yet, even still, the gulf between me and the Timorese is cavernous. Worlds apart. So it is with a tinge of guilt, yet a wonderful sense of joy, too, that I step under this shower.

Once I'm dressed, I pop the US$100 into my bag, close the door behind me and float down the stairs into the foyer where I bump into Viktor. He's on the phone. He ends the call. 'Oh hello,' I chirrup.

'Hello.'

'What are you still doing here?'

'I just have a coffee?'

'Everything okay?'

'Of course, why not?'

'The phone call.'

'Of course. I pay for room now, you go to breakfast.'

'Actually, don't s'pose I could catch a lift to the Metro Café to meet the street kids? It's almost 9 am.'

'I have to get to my camp.' I am aware that he is under a lot of pressure now and I am making significant demands on his time.

'Sure, of course, I just thought I might as well ask. That's fine. I'll take a taxi' (and get there in a couple of hours with burst eardrums).

'Okay, I take you, of course.' We drive through the near

abandoned streets and arrive at the appointed meeting place. The children come running towards us. The two of them have obviously put their fortuitous experience out onto the grapevine because there are a few more kids here than expected. It's difficult to order the interlopers away but it is managed with a few commands barked by an impatient GNR captain, which cause us all to jump and some of them to scamper away.

'Do you want to come with us to buy the bikes?' It seems a reasonable question because the original two street children have clambered into the back of his car and sit there.

'I have to get to my camp.'

'Sure, but we'll be quick and it could be fun. Sounds like you could do with some fun.'

'Okay, I come, of course.' We're motoring around the city of Dili, two excited children in the rear, one of them reaching around the back of my seat to hold my arm.

Then, 'Where is the shop?' snaps the short-tempered driver. 'I have to go back to my camp, you know this.' He can't understand the Tetum we're speaking.

'It's just down here, not far, we shouldn't be too much longer.'

'Are they taking us some long way?' Maybe these children also expect a diversion from the route. After all, there are paedophiles in Timor. I know of two — one who works for a UN agency, the other's an Australian government employee — and they prey on children like these who will go with them for just US$10. On this day, however, they can feel safe that our gifts come with no price attached. And they must sense this because I feel a little boy kiss me, innocently, on the back of my head.

'No, we've been past one shop. It was closed so we are heading to the next one. It's on the way to your camp. You can just drop us off if you want.'

He looks at me then at the boys and their faces peering out from between our seats. 'No, I come, of course.'

Pulling into the car space just in front of the open doors of the bicycle shop and the two children jump out of the car, they run up to the bikes, make selections so quickly it appears they fear we will change our minds, and they ride around in circles in the dust, squealing with delight as Viktor and I watch on, unhurriedly — no one in their right mind would rush a moment like this.

Bursting with glee the children present their very own BMXs. Viktor enhances them with optional extras like lights and little sirens for the handlebars. The Timorese proprietor performs the requisite adjustments with the children supervising, authoritatively giving him advice, and, when all is in readiness, I give them some safety instructions and then they're off, waving, wobbling, and instantly they're almost hit by a car in their haste to ride to their friends! Turning back to the counter, the storeholder takes my hands and tells me in his language that I am very kind. Kind? God, it is easy for Viktor and me to be kind when we have so much to give. Privilege is easy to share.

With very satisfied customers, the transaction is completed and a receipt is handed to my suitor who turns it over, asks to borrow a pen and writes on the back: 'We buy the bikes to "our" kids. It's so nice . . . I ♥ you. Viktor', before he gives it to me.

It's night-time and we're hidden inside the private opulence of the Hotel Timor again, where I turn on the TV and jump on the end of the bed, pointing the remote control and flicking through satellite channels. Victor, meanwhile, serves cake. He sits behind me. I'm living the cliché: I have my cake and I'm eating it too, damn it.

After a succession of Portuguese game shows (Jesus they

like those things), I find MTV Asia which is broadcasting a blast from my past — now my present and my future — and Cyndi Lauper's walking away, the goodbyes have been said in a televisual analogy to a moment we'll be sharing soon. I turn around to look at Viktor who is reclining against the head of the bed with a glass of wine in one hand, a piece of carrot cake in the other, and I expect to see a look of horror on his face, the effect of my voice singing at full volume but, rather, he's crying. 'What, sweetheart, what?'

'Lynne Maree, it's the last time I feel this in my life, the last time.'

I lie back to where he is and take his head in my hands, 'That's the whole point of love.'

'Yes, but I never feel this again in my life,' he repeats, as I gently wipe away his tears and kiss the lid of each eye.

'You're not dead yet, Viktor.'

'No, but you go home to Australia and you feel this again with someone else.'

'Stop.'

'But for me, I am 42 years. I know I never feel this again.'

'I don't want to think about feeling this with another man, Viktor.'

'No?'

'No. I want this to be the last time. And I'm not going to cry until you're leaving and I don't want to think about your departure yet.'

'Yeah?'

'Because I know that when you leave, when your helicopter flies overhead, my heart will break.'

25

THEY SAY JOVE LAUGHS

How much life can be sucked out of a single day and night? Can a 20-hour period of time be made to equate to a lifetime? These questions of science are in good hands for I intend to discover the answers today.

Waiting in the plush foyer of the Hotel Timor I have a bikini on under my sunfrock, pigtails in my hair (I so need a beachball), and a superhero's determination to overcome seemingly insurmountable obstacles in making this the happiest day of my life — call me Super Woman, or Super Annuated, if that's more suited to the look.

I perch on the edge of an enormous sofa, watching through the huge plate-glass windows for my man to arrive out the front. Inside it's all cool, regulated temperature, white-tiled floor, crisply uniformed staff, requisite quiet of the five-star establishment, while outside a pig perambulates by. Viktor, in a hire-car for anonymity, dodges it nicely. (There is a US$100 'tax' payable to the closest and most nimble Timorese person by any malae who runs over any local wildlife.)

'Hello, you'd be my guide. Are you one of the day's attractions too?' I say when I reach him out the front, ready for our ultimate adventure, restraining melancholy, and he lifts the back hatch door of the car to show me that inside it's loaded with firewood, a tray of marinating pork, freshly baked bread, an Esky that's chilling bottles of his favourite vinho verde, a barbecue grill and all the other necessities for a wonderful trip outside this metropolis and away from scrutiny or interruption. Just the two of us. Melancholy is effectively erased by these picnic preparations which confirm for me every single romantic stereotype of the Latin man.

This is serious sociological research and the results are in. I've put myself on the line to participate in a highly revealing qualitative study (can I emphasise the quality?), going under the covers in the cause of investigating, once and for all, the claims vis-à-vis the Latino lover. And, let me tell you, it's all true. The legend is fact. Fairytales can be found in the geographical reference areas of southwestern Europe, South America, parts of Florida, Bondi Beach, some African nations and, obviously, East Timor.

'I think you should speak Portuguese exclusively to me today,' I say.

'But you don't understand.'

'Oh, I understand, darling, don't you worry about that,' I purr, nestling into the crook of his shoulder and he pats my head, as the car starts up and purrs along with me.

Out of town we motor. Eastward, in fact. Then, turning right and travelling past the house of a Foreign Affairs Minister who has been flitting around the world, up onto a steep hill with the vivid blue expanse of water to the left, and way below we can see the beach on which we had our very first date — the white sand kissing the sea in a suitable analogy.

It's a beautiful 30 degrees Celsius, the humidity is low, a wind scented with clove cigarettes and wood fires rushes through the car window, as I ride with my feet up on the dashboard and a hand outside, playing against the air, the other on the gear stick changing from second to third, back to second again when required, 'See, it's an automatic!' I say and he smiles at me and shakes his head as we reach the peak.

At moments like this it is utterly impossible to believe that we are in a peacekeeping mission. I mean, look at that view! Feel the freedom! There is not an armed, uniformed individual or a burned-out building in sight, so we can trick ourselves into believing that we are in a tropical paradise, on a honeymoon, as mountains, ocean, palm trees, beaches and a Christo Rei all combine to create a vision that proves God's benevolence. I've certainly been granted a pretty blessed life above and beyond the one I deserve. What right do I have to be the beneficiary of all this privilege? Don't God, Mother Nature, Fate have some other more worthy heroines to work on? Although, don't get me wrong, I do appreciate that they've collaborated on this vast panorama that performs prettily for us, as we zoom downwards now.

See, life is a matter of perspective. We could lament that soon we will part, but instead we've chosen to celebrate this day together, sucking the life out of mere hours, an hour of which passes before we turn left at a dirt road and slowly make our way past a row of UN cars lining Dollar Beach — so called because the locals used to demand US$1 for use of the sand, a practice that's stopped (charging admittance, that is, not the sunbathing). We want greater privacy, however, so we continue on around a hillock to a secret piece of beach that's ours alone, and the car bumps along a rough track, passes through the gateway to nirvana, and pulls to a stop.

The only problem in nirvana is a wind that tests our hero's fire-making skills. What is it about men that they must succeed at activities like lighting campfires? I'm happy to just be here with him. I don't need to eat marinated pork. Is it the Neanderthal in every man? Because I'm watching on in increasing mirth at a Viktor who is becoming gradually blackened with soot, wet with sweat, and aggrieved at the audacity of the elements to spite him on an otherwise perfect day. Actually, on second thoughts, I'm quite happy with this rather manly fight against the elements. It's just one man (and his lighter, paper, kindling, firewood) against a lovely breeze.

'Look at this!' He indicates the filth and starts to wipe himself down. There are some things even a Latino man needs to learn I'm thinking, as I chase an errant wicker mat, kicking my toe (at least he's noticed the green bathers!). And now he is rescuing pork ribs that have fallen into the smoking fire, burning a hand. So one of these ridiculous individuals simultaneously yells with pain and doubles over in laughter as she nurses her foot, and the other stews furiously because it was all supposed to be perfect

'It is perfect! Don't worry about it. We have too much meat anyway. It is a lovely day, made lovelier by the comedy of errors, really. Oh, no, I didn't mean it like that. I mean, it is fun and, hey, we're not experienced in living in the wild, we're from big cities in developed countries. Yes, I realise you are a GNR but I'm afraid you are fallible and this whole day has been wonderful as a result.'

We sit in the shade together on the wicker mats that are secured now with many large boulders, drinking vinho verde, talking about world politics, solving the problem of war, devising the answer to poverty, mapping the creation of a world of freedom and happiness just like ours, inventing the key to equality. And with every glass it seems inconceivable that the world would reject our ideas for a universal nirvana, if only we could run it.

Some little faces appear in the trees, looking over at us. I cover my body with a sarong in deference to the culture and adolescence of these Timorians. They timidly return Viktor's wave. He calls to them to come. They resist. He goes to the barbecue, gathers up meat and bread and takes it to them.

You know, really, it's his kindness that's the most attractive feature of him. Despite my talk of biceps and caramel eyes, it's his heart that's drawn me to him. It's a rare empathy that he has and it is irresistible to me. See, he knows that everyone in the world should be as happy as we are right now, and that they could be. It's such a small token from us, yet even the barbecue food has placed broad smiles across previously uncertain faces; plus they get a good look at a malae chick in a sarong as an added side dish.

Once they've left, Viktor rubs sunscreen into my shoulders. 'I will miss my green eyes, Lynne Maria.'

I turn to face him. 'Your green eyes will miss you too.'

'I don't know what will happen. I can't be without my green eyes.'

'Come on, let's have a swim.'

'You want?'

'Sure.' Hands holding hands, wine glasses in the others, down to the waterfront. It might have seemed a good idea at the time and the view did seem appealing but it's a rocky path. 'We shouldn't talk about it today.'

It's low tide and it is a painful walk into the shallow pool of water. 'But I want you to know I will miss you. I miss you when I go to my camp, one hour away and I miss you. How can I leave tomorrow? This is impossible.'

'I'll miss you too but Viktor, for now we're two young lovers on honeymoon!' and I splash him.

'Hey!' He hates the cold and today the water is only tepid.

'Oh, big GNR commander can't handle a bit of water!'

Bad move, I'm in trouble, here it comes, and I squeal as a tidal wave makes its way to me. Despite himself — the melancholy he's finding it hard to ignore and the hatred he has for cool ocean water — he laughs playfully when confronted by my very real threats to retaliate but he says, 'Stop, Lynne Maree, enough.'

'Okay, grown-ups. I can do that. What's up?'

'I was thinking how to make you remember me. I am so frighten you forget me.'

'Oh, sweetheart, don't worry about that.'

'No, I think about this a lot and so I'm thinking about how to make you remember me and then I think of our first day together.'

'I'll always remember that too.'

'No, wait, so I ask my deputy to help me, I tell him I want to give you a puppy.'

'Oh my God.'

'Yeah. So he finds some and he bring the litter to my compound.'

'You had puppies in the GNR compound?'

'Yeah, such nice puppies. There was one, I knew he was right for you, so nice. But then I think this is irresponsible, that maybe it is not such a good thing to give to you.'

'Sure, it would have been completely irresponsible but it also would have been the most romantic gift in the world!'

'So you will forget me, Lynne Maria?'

'No, I won't forget you, Captain Viktor Carlos Mesquita Fernandes, how could I? It's simply impossible. Puppy or not — but the puppy would have been a help. I'm joking! Of course, I will remember you.' I don't want the tears to well and so I craftily send a foot out of the water and down with careful strategic placement in order to splash him right in the face.

He can't help but smile, shake his head and make as if to drown me, so I run and he chases me, 'Ow, ow, ow,' over the rocks and back to the wicker mats, to a fire that is burning low now and to the last of the bottles of wine Viktor brought with us today. No wonder we are soon wrestling and kissing on the mats, in peals of laughter and, with drying hair and bellies full, he lies down and I place my head on his stomach, giving him ample opportunity to play with my blondie locks, as the sun moves downwards towards the horizon and we watch it, giggling, while completely aware, on some heroically suppressed level, that it is dropping for the final time on us.

With the day's end and it alone prompting us, we unwillingly rise to leave. Packing the car, still giggling (my God this is mind over what's the matter), and with me behind the wheel, we manage to negotiate left and right with cliffs dropping away all around us and we're moving in the direction of whence we came. 'You have to buy little bags for your daughters!' I announce, as we drive towards the Metinaro market stalls, where wicker baskets line the roadside.

We pull to a stop and an extended family of Timorese women runs towards us, 'Malae, malae!' 'Hello Missus!' they cry.

'Botardi Senhoras,' I reply to them. They hold handbags in pink and lilac to my face. 'Which do you like?' I ask Viktor. He inspects the collection while I talk to the women in Tetum about price. Sure, he's pissed but, regardless, his Portuguese wouldn't have been able to assist too much. Here, in the foothills of the real Timor, these people can't speak in Viktor's tongue, they speak in theirs with a little bit of mine. So with theirs and mine, I tell them that money is no object when it comes to my companion's adored girls. Then, with the prettiest selections made, he points to a big weaved basket next to him and he hands them money, then he turns to me and says, 'It's for you. But it's not a puppy.'

'I suspect it'll be easier to take care of,' I reply.

'It's something you can keep forever,' he says. 'To remind you, if you ever do forget.'

I'm awoken by Viktor. He's urging me into wakefulness. And as he does, it dawns on me in tandem with the dawn of the day that he's leaving and I'd really prefer to be asleep, actually, ignorant to it all. I want my life with him to continue, however unrealistic that may be. I want it to last forever. I don't want to wake up. Waking to the realisation is simply too painful, if inevitable, yet he's shaking me, gently now, and so it's here. Today. I open my eyes a little bit in this room in the hotel I stayed in on my first night in Timor. He's already dressed. I must still be asleep because this is a nightmare.

'Lynne Maree, you have to wake,' he whispers in my ear. I feel his breath on my skin.

All right, here we go, it begins. 'Remember I told you that I wouldn't cry until the day you leave?' I say.

'Yeah.'

'Well, it's here now.' And the tears fall. I suspect they'll never stop.

Both of us are crying now. Holding each other. Stroking the other's wet face. Both of us dreading and yet anticipating the moment at which we will disengage for the last time.

We can't let go. We're kissing each other and tasting tears until I almost wish it over but, no, I don't, ever. This anguish is better than nothing, than the inevitable. Then, inevitably, he says, 'I must go.'

'I know.'

'I don't want to go.'

'I know.'

'I have to go.'

'I know.'

He releases me. Then he takes me up again into his arms. He releases me. And my arms continue to reach towards him as I watch him walking slowly, as if in great pain, away from me before he turns at a door open now and we stare at each other.

I try to remember every feature of him, the cowlick at his forehead, the little lines beside his eyes, his bow-shaped lips, the colour of caramel, and then, with time directing the scene, he says, 'I love you Lynne Maree,' and, as I reply, 'I love you Viktor,' the door closes behind him and he doesn't hear my words.

I stare at yet another ceiling for a moment, but unable to just lie there, I dart out of bed, throwing open the door to the balcony and I see him walking through the carpark in the morning mist. I call his name: 'Viktor.' He turns at the sound and comes to beneath where I am and stands below me. Night turning to day, we look at each other for what seems a lifetime. If only it was. For both of us. Lifetimes together.

This time he hears it, 'I love you,' I say and blow him a kiss. He blows one back to me and, with my hands, I catch it over my heart. He smiles and shakes his head and then he turns once more, and walks to his car. He opens the door, he hesitates, he turns back towards me. A confused, hopeful, silly heart starts beating furiously. He walks towards me, why? With an arm behind his back he comes and then, beneath where I stand again, he brings a hand forward and in it is, merely, my cardigan. Standing still, he lifts it to his nose, inhaling the remnants of my scent with closed eyes and, having consigned them to memory, he throws it to me.

Imagine having it all, then watching it walk away. Imagine wanting to scream to your dream, demanding that it stays. Yet you can't. That's what happens now. And there's nothing I can do.

So I stand in the cool morning air on that balcony, impassive, with a cardigan in my hand. The hotel is still. No one watches. The world is oblivious to a minute in time that is defining the paths of two lives. Separating them when before they were joined.

Returning to our room, I look at the bed that so recently held him and me and, with a crazed urgency, collecting my things, I run out the door, allowing it to slam behind me as I sprint down the corridor, the stairs, across the carpark, tracing his steps, then out the hotel gate and into a world that is starting to awaken now that a new day is beginning and his car is disappearing into the distance, to a Dilitown bathed in red, and staring after him I stop, bereft, I stop, in the middle of the road.

Then, after a period of time, I continue onwards to the very same beach on which we had our first date and, with the realisation washing over me, I fall to my knees in the sand, oh God, it's true, and, just as I did on that first morning in Timor, I remain there as the hours pass, managing only to chain smoke on that spot, creating a pile of butts beside me, as the scrawny dogs come and sniff at my legs, they look as forlorn as I feel, Timorese children wander past me, slowly, staring at the peculiar sight, 'Malae, malae,' they say and still I kneel there in the filthy sand until, after a period of time, with the sun shining brightly now, I see it, a UN helicopter, and it flies towards me, skirting the oceanfront at low altitude, moving along quickly, whump, whump, whump, and, with tears streaming down my face as it looks upwards, I'm peering at the little round windows, desperately hoping for one last glimpse of him and, with nothing I can do, it passes over my head and, as it does, as predicted, as I knew it would, my heart does break.

26

GETTING THE MESSAGE

Beep, beep. Beep, beep. My phone. Joy! I'm sitting in the sand with my phone in my lap, anticipation ending as I snatch it up and look to a message that has to be from Viktor. **1 new message.** I press OK. But it's not. Which individual can provoke a diametrically opposed reaction in me? It's BH1. And, to make it all the more astonishing, his message is: **How could you do this?**

Now, I'm no Einstein but even I can guess what he is referring to. How, indeed, could I have had the audacity to fall in love with someone other than him? Gee, let's contemplate that one for about two seconds. Jesus Christ, even a person with the mental acuity of an Australian police officer can see that there are some large barriers to me loving him: firstly, there is the small matter of his forceful seduction techniques; and, secondly, it's all fucken irrelevant because I'm in love with someone else, a man of my choosing.

Talk about interrupting the moment. I was perfectly happy mourning away in the grotty sand on my own (except for the company of a few stray dogs who've indulged me nicely by letting me talk about my pain in a stream of consciousness for the last couple of hours), until that arsehole had to force his way into my consciousness. He had to layer some more shit onto it because he hasn't contributed enough, has he?

How could he say how could I? I have the right to live my life as I bloody well want. I have put up with more than a woman should. Why? Because I was genuinely thankful. I was genuinely scared. I genuinely thought him a friend. But as for his: 'How could you do this?', that man has a perspective that is seriously askew.

I'd suspected he might hear whispers at some point and I'd come close to getting away with my double life, until the final morning! But he's discovered my secret love. Great. Just as I'm going back to the compound.

I'm standing beside the road, waiting for a taxi but it appears they don't tend to frequent the oceanfront all this way out of Dili proper in the early morning hours. Minutes go by. Then more. Here I am in the clothes of last night — with the cardigan on despite the stifling heat for fear of showing off my shoulders in a halter-neck top. God, it's hot. I pull at the collar. I may not be showing my shoulders but in this black get-up I look like a Darlinghurst hooker, nonetheless. Whatever. Can I really care about my appearance when I have so much going on in my mind?

What am I going to do about the BH1 issue? Especially as tonight is the dinner we've arranged to discuss What Happened Between Us.

I'm in a taxi now and the fourteen-year-old driver turns up the booming Boney M and lights a clove cigarette from the one that's burning to its end in his hand and he takes me on a tour of Dili. Do I want to listen to Boney M at maximum volume right now? Not really, but I don't have the energy to fight it when I can't think straight and I can't remember a word of Tetum in this state, so I sit in my moving cocoon with the thumping beat providing a background to the view of dusty streets, wildlife and dilapidated buildings before, eventually, he drops me off at my base where I run in the gate, across the empty common area, through my container door and dive onto my bed, bursting, as I do, into wretched tears. And the tears seep into my pillow as I cry out aloud, just like a child, weeping without restraint.

I know this is the worst of it. I am aware that this is the day I was expecting and I have to accept that it was worth this pain. It's better to have loved and lost, I try to convince myself. That was the choice I made long ago. I knew I would be here, sobbing, at this point, so I can't rue my misfortune, for it is the fortune I chose.

I lift my head and wipe my nose on my hand (a demonstrably inadequate surface), rise and power up my laptop. I know it will hurt me but for some ridiculous reason I need to make it harder. So I press PLAY on the CD Viktor gave me then, thanks to some inexplicable sado-masochistic impulse, I look at the digital photos of us in Maubisse, the ones from his camera which he forwarded to me. Great, we look so happy at our mountaintop resort.

It's an odd human condition that's makes me do this. I know that I am compounding my misery by acting in this way but I am compelled to look at the patch of the Portuguese flag from his uniform which he removed for me; to expose myself to thoughts of puppies and bikes bought for street children, all the while listening to his music as his face stares at me from my desktop. Just as I was compelled to love him.

Beep, beep. Beep, beep. My phone. I scramble for it. Where the fuck is it? I rummage through my handbag. Why do they make these things so small? Found it! I look at the screen. **1 new message.** It's Viktor. Thank God, it's Viktor. His helicopter must have landed at the airport in Baucau, where he'll be joining his chartered flight for Portugal. I press OK. I read: **I can't leave this way. A fairytale so sweet. I love you. I want spend my life with you. What you say?**

27

MALICE IN WONDERLAND

Hours later I interrupt my musings. I need to go to the doctor because my skin is corrupted thanks to some water-related bug. Women are particularly susceptible to complaints of this kind here and a real concern for me during this unanticipated period of unemployment is that I have no access to any UN facilities. Those who are not a part of the UN in East Timor are excluded from essential services, like the medical clinic. Today, however, I have a doctor's appointment at 10 am — an appointment, ironically, organised by BH1 in yet another thoughtful gesture. Obviously, he is ignorant of the specifics and generalities of my condition but he was charitable enough to discover that the Australian Embassy has a doctor on site and that I can consult her.

So it is that at my appointed time I head down to the magnificent seafront compound, pass the sign that tells people to dip their headlights, walk briskly between imposing gates topped with razor wire, throw a 'G'day' to the Timorese security guards (all that's required to prove credentials), thereby stepping through the looking glass and straight into a wondrous and magical First World.

To the left and at the end of a road bordered by manicured gardens is the surgery. I talk to the receptionist and look around at environs which are all very familiar in appearance, from the posters on the walls to the phones on the desks. It's Australian from floor to ceiling and everything in between, including me.

In the consultation room now and I'm greeted with just such sentiment by a kindly doctor behind her desk, 'Welcome to Australia,' she says.

'Sorry?'

'According to international treaty, so you are technically on Australian ground right now.'

'I wish.' Although, it *is* nice to be in this tiny approximation to home.

'How can I help you?'

'Well, you see, I've got this problem and, um, it goes like this . . .' In opening my mouth, though, medical problems *per se* are pushed aside as a torrent is unleashed and within it comes the story of BH1. In a gush, finally, it has been allowed to surface from where it was submerged. These things can only be locked away temporarily; even the strongest individual needs to come to terms with events that disturb one's sense of, well, decency, actually. Imagine, then, the catharsis it is speaking to this woman, a qualified woman without agenda or involvement. Imagine how therapeutic it is for me to have someone listen, really listen. She's validating what is valid. And she's allowing me to shed the fake smile and amiable exterior — it's a curative exfoliation. She's allowing the release of all those nasty built-up toxins, such as hate, from just below the surface.

Right in the middle of all this, wouldn't you know, my phone rings and irrespective of the value of this appointment and its flood of relief I say to her, 'I'm sorry, I have to take this call,' because I can see from the screen who is calling. She doesn't mind, she says, 'Come back when you're finished.' A professional behind a desk is being just that — I have left East Timor, haven't I?

I go out the door quickly. This will not be a missed call. 'Hello'.

'Hello, it's my Lynne Maree.'

'Yes, it is, Viktor, hey! How are you? I didn't think I'd talk to you again.'

'Yeah? Did you get my message?'

'Message?'

'The message where I say I want to spend my life with you, you got this?'

'Oh, that one, yes!'

'What do you say?'

'Oh my God, you weren't being rhetorical, you were being literal?' I'm stating the obvious. Why?

'Yes, I want to know, you want to spend your life with me? I want this. I cannot leave, I miss you, Lynne Maria. I am missing you so much, so much. This cannot be all, there must be more, I cannot believe I miss someone so much but, Lynne Maree, I love you. You understand?'

'Yes, I understand.' I'm walking around in the sunshine, my ear to my phone, the ocean-view bungalows of the Australian Embassy staff around me, all luxurious, about sixteen of them taking up a large section of the Dili waterfront, carports containing large 4WD city cars, imported wooden furniture on each empty veranda with lonely fans whirling around for no reason other than to show that these people are not conservationists. What they are is lucky, though. People of every nationality wish dearly that they could live here, because it is far more lavish than the living quarters of the staff of any other institution and country. For that reason it breeds intrigue, envy and contempt, of course — and the exteriors alone promote these things. God, if people only saw what was inside.

I happen to know that inside each house is all the affluence promised by the exteriors: state-of-the-art technology for one's guests' entertaining pleasure; an epicurean's kitchen for best hors d'oeuvre facilitation; toilets appropriate for delicate First World bottoms; recirculating ducted air-conditioning because one wouldn't want to break a sweat opening all those bottles of imported Australian bubbly; laundry with the latest white goods for the satisfaction of the most discerning maid; sheets free of floral pattern — a near miracle in this country — oh, look, the attributes are endless. And each staff member gets one house of his/her very own.

The whole extravaganza is bounded by gardens and right now I'm watching the Timorian gardener as he tends to the birds of paradise, the hibiscus — no, tiger lily — and over there, a little further away, I can see the in-ground pool and undercover bar ringed with Australian native plants. The sun is searing into me as I walk in circles, kicking gently at tufts of grass and prodding mounds of dirt with a toe in the common gait of the mobile phone user.

'So, what you say?'

'Um, what do I say? You want to know my answer, if I want to spend my life with you?'

'Yeah, of course.'

'Yes, Viktor, I do.' Interesting choice of words.

'I don't know what will happen but I must be with you. I don't know what will happen. I miss you, so much.'

'I know, sweetheart. I miss you too. So you're in Baucau?' I can't talk about all that emotion caper when I can't really see any way for him and me to have a future. I have this sense of running and running, faster and faster and not getting anywhere at all and I'm not even sure of my destination.

'Yeah.'

'You're leaving soon?'

'Yeah, I am at the airport watching the plane, my guys are all here. I send my deputy to get this phonecard to call you.'

'That's very nice of him. Once again the loyal deputy comes through for us.'

'Yeah. The plane is loaded, I watch now for them to say we go but I have to call you, I need to know if you feel this way.'

'You know I love you, Viktor. I do. This has been a fairytale for me too. I am devastated that you've gone.'

'Yeah?'

'Yes! Of course, I want you here with me. I would give anything for you to be here. I hate that you have to go home.' I'm laughing as I speak, trying to bring some lightness to a conversation that is overwhelming me. How can I possibly make plans for life with a man who is standing on a tarmac waiting to board his flight to Portugal and away from me? It may have been a fairytale in many ways but I wonder about the happily-ever-after business; it's always proved so elusive to me.

'I never hated my job, Lynne Maree, but I hate it now. I hate the GNR. I want to stay here with you.'

'I wish that could be true.' I do. (What, again?)

'I must go. They call me now. I must go. My guys are on the plane. I don't want to go but, Lynne Maree, I will see you again. I love you, so much, so much.'

'I love you too.' With all that established quite clearly, I press END, then, turning, I walk up the stairs and into the surgery again, where a doctor continues to accommodate me.

'Lynne, do you know many people in Timor?'

'Well, as you know, the thing about missions is that people are always leaving. I always seem to be saying goodbye to people who are ending their tours of duty and I hate it. Most of my friends from UNTAET have left now, there are only the police officers and obviously that comes with issues.'

'Next door to here is a woman who used to be a police officer and her husband is a police officer working with the embassy. Have you spoken to her?'

'I've met her,' through BH1, 'and I like her but I don't know if I can trust the police any more; they are all mates.'

'But she is a woman. And she'd have to be confidential and impartial, as a requirement of the job.'

'Sure. Look, really, I don't know whether I should tell her. What could she do? The risk is too great if she breaks my confidence. I really don't know. Do you think I should?'

'You should tell someone who can give you some protection in future, someone to call if you feel at any time that it could happen again. And while you are looking for a safe place to move into, you need someone who can keep an eye on you.'

'He's going on leave the day after tomorrow.'

'That's still two nights. And you need someone to talk to, Lynne, a friend.'

'I'll think about it while I'm walking the 10 metres from here to next door. I don't know if I can trust her but, you're right, I should. Go the sisterhood.' Awkward giggle. 'Thank you so much for your help. I'm glad I came. Apologies for the interruption in the middle.'

'Any time.' Now *this* is service. 'That'll be $25.'

'Sorry?'

'It's $25 for the consultation.'

'What about Medicare? If I'm in Australia I want to bulk-bill.'

'No, I'm afraid that's not possible here.'

Right. 'Not even a rebate?'

'No, actually.'

'Twenty-five Australian dollars we'd be talking, wouldn't we?'

'No, US.'

That's a pretty nifty example of the global political economy, I guess. Why be jingoistic, after all, when the world is one big happy chessboard . . . and there are currencies worth twice as much as your own. Although, you may be wondering why the US dollar is being used in this geographical spot at all. Is Timor (and Australia) lining up to become the 51st (and 52nd) state(s)? Well, the rupiah was the currency traded during Indonesian times and it was quickly replaced post -'99 by the Australian dollar, which was thought to be far more valuable and stable. It was. So, given the success of that experiment, some optimistic bureaucrat (or mercenary idiot) decided to aim even higher and the Australian dollar was switched for that of the United States.

What occurred immediately after that move was nothing, really, on the part of the shopkeepers who left all the pricetags undisturbed. Thus, items available for purchase in Timor doubled in value thanks to the strength of the US dollar against the Australian at the time. Instant wealth for some and a mortified face on me when I locate, amongst sparse, dusty shelves, a commodity I need, say a bottle of hair-conditioner brought in from Indonesia, and the $3.99 marked on the object isn't really the fair and reasonable $3.99 I'm accustomed to paying in my nation's money, it's actually $3.99 in denominations of green that all look the same, deriving from a country with a population that is better able to afford a fee like this. I've never felt impelled to SMS the prices of supermarket items in my life but there are times here when I really must send a fascinating transcontinental message to my mum such as: Lettuce — US$4.00.

For those outside the UN system, basic facilities are non-existent, rare, or prohibitively expensive in Timor. Still, at least I can check my email, I'm thinking, as I head to the Telstra Australia shop where I'll paying US$2 for each quarter of an hour that I wait for a page to load.

Telstra has a history of moving into shattered countries in Asia Pacific and quickly establishing a telecommunications infrastructure. It is rewarded well by identifying these new markets, tendering and signing up deals with an urgency that these countries (and the UN in them) desperately need . . . and the Australian government gets the advantage of being able to monitor the calls of the Third World leaders. Should we look at this as preying on the misfortunes of others or should we view it as providing essential expertise and equipment — fast?

I'd answer these questions objectively if I felt able, however my monthly phone bills leave me incapable of doing so without bias. It's the reason for the dependency on text messages here, which makes it rare to go anywhere in Dili without hearing the familiar 'Beep, beep. Beep, beep'. Including the shop where I sit now, waiting to access my inbox, looking up at the blue and orange logo on the wall which is probably more well known than any national flag in these parts.

I guess we are lucky to have Telstra here, in a simple and mountainous half an island, and sometimes I do marvel at the incongruity of having this service, such as when I'm punching in an SMS message and a goat meanders by.

Regardless, Telstra is preparing to pull out. Portugal Telecom is the carrier preferred by members of the Timorese Government and has been awarded the role as national telecommunications carrier. An outcome publicly known long before the deadline and tenders closed. Thank God, here's my inbox and, shit! It'll take me US$20 to clear out the spam.

I scour the list of names that have downloaded onto the screen and see that Maluco has sent an email. What does it say? We'll have to wait and see . . . finally it appears, allowing me to read a hope-everything-is-well note. That's nice. I wonder if we should resume a friendship — doctor's orders, after all. I dearly need to diversify the company I keep and he may be the better of evils. Should I reply? I'm wondering this while I empty my inbox — I don't need to elongate my penis, thanks; celebrity porn isn't really great viewing in a Telstra shop; and those girls from Scandinavia may or may not be luscious but I'm afraid I need to delete them all before my bill reaches an all-time climax.

When I eventually walk out the door and along the street, I'm mobbed by street children, 'Maria! Maria! Viktor nebe?' they yell.

'Viktor ba Portugal,' I reply sadly. Great. Just to reinforce to me that he's gone, they have to use his name for me and they have to ask me where he is, which requires me to tell them that he's gone home.

'Viktor nebe?'

'Viktor ba Portugal!' They are trotting along beside me, 'Maria! Maria!' Then a crying boy tells me that the bikes were stolen by bigger kids, as he tries to hold my hand. Oh God. I don't know what I can do. 'I'm sorry', I say, as I hail a Timor taxi and hop in and the children bash on the window, yelling, 'Maria! Maria! Dollar Maria!' while it pulls away.

In the compound, the incumbents are sitting around having their customary mad coppers' beer party as they do every eve at approximately 5.07 pm. I join them for a bit of banter and, watching them, I have to say that sometimes I do feel a fondness for them and a sense of safety in their midst. The brothers, as they first became known to me. And they're lifting my spirits with the story of BH5, who did indeed tie those six roosters to the landlord's door.

'You should have seen his face when he flung open the door going, "What the fuck?"' says one. Booming guffaws around the table magnified in volume by the corrugated-iron roof above us.

'The fucken things were taken away within hours,' says another one.

'Why do the fucken roosters in this country crow all day and night?' queries one more.

'I asked a Timorese person that very question one day,' I reply, 'and I was told that they are all still traumatised by '99. But what on earth is the lifespan of your average rooster, especially in this country?'

The roof's going to come off with all the fucken laughter, but despite it I hear the tell-tale squeal of the faulty fan belt on BH1's UN Land Rover as it pulls up out the front. Soup's up, I guess. It must be near dinnertime and I seem to have lost my appetite and this time it's got nothin' to do with love.

I did follow the doctor's advice and tell the policewoman at the embassy compound and she said I could call her if I am fearful tonight, but I don't know if she wants to be involved and I wasn't even convinced that she wanted to hear it. I felt that she wanted to put a finger in each of her ears and go, 'La, la, la!' as I was speaking.

It's a relief, nonetheless, to have her number in my phone as I step up into his car. I turn on the police radio. I figure it could replace the need for conversation, and, on cue, the East Timorese police officers responsible for staffing radio central start up with the whistling and the singing, then it occurs to me — God, I hope they can refrain from simulating sex! Talk, now, loudly, 'Creative driving skills,' I say of the traffic, a very platonic subject matter. A Timor taxi pulls out from a T intersection into our path and its driver lets off a spurt of siren sound at us.

'Every bugger in this place has a siren, except the police. Gives me the shits,' says BH1, and we dodge and weave through the anarchy on the roads, made worse at night-time because the Timorese prefer not to use headlights in an attempt to save petrol.

It's thanks to some competent defensive driving that soon we're pulling into a car space over the road from the Turismo — the place of a magical meal betwixt me and mine, just before his departure, when I was wearing a red dress and fresh flowers in my hair. Tonight is no comparison: I'm in the dowdiest clothing I possess (in public!) and the circumstances are far from romantic. And I am miserable, in that stage of grief when every single place, song, phrase, smell, taste, sound, activity reminds me of him. I can't get him out of my head. He is occupying it each day and every night. And, while I love seeing his image in my mind and I am fearful of forgetting every nuance of him, I'd really like a break from the memories, just an hour from the pain.

All of this causes me to be rather wistful tonight, as I look around at the environment we once shared, at the cats (Viktor threw food to those cats), at the tables among the tropical foliage (Viktor and I sat at that one over there), at the candlelight flickering (Viktor lit ours, then a cigarette which he handed to me), at the food (Viktor and I had the fish). I'm not really paying attention to BH1 other than occasionally throwing in a question such as 'How are your children?' or 'How are your children?' Although I sit up and take notice when he broaches a subject of interest. 'Lynnie, I want to know what's wrong? You seem to have pulled away from me recently. Is it something to do with What Happened Between Us?'

'Nothing happened *between us.*'

'Of course it did and I want you to know that it really did mean a lot to me and it made me the happiest I've been in this place. But I'm worried that you've had second thoughts about it all. Are you okay about everything?'

I am having a conversation with a character more wacky than anything Lewis Carroll ever came up with. 'Nothing happened *between* us,' I repeat.

'Lynnie . . .' I am speaking to a stoned caterpillar. I must be. Still, I can't confront him and his brothers. And I am finding it difficult to switch off every strain of feeling for him because, for a long time, he was my benefactor, a trusted companion. Then he went and ruined it all in one night. So, while logically I'm outraged, I pity him too and I can't bring myself to hurt his feelings! Yet I can certainly avoid him until he goes on leave. Yes, avoidance is a nice passive-aggressive approach. It's an approach that's *en vogue* too because he avoids any mention of his text message: 'How could you?' too. (Viktor's not off with the pixies.)

Therefore, soon enough in my continual container-room shuffle, I find myself approaching the door to BH1's bedroom with *en suite*, the scene of the crime. My complicity in agreeing to move in here while he is away almost makes me feel like his mistress, as I kick off my pretty mother-of-pearl sandals at the doorway, deposit my belongings inside and look around. Is that chill caused by the air-conditioner? But it's only for three weeks, then I'll be gone from here forever.

To where? No idea but will work it our I'm thinking, as a case of Portuguese wine arrives addressed to: 'Lynne Maree.' I'm instantly filled with his warmth. (Viktor *is* perfect! Well, other than his geographical shortcomings.)

Viktor and I have been speaking on the telephone most nights. Emailing most days. Is it prolonging a hopeless agony or is it lovely to read his protestations of an, apparently, enduring love?

— Original Message —
From: 'Vitor Fernandes'
Dear Lynne,
I'm allawys so exciting when i write you that, sometimes, i, realy, don't know what

can i say to express all my feelings about you . . .
I miss you so much that it's impossible to write in a E-mail what i think about you and us . . . I have you allawys in my mind and i'm trying to leave, day by day, with my girls, with you in my mind. It's very strange for me but, at the same time, it's an incredible feeling.I miss you so much that I usualy use all the things i feel and i see to remenber you . . . I miss 'my' eyes, so much, that i'm allawys trying to to see them in diferents ocasions and places.
Yesterday i heard a music in my car and now i nominate that song like 'my' and 'our' song, here in Portugal. It calls: 'Inflatable', from the band 'Bush'.
I wish you all the best and i want that you know, with no doubts, that I miss you so much, that i love you with all my heart and that will do everything i can to have you in my life.
I kiss your eyes,your face, hair and your special lips, and i send you the bigger kiss on the universe, to you my special and unic women, that i love so much,
your VIKTOR

How can I doubt my future now? It has to be linked with this man. Surely I can believe in the candour, honesty and integrity of a partner who loves me because I am 'unic', I'm wondering, in the early hours of a Saturday morning at the Purple Cow disco (Viktor stood over there near the bar one night), swaying to the sounds of King Africa's 'La Bomba' and Aqua's 'Barbie Girl'. Over and over again. They're favourites here. I find myself distractedly singing, and I realise what I'm doing before all street cred is completely eradicated. Jesus, it's one thing to enjoy the music as best I can, begrudgingly, but quite another to have a taste reversal and like the stuff! I do thank God for pocket-sized mercies who, like me, can't get someone out of her head, and it's true, all right. Especially tonight because it's his birthday.

A few times during the night I've slipped away from the group of Oz cops and submitted myself to the indiscreet stares of the other patrons while calling his number in Portugal. But each time there's no answer. Sigh. I wonder why? as I resume my place and take up my glass of personality again after another try. Surely he would know I'd be calling on such a special day?

As a visual spectacle, the Drag Queen Strumpets are here and for some reason one of them says 'Slut' to me as they prance past. And all I was doing was minding my own business (albeit while looking aghast at the mock leather/lace/denim/Lycra construction she'd managed to strap herself into tonight, topped inexplicably with a gangster's hat; remarkable).

On the dance floor I am feeling the certain freedom that comes from moving to music, the beat infecting my body together with the humidity and the view of a beautiful ocean, while my companion, one of the brothers, holds his VB stubbie in his hand as a protective talisman and awkwardly places a left foot there, a right foot here, the hips waving a bit awkwardly — why can't Australian men dance?

It's now that I notice the Drag Queen Strumpet beside me moving melodramatically to the beat, trying to impress the hundred or so men watching her wild antics and she's belting out the words, incorrectly. She seems to be challenging me to a dance-off. Less is more, honey, I'm thinking, as I move with restraint and sing the lyrics, correctly, in my language. Still she gesticulates with her arms and wobbles her bum as she spins around, eyes boring into me between her demonstrative pirouettes. She's just like Jennifer Beals in *Flashdance* on acid.

I've been caught up in some mating ritual she's performing for the guys, and it must be a mating ritual peculiar to her country because my dance partner looks at me, looks at her, looks back at me, raises his eyebrows and looks plainly petrified. 'Er, it'd be my round,' he says and takes off for the bar like a cartoon character in a hurry with legs a blur beneath him.

I escape from under the palm-frond canopy, onto the pebble-covered table area and towards the gate (behind which the Timorese stand, watching) where I call again, pondering the activities I've just been witness to. What was that all about? No answer. I am concerned about this but I'll file it away for a little bit and hope for the best. Things are never as bad as they seem, are they? His phone could have been dropped in the water during some dramatic air/sea rescue for which he'll win a bravery award, or perhaps it's turned off because he's decided he can't live without me and he's currently flying back to Timor and into my arms? I'm deciding between these options when one of the cops, hoping to lend clarity, provides the sensitive observation, 'Look Lynnie, live with it, you were just his Dili fuck.' But it's an offering that isn't entirely helpful.

Is it the oppressive heat, is it the sadness I feel, is it the professional circumstances? Whatever, the days are melding into one long, tiresome slog. With only subtle differences to distinguish one from the other. On this day, as usual, the mobile phones are active. A few of the callers are offering the common refrain, 'It's a hardship mission, you know,' to their respective spouses as I walk past. I stifle a laugh. How hard it can be when you are a big white bloke with a gun who's being paid a tax-free fortune to be here. They don't even bother to learn Tetum and I'm wondering what they would think of anyone who lived in Australia for so long and didn't deign to speak English (Viktor is multilingual). They're doing better than most here, but I guess that information would do nothing for their fearless and heroic reputations back home.

Giggling to myself I go to the kitchen and make a cup of tea. 'Anyone for a cuppa?' Of course, not, it's beer o'clock in these parts — yeah, hardship mission. 'Whaddaya want for dinner? Which seafood restaurant?' I say, and I'm told to 'SHHHHHHH!' Oooh, tetchy.

Sitting at the table with Jill Jolliffe's *Cover-up: the inside story of the Balibo Five* in my hands I'm not paying an enormous amount of attention to the blokes who end phone calls and take seats at the table. Instead I'm remembering the time I went to Balibo with Ramos-Horta. It was his first time back in that village towards the western border since he'd dropped the Australian journalists off, just prior to the Indonesian invasion in 1975. The journalists, as we know, were killed. And two and a half decades later José was clearly shaken when our car within his motorcade stopped in the town square and he surveyed the house in which they'd died, reporting on the war and highlighting to the world the Timorese struggle.

I'm caught up in my thoughts when suddenly the table lurches and, rescuing my mug, I sit up to watch BH5 and BH9 engage in that proud Australian custom, the biffo. It's a struggle of a far less profound kind than the one I was contemplating. Punching, pushing, chests out and eyes staring into other's. 'Yeah?' 'Yeah!' They pull away, circle each other, in movements that resemble a dance and, keeping true to the traditional steps, the more manipulative one moves away, although he's careful not to be seen as the submissive participant (lest it diminish his masculinity) and he throws an insult under his breath designed to be heard, causing the other to launch (thereby making him appear the aggressor), and so it begins all over again. One, two, three; One, two, three.

Some nationalities have the salsa, others the waltz. Some people like to tango, flamenco, jitterbug, jive. Aussie blokes will tell you they hate to dance, but you'll find them engaging in this particular one often enough. And it's an even more spectacular display when the blokes wear our flag on their arms — I can imagine this in the national dance category at multicultural festivals: the Cossack hopak-kolo, the Irish jig and the Australian biffo. (Viktor and I did the Latin salsa.)

It's almost a relief to fall sick. I don't even have to pretend to be positive. I can lie in my sweat and curse each boring bloody hour as it passes in slow-mo. I don't leave the room for days. I'm worried I've contracted dengue, when I can be bothered to put any thought into it, as I slip in and out of sleep. I suspect that a mosquito injected it into me. And I don't know when I was infected because, irrespective of the amount of repellent (Dili perfume) I put on, I can't give myself coverage 24/7. Every day a few mosquitoes get me; it's inevitable. All I can assume is that I was probably bitten in the morning because that's when dengue mosquitoes are active. Malaria mosquitoes bite for the rest of the day and at night. A curious natural demarcation line.

The mosquitoes are the curse of this and many Third World nations. They are floating killers, droning consistently, taking the lives of those who can't fight back — the poor, the young, the old. I'm none of these things even if I feel 100. I've got the immune system to survive.

Thank God there are water bottles in the room and I reach for one through barely opened eyes. Oh, that hurt. Too much light. Too much movement. I am exhausted, my muscles are consumed by apathy, aching intolerably. I'm unable to sit up or stand, nor can I read; I can only occupy myself by replaying my time with Viktor on the backs of my closed eyelids, in the dark. I'm too ill to go outside, to go to the doctor — although the US$25 is another impediment. I'll just see it through, I'm too tired to care.

And, in all those days that I lie in the room, bathed in perspiration, humming to myself, eating BH1's biscuits when I can, remembering stories of skipping along beaches in a state of glowing health and hallucinating about a mountaintop tryst, not once does someone come to the door to see if I'm okay.

Miraculously, it shuffles to the common area and takes a seat some days hence. Dark bags under the eyes are a fashion statement to rival heroin chic, honest. The blokes are sitting around discussing the landlord and his sixteen-year-old Timorese girlfriend who want to move into another room. No one takes a great deal of notice of me. (Viktor thinks I'm unic.) Currently the landlord and his adolescent girlfriend live in a basic bunk-bed container room in the compound and they need more space. Which room should be made available for them? I speak up and suggest that they could have the one with access to a private bathroom.

'Why?'

'I think it would be good for her. Then she wouldn't have to walk across the common area in a towel whenever she's going to the shower and back.'

'Why is that a problem?'

'Well, of course, it isn't ideal.'

'What are you saying?'

I am stunned that I need to explain this. 'Um, well, she's sixteen. I'm sure you agree that it would be better for her to have her own private bathroom, that it could be somewhat intimidating for a Timorese girl to walk across the compound in front of a mob of big Australian cops when she's in a towel.'

'Is that right, is it? Let's ask her. Hey . . .'

'Hang on! What's going on? I'm not completely certain why this is an issue. I mean if she had her own bathroom she could lock the door behind her. She is too timid to lock the door to the communal shower container behind her . . .'

'Yeah, and we fucken hate the way you do that.'

'Why?' Mosquitoes are preferable company to these blokes today.

'What are you saying when you do that? Are you saying we're a bunch of perverts?'

'No, but prevention is better than a cure.'

'Really? Prevention of what?'

'You're the police officers. Rules and laws don't presume that every member of a community is a bad egg, but you never know . . .'

'Ah, here we go. What are you saying?'

'Surely it's better to err on the side of caution? That's good for you, too, because it protects you, then nobody could even suggest you are perverts. I mean, I don't go into the toilet block if any of you are in there — and that's most of the time — because you have every right to some privacy without a chick going in there and making you feel like you have to be quiet when you're on the loo, or that you've got to get dressed in a wet shower cubicle. I hear no evil, I see no evil, I smell no evil. It's all good. So all I'm saying is that a tiny bit of compromise can't be a bad thing. I can't see the problem with that.'

'You've got a problem with her, haven't you?'

'What? What kind of a problem could I possibly have with her? I am trying to look out for her best interests so clearly I don't have any problem with her at all.'

'Yeah, you've got a problem with her. What, you don't like her? She's younger than you? She's stealing some of your attention in that towel, hey? Is that it?'

'What on earth? Have you gone mad? I don't understand why we are having this conversation or why this conversation is quite as antagonistic as it is. I just believe that women have a right to be comfortable in their own private space.'

'So you're not comfortable? is that what you're saying?'

'No, I'm not saying that. What I'm saying is that we could take care of her a bit. She's a Timorese teenage girl! She's from an extremely patriarchal society and you guys are over six-foot tall and white and loud and it would be a good thing to offer her. I have advantages she doesn't have, I'm Australian, I speak your language, I'm an adult, I am able to lock the door to the shower container.'

'Which pisses us off.'

'Why? I'm not in there for long, I ask you if anyone needs to use it before I go in there, and why should I shower behind a flimsy see-through shower curtain with anyone able to come in and use the toilet cubicles? That doesn't make sense to me.' I hardly have the energy for this and I certainly don't have the will.

'Doesn't make sense. Did you hear that boys? Doesn't make sense to the poor princess. You don't like having to justify yourself, do you, Lynnie? You don't like that you haven't got us all twisted around your little finger, do you?'

'Right, now I understand. You have no idea what you are talking about. Presumption is a dangerous thing; you are all coppers, you of all people should know that. Anyway, I've had enough of this, conversation over.'

'Don't you walk away, girlie.'

I continue to walk.

'Oi, girlie! You heard me. Don't you walk away when you haven't been told you can go,' says BH2.

Excuse me? I continue to walk and, reaching the room which was once my curse and is now my private space, I enter through it and this time the click is a comfort . . . Until there's the warrant knock, BANG, BANG, BANG! I ignore it. Again, BANG, BANG, BANG! Jesus Christ, what is going on? This is crazy. Why would a grown man follow me to my room to continue a preposterous conversation that has no real benefit to anyone at all? BANG, BANG, BANG! Opening the door a slot I stick my nose to the crack and say, 'I really don't think we should continue the conversation, it's doing no one any good.'

'I'll tell you whether this conversation is continuing or not, girlie,' says Tweedle Dumb.

What? 'Look, I think it is better for everyone if we just stop it here,' and I go to close the door, which seems a wise approach — to me anyway. Unfortunately my opinion in this regard isn't shared, because I am knocked back with the shock and force of the Australian-issue police boot that kicks its way in. Okay, we've now skipped straight into the realm of the absurd.

'All right, you want a blue, don't you? Not my preference but I won't be intimidated by you. Give it your best shot.' I walk out of the room and face him. Actually, in truth, I look up at his six-foot-high face wondering if he has dengue of the brain.

'I'm gunna call your father and tell him that you should go home,' he says.

'What?' Okay, this man has actually gone bonkers. He's prescribed sentence first. Here follows the verdict.

'I'm gunna call your father and I'm gunna tell him to tell you to go home, that it's about time you stopped running away from whatever it is you're running from.'

'Mate, I'm actually going to respond to you with a little more respect than I'm getting from you and I hope it can change the tenor of this dialogue to a somewhat more constructive one. I'm going to address your allegation. I'm going to point out that the job I've been offered by the Prime

Minister of this country is an opportunity for me. It is a job that'll use my skill and it is a career development for me. And, quite frankly, I think it's worth waiting for the very new government of this country to organise the work contract. I can't expect it to happen in First World time 'cause we ain't in the First World.'

'Go home. Go home and stop running away from what you're running from.' I could tell him to stop running from whatever he's running from, to go home to his wife and four children who've been sitting there during how many — was it six? — missions but that might be even more inflammatory.

'You're not listening to me. I've told you that I have come here for different reasons from you! I know it's almost incomprehensible for you to imagine that someone could choose to come to Timor because they want to work here and contribute to rebuilding this nation but I am one of many people dedicated to a thing called humanitarianism.'

'I'm gunna call your father and I'm gunna tell him to tell you to go home.' Oh God, I'm having a dialogue with a character who still occupies a world where women apparently care-give in aprons and very little else, defer to the men in their lives, with their only ambitions a new Canberra townhouse, top-of-the-range Ford Falcon, in-ground swimming pool and a bouncy baby boy.

And even though my body is depleting its stores of adrenalin and feels ready to collapse, I'm loath to faint into his arms right now because it may very well illustrate his point versus mine. I reach into deep reserves of defiance. 'I'm sorry, Constable, but how dare you! Although, on second thoughts, let me get my phone and dial my father for you, shall I? Yeah, hang on, let me just get my mobile and I'll hand the phone straight to you and you can tell him whatever you like. But you know what he'll say to you? He'll remind you of the bleeding obvious, that I am professional woman of a certain age who makes her own choices in life and that if he were ever asked, not that he needs to be, he would say he's proud.'

'Bullshit.'

'And while we're talking about fathers and daughters, imagine that your daughter is overseas, and she may very well be one day, and some bloke treats her like this. Have a think about that.'

'My daughter wouldn't be a sponge.'

'That is something you need to take up with a colleague of yours, not me. You can't rescind an offer of sanctuary the minute he's on leave. But don't worry, I'll leave — the compound, but not this country. Now if you'll excuse me, this conversation is over.' (Viktor would have punched his fucken ignorant lights out.)

The door slams behind me and with a certain desperation, I call anyone I've ever met in Timor. Will they even know who I am? Still, I need to reach out to the world beyond the compound, an unfamiliar world but unlikely as strange as the one in here. Hey Lynne, yeah, says someone who knows of a room in a house in Comoro, it's sharing with an English couple that runs a scuba-diving operation and they are abusive alcoholics, if you think you can put up with that then, sure, there's a room for you right now. It sounds like a picnic compared to where I've been living, I'll take it!

I'm busting out! Let's pack up the baskets and bags of accumulated possessions including Balinese homewares, gifts from my former kolegas, a watch given to Viktor by the GNR for his 40th birthday (Viktor used to wear it), a blue UN beret, a Brazilian military belt, all of them special to me, and then there is the Australian police uniform that I was presented with by BH1 some time ago which I might just leave behind. Packing up hurriedly, I'm thinking of placing a burned bra over BH2's doorknob when my phone rings, 'Hello.'

'Hello Miss.'

'Sweet Jesus.'

Actually, it's not, but the man who is, instead, on the other end of the line tells me of the travels he's made, including to the World Cup opening ceremony, and the important international meetings he's had to further the cause of peace and democracy in his country, yes, yes, yes, it's all very consequential but, wait, I have to tell you what I've been up to, José . . . and, soon, arriving in the driveway of the Australian police compound in Dili, East Timor, is his car (numberplate '2') together with his driver, 'Hello Missus Leeen.'

'Botardi Celestino. Obrigado!' and it's time for me to choose to stand up to my full size and head for some new lodgings with an alcoholic English couple, in style. So, with the car loaded, I jump into the front seat of the Minister's car and it's the fitting time to bid these boofheads I've been living with in this wonderland of theirs a happy '*adeus* = bite my fat arse'. (Viktor has a lovely bottom.)

28

IT'S A SMALL WORLD AFTER ALL

Darling Viktor,
I wonder: is love a gift or a curse when the wonderful man I love is 16,000 kilometres away?
Sometimes I feel like the luckiest girl in the world because I met you, at others it seems that I am in purgatory.

Oh, look, this is bloody ridiculous. It's gone too far. It's about time I just got over it. I mean, I'm listening to Shania Twain. On repeat. And I know the words. Things have gone too far. But still I press PLAY again. Oh God, I am deliberately and consciously torturing myself. A once rational woman is doing her own head in.

Why do so many songs sing about love and lack thereof? Doesn't it show a marked lack of imagination on the part of songwriters? What about sunsets as an alternative subject matter? They give joy, are consistent, stable, they rarely let you down. What about a great meal? Isn't that a gift in a life, a sustaining, valuable gift that many in the world go without?

What about shoes? Surely there could be odes to shoes, things that genuinely bring joy, until you choose to upgrade? Let's face it, shoes don't leave you; *you* discard shoes when you are good and ready. That's worth singing about, isn't it? Instead I'm singing melancholic lyrics to myself as I come into the kitchen.

'Aven't ya go-h any uver fuckin music?'

'Sorry?'

'Tha-h fuckin music ya play on repea-h. Ya don'h 'ave anuver fuckin' song in 'ere?'

I need Morse Code talking to Wayne sometimes. 'Sorry. I didn't realise you could hear. I've been trying to be quiet,' because, even in my grief, I am aware that I am ridiculous, which is why I am embarrassed to learn that I have been heard screeching like a mournful cat to Shania Twain.

'Ya fink tha-h's fuckin quie-h? All day and nigh-h long. Ge-h yaself some new fuckin CDs, why don'h ya?'

Ay, the world is made up of all kinds; all kinds of fascinating people with distinctive tongues. I speak the same language *per se* as Wayne but often I'm just left looking at him — blink, blink — as he takes it to a whole new creative level.

The special linguistic skills of Wayne stem mainly from his Souff Lun-dun background, which paid little attention to the letter 't'. In fact, in most instances it is eliminated, certainly it is considered dispensable within phrases pertaining to most things. I, however, am rather fond of the letter 't' and, frankly, some words just don't have the same ring without it, such as 'letter', 'sentence' and 'alphabet'.

Aggravating the issue of pronunciation is a hearty appetite for the grog. And don't presume, just because it's ten in the morning, that he's not drunk. Why be shitfaced for only five hours of an evening when there are many more hours in a day during which one can be oblivious to it all too? 'Ya go-h any beers in 'ere?' as I lean into the fridge. Colonisers appropriating from the Antipodeans, as usual. When's the next chance to vote yes for a republic?

I go outside to where his bride is supervising the Timorian gardener with a VB in her hand for breakfast. 'Morning.'

'Morning Missus.' It's a peaceful scene. Ann is here, among her friends, the plants — bougainvillea, papaya, rocket, basil, custard apple — and six puppies. She speaks to them as she meanders around and a day begins, drinking her breakfast and smoking her menthols. 'How are you then, Missus?'

'Good, good. Well, a bit maudlin but otherwise, you know, chipper,' I reply.

'Don't talk to me about the Portuguese lover. I've told you, I don't want to hear it. I've heard it from too many women before you.'

'Well strictly speaking I wasn't. Anyway mine's different. You don't know him.' How did we get onto this, as always? It infuriates me that she is so dismissive of a very real love in my life.

'Bah! Different? I told you, I don't want to hear it.' For someone who doesn't want to hear it, she spends a curiously large amount of time talking about it. 'The number of otherwise intelligent and discerning women who fall for all that never ceases to amaze me.'

Hmph. I'm scowling now. She doesn't know. She's never even met him. I haven't told her any detail at all. She has just assumed that Viktor fits into some stereotype of the Latino braggart, a Lothario, which I think is unfair. 'Look, I appreciate that you . . .'

'Appree-SEA-ate, not appree-SHE-ate.' Ann has much better diction than her husband and she likes to correct mine in what I assume is some sort of misplaced passive-aggressive response to Wayne's appalling elocution. Ann's is pretty posh, actually, and yet she is the former pole dancer, if I can submit to a stereotype for a minute, whereas he was a war correspondent covering most of the conflicts of the last couple of decades — no wonder he prefers to be drunk and oblivious to his memories.

Still, their differences and contradictions have combined to form a committed twosome. Peas in a pod. Together they have the bond of two alcoholics versus the world, with an understanding they alone share. So despite the bitching and insults, the screaming and sulking, theirs is a marriage that'll last a lifetime, and I have some grudging respect for that. Yes, it works. I don't know why, but it works.

Their compatibility is of an original kind: 'I know I'm ugly,' Ann said to me once, as we sat on the veranda.

'Ah, yeah, luv, bu-h ya go-h the best tits in the business,' came the response from the bar fridge inside. (Point of interest: that he can pronounce the word 'tits'. Practice makes perfect.)

The odd couple opted out of the fast and furious lanes and came to Dili to open a scuba-diving business which they had hoped would take advantage of the natural beauty of the underwater world along the coast of Timor and snare a healthy chunk of the massive UN wages. Unfortunately, the idea wasn't an innovative one and so Dili has a startling profusion of scuba-diving centres all competing for share of a temporary market.

'Anyway, I'm the one with troubles. Just you imagine what it's like selling up and coming here, putting everything into a business, helping the economy in this country, and to be on the edge of going broke, losing everything, hundreds of thousands of pounds. That's when you've got worries.' Ann's conversational repertoire is limited to only a couple of subjects, her financial problems, understandably, chief among them.

The Timorese gardener hoses Ann's wilted plants in the hot sun, the water evaporating as it hits earth parched from the dry season combined with a drought. 'Yeah, I know. I do appreciate . . .' oh, fuck.

'Appree-SEA-ate, not appree-SHE-ate.'

'Okay, okay. I'm off then.'

'Where are you off to?'

'I'm going to the Prime Minister's office. Phone calls aren't the most effective way to get things done in this place so I'm going to force a meeting.'

'Good luck. Champagne's on you.'

'I appreciate that,' I giggle, trotting quickly up the road before she can turn around.

I hope you can see that I am true to you. Love is not flippant to me, it is a rare, special and intimate gift that I cannot erase and which I cherish. There are no other men for me here. Only your memory, and that is enough . . .

Past the filtration centre that provides water for the UN peacekeepers I go. Soldiers are filling up their trucks but they interrupt proceedings for a moment to catch the sight of a woman's arse. I try to wiggle it as little as possible, despite contending with the rocky road in my sandals (accompanied by my best skirt and the shirt with the least amount of discolouration that covers my shoulders as well). A scooter, laden with five people, including the requisite breastfeeding mother, motors by, 'Hello Missus.' A taxi slows down beside me but I think it best to wave it past, given that there are already three Timorese men inside.

Coming up onto Comoro Road I stand underneath a frangipani tree in front of one of the many kiosks selling cigarettes, brooms, instant noodles. 'Hello Missus, fuck, fuck,' comes the greeting from a group of teenagers under the tree next to mine. They snigger.

'Bondia,' I reply.

'I love you Missus,' comes the chorus and they collapse into peals of laughter. Thank God for the sound of booming bass that heralds the approach of a Timor taxi.

This is an important mission of my own today. My finances are perilously low. I have now entered a fearful stage — I no longer have the money to fly home to Sydney, so this job had better come off. Which is why I make my way into the main foyer of the big white government building and the security guards say, 'Hello Missus Leeen!' A diversion first — I poke my head into the Ministry of Foreign Affairs, which is on the ground floor just off to the right, 'Hello Lynne!' they say. José really did get the cream of the crop when it comes to staffing. Many of the people who were working for the resistance movement in Australia are working in this office now, bringing their multilingual education with them. I love coming in here, kisses on each cheek, before ducking in to trade words with the internationally renowned statesman, racouteur and rake himself. 'Hello Miss.'

'Hello Minister.'

He stops tapping at his laptop and turns towards me as I sit in the chair opposite him.

'How are you?' He smiles that unnerving smile, the one that suggests he wants to eat you up.

'I am well, thank you very much for asking, that's very kind of you. And how are you and your nation going?'

'Very good, thank you. Listen, I've spoken with the Prime Minister again about your position. He says he is waiting for the paperwork and he'll sign it.'

'Paperwork. Well, that's for his office to organise. I'm on my way up to talk to his adviser: he with the phone that doesn't dial out.'

He breathes his laugh, 'Is that right?'

'Like, yeah!'

'Do you need some money?'

'Sure, but I'm not going to take it from you. Heaven knows what I'd have to do to repay you.'

'Well,' he says in that deep gravelly voice of his, 'I'm sure we could come to some arrangement.'

'I'm thinking that arrangement might suit your, um, requirements more than mine, so I'll just go hungry. And, hey, it's showing solidarity with your people.'

'Is it?' He grins as he leans back in his chair against the backdrop of countless tais interwoven with his name while, stuck to a glass door on his left, are the security passes and name tags bearing his visage and moniker from hundreds of international events around the world.

'Yes. I'm going upstairs now. Thank you for going up there earlier. At least they will have been reminded that I exist.'

'You're welcome, lady,' he rises and moves around his desk ostensibly to give me the requisite kiss on each cheek. 'God, you look beautiful,' he says as I stand up. 'Is this for me or the Prime Minister?' He sees my frown. 'What?' he laughs.

'I'm going.' I lean down to give him those requisite kisses and he takes the opportunity to place his arms around me, pulling me to him with a thump. I disengage, the brow particularly furrowed now. I am starting to realise why these Latino nationalities prefer dual kisses. 'Goodbye, Minister. And by the way, people just saw that through the glass window.'

'Impossible.'

'It may be frosted but I can make out their shapes and one can assume vice versa. You could do with exercising better discretion.'

'Lynnie . . .'

'What?'

'Come round for a drink this week. You can tell me what the Prime Minister's office said.'

'I don't have transport. It's not safe to take a taxi at night here, I've told you that.'

'Don't be dramatic.'

'When have you ever taken a taxi in this country?'

'Okay, I'll send my security car.'

```
I want you to know that for me this love is
real, it's not 'mission passion'. You are
Timor for me, you are love for me.
```

I walk into the Prime Minister's office to meet his political adviser, a longtime UN staff member and Portuguese-speaking Briton who subscribes to the common manner of UN workplace interaction: see, the high wages and internationally respected jobs make it a competitive shop floor. People guard their positions and influence doggedly, to the exclusion of social niceties. So much so that Sergio Vieira de Mello once sent out a memo urging staff to be nice to each other. To no avail. So even though we are discussing my livelihood, my access to essential services and my ability to get home, I'm told bluntly by the PM's adviser that he has 'forgotten' to arrange my contract.

At least I'm front of mind now, which forces him to comment uninterestedly, 'I'm not sure I know how we can pay you what you should be paid. I'm sure you wouldn't want to be a UNV.'

What he sees as a problem is a solution. 'I'd be happy to be a UNV! I haven't come to East Timor to enrich myself,' I reply and beam — word and deed combining to make me terribly atypical in these parts.

'All right, I'll talk to UNDP,' he concedes in frustration because he can see that a crazy woman has ensconced herself and isn't going anywhere; she's just going to sit here in front of his desk with a smile on her face, clutching her handbag and scratching at mosquito bites.

Although hang on: 'The UNDP positions need Portuguese fluency, don't they? I speak some Tetum but other than that only English, and the government is officially operating in Portuguese, isn't it?' I say.

He shoots at me, 'The decision to bring in Portuguese is simply unworkable. It won't last long.' Therefore, I'm going to be one of the 200 UNVs employed by the United Nations Development Programme to capacity-build the Timorese in the skills required to govern and administer their nation. So my job title will be the Adviser to the Adviser for Public Information to the Prime Minister of East Timor and the Council of Ministers.

The whole intention of this mission is theoretically to work your way out of a job, to train your Timorese 'counterpart' to be self-sufficient, to transfer your knowledge and skills to them through day-to-day mentoring, because the Timorese can't be expected to know how to run their country when they've never been allowed to do it before. In the previous mission the UN did the governing and administering, it *was* the government. But thanks to this new mission and the year or two it intends to spend capacity-building Timorese counterparts, the UN can pull out one day, leaving behind a competent and experienced local government and public service. It's a great idea and I can't see any hurdles. Well, other than the careerism (and recall issues) of UN staff, and the predisposition of Timorese counterparts to sleep and/or meow.

`I miss you deeply. I cherish hearing your voice on the phone. Still, I want to see you laugh, I want to touch you, I want to talk and talk with you, I want to dance with you. It is unbearable to me that I cannot. I don't know what to do. I am XX* years old and yet I remain a teenager.`

*Precise age suppressed by publisher under threat of legal action by the author.

There is a lot of woofing going on here I'm thinking, while I sit, trying to read on the back veranda. Moments later, I'm mobbed by the puppies that follow around Ann, the Pied Piper of Comoro, who comes upon me with her menagerie. 'Hello Missus,' she says from within the din.

'G'day Missus,' I reply, as I surreptitiously sit on an envelope with a Portuguese stamp on it (I really don't want to have an encore discussion with her) and fend off creatures.

'And it's appree-SEA-ate, not appree-SHE-ate,' she throws at me from the kitchen door they're all entering and I hear her beloved's sweet talk from inside, 'Allo luv, wha'h's fuh fuckin dinnuh?' while I remove an errant pup, named after a former Associated Press correspondent to Timor, from on top of a borrowed magazine. A women's magazine! Filled with clothes, shoes, accessories, cosmetics and celebrity gossip — who are Ashton Kutcher, Brittany Murphy and Sophie Ellis Bextor, anyway? Goodness, I have been away from civilisation for a while.

Beep, beep. Beep, beep. My phone. It's been going mad ever since I got home. **1 new message. I think you are falling in love with me**, it says.

I reply, **Oh dear, you've caught me out, Minister. Now go and SMS your Australian Embassy girlfriend.** Anyway, José knows perfectly well that I am in love with Viktor, a love that transcends innuendo, that is what it appears to be. One of those rare Sharon Stone–Phil Bronstein, Uma Thurman–Ethan Hawke, Cameron Diaz–Jared Leto, Halle Berry–Eric Benet, Lisa Marie Presley–Nicolas Cage, Liza Minnelli–David Gest connections. Unbreakable. For ours, too, is a genuine, enduring and concrete union. And distance is no challenge to our determination, it seems. A fact illustrated by the gift I've just received in the mail. Better than the most effusive and prolific of email correspondence, this *communiqué* of old-fashioned romance came thanks to Correio Aereo Portugal: the post.

I've been looking forward to it, the mystery present, for weeks now. Viktor has been emailing and calling me, asking excitedly, 'You receive my present?' Frustratingly, it took a very long time to make it from Oporto to me, a time during which he informed me that: 'It will show you how you mean to me.' Of course, that only served to drive me crazy with anticipation as I waited impatiently.

And so it was that I swooned at the sight of his handwriting, prised opened the padded envelope, found the card with the blue bow on the front that read, 'I MISS YOU . . . I LOVE YOU . . . MY GIRL'. Then I see the box. What could it be? And it's such a small box, too, yet representing so much. Inside that box . . . oh, I'm bracing myself with cinematic suspense . . . I . . . find . . . a . . . watch. Another one? It doesn't seem terribly romantic as far as declarations go, *except* that this is a watch with babies printed on the face *and* the band. Babies! Sure, if I were to be completely honest, I would have to describe it as the ugliest watch I have ever seen, but right now I think it is simply the most beautiful in the world, because it tells me more than the time. Thus, henceforth, it is known as my biological clock.

```
Last night I saw the most beautiful sunset
that I have ever seen here.
  I stopped my little car by the side of
the road and just watched as the sun moved
from shining on me here to shining on you
there . . .
  Oh God, I'd better go, I am starting to
cry in the Telstra shop!
  And so I love you.
  Lynne Maree
```

29

SPEAKING IN TONGUES

My Captain,
I am so happy that I heard your voice tonight! It is 12.30 am here and I want to write to you to say that I feel so excited. Your laugh can make my heart soar.

I can't sleep and it's got nothing to do with a soaring heart. My throat is painfully constricted and I suspect I might die from suffocation if I do. All due to a packet of noodles. Which was apparently infested. With fireants. Those rotten near-invisible insects that seem particularly fond of me and cause inflamed welts on my skin. They obviously have a similar impact on the insides too when they're an addition to a serving of Super Mie. An unintended optional extra. I hadn't even noted their (omni)presence when preparing a mie goreng on the gas stovetop. But then I was working by the light of my laptop monitor because the electricity was out and I was hungry and out of candles.

Now I am sitting up in my single bed, leaning against the wall, writing to Viktor on the lit screen and I'm not brave enough to lie down for fear that my oesophagus will close up completely.

This place is Noah's ark I think, as I look around at my room through the mosquito net that wraps the circumference of my tiny mattress. Timor is filled with animal life. Although, I do wonder why Noah went to the trouble of ensuring the survival of two of some species. I mean, what possible benefit does the fireant have? They can't even be constructive members of the food chain because you can't fucken eat them.

While swallowing awkwardly with my poor be-stung gullet I can hear the zzzzz, zzzzz, zzzzz that provides the bass line of the soundtrack to this country, as the mozzies head-butt fabric trying to get to my tasty blood. Great, I know that soon I'll need to get up and use my well-practised and deadly accurate hand claps to rid my room of them completely — well, for the hour it takes for their sound to start up again, zzzzz, zzzzz, zzzzz. Outside, the lead vocals are provided by the roosters that are crowing, as always, with a vocal range that puts Britney to shame. It's supplemented by a call that gives a nice R&B edge to the whole thing from the geckos that climb around the walls on their suction-cupped toes and look like little lizards with big eyes, and are the cutest things until they shit on your head, which they regularly do. Percussion comes from the dogs which roam the neighbourhood and six puppies, adding their opinion on the goings-on. And, suddenly, just as the laptop adds its beep, beep, beep to proceedings warning it's running out of battery (an apt techno contribution), the lights burst on and the streets around all resound with a cheer from the Timorians who've been sitting quietly in the dark out the front of their dilapidated homes.

The electricity has only been out for five hours this time. Still, we'll throw out the entire contents of the fridge (except the beer which my English flatmates are happy, of course, to drink warm) and restock it again. It's routine now, anyway. It's grist for the Third World mill. '*Lae problema* = No worries'.

I am even getting accustomed to the single bed. When was the last time I slept in one? No idea. Whatever, I can't complain because a double bed would have taken up the bulk of floor space in my room with its total square metreage equal to that of the average Australian bathroom.

It's quite nice in here, really. To create a tropical atmosphere the walls are painted green and the floor is covered with palm-frond mats that give off a lovely scent and provide a frisson of danger on those nights when I'm using candlelight. Also, despite the wafer-thin walls, it's private. And it's mine, a luxury I haven't had for a while. I just have to listen to my new pirate CDs, on repeat, very, very quietly, or I'll have the belligerent Pom having a go at me in his exclusive idiom.

Ah, Wayne. At 6 am the banging starts up. BANG! BANG! BANG! Silence. 'Ya fuckin cun-hs!' BANG! BANG! BANG! It's so habitual it should be comforting in its familiarity. However, 'Huh!' I jump upright in bed — God, and I fell asleep just minutes ago! — clutching my throat to make sure it remains operational. BANG! BANG! BANG! Silence. 'Ya fuckin cun-hs!' BANG! BANG! BANG!

Why am I the only individual who seems to hear this? So I have to do what I'm doing right now: I have to get out of bed, throw on some clothes (where are my thongs?), find my keys, walk through the house, open the back door and immediately bend down to prevent a pack of squealing puppies which is bouncing over and around my arms from entering the house, the rooster crow competing with the protagonist who contributes his voice, 'Wha'h took ya so fuckin long?' as he bumps against the doorframe, 'Bin ou-h 'ere fuh fuckin 'ours,' and staggers towards his bed, singing his favourite karaoke song of the night, 'Hotel California' this time, which I consider poignantly appropriate. And so the day begins — for me.

Sometimes it varies. On other occasions I open the d[illegible] the back veranda to find Wayne asleep on the couch out there, which means he was too pissed to knock. At the sound of me and the wildlife, he awakens and the situation with the dogs and his inimitable rendering of the English language begins, him bumping, swearing, singing his way towards his bedroom while I contend with little spotted pups.

Sometimes the bride and groom come home together and that's when I put a pillow over my head to give them (or me) some space (thankfully, she always has her keys) during the times when she's weeping, 'No one likes me,' as he comforts her and insists that she is his one and only whom he adores. Well, that's what I think he's saying but it's hard to be sure without semaphore.

Regardless of the scenario, he always drives away in the morning to take a group of divers to see Timor's underwater paradise at high-risk and high-cost while under his supervision. Then the whole troupe goes to the pub, often the Dili Club (an Australian establishment on the waterfront), and it starts all over again.

And so I think we were crazy! We were crazy to fall in love! How long will it be before I am happy to sleep alone again? How long will it be before I don't think about you every minute of every day? How did you do this, Viktor? How did you bewitch a grown woman . . .?

Tonight the newlyweds are throwing a party, the launch of a new price list for their submarine services. I wonder how effective an advertising exercise it will be, given that the proprietors of the company are destined to get rat-arsed in front of any potential customers. Especially as insurance is impossible to get due to the country's status as a peacekeeping mission.

I've been asked to invite anyone I know who could be recruited as clientele and, while this might seem rather irresponsible of me for a number of reasons, I ask Maluco. At least he is a trained scuba diver.

Now, when was the last time I saw him? It was a night last week when I had explained to him, in the gentlest of ways, that we don't have a future but I'd like to be friends. It was news he'd taken well, it had seemed, until I'd gone to give him the requisite goodbye kiss on each cheek and he'd leaned in too, then with a quick twist of his head, he'd neatly and effectively stuck his tongue down my throat. Despite his interpretation of friendship, I'd still prefer it to having him as my enemy.

He arrives on time tonight and I can see immediately that something is odd. Uh-oh. We talk, 'Would you like a drink? How was your CTO? What do you think of Australia? I trust my nationality was hospitable. Um, another drink? No, no, let me get it.' I'm pulling teeth. Why is he awkward? His phone beeps, punctuating my efforts. Then it dawns on me. He has met someone else. Who would've thought? Although, as the realisation hits me, I am overwhelmed by an enormous sense of relief. Oh my God, I am so happy. Uh-oh. Wrong response! He is infuriated by my goodwill.

Away from the extreme-sport scuba divers I direct him, and onto the back veranda where he spits at me (abridged version): that he knows all about me, 'What do you mean?'; that I devastated him, 'I didn't mean to'; that I am a whore, 'No, I'm not'; that I have no morals, 'Yes, I do'; that I am nothing but a mistress, 'Absolutely not'; that I was off gallivanting with a married man, 'What has brought all this on?'; that he knows everything because he's seen the photos, 'Ahem, excuse me? Can you just repeat that last bit for me?'

'I've seen them! They look like you are on honeymoon!' He screams. I daren't tell him how spookily accurate his terminology is for fear he'll really manifest his anger-management issues. 'You look at him with love in your eyes! How could you fall in love with him!'

'Um, well, because he's a somewhat calmer individual for a start.'

'You patronising me!' He's gone bananas. He looks like a Muppet waving his hands over his head like that.

'I'm not patronising you, strictly speaking. I am making an accurate statement. Calm down.'

'Calm down? You cannot tell me anything. I have seen you like a slut.' Yes, he's already made that point clear.

I retaliate, angry too now: 'You know, right now I'm tiring of this whole thing and I have to say I really wish I hadn't taught you such good English if you're going to use it like that at me!' Ooh, that was ill-advised.

A volcano erupts in a face contorted in rage. His veins are engorged, he is bright red. In his language he yells what I assume are rather unflattering descriptions of me. Even though I can't understand a word, it is more disturbing than any tirade in a vernacular I know. And he's armed.

'Um, calm down. I'm sorry. Calm down. It's okay. You're right, I'm sorry I patronised you, I won't do it again.' Of that I am certain.

After I coo and beseech and apologise, he segues back into English. 'How could you, kitten?' he deflates but his expression remains one of absolute antipathy. I've never seen a person so consumed by loathing as he is when he loses his temper, which he does, let's face it, disproportionately often and with devastating effect.

'I honestly will answer your questions but I'm not completely sure what you're referring to. Tell me what you saw?' I say softly, passively.

'You know. The photos. You took them with him. Where were you, Maubisse?' He looks at me with disgust.

What? 'Where did you see these photos?'

'Fuck you.'

I feel like I'm being yelled at by someone who's read my personal diary and found the contents not to their liking. 'Tell me, I have every right to know.'

'You don't tell me what I do.' He wants me to beg and I dearly want to know the answer. How's that for a transaction?

So it appears that Viktor left the electronic versions of the photographs on a computer in the old GNR compound. It's a bizarre oversight from a commander within a paramilitary organisation, although he was distracted at the time and I take responsibility for that. As a result, our photos are being distributed around Dili. I feel like Pamela Anderson (well, as much as a, er, B-cup can).

The images Maluco viewed are romantic. Some were taken in front of the swing! And it's the fact that their intimacy comes from emotion, not nakedness, that makes me feel so violated. Who on earth would do this? 'Maluco, who showed them to you?' He glares at me. Whoever it was, obviously hadn't ever seen him holding a gun to someone's head at point-blank range. 'I have a right to know, please.' Or, perhaps, she had. Because it was the Drag Queen Strumpet.

Despite the distance, your smile, your laugh, your kisses, your grace and class, your delicacy, your conversation, your touch are all still so clear in my memory. I am terrified of them fading. But for now I am happy that I can see you in my mind's eye.
And so I continue to love you,
Lynne Maree

30

FOREIGN AFFAIRS

How lovely it was to read your beautiful words. Sigh.

I have been filled with doubt during the last few days, wondering if it was merely a game, thinking that it would be less painful to walk away.

I lay awake all night trying to convince myself that I should move on emotionally . . . then I was reconverted to a teenager when I read your email. What a primitive creature I am!

'So, how is the Midget Cop?'

He and I look at each other and, while I'm trying not to dignify that statement with a reaction, I am finding it hard to stifle a smile. 'He's well, thank you, José. We talk often, email, I continue to love him, thank you for your interest.'

'Wow, love.'

'Yes, love. You should try it sometime. Ridicule it all you want, but my relationship with Viktor is legitimate and genuine.'

'His wife is happy about this?'

'He's not married any more.' Sigh. How tired I am of justifying this point. Why are so many people interested? Why do so many people feel it's any of their business? And why are so many people rather insensitive in the way they discuss the matter with me?

'God, you are so naive. I never thought you were so naive. You look like you should be smarter. You always told me you are intelligent.'

'I get your drift. Thank you for your concern, Minister, but I am fine, happy and unic. End of subject.'

'You're defensive. It shows that you know he's married but you don't want to admit it.'

'Gee, I like what you've done with the house. How's the roof? Is your termite problem going to bring it down on my head?' Or, preferably, his?

'God, the insects. My roof has to be completely replaced.'

'That's terrible. Didn't you have it treated when it was put up?'

'Those stupid idiots who built it, they treated it but with what?'

'Sugar?'

'Months later and it's infested. The whole thing has to be taken down, start again. So expensive. Thousands of dollars.'

'That's terrible.'

'Like adultery.'

'How long will it take to fix?'

'Your morals?' I stare at him again but this time no grin spreads across my face. 'What?' he says, 'You're the one who broke my heart so why are you angry with me?'

'My emotions are not a game.'

'What?' he breathes his laugh, 'I have been true to you, waiting here, while you were off fucking a Midget Cop.'

'José, as much as I can see that you're enjoying yourself at my expense, that's enough.'

'I know he's married.'

'That's enough.'

'I know.'

Right. 'Of course you do, you and every other person in this city. You're all experts on my life, aren't you? You all think you can tell me that I'm a fool and he doesn't love me and I've, apparently, got to sit and listen to it all. Apparently my life is for public consumption these days and it's something I've just got to cop.'

'Midget cop.'

I stare at him again. Then send a coaster in his direction but it misses its target and thumps, instead, into a pillar holding up a massive termite-ridden traditional roof, 'That's enough . . . please.'

My tormentor's expression seems to soften a little as he says, 'Lynnie, I know he's married.'

'How do you know that?'

'I had his file pulled. I can do this, you know. I wanted to know, for you. He's married with two children, daughters, no?'

It's a stomach punch but I am resilient. 'That file may not have been updated since he separated from his wife.'

'He's married, Lynnie.'

I have to protest for what I know to be right. So I decide to call his bluff. 'Well, I'm afraid I have no choice but to immediately dismiss the results of your investigation since I'm sure your information actually came from a gossip while jogging with your Latino bodyguards — I'm guessing Jorge,' I can see by the expression on José's face that I'm right on the mark. 'And, as it influences the accuracy of your case, I'll mention he's tried to get into my knickers. So, once again, I thank you for your concern but the subject is now, officially, closed.' And my stare this time is definitive and defiant.

'He is very short though, no?'

Surely José has far more important things to focus on than my paramour's relative size. Although, maybe a little diversion is precisely what he needs due to the growing political and economic instability in his country. With independence has come disenchantment among the people. A threat of protest lies heavy over the streets, as the memories of the celebrations fade and thoughts turn to poverty — a poverty that's deepening now that the society isn't being subsidised by the Indonesians and UNTAET. Even most aid organisations have pulled out and moved on to other areas in worse crises. Therefore, the contribution here now pales by comparison and has left many Timorians unemployed, in the dark, with a new user-pays school system, filthy water, and many of their hopes dashed.

East Timor is the eighth-poorest country in the world — quite a statistic — and they don't like it. They don't like that they are free but they are poorer than before. After all, they are a democracy and democracies bring wealth — don't they?

I saw the same disappointment in a place that some of us remember as the Eastern Bloc. As I travelled around there post-1989, with country after country acceding peacefully to Independence, the favourite television program was *Dynasty*. The Polish, Hungarians, Czechoslovakians et al, simply couldn't understand why freedom hadn't brought them sweeping staircases, swimming pools, couture frocks with giant shoulder pads and jewels. In their place, they had skyrocketing rent, quadrupling food prices, escalating unemployment — problems that had all been controlled during communism.

Once the memories of celebrations had faded, families were forced to occupy tiny dwellings, students couldn't afford to stay at university, and crime became a career in these new market economies. The population may not have feared being transported to Siberia any more, but they came to fear dying from the cold in their homes. Memories of the now defunct oppressive regime became curiously affectionate, hindsight prejudiced by an inability to pay for heating during the freezing winters.

The weather may sit at a consistent 30 degrees Celsius in East Timor but otherwise the story has parallels. History is repeating in this little half an island, as it often does in international politics and foreign affairs. Every piece of disillusionment and each additional person living below US$1 a day could have been very easily predicted. A post-Independence period is always going to be somewhat testy.

Especially if the gap between rich and poor is stretching to a gulf. The Timorese want to be able feed their families, and they are pretty pissed off at the remaining malae who sup in style at oceanfront locales, enjoying vinho verde and barbecued seafood (most of it imported), with the extravagance of filtered water and lights powered by generator. And they're also pissed off at a few Timorese families, particularly the Prime Minister's, that seem to have lifestyles in a similar vein.

'How can you talk, anyway? Your Prime Minister is rather petite.'

'Yes, from what I hear he is very small.'

'In physique, José.'

'Yes, he is in proportion.'

'You know, he's actually known as the Prime Miniature to me.' Now he's staring. 'What?' I laugh, 'He can't be much more than four feet tall. Viktor's at least a foot taller than that.'

While democracy doesn't guarantee instant riches distributed equally throughout a society, it does allow protest against a prime minister perceived to be getting too big for his boots. But just how violent will these protests be? In Australia, protests are touted as violent if there is a scuffle. In Timor, politics have often been influenced and enforced through violence. Many Timorese see violence and its threat as a means more powerful than the ballot.

East Timor is a nation of battle-scarred people. They've seen terrible things. They've all lost loved ones. Their education level makes it difficult for them to understand that democracy should give them other avenues of public debate. Their poverty makes them desperate. They have done terrible things too. Indonesian occupation lasted 24 years and, during that time, some of the male population was engaged in a guerrilla war against the oppressors. Many Timorese men spent time in the mountains, living as Falantil freedom fighters — an emotionally charged name for people who, for a cause, committed murder.

Then there is another group in Timor with the very same skill, the former militia members. Around the world, we saw the brutality of these individuals in '99, in massacres sponsored by the Indonesian military. We saw the Indonesians organising proceedings — in Suai and Liquica and elsewhere — where the Timorese mobs rampaged, and supposedly safe havens became awash with blood. But we also saw that the actual perpetrators were East Timorese. Yes, they were pro-Indonesian or manipulated by the occupying force, but I'd like to think that placed in the same circumstances and despite offers of cash and the provision of weapons I'd be disinclined to slit the throat of my next-door neighbour. I'd certainly be unlikely to disembowel a pregnant woman I'd known since childhood. In East Timor, however, for whatever reason — poverty, fear, an acceptance of violence or a disrespect for human life — murder has been a political instrument. And its spectre hangs over us now.

Although, there is hope that the population will remember back to a time when it exercised profound restraint and, instead, used the instrument of peace. 'José, in '99, why didn't Falantil fight back against the militias? They'd been waging a guerrilla war for decades and then they put down their arms when they were needed most and they watched on as their families were killed.'

'It was the decision of me and Xanana. We told them they couldn't fight, there would be no violence.'

'But it must have been horrific, I mean you must have felt terrible responsibility for the people who were being murdered each day and Falantil must have been going crazy. Surely they wanted to fight back.'

'Of course. It was the worst time in my life. God, many phone calls from people begging me and Xanana to let them fight back, every day hearing the stories of the massacres, stories of barbarity.'

'Did you make that decision so the message of your struggle would be validated? It seems to me that a deliberate decision was made to lay down arms so there could never be any suggestion that it was a civil war, and that the Timorese could not be accused of merely being violent guerrillas, because then the international community wouldn't intervene, is that right?'

'Yes. It was important that the international community see the actions of the Indonesians. How many media interviews I gave then, thousands. God, the stress, not sleeping, hearing the stories.'

'And feeling a little responsible?'

'It was the most painful time in my life but we had to be strong.'

It was one of the rare times in history when peace was used as a powerful political tool. It was used deliberately for a certain outcome. Is that cynicism? No, rather Realpolitik. And it came with remarkable bravery — because it takes greater courage to use peace and not war. Gorbachev, José and Xanana; there are few examples in contemporary times of this type of valour and, rather than indicating weakness, it shows rare strength. As a general rule, borne out in the history books, men prefer not to retreat; power and machismo usually prohibit the laying down of arms; but, see, these can be used effectively and, in doing so, provide the measure of the true statesman.

'You know, your people wouldn't protest any more and they'd be more satisfied if they knew what was going on. The Prime Miniature isn't talking to them. I know he believes he has been handed a five-year mandate but democracy requires him to be transparent and answerable, whether he likes it or not. His silence confuses the people and the arrogance angers them. This is basic public-relations strategy so I think I need to be employed immediately.'

'Well, as you can save our country . . .'

'Too right.'

'. . . I'll talk to the Prime Minister again, tomorrow. Although, we'll need to negotiate the terms of how you will repay me. You will like them.' Ah, corruption comes in many guises.

'There will be no sexual favours paid. You will do this because it is the right thing to do and because I have professional skills required by the government.'

'What if I offered you a million dollars also?'

'My love is not for sale; it's priceless.'

'But a million dollars?'

'US or Australian?'

Days later my position is announced by the Prime Miniature to the Council of Ministers of the Government of East Timor, upon the recommendation of the Minister for Foreign Affairs and Cooperation.

What will be will be. I know I probably will never see you again but I do dream of being with you once more. That is my indulgence.

31

GOING TROPPO

Is it just me or has the whole place gone troppo? I go to a party at the US Embassy, a barbecue with cocktail snacks, tubs of beer and a combination of meats providing a carnivore's delight. It's an interesting time to be celebrating at this compound due to the scandal surrounding the Americans working for the UN here and in every mission worldwide. I feel like I've crossed a picket line.

Americans are threatening to pull out because they don't want to be under the jurisdiction of the recently ratified International Criminal Court. Will the UN stand firm and make all Americans accept the same conditions as every other nationality or will it back down and accept that Americans should receive special treatment?

The US is accustomed to having a certain amount of control. It achieves this by refusing to pay its contributions to the UN's operational expenses. Other countries pay the amount they must but the US, which has the largest bill thanks to its GDP, prefers to use non-payment to wield influence. For years it has said it won't pay unless decisions go its way. It has brought the UN to near bankruptcy at times, as a result, which is why it usually wins. This time, the UN has said it will stand firm and rule in the interests of all countries in the international community, without allowing a country to be renegade. The US, however, is immovable. That may sound troppo in itself but, bear with me, the madness is yet to begin.

As I'm leaving I say goodbye to the host, a young diplomat with a Texan twang. He's in the kitchen and he insists I stay for a body shot. 'What's a body shot?' I ask.

'You don't know what body shots are?'

'No, I've never heard of them.'

'There, you can't go! You have to learn about body shots!'

'I'm sorry, I *have* to go. Another time.' Which is when I, ignorantly, arrange to go with a group of people, including the young American diplomat, to Maubisse. Yes, Maubisse, to the Pousada, where not so long ago I told a man I loved him.

A forward party left at dawn to climb the highest peak in Timor, Mount Ramelau, but given my disdain for physical activity I drive up at leisure with an Englishman, Jake, the spokesperson for the United Nations High Commission for Refugees and the survivor of a massacre of three colleagues in West Timor a couple of years ago. He and I have planned to meet up with everybody after their hike to the summit, in nearby Maubisse.

In his enormous car with the UNHCR flag flying from the big pole on the front, we weave our way above Dili, through the lush foliage, along the uneven roads, past Xanana's new house in the hills overlooking the city, higher and higher, with the ocean twinkling below us. Once again, it is a breathtakingly beautiful journey.

Particularly in this car. The important thing to note about UNHCR is that it rehoused many of those displaced during the chaos of '99, so the country seems covered with tarpaulins bearing that blue-on-white symbol. But the true testament to the work this organisation has done in East Timor is the reaction of the people when the symbol drives toward their village and men, women, children come running to greet the car, waving at their saviour. Jake waves back to each and every one of them.

It is a slow and profound trip up to a place I'm dreading to arrive at. Maybe I'll get some closure in Maubisse? I don't even know if I want closure yet. Viktor tells me to ignore the gossip, saying I should only believe what he says and he says he loves me. And what I do know is that I miss him with a deep yearning that hurts. Missing someone is one of the most painful of human feelings. I wish it would stop. But I seem condemned to walk around in its grip. So it's with mixed feelings that we continue on to the resort on the mount, the car winding upwards as Moby adds to the poignancy with his atmospheric refrain.

Too soon we arrive at the Pousada and I am pleased to see that we are staying in a completely different annexe from the main resort. That'll prevent some comparisons with my last stay here I'm thinking, when, in the corner of my eye, in the delightful garden, I spy the swing and my heart takes a dive — a triple somersault in a pike position with a difficulty of 6.3 ending in a bellyflop — that comes close to doubling me over. It's a blow, I can't deny, but I'm on my last weekend away before I start work and I'm buggered if I'm going to allow myself to be found, in hours to come, with a bottle of vinho verde in one hand, as I fly up and down through the air, drunkenly beseeching the heavens '*Why?*' when I may as well enjoy this trip as well. Mind over mind so Jake and I settle down on a balcony with tall glasses of vodka, and my companion reads me his book aloud, reciting all the characters' dialogue in voices he imagines fit, all of them variations on his frightfully posh accent. I succumb to fits of giggles, while the sun sets over a mountainous landscape and the big pink church. Viktor who? (Bad, Lynne!)

Hours later the others arrive and we are swamped by people exhilarated from their climb. There are a couple of English diplomats, a lovely World Bank staffer, an Australian aid worker, and the young American diplomat, who takes my hand saying he has something to show me. 'No, no, no, I want to stay and chat.'

'You have you see this.'

'No, I don't want to go off when everyone has just arrived.'

'Come on, I brought it specially for you,' all argument ending when I am propelled out across the carpark and into a room on the other side.

As we enter, the lights are off and they remain this way. The door is locked behind me. Is this *déjà vu*? It won't be, I can tell you that much. My humour isn't quite as elastic any more when it comes to men taking liberties with my time. 'What's going on?'

'Wait a minute,' and he says he has to make preparations, that I am about to do my very first body shot.

'O-kay.' But what is a body shot? As he moves around his hotel room, I can barely see the shape of him at the desk opening plastic containers and he explains that a body shot is a variation of the tequila lick, sip, suck. Can I do that, he asks? Um, sure, but usually in an illuminated space. And while that explains the shot, the most important question has to be: where exactly does the body come into it? Well, he says, each part of the lip, sip, suck sequence is performed with the ingredients placed on a lounging body — so you, Lynne, have to locate them and when you find the salt you lick it, then the alcohol and you drink it, and finally the slice of lemon, wherever it may be, and you have to suck it. Apparently there are many different body parts that can be used to hold these different substances and a quick mental inventory of a man's components has me concerned.

I can make out, through a darkness that is testing my eyes and revealing only a grainy, undefined room filled with vague contours, that he is reclining on the bed now and, after the sound of movement lasting a few more minutes, he announces that he's ready. Although, just to be clear, he points out that the lick, sip, suck has been altered slightly by the absence of salt in his pantry, meaning that on this occasion he's substituting olives for the purposes of the lick.

'What? Olives? Pantry? Do you mean you prepared all this before you left Dili at dawn this morning?'

'Sure,' comes the Texan twang. 'Come on, it's time for your first body shot.'

Right. The situation is very unsettling and just to illustrate the point there are knocks at the door which my companion ignores. 'Come on,' comes the Texan twang and I wonder if I am being a prude. Should I just try this thing called a body shot? What's the harm? I do seem abnormal in not knowing what this phenomenon is. I have no reason to distrust the young American diplomat either. I'm sure my fear is merely paranoia grown out of a recent coincidental situation. Oh, Lynne, do you really need to overanalyse a body shot?

I breathe in and lean down and, as I do, my eyes adjust a little to the light down at this level aided by the close proximity of his body now and into view is the vodka, which I spot in his belly button . . . and a lemon slice that is in his mouth . . . then, indeed, I do see the intended object of the lick in the shape of an olive and it's balanced just above the top of his unbelted pants — against his erect penis. I guess this is the true definition of the cocktail snack.

Does the US see itself as a law unto itself? It *is* precisely that, in actual fact, because the UN backs down, allowing staff from the US to continue in this mission and others without being subject to the jurisdiction of the International Criminal Court. Which means that this particular nationality can behave according to its very own view of right and wrong.

On Sunday I was standing at a window, watching Timorese children playing on the road outside, consumed by my thoughts when a friend came up behind me and said softly, 'You miss him, don't you?' Yes. Yes, I do.

The Purple Cow disco, which should be called the Mad Cow, has salsa classes on Wednesday nights. I can't see the need to place myself in an environment in which I'll appear available to men, given my recent exposure to them, but I go along to watch my friends nonetheless.

As they step backwards, forwards — one, two, three, four; one, two, three, four — on the dance floor, I sit at a table, smiling at the insincere coquettishness of women who came here with the deliberate intention of picking up a Portuguese or Brazilian man. Lord knows it's easy to do. There ain't no challenge to it. It's only as complex as possessing the requisite apparatus. Still, right now I'm reminded that many women thrive on the attention.

I guess it's no surprise. Imagine arriving in a place where you are told daily by many men that you are beautiful. Now, sure, initially on some intellectual level you might understand that they are in the grips of a troubling primal lunacy brought on by circumstantial sexual abstinence. But, over the months, you could come to believe that their words are a true reflection of a beauty that mysteriously emerged on the flight over from Darwin or Denpasar.

Therefore, women who would never be considered attractive in their countries of origin are worshipped by platoons of men here. And it seems to compensate for every insecurity they've felt before. It's a win–win situation. The men get to relieve some of their bio-physical frustrations while the women feel like Cinderellas surrounded by balls. And, thus, let me introduce you to the variety of woman known as the Dili Princess.

The Princess, though, is an organism spotted not only in the environs of Dili but, alarmingly, can also be found in Kabul, Pristina, Kinshasa etc because she's a creation of peacekeeping missions. There is an urban myth that says: a planeload of UN workers were flying from one of any missions and, as they crossed the border into a First World nation, the pilot's voice came over the intercom to inform them of their revised situation — the altitude, temperature, arrival time, and that the women were all officially ugly again.

For some girls the talk of their charm is intoxicating, and certainly they must be drunk on sperm to believe it. I mean, you could loudly fart during the main course on a first date and your Latino peacekeeper would still lean over and say you're beautiful. I can see the appeal of being perceived in this way, of course, but my brain can't get past the knowledge that most of the men in UN missions around the world are walking hard-ons — and I should know, I've had enough pressed up against me on the dance floor of the Mad Cow.

Anyway, it all makes for a good spectator's sport, I'm thinking, when my attention, along with that of everyone else's in the room, is diverted by the appearance of a figure arriving on her own. And a striking figure she cuts. I often see her like this, entering alone, men leering and women whispering behind their hands. It's Marilyn. And her breasts.

Marilyn is singled out for catty treatment by those women who manifest an unreasonable competitive instinct. Her breasts, her characteristic flounce, her sexiness all combine to create a potently alluring honeypot. This girl is the Dili Queen! Which is why she is victim to those afflicted with feline distemper. But, for God's sake, there are simply thousands and thousands of desperately available men who all want to get laid.

I go up and invite her to join my table. She seems surprised. With urging she does. And she's a nice, intelligent, multilingual UN staffer who has worked in Timor for years and has a soft spot for a swarthy-looking man. She's just as insecure as any of those girls up on the dance floor, trying to catch bees. And she, too, wants to be called beautiful. Which is why, as we kick on to the karaoke bar down the road, she asks an entire battalion of peacekeepers to join us.

Still, I will continue to write because you want me to – how touched I was to hear you say that my letters are like 'oxygen' to you. But, Viktor, I too need oxygen to breathe.

32

BECAUSE FORTUNE IS A WOMAN

Timor is the popular place to be now: witness the arrival of a boatload of Sri Lankan refugees. They originally wanted to go to New Zealand but that nation said, 'We're rather full of Afghanis and similar', so the exiles put down anchor off the coast at Taci Tolu, proving that people do migrate to the Third World. Maybe they'd heard of the Dili Princess.

As a result, the East Timorese Government is in chaos. The Prime Minister prefers a rather familiar approach of the 'You're all middle-class queue jumpers' nature. I beg to differ because these people are actually the only ones in the queue, but who am I? The Foreign Affairs Minister, meanwhile, is pointing out that Timor signed on to various treaties as recently as May and is still relying on UNHCR to repatriate 30 000 East Timorese refugees from West Timor, therefore the Sri Lankans should be allowed to land their boat. And that's his final comment on the issue, which is why he is screening the PM's calls.

In the middle of this intrigue, I'm contacted by Jake from UNHCR who is in a panic because the boat has sprung a leak. 'You have to help me. We need to meet with the Prime

Minister. This matter has to be resolved tonight, it is urgent!' he cries.

'Jake, you do realise that I haven't started my job yet, don't you?'

'Yes, but you're my last hope. We tried, with no luck. You have to help us!'

'If the Prime Minister is refusing to meet with UNHCR then I really doubt I'll have any success.'

'This is *urgent*!'

'I'll see what I can do.'

I call the Prime Miniature's Timorian adviser, José. Thanks to my weeks-long campaign to get my job contract signed, I am an expert at getting in contact with the PM's office, which is no mean feat because, as the adviser to the UNMISET Deputy Special Representative of the Secretary-General (DSRSG) said to me, 'The Prime Minister's office has ceased to operate.'

That's not quite true because half an hour later I am stunned to answer my phone and it's that very office. I'm asked to organise an audience between all the stakeholders for later tonight. I call the Foreign Affairs Minister, who says he is washing his hair or doing his nails, but he does give me a message to pass on — tell the Prime Minister that I'll quit unless the issue is resolved in my way (I decide to renege on that demand). The Timor head of UNHCR is joined by his counterpart at the International Organisation for Migration and, in a meeting in that big white building on the Dili waterfront, it is decided that the boatpeople can be liberated onto dry land.

I'm very relieved; I hadn't thought it a prudent international public relations strategy to have 56 people drown in an inlet 100 metres off the coast of East Timor. So I'm glad I could help, especially the next day when my phone goes, Beep, beep. Beep, beep. **1 new message.** It's Jake. **Thank**

you — you made all the difference yesterday! You made 56 men feel human again. (Now, if only I could use my negotiation skills, contacts and sheer bloody-mindedness to get my contract signed.) And precisely what did my friends from the subcontinent do when they were able to feel human again? They requested a cricket set. The New Zealand Consul-General was only too happy to comply with this request.

Following orthodox thought, have we opened the floodgates? Not quite. In addition to the first lot, a geographically challenged boatload of refugees arrives in West Timor and asks around for someone to take them to Australia. One man says, sure, I'll drive you for US$1000. He drops them off at the border with East Timor, says welcome to Australia, turns around and drives home.

Then there is a Russian man, his Ukrainian wife and their children who move into a shack on the beach after inexplicably arriving with no prior knowledge of a country called East Timor. The weather is better than anything they're accustomed to and they can't afford to go anywhere else, so there's nothing for them to do but stay. Plus, the Slavic UN workers have taken them into their affections and are subsidising their lifestyle; the woman is applying for a P position with the UN (her nationality should make her a shoo-in); and they've been invited to the Foreign Affairs Minister's house for Christmas.

Most of the refugee issues in Timor, however, don't relate to the incoming but to the Timorese who have left. Those who were taken in by Australia want to stay where they are! They don't want to return. They prefer toilets that flush. They choose to stay in comfort rather than bring their new First World education, language skills, and computer literacy here to assist in the rebuilding of their nation, alongside all those people from other countries who have no cultural connections but have done exactly that.

And there are those in West Timor who fled over the border in '99 and have been living in camps in Indonesia, despite the best efforts of the UN, Xanana and various animal sacrifices to bring them home. Because they, too, want to stay where they are! There is effort being put into returning the reluctant, but irrespective of the incentives offered by the international organisations ready to rehouse them, and whether we can understand it or not, those tens of thousands of people prefer to live in Indonesia where the government is the one they know and the official language is the one they speak.

It all reinforces that the world is such a transient place these days. Globalisation extends beyond technology and economics to include the movement of people. Peoples all combining and interacting, seeking love, career, home, safety and happiness. Some more vulnerable than others. Some more legitimate or less. All of them contributing to a rich international mix of beliefs, cultures, faiths, ideas, principles and ethics. East Timor adds to the interaction, both incoming and out-gone. Which is why these days I find myself fantasising about life in Portugal.

. . . what I have learnt through writing to you is that I am not Shakespeare, my words are ultimately powerless because I cannot control your interpretation fo them. I want them to make your heart soar too – how frustrating it is for me when they fail in this! My craft is unable to close the 16,000 km gulf between us.

'You really should take up diving. You'll love it. It will change your life.'

'No way. I have no interest in diving. I appreciate that you love it but I was at an impressionable age when *Jaws* came out and my fear of sharks stops me from ever going deep underwater dressed like a seal.'

'Appree-SEA-ate, not appree-SHE-ate,' says Ann. It had never occurred to me that the word 'appreciate' is fundamental to my vocabulary but it seems to be and I wish I could eradicate it completely and replace it with others; however, my brain defaults to 'appreciate' and Ann just can't help herself — restraint isn't common behaviour around here.

Ann and Wayne must be going through another financial rough patch because the recruitment drive for their dive 'safaris' is, once again, focusing close to home, like the back veranda. 'Ya fuckin pussy. Ya scared of fuckin fish? Ya can go wif me' (heaven forbid) 'and I'll show ya' (put my life in his hands?) 'fuckin whale shark as close as 'ere' (he tries to touch his nose but misses and hits his cheek). 'Ya go-h any beer inna frige?'

'Wayne, I'm not interested in diving, despite your persuasive argument.'

'Ya fuckin pussy.'

'Look, if a whale shark came up to here' (I touch my cheek) 'while I was diving, I know I wouldn't see it and think, "Oh, look at that magnificent plankton-eating fish," instead I'd see this gigantic thing with a great big fin on its back and immediately have apoplexy and die. No alternative. Now, I appreciate your right to love it but you need to appreciate my reasons for not going there, ever. So can we drop it?'

'Appree-SEA-ate, not appree-SHE-ate,' says Ann.

'Fuckin pussy,' says Wayne.

I do appreciate the reasons for their enthusiasm. Impending bankruptcy is a powerful motivator. And I do feel sympathy because their financial concerns are not really of their own making — well, other than in their decision to invest in this country. They are actually prevented from making any real return on their investment thanks to the many impediments that are stacked in their way.

Since Independence a ramshackle taxation system has been put in place that slaps around 20 per cent on the cost of many items any malae might want to purchase. The application of the tax is arbitrary, and some Timorian business owners just charge whatever they like and put it all straight into their coffers. The government can't realistically supervise the implementation because it doesn't have enough computers, and capacity-building requires time. Then there is the problem of foreign ownership laws — that they can't own land, so malae homes or offices will never really be theirs and can be repossessed at any time. And the security issue may see the theft of anything that's not nailed down — take the case of the individual who slipped into the offices of an Australian company under cover of night and carried out its filing cabinet. Plus, the burgeoning business of corruption can lead to anything, from the rental of warehouse space to the assigning of tenders, going for an additional gift of cash. You can't get a residency visa, which means you can be kicked out of the country at any moment and you'll have to leave it all behind. Also, the legal system is in such crisis that court cases are presided over by inexperienced Timorese judges, none of whom has ever worked as such, some of whom were law students until Independence, and the appeal court is not operational. Not to mention the confusion that comes from language issues caused by a general population which speaks Bahasa Indonesia, a government insisting on Portuguese, and foreigners using English and anything else that can make sense of it all. Then there's an anti-malae sentiment. Risky business plan?

Many of the international businesses here are bloody worried about the future and they don't seem to be getting adequate support or answers from the government, but then the government is in chaos, expending its energy on playing internal politics rather than on the grown-up game of governing.

Beep, beep. Beep, beep. My phone. **1 new message.** It's José, a man who isn't aligned with any political party in Timor, has a very developed idea of First World business practices and is an impressive statesman **(Thou misseth me?)** of the Renaissance period, perhaps. Certainly, at the moment his language is littered with 'forsooths', etc, and he is also having a renaissance in political reputation because, even though his authority is lower than that of Alkatiri, he is seen by many as the communicator. He listens to the people and mediates on their behalf.

It's quite a rehabilitation for a man who, in 2000, returned to Timor after 24 years in exile and rode around the devastated streets on a big black Harley-style motorbike, alienating every poor Timorese person who thought he looked rich and/or like a wanker.

Beep, beep. Beep, beep. My phone. **1 new message.** It's the great hope of the Timorese people again, **I knowest thou loveth me.** Love? Hardly. But like many Timorians and malae I do have some fondness for the man because he alone listens and mediates on my behalf. With UNDP blaming the Prime Miniature's office for the delay in my contract and the Prime Miniature's office blaming UNDP, I have even gone to the extent of riffling through every one of the enormous and unruly stacks of paper in the PM's office looking for my lost contract, only to find it and have it promptly lost again. Eventually UNDP said it will accept any format of contract, just so long as it has my name, the date and the Prime Minister's signature on it — even if it's the back of a beer coaster.

Imagine my surprise, then, when the Prime Miniature's assistant called me the other day demanding to know the reason for my delay and to get myself into the office immediately to counter a scathing article published in the *Australian Financial Review* on the corruption, legal problems, anti-malae bias in the new nation. I'm assuming that the Prime Miniature has signed the contract, then? No. Nobody knows where it is, and the PM is going overseas on yet another jaunt and he'll be gone for quite some time. *PANIC!*

Not to mention that protests are coming up and he should remain to face them. People are demanding answers to questions they have every right to ask. They are accusing him of silence, arrogance, nepotism, corruption and they're saying they'll overthrow him if they're unsatisfied with his response. The word is on the street and the local newspapers are reporting it all so it's nothing he doesn't know. Don't you think his absence from the country might antagonise them a little? (Not to mention me.)

That's where Renaissance Man comes in. Soon afterwards I hear on the grapevine that at 8 am on a Sunday morning, a Foreign Affairs Minister called for his motorcade and travelled to the house of a Prime Miniature who was due to fly out in hours' time. And he presented a piece of paper to him and on it was written my name, the date and a great big asterisk indicating where he should sign.

Sitting on the back veranda, I text message José who is now at a conference in Malaysia with sixteen Timorese ministers and secretaries of state, and I say thank you, as well as pointing out to him that with most of the government away it is a perfect time for a coup, so they should all come home. Beep, beep. Beep, beep. My phone. **1 new message. Thou doth misseth me!**

The waiting game is almost over. Soon I'll be gainfully employed — in an office under siege by desperate protestors inclined to violence, sure, but every job has its downside.

Actually, I'm pretty stupid to think that armed and hungry protestors are the real threat to a constructive workaday here because ring, ring. It's my phone. 'Hello?'

'Hello, Lynne Minion?'

'Yes, it is.' It's an UNMISET adviser I've met a couple of times. 'Hi!' I chirp.

'Lynne, I've just had a call from an ABC journalist in Darwin saying you've spoken to her.'

'Oh, really? I don't know any ABC journalists in Darwin but I'm happy to help. What's it about?' I really am so stupid.

'She says you've leaked information about protests aimed at the Prime Minister. She claims you are her source.' This is so odd. I mean, no quality journalist would reveal her source.

'I have no idea what you're talking about but I think this is great. I'm happy to try to get a comment from the government for her.'

'Did you hear me? I'm making serious allegations against you and your professionalism.'

'Professionalism. Right. I haven't been paid for months, actually, so if we want to get picky, whose professionalism are we referring too, exactly? And I can't see what I could possibly "leak" when everything anyone would want to know about any protests are on the public record already, like the front page of the *Timor Post*,' which is one of a couple of independent newspapers in Timor.

Man, I continue to find it disgraceful that UN staff are so rude. And this whole discussion is outrageous because it shows that the UN remains determined to control PR spin in East Timor. It wants the world to continue seeing the East Timor UN mission as a shiny success story, even if the people are protesting on the streets. 'The media is not to be involved in this. I told the journalist that nothing is going on.'

'And she believed you? Surely she'll go and get an interview with someone else who will be more forthcoming? Then we'll have a problem.' Basic rules of journalism — speak to the other side of the story and be well aware of the propaganda machine of any organisation.

'Not a chance. I have diffused a problem caused by your conduct.'

'What? I think it's a good thing that the media internationally is calling for comment. Particularly a quality broadcaster like the ABC. I'm happy to arrange for someone in the government to answer allegations and communicate about the work the government is doing. That's what the people want. Silence is the reason they're protesting . . . and they *will* be protesting.'

'I've told her there is nothing going on and I don't want to hear that you have had any more contact with any media or said otherwise.' Despite the fact that it will be my job? Or the job I thought I would be signing up for.

'You told her what?' Basic rule of public relations: always tell the truth.

'We will not have any coverage about this, any beat-up. Dili is a town of gossip and the media doesn't need to react to every ridiculous story. That's what you need to learn.'

I guess so because I happen to think that the matter of people starving isn't ridiculous and, for the life of me, I can't see why, if there is nothing to hide, media coverage is being suppressed. It's undemocratic and paranoid. And it's interference — the UN doesn't run East Timor any more, this is a free country. As for the suggestion that there's nothing going on . . . there *is* something going on! Critical articles — *sans* UN and government comment — are popping out all over the world now, international investors want to know if they should cut their losses and run, and Timorese people are travelling into the capital at this very minute, spilling out of the backs of trucks, sitting precariously up on cabin roofs, to confront the Prime Minister about their poverty and ask why they don't have jobs, why they can't feed their families, why they have to pay for their children to go to school, why they are worse off than they were before the independence they fought so long to have.

And, anyway, the story is not all bad. Surely there's no reason for shame already, is there? It is important to show the world that this democracy *is* developing. The mere fact that people can come out onto the streets and demand these answers shows that this country may be poor but there is hope, because for the very first time in their history the Timorese are using their right to protest against their very own government.

33

HUMANITARIAN AIDS

The problem is that you made promises to me. You used the word 'Forever', you said that you are trying to come back, you wished we could have six months together, you wrote that you are doing everything you can to have me in your life.

And I believe that love can overcome every obstacle placed in its path. And I know that I have found it so difficult to forget you and I want you in my life. And I feel this so strongly that it overpowers reason. Logically I feel that I need to walk away because a relationship cannot be merely yearning and insecurity, occasional phone calls and rare emails – but my heart won't let me.

I actually need a heart transplant but, instead, on this occasion I am at the UN medical clinic in Obrigado Barracks to have my pre-contract medical examination. I sit and watch the condom bucket because it has fascinated me ever since the nurses told me about the Singaporean who asked them for a smaller size. And no matter how covert I am, I never see a man go near it — oh yes I do! Thankfully, today, some enlightened individual has used this important resource. Although, now that I've seen someone do his surreptitious grab I'm perturbed by the question of where he'll use his supply, what with the population of female UN workers in Timor having dwindled to such a low count. The UN is hardly an equal-opportunity employer and the administrative complement of UNMISET is currently running at around 20 per cent female. So much for the UN having an agency, UNIFEM, specifically designed to raise awareness of gender inequality.

Women are a constructive addition to every mission, as well as to its host country for many reasons; certainly today's condom recipient would agree for just one. Maybe he's one of the lucky few men in a relationship here? Or there's always the roaring trade in prostitution. Just yesterday I was sitting outside a new sushi restaurant in town, Ryoshi, being entertained by the taxi-loads of off-duty Portuguese soldiers disembarking then ducking into the day spa where the cooperative masseuses are known to ask, 'You want massage with happy ending?'

The industry is certainly booming. So much so that supply can't meet demand, leading to a UN investigation into allegations that Portuguese peacekeepers have attempted to ship Thai prostitutes into East Timor, which I see as one of the few wise international investments in this country because the customers are guaranteed to just keep coming.

Right about this spot in my musings I am called into a consulting room where an African doctor says, 'Hello, how can I help you?'

'Hi, how you going? I just need my UNDP medical done, thanks.'

Blink, blink, 'I don't know this.'

'Um, every person under a UNDP contract has to get a medical first from this clinic.'

'I don't know,' the doctor says with no interest.

'There have been thousands of them done and you're responsible for doing mine today.'

'I can't help you.'

'Well, you have to. I need to go back to UNDP with a completed medical saying I am fit for duty.'

'No, I don't know.'

Everything in Timor, simply everything, has to be that little bit more complex than necessary. Every single day, the easiest of tasks are made frustrating. It requires the development of a hardy patience, tremendous resilience, innovative problem-solving techniques, tenacious perseverance, and a fateful sense of resignation. I even daydream about the ease of dealing with an Australian bank teller, which shows how deluded I've become.

'Perhaps you could find a template on the computer or ask another doctor or make an educated guess because I'm not leaving until I have a medical,' I force a smile. This is where the hardy patience is handy. We have some success when the doctor stands up and takes my blood pressure, which at this point is frightfully high.

'That's all. I will sign this.'

'That can't be all.' How could a doctor possibly be prepared to sign off on a medical test that has recorded a blood pressure so high it indicates an imminent brain haemorrhage? Although, that's not my real concern. 'I'd like an AIDS test and, also, this is my second contract in Timor so I should have a pap smear too.'

'No. This is not possible.'

'I beg your pardon? These are particularly important tests and it's particularly important that they're done.'

'No, impossible,' comes the reply.

'I find it very peculiar that I can't get female health examinations. Pap smears are considered quite vital in my country.' So much for women's issues, I'm thinking, while exercising tremendous resilience.

'We do not have the laboratory for the pathology so we cannot do this.'

'Right. Then you should have a laboratory. A pap smear isn't an elective examination. I certainly don't do them for fun. But I can't believe that the UN doesn't have mandatory AIDS testing at the beginning of contracts.' No matter how tenaciously I persevere, I usually lose.

'No, it's not possible.'

'Surely you agree with me that this is mad? I mean, you have a full-blown epidemic on your continent!'

'I cannot do these things for you. You have to go yourself to Darwin and go to a doctor there.'

It was in Darwin that the alarm first sounded that the UN mission had probably introduced HIV to East Timor and was certainly spreading it. The number of aid workers and peacekeepers presenting with the disease to Australian doctors caused the concern, and it was soon noted to correspond with a similar increase in diagnoses in the other popular R and R destination, Bali.

This information has been widely known for some time now, which is why I expected a mandatory AIDS test today. Yet no changes have been made and no responsibility taken, and so Thai girls are infected and they infect others and then it gets into the Timorese community. And while you may think this surprising — certainly it is an unacceptable tragedy — it's made worse by the fact that the UN unleashed a plague of the very same kind in Cambodia ten years ago.

Some nations, including Australia, impose compulsory pre-deployment medicals, which include an AIDS test, on their police and peacekeeping forces. Others don't. This is a void the UN has to fill as a matter of urgency and conscience. How can it afford it? Diverting the budget used for the staff's bottled water would be an easy solution to the problem.

In this country there are fears of an epidemic exacerbated by the poor education level of the population and an extremely patriarchal society which sees women with no power and little voice. If a Timorese man wants to have sex with a Timorese female — whether his wife, his sister, his child or otherwise — he will generally do so. Those demands are unlikely to change if he has HIV. And he won't be wearing a condom, thanks to the Catholic fundamentalism in East Timor, which doesn't support the use of contraception.

The HIV/AIDS message is difficult to disseminate even in the most aware and secular of nations. Australia has conducted a long and non-judgmental education campaign and even men from there, especially those over thirty, are unlikely to use a condom without the annoying, pressuring, pre-penetration let's-go-*au-naturel*, I'm-clean, it-feels-good-without-one issue raising its ugly head. And they are supposed to be enlightened!

Even worse, many nationalities have not had the luxury of being exposed to anti-HIV/AIDS advertisements, so their education has yet to begin and, thus, they bring their ignorance and even their infections along with them to a place that isn't able to understand or fight the disease. Conversely, some of the ignorant take new infections home.

In a case of too little too late, the UN has employed a Ghanaian woman to teach staff in East Timor about using condoms — she even demonstrates the application using a plastic penis. Imagine how many nationalities find that offensive. Imagine, also, how many people can't be bothered. And then, given that Timor is a chaotic place filled with incompetent individuals, imagine how many people don't ever get invited — like me. This provides an idea of how many people are swayed by her message.

This is where the sense of resignation comes in, because I have to be satisfied with my medical certificate, such as it is. Sure, the UN does have an agency specifically mandated to contend with this disease worldwide, a disease that it claims is causing a disaster of catastrophic proportions, that is destroying people, communities, cultures and nations, especially in the Third World; and this UN agency goes by the usually unambiguous name of UNAIDS, which in the case of East Timor, seems a little too close to the truth.

34

NOTHIN' GOING ON

I've organised a lift into work in a Serious Crimes Unit UN vehicle, hoping this will deter any mischief-makers from targeting me because I'd consider that to be a bloody serious crime.

I didn't have to come in today. I was advised by the Prime Miniature's office to take some time off for safety reasons but I knew I'd feel pretty cowardly lazing on Arieia Branca when the Timorese staff are in here and the PM is, indeed, flying back for the occasion. So I arrive and announce my intention to stand shoulder to shoulder with all of my new kolegas in the face of the protests.

And I would, except that half of them have decided not to turn up. 'Um, how is everything? Anything I can do?' I ask of those in attendance. Some look at me as though I am an alien then go back to playing solitaire on their computers, trying to look unconcerned; others are huddled, near-hysterical, exchanging the gossip they've heard from within their communities overnight. Meanwhile, 2000 Timorese men have gathered in Dili for quasi-military marching ceremonies, and they may or may not descend rather soon on the big white government building we're all currently standing in. I expected some frenzied meetings, yelling into phones, frantic solving of a rather substantial problem, but a game of solitaire seems a far calmer way to prepare, really, and then there's always the frightened gossiping as an alternative, although that doesn't seem to be generating any calm. Timor Whispers can be sinister. But it's all they have when the official UN line says nothing is going on, and yet bandana-wearing men are revving motorbikes and riding through the streets, holding weapons aloft, yelling their call to arms and getting drunk on tua mutin each night.

It's a fear compounded by a mass breakout from Becora Jail that occurred a few days ago when some of the very most dangerous prisoners in this country, 190 of them, checked out; and they might just turn up here today. If they do, the assumption has been made that these particular characters may not be peaceful protestors.

I put on my own very best nothin'-going-on face and comfort those who are scared. They experienced such terrible violence in '99, after a vote that the UN had promised would be safe. The memories of that horror are fresh, and I put my arms around some of the women — they are the size of eleven-year-old Australian children — and I tell them that the UN won't let that happen again. 'The UN! This our country! This Independent Timor-Leste!' Seems that people in here have sympathies in kind with those out there. 'In the commoonity they talking all night. I know my country!'

'Hey, it's okay, I know it's your country, of course I do. And I also know it will be okay today, everything will be okay, because today we will see your new peaceful democracy at work.' I see a smile through terrified tears.

The protests are aimed at the UN, the malae, and the Prime Miniature and, as the only UN malae working, not merely in this building, but actually in the PM's office, I might be in the wrong place at the wrong time (the British adviser has quit). Many men have said they'll be looking out for me and, to be honest, this is one time I've appreciated the gender imbalance.

Many of the Timorese staff members, however, have spent the last few days placing their children in safe locations, packing up those few items they can't bear to have looted or burned again . . . just in case the Timor Whispers are true, again.

The peacekeepers and UNPOL also seem to disagree with the official line of UNMISET, I can see, as I walk out onto the balcony of the Prime Minister's office and view an accumulation of forces from around the world. The peacekeepers wear their various camouflage prints in greens and blues (blues? what are those Filipinos thinking?), the police are represented in their diverse national uniforms, flags are displayed on each arm, and all are carrying semi-automatics or handguns.

I'm prepared for the worst-case scenario too. A bodyguard has told me about the secret exit from the PM's office and, while I'm not strictly allowed to use it, if it comes to a decision between life and death I might just let protocol slip. I'm also wearing flat shoes with good grip on the soles, a skirt with adequate movement, a shirt with a lot of shoulder space just in case I need to run anywhere or jump over anything, at speed.

Looking at the armed presence, though, I'm reassured that everything will be fine, so I go for a chat with the new New Zealand peacekeeping contingent commander, who is laid-back despite the occasion, as he stands on the balcony being continually updated on the movements of the protestors by his intelligence operatives placed throughout Dili. We're joined by his Portuguese equivalent, who seems very excited by it all, thanks to the adrenalin and testosterone coursing through his system. Meanwhile, I'm starting to enjoy myself.

There's something romantic about being under siege, and I think I'll happily allow myself to be rescued today; which is why, whether it's appropriate or not, I am now cursing that I dressed for safety over allure. What a time to let my standards slip when there are all these colonels around!

It is such a dichotomy, this moment and this place. Leaning up against the whitewashed concrete parapet underneath the majestic arches talking to the contingent commanders, I leisurely watch the armed and uniformed troops arranging themselves just below me, and beyond them I can see a view that is undeniably beautiful, with its yachts on a bright blue ocean and the grey–green island of Atauro out there, even at a time like this. Menace in paradise.

The New Zealand commander surveys the scene and talks to one of his men in the field. 'They're on their way,' he says to me, before adding, 'You know, Lynne, if you took a New Zealander, an Australian and a Timorese and put them out in the middle of the bush with no resources what would happen? What would you find if you came back a year later?'

'Um, I don't know what you mean.'

'Well, the New Zealander would have built a home using palm fronds and wood with a solar-powered electricity system and organic garden to sustain him. The Australian would have created a luxury home with slat windows, wooden floorboards and essential mod cons powered by some innovative natural method. The Timorese, however, would be in the very same state as he was left until someone came along and saved him.'

The cynicism has a source: see, some Timorians want the UN to leave, but they want the jobs and money to remain. In other words, they want to be handed the hundreds of millions of dollars the UN brings here to do as they will, without malae interference, which they see as re-colonial. Somewhere along the way someone should have explained to the population that this UN mission is here to give them responsibility through training. That the UN is providing experts who are employed in capacity-building now, that it is no longer ruling the land.

The main complainants are the former Falantil fighters, who say they are trained soldiers and security experts so there is no need to have the malae peacekeepers or police here any more, earning fortunes. The ex-rebels are angry that the Timorese defence and police forces have been recruited from the younger, fitter, more educated Timorese community, and they won't accept that the UN is here to train them in more appropriate ways of fighting bad guys, restoring order and securing borders than techniques preferred by guerrillas. And they don't understand that the new nation's security forces cannot take on anyone illiterate and physically affected by years in the mountains or that sentimentality has no place in a vocation requiring mental and physical agility.

It's a terrible paradox and each side has a point I'm thinking, as I make my way downstairs where suddenly I hear an almighty commotion coming from outside and big, fat Australian police officers bounce towards the front of the building.

Inside, bodyguards from worldwide propel themselves around the building, evacuating everyone from the offices facing the street, 'Get away from the windows!' It's a phrase we'll hear again and again today. Protestors are arriving on motorbikes, revving their engines and screeching their tyres to the cheers of others on foot who are sprinting up the street to join them.

The crowd is swelling out the front and I'm being shepherded away by security yelling at me to 'Get away from the windows!'

I'm trying to coax a Timorese Government employee to get up from a game of solitaire or whatever it is she's doing at a time like this, 'Come on! It's for your own good.'

'You no tell me what I do, I am in this my country!'

This is no time for the Malae Syndrome. 'I know it is, but let's just go upstairs. I'm not really telling you what to do, it's the police who are evacuating these offices so you have to come with me.'

'No! You go, all you UN people, you go, you always go like you do, leave me here!'

I'm looking at her agog, I know she's right and wrong all at the same time and I don't know what to say . . . 'Lynne, what the fuck are you doing?' a bodyguard yells at me. 'Get her out of here and you out, NOW!'

'But . . .'

'You hearing me? Get out of here now, they are one metre away from you through that window, girl. You want them to smash through, you want them to see you in here?' My Timorese kolega throws open the curtain. Sometimes the provocation goes too far, you know. 'Jesus, get out of here, NOW! You too!' he yells, grabbing the curtain back into place and he directs us out the door before heading to the other offices along the row and, as he does, my kolega glares at me and returns to the room whence we've come.

What can I do? I tell the police there is someone in that room over there and then sprint up the stairs and down the corridor, into the Prime Minister's office and out onto the first-floor balcony again, breathless, watching the anger below. There are about 500 of them now and they are surging towards the grand front doors, chanting in Tetum. The tempo is rising. Just how angry are they? What are they capable of? 'Hello Asim!' I yell at my huge Bosnian police-officer friend who is moving towards them, whom I know will look out for me. Then, shit, I lean backwards realising I should make sure the protestors don't see my white skin up here. I don't want to be seen to be presiding over them — a foreigner at their hub of decision-making.

I duck back into the Prime Minister's office and that's where I see him, he's arrived. He's standing alone at a window, looking at the scene playing out at ground level just beneath him. They are calling for his resignation, they have been for weeks, this is the deadline for them and him, they scream, meanwhile he watches on. Pensive. Distant. Lonely.

An uncommon maternal instinct directs me (probably because he's the size of a well-nourished child) and I go and stand beside the Prime Minister in a show of support and solidarity. We're silent, both of us, looking outside at the mass of his people and listening to their chants, 'Alkatiri nebe?' 'Alkatiri nebe?' Where is he? He's standing here, watching them.

After a while, I look down to my left and say, 'You know, if my Prime Minister spoke to every mob that protested outside his office he'd be out there all day every day.' Mari Alkatiri laughs. He glances at me out of the corners of his eyes and then, after observing his democracy at work outside his window for a minute or so more, he turns and leaves. And I mean that literally: he leaves.

At first we all think he's gone to the loo. 'Alkatiri nebe?' his staff asks. Finally some people are jumping on their phones — albeit without luck — trying to track down the executive leader of the country. In the meantime, the crowd outside is growing more insistent, 'Alkatiri nebe?' It wants answers from him, everyone does. But it appears he's not going to provide any because he's taken his private exit and gone home, despite the hundreds of people below his window, combined with those inside this building, plus the children hiding in safe houses, the malae at the beach, international investors, donor nations and a handful of errant refugees, yes, all of them want to know what on earth is going on in this country of his, as a democracy demands, but Alkatiri nebe?

He misunderstood! My comment wasn't meant to suggest that he should bugger off. Sure, I may not have felt it wise to place him out on the balcony with a target on his forehead but I'd never imagined he'd leave without saying a single word via less risky media.

Whatever, the rot has set in now. Curious, I want to gauge the reaction to his disappearance. Going out into the corridor and opening doors, I see some terrified Timorese staff gathered in the rooms on the other side of the building from the windows facing the demonstrations. 'It's okay, it's okay,' I say, closing each again with the noise from outside gaining in pitch and fever, and I'm drawn downstairs to a foyer which is filled with the sound of chanting now. Furious Timorese protestors are banging against the windows along the front of the building, reaching their arms through the bars across the entrance, pushing, banging, screaming. Police yell at me to leave, NOW! as I approach. I have no intention of leaving — everything I have ever studied, learned, reported on is occurring right now in front of me. The result of all those words and principles is unfolding here at this moment and I want to see it at work. So I hide out of the way on the stairway, as the people and police come face to face. Yelling, demanding. Both sides. I'm fascinated by a group aggression I've never witnessed before. Then I notice Maluco glaring at me just as his principal, the minister he is employed to protect, moves from his ground-floor office area and the bars are opened for him to move outside, into the seething throng.

Entering the mob, José is jostled and he speaks via a loudhailer to the crowd in Tetum. He says he wants to listen to their concerns and he is prepared to be the mediator for them. 'Alkatiri nebe?' they chant and jump up and down, while some, the literate presumably, brandish banners. Their voices fade to allow him to speak again. He's placed himself in the middle of a dangerous melee, the Prime Minister long gone, his bodyguard preoccupied with the woman who hurt him, the peacekeepers only able to watch on because their mandate doesn't include intervening in simple law-and-order issues.

To the desperate crowd José pledges to hold a public consultation, a forum for the people to get the answers they need. The people chant, 'Alkatiri nebe?' The response comes, 'We'll see. That is up to him.' Despite my basic Tetum language skills, I can tell that all participants are frustrated by their leader's absence.

Still, they calm at the offer to be heard and informed, so the Foreign Affairs Minister makes his way back through the crowd, safe despite a distracted bodyguard, and through the arched doors. As he enters the foyer the bars close shut behind him. With the noise dissipating and the crowd benignly milling now, I stand up from where I'm crouching and walk down the stairs, catching the eye of the man who has just performed this remarkably brave feat, 'Congratulations on your promotion to Internal Affairs Minister,' I say. And he, too, laughs.

35

SEAT OF GOVERNMENT

There are some selection criteria worth mentioning to prospective applicants for a position of adviser to the Prime Minister of East Timor: that one possess unwavering serenity, heartily enjoy passive smoking, boast advanced handyman qualifications and a background in office administration, while providing all one's workplace resources. A penchant for stiletto-heeled sandals and faux leather handbags imported from Indonesia advantageous. Plumber's certificate desirable.

I drive beside the oceanfront on my way to work in my Governu Tata. Yes, I have a Popemobile of my very own! I know I've made it to the heady heights now that I can bounce fully exposed in my big square box on wheels with the tintless windows and absence of accessories (what were there have long since been looted) down the pockmarked thoroughfares of Dili. It doesn't have brakes, my Popemobile, or many other safety features for that matter — like lights or indicators or window wipers — so right now I'm moving down through the gears preparing to corner (praying that no dog, pig, goat or Timor taxi appears in front of me).

My morning-time travels take me along the beach, skirting the broken footpath and a small stone wall, the fishermen with their handmade wooden canoes plying their trade here and there in the high tide, the startling radiance of the reflecting sunlight of the new day investing a glittery glow. The Tata's windows are down, Ah, this is the life, I acknowledge, dodging the oncoming Timor taxi that drives into my lane as it chooses to overtake a scooter (bearing family with breast-feeding mother). UN Land Rovers overtake me at extreme speed causing all sorts of vehicles and animals to scatter. Then a motorcade screams up behind me with honking horns and flashing lights — it's my boss, I know, because his is the very most extravagant motorcade. So, respectfully, I pull over with a nimble whiz down through the gears and a tug on the handbrake, and past me scream the one, two, three, four, five cars in a motorcade fit for any Third World dictator. Look at that for a spectacle, then. With all those bells and whistles he's certainly alerted any assassins who might be lying in wait — quick, aim and fire now!

Yes, it's an obstacle course driving in this place but I'm happy to get back out there amongst it, and I push in the spongey clutch, put her into second gear and with a screech and a bunny hop we're off bouncing over the potholes again. This car's so temperamental it's like riding a skittish colt, but I enjoy the challenge, and the scenery as I putter by it: G'day! to my new Ambassador; Howdy partner! to the friendly folk at the US Embassy; Bemvindo! to the new SRSG. The picturesque lighthouse that seems made of gingerbread appears beside me on the left, then the shipping docks provide a blemish upon the otherwise picturesque semi-circle that is Dili Harbour. Merging into a traffic of overladen microlets, up through the gears, down again as the car squeals (it's labour-intensive getting to work), and I turn right, up a small block, a hard left, then I'm bouncing through the dirt carpark until, with a flick of a wrist and a wrench of the handbrake, I find myself sliding neatly into a spot facing the entrance of the magnificent white government building. Safe and sound.

The early morning adventure completed, I turn off the key, wind up the windows and lock the doors manually (forget what world we're in, what century are we in?) and wander away from my death-trap-with-charm and the engine stops with a shudder that seems like a great exhalation after the effort of transporting me to here. To the edge of the road in front, waving on the taxis that slow, horns honking, and I run over, careful not to break into a sweat in the hot humidity, and walk through the official cars parked in front of the building '1', '2', 'TL1' — Alkatiri, Ramos-Horta, Xanana — it's an effective advertisement of which leaders are inside. Even more effective, the absence of cars out the front shows which leaders spend most of their time overseas and, in fact, it's quite customary to arrive and see no official cars here at all. Anyone can wander past the cars, between numbers '1' and '2' or whichever configuration is in attendance, park alongside them, have a casual look inside at the upholstery of the often unlocked luxury vehicles, because we are yet to reach any security zone. Under the terrace I go, and sitting on the steps or down on their haunches in traditional style are the chauffeurs who greet me as I stride up the steps, 'Bondia Missus Leeen.'

'Bondia Celestino, diak ka lae?' I say.

Into the cool waiting foyer, the scene of so much drama during its years, past the green uniformed security guards, 'Bondia Missus,' they say before they resume their gossip. Left and right are corridors, both now co-opted by the Ministry of Foreign Affairs, which means that his bodyguards stand to the right-hand side, watching a large-screen television that plays all day, their attention leaving it only when their principal leaves his office or a chick comes into view. And it's at this point that my day becomes good or bad when I see who is on duty — if it's Maluco, I know I have to duck past him and up the grand stairway while he turns, crosses his arms, and glares at me; if it's one of the others I know I'll receive a hearty 'Hello!' and a quick compliment on my apparent beauty to send me on my way.

The stairs curve upwards to each side and I take the left, stepping over the Timorese journalists who sit here waiting, hopefully, for a comment, something, anything, from Alkatiri; usually they wait in vain. When they saw me here the first time they hugged me in congratulations, and now they are the next wave of greetings I enjoy of a morning. 'I'll try, I'll try,' I say to them, and we laugh because we know the Prime Minister will avoid them at any cost and the only time they'll see him is when he sweeps up and down these stairs while they scuttle out of his path.

At the top, I could turn left to go to Xanana's suite of offices but instead I turn right and head past a generally unattended reception table and some doors on my left (one of which has the PM just behind it and a stickytaped sign telling you to use the next one along). I grab the correct doorknob, as instructed, and it's locked, as it is most mornings. I don't have a key, which requires me to wait around, side by side with the two maids, 'Bondia,' we greet each other and go out the door at the end of the corridor, walk around to the balcony in front, and settle down, enjoying the view for however long it takes until one of the assistants arrives and opens the French doors to let us in.

There's no desk in here for me. I'd like a desk, actually. Generally I find them to be useful items in the workplace, on a par with a chair and I don't have one of those either. Still, I guess I have to patiently accept some difficulties because I'm not in Sydney now, am I? Indeed, protests are the least of the difficulties I'm facing, God help me.

In the meantime, I perch on a tiny temporary desk that I've carried in. It doesn't match the rest of the designer furnishings at all, and I've had to place it in the only free spot, which is on the way to the French doors — a hazard for anyone who wants to go through. It's also a nuisance for anyone who might want to sit at the meeting table: 'Lae problema,' I say all day to those who bang chairs into my arrangement whenever they take a seat. Luckily, most of the time only the Timorian bodyguards sit there, talking to me in English, excitedly, because they want to study in Australia one day, 'Missus Leeen is from Sydney?'

'Yes but please call me Lynne.'

'Ooh, Sydney very beootiful!'

'Yes. And we have desks in Sydney, lots of desks.'

'Squeeze me?'

'Nothing, nothing at all. I'm just going mad over here, just a mild case of claustrophobia,' brought upon by being pressed up against a wall by a tiny bloody desk. Maybe I should swap mine with the Prime Miniature's, that would be more size appropriate.

I'm also not provided with a telephone, my little deskette doesn't come with an internal extension, so I guess I'll use my mobile for calls until that's sorted out . . . As for a computer, well that came about from a morning of putting together a jigsaw puzzle of components discarded in a pyramid in the corner resulting in a sporadically operational system. And email hasn't been put on in here, so I mire myself in the bureaucracy that'll furnish that indispensable device.

By 8.30 am each day the assistant to my right, who speaks no English at all, has had her third cigarette. To my left in a cosy arrangement is another assistant, Rita, who happily complains to me about the chainsmoking colleague, 'Smell Leeen, she *dis-gust-ing*, I hate her!' and she laughs, confident that The Chimney can't understand a word before launching into a stream of delightful and downright scandalous stories about anyone at all.

There are two cubicles further to the right and one of them is empty — that's right, desk, filing cabinets, phone, all the paraphernalia I'd love are actually lying vacant. However, I can't sit in there, according to the Prime Miniature's Timorian adviser, José, who sits at the next desk along, because the UN should give me what I need to do my job, which would be a great suggestion except that the UN says it has provided my services to a new Independent East Timorese Government that needs to provide its own resources from now on. Hence the cobbled-together deskette arrangement I've managed to construct in front of the French doors. I'm a professional bag lady — all I need is some cardboard boxes for my files.

Beyond José is a door that leads to the seat of government and the Prime Miniature's large desk, and occasionally the man himself when he's not off overseas.

And that's it. Other than that other seat of government, the toilet, that is. Yes, we all share the throne. Unfortunately for the Prime Miniature, he has to share this intimate space with the proletariat — although, he makes the bodyguards clear it out before he goes, which always has me concerned that I'll be caught mid-performance.

The main cause of my performance anxiety, though, is that my job is to train a Timorese counterpart but no counterpart has been hired. Now, theoretically, I am not supposed to perform the role of media adviser because that would be contrary to the role of the mission, which is to build the competency of the government and its employees, so the absence of a counterpart makes my job, therefore, impossible.

I've been trying to get a meeting with the PM since I arrived. I want to formally introduce myself and explain my role, talk about recruiting a counterpart as a matter of urgency, present him with my ideas for the media unit representing him and the Council of Ministers, and get his approval to proceed. Every day I request an appointment from his José and every day I seem to be bumped off the agenda. I think it's important for him and me to work out how he can communicate with his people and prevent future riotous protesting. My enthusiasm isn't shared.

So I head off in my Popemobile — the only resource I've been able to annex because the Timorian staff can't drive and there are literally hundreds of dilapidated Tata cars left languishing in the wake of the UNTAET mission — to see my project manager at UNDP, asking him to arrange an initial summit. 'What? I can't just waltz in and request a meeting with the Prime Minister of the country!' Terry replies, aghast!

'But you have the imprimatur of UNDP behind you.'

'Look, usually we hold an introductory meeting with a new line manager at the start of a contract to explain the job and what will be achieved and how they need to participate in it . . . but in your case the line manager is the Prime Minister!'

'Even more reason for you to hold the meeting.'

'No way. I'm not going in there!'

So I just keep putting my name on the diary list. In the meantime I go about writing a project plan on how the media unit could operate, with ideas for messages, objectives, funding of resources and communication lines between the unit, the ministries and the media, in between giving language lessons to the bodyguards, listening to Rita's wonderfully salacious hearsay, eating the Indonesian pastries she feeds me, greeting the English-speaking VIPs with the words 'I'm terribly sorry but there seems to have been a mix-up, you're not on the Prime Minister's diary list for today' (which always makes me see that I'm not special) 'and he's heading off on an international trip that'll last for weeks. How urgent did you say it is?' while The Chimney stubs out the latest of many fags and sets about lighting the next.

At other times I can be found trying to fix the fax machine, air-conditioning and printers. When the seat of government goes down I draw the line; my expertise does not include cisterns.

To understand the position of the PM, however, it is important to accept that he is distracted. The post-Independence honeymoon is well and truly over and I have walked into a hornets' nest. Divisions have opened, great cavernous gulfs, between the Prime Minister's faction of 'Old Fretilin' party allies and the rest: the members of other parties, the independents, the rest of Fretilin who want the old hegemony to end, and a proportion of the people.

The division is made clear when the Prime Miniature attends the public consultation promised to the protestors by Ramos-Horta. The audience is a malae-free zone, so I'm excluded from proceedings but, afterwards, I settle down to watch a video taken by a bodyguard and as it begins I can see the leaders standing on the floor of the venue while a crowd of thousands fills the auditorium to capacity. On one side of the floor space is a collection of leaders in conversation, including Ramos-Horta, Xanana and Bishop Belo. On the other side, the Prime Minister stands with a comrade, just the two of them. After an awkward period, the Prime Minister walks across towards the other group and, as he does, Ramos-Horta and Xanana move away, leaving only the Bishop, who benevolently stays.

It's all very telling. The discord within the government is profound and some powerful political leaders have shown to a packed public venue that they, like the protestors, have tired of Alkatiri's arrogance. The seat of government is a lonely place to be right now; it's time for it to be shared in an open and democratic fashion, if only I could fix the cistern.

36

PRIME MINIATURE'S SHOE AND HANDBAG EMPORIUM

A towel around my torso and thongs on my feet, I unlock the door of my tiny green bedroom and flip-flop out in the direction of the communal bathroom, yawning, rubbing my nose with one hand, holding my towel up with the other. That's when I focus for the first time today and, unfortunately, as I do I see in front of me a collection of short, squat uniformed Portuguese peacekeepers all staring directly at me. I wish I could say it surprises me but, alas, it doesn't. Instead it causes me to declare them 'Perverts' then run as fast as thongs allow while adopting a vice-like grip on my covering.

Ann has decided to open a café in the front room of the house, hence the early-morning callers. The proximity of the house to the UN water-filling station has provided a rush of custom, drawn by the added incentive of catching a glimpse of a chick in a towel. Four women live here — quite a statistic for Timor — and our daily comings and goings provide organic advertising that is equal to the most powerful campaign in the world. My landlord thought it financially prudent to harness our natural resources, and so the soldiers have taken to popping in for an espresso and a perv as the froth on the top. A nice macchiato with which to begin the day. Although I'm surprised the breakfast special isn't a VB for US$5.99.

As I stand under the trickle of water in the shower, safely locked into the bathroom now, I feel a pall of sadness at the memory triggered by the Portuguese flag on the perverts' shoulders. Usually I can ignore it but sometimes, still, the grief is overwhelming. I wish I didn't pine for him, yet I do, despite the passage of time or perhaps because of it. I have continued to allow hope to rise every now and then — generally coinciding with Viktor's loving emails to me — but maybe I should just cut my losses and embark on a determined healing process alone? He's currently sitting on a Spanish alp with his daughters, contemplating the future. Will I be a part of that future? Do I want to be a part of that future? At what point was he handed responsibility for my future?

Leaning up against the wall on this morning I can't see with clarity. All rational thought seems overwhelmed by emotion. I can't make sense of the past, the present or the future. I no longer know what the past was, despite having lived it alongside him, the present seems rather foggy to me even though I'm showering in cold water and, given all of that, I daren't look forward.

On one level I know that it was probably all a silly dream foolishly brought to life. On that level I can see that it's unrealistic to believe there is any hope for us. It's hard enough finding a relationship with potential, let alone adding an impediment the size of half the world. And there was no time to really get to know Viktor, which is why I can't be sure that he is a deserving object of my love. I tried to assess him carefully in the beginning — his morals and ethics — however, my past shows that I'm not a great judge of character and, hey, my ideal men are Hugh Grant and Robbie Williams so I'm clearly not attracted to commitment-orientated individuals. Those are the thoughts occurring on the one level that is probably the more rational.

On a far more emotional level, I still cling to that dream, whatever it may be, because sometimes . . . well, rarely, actually . . . in truth, once in a lifetime, probably . . . a man slips under your defences. That man was Viktor for me. He snuck right under my guard with all of his 'blondies' and 'my green eyes' and 'I don't know what's going to happen'. All of it so endearing, suave, clever and masculine that I simply couldn't resist him. Still can't. I liked feeling unic. It felt so good that I can't throw it away, even if it has felt like shit since he left.

It's time for a heart-starter I realise, which is why it is helpful for me to bump into Ann while I'm darting out of the bathroom ('Morning — Mornin' Missus'), because it gives me the opportunity to order a long black from the café. I'm continuing by in a rush to minimise the show for the troops when I hear, 'That'll be one dollar,' which the proprietor calls out after me. I have to pay US$1 for a coffee from a café that's invading my privacy? Let's not forget the amount of promotion I do for the franchise when I walk around in a towel, like right now. I should be awarded a share of takings, a rent reduction and free long blacks if I so choose. Whatever, this is an emergency, 'All right, all right. But it'd better be strong.'

Coffee, conservative business attire, Dili perfume to keep away those rotten mosquitoes, blast of deodorant which promptly turns to dust (as it always does) over my conservative business attire, affix confident demeanour of professional person with intact heart, another US$1 coffee, then I'm off in the Popemobile for the drive into town to beat my head extremely hard against a brick wall for a workaday. Wish I was on a Spanish alp. Well, I wish my body could join my heart on a Spanish alp.

I'm not in the Pyrenees, though, am I? So I try to force my mind onto the job at hand. I've tendered the project plan for the media unit to the Prime Minister for approval, which required me to place it on one of the very big piles of paperwork on José's desk, and while I wait for that pipe dream to come true in contravention of the immutable laws of Timor, I busy myself with organising media training for each ministry. To this end I take it upon myself to write a memo to the ministers, introducing myself and announcing that I'll be popping in for a visit with each of them this week. As we've discovered, phoning doesn't work in Timor and assistants don't either — The Chimney inhales from her fifth cigarette of the day beside me to illustrate my point — so I know better than to wait for meetings to be scheduled. Which is why, to streamline the process, I'm going to just drop in for a chat with those in charge of each portfolio and discuss ways in which they can communicate with journalists and therefore the population, using me and my soon-to-be-hired counterpart as the conduit. It's a flawless plan. See how easy it can be to do business in the Third World? Yes, it's just a matter of accepting the limitations of the place and working within them. So right now I'm alerting them to my impending arrival . . . put out the Iced Vo Vos and stick on the kettle, I'm on my way! My personal life may be foundering but at least I can succeed in my professional life.

Now then, I need to create a prime ministerial letterhead: with no template in the office, I take the government's symbol — a crest of crossed swords and the motto 'HONRA, PATRIA E POVO' — place it at the top of the page, and beneath it I paste the words 'PRIMEIRO GOVERNO CONSTITUCIONAL DA REPUBLICA DEMOCRATICA DE TIMOR LESTE', then 'GABINETE DO PRIMEIRO MINISTRO' in the most authoritative font Microsoft provides. There can be no doubt that this dispatch will convey tremendous weight to the few people in this country who can understand what it says — and to the vast majority who can't.

I've been careful to use Portuguese. The Prime Miniature insists, apparently (what would I know? I'm hardly his confidante), that the Portuguese language be strictly adhered to as the language of government. This requires documents to be translated and retranslated and translated again, time, energy, manpower and money as an additional problem for a student administration. Imagine the law courts when they are operating! Testimony given in Bahasa Indonesia — the language of the people — translated into English — the lingua franca of the UN and aid organisations — translated into Portuguese — for the benefit of the leadership who spent 24 years out of the country and speak the latter.

I've been at meetings at which a question is asked by a Timorese person in the language he understands, Bahasa, and an answer has come back in the language he can't, Portuguese, from a Timorese minister. It all gives the Prime Miniature and his cronies an advantage over the people who remained here during the Indonesian occupation, which is why the Prime Miniature determinedly holds on to his Portophilia.

Any wayward usage of the nomenclature 'East Timor' could get me sacked so I make sure to use 'Timor-Leste'. Timor-Leste, Timor-Leste, I'm reciting, while thinking that I really should start putting my foot down when anyone thinks they can get away with calling my country Australie or arrogantly adding any of their ethnic inflections over the letters (Austrália indeed!) and I'm thinking how curious it is that the PM refers to Germany as Alemanha when it should be Deutschland, and Switzerland as A suiça when it should be Confoederatio Helvetica, if we are to follow the Timor-Leste example.

Oh look, I'm sure my boss is right and the world should see the tremendous power of the Portuguese language. The Internet should switch over to it immediately. After all, I wish I was fluent in Portuguese. I have incentive. If I could speak that language then Viktor and I would have a greater chance at a future. Yet I can't because it is a complicated language, and conjugating verbs with any enthusiasm is something I can't quite master. So, for now, I prefer Tetum because it's easier to learn.

Tetum is the second new official language, according to the Constitution, a more indigenous choice for those in the Dili area who speak it. However, it comes with problems of its own. Timorese people in other regions speak their own dialects and languages, so it's not an all-embracing alternative to Bahasa. And it was a language spoken by a generally illiterate people and, therefore, had no official written form. It's now being used in translations of government documents and, when it comes to the legal papers, for example, the language simply doesn't contain the words required. In fact, as a language it is rudimentary. Verbs don't change according to subject or tense (has gone/is going/will go to trial) and instead a tone or gesture indicates whether something has occurred, is occurring or will occur — and this isn't easily represented in the written form. Then there is the added disadvantage that the language doesn't have a great deal of reach, given that it's not spoken in any other country in the world. So much for my lessons.

Actually, I recant from the latter point because my lessons have been invaluable — Tetum helps me in my Timor-Leste workplace because I can listen in on Rita's gossip with the maids, as I sit at my deskette until there comes a time when I need to interrupt, I'm sorry to say, in English, 'Rita, where's the OUT tray? I want to send my memo.' There's no literal translation in Tetum: the language of subsistence farmers who had no need for words meaning memo. No, memos are the invention of the First World in line with other signs of development like introductory meetings.

Not to worry, Rita loves to practise English because she's realistic and she may be going on a training course in Australia for personal assistants soon, and I want to help her get there as much as possible because, Jesus, she could do with it. 'Leeen, not possible,' and she rolls her eyes. She's always rolling her eyes at me.

A maid places a cup of black coffee beside me. She can see that I've finished the one before. 'Obrigada,' I say to her with a smile then go back to the task at hand, 'Rita.'

'Yes, Leeen?' she smiles at me with those huge teeth she has.

'Rita, how do I send mail then?'

'Leeen, you take mail,' she mimics the movements. 'You go to post office, you take stamp,' she licks the air, 'you give to them, they send it, weeeee!'

Right. 'So each time I have a letter to send I trot off to the post office over the road and send it?' She rolls her eyes. 'O-kay. We may have to change that system down the track but for today I'll do it. Where's the petty cash?'

'Nooooo!' Rolled eyes. 'You pay!' and she translates into Tetum for the benefit of the maids and they all laugh at me. I'm not surprised, I'm paying for the petrol in the Popemobile too, because nobody seems to know where the vouchers are.

'So, can I assume then, Rita . . .'

'Yes, Leeen?'

'. . . that there is no IN tray either?'

'Nooooo!' I roll my eyes too, along with them, then I look away as Rita gives me a good-natured hug. I'm sitting, she's standing, which is a confronting configuration because the woman has a raunchy sense of fashion that often makes me blush. I can't imagine how the Prime Miniature feels about the coloured bras through sheer shirt fabric, the tight trousers clinging to her arse and sky-high stilettos that bring her clip-clopping to his desk when she's summoned. Clip-clopping and gossiping, we always know where our Rita is in the big white building on the harbour foreshore at any given time. Big mouth, big teeth, big heels, big tits and a big laugh. And she certainly never allows work to interfere with her day, which is a reason why the office has ceased to operate, unless you like shoes and handbags.

You see, Rita has started running a shoe and handbag catalogue service from the Prime Minister's office, which means that these days it gets a little crowded around the meeting table, and from my confined spot I watch on, fascinated. Indonesian catalogues are being passed around a group of excited women who are pointing at their selections, shrieking with joy at each turn of the page.

Now, I'm an advocate of shoe appreciation, of course, and there are very few priorities that I place above shoes, but I have to wonder about the appropriateness of dealing in mail-order shoes from the meeting table in the middle of the office of the leader of the nation. Although, I concede it might be nice for VIPs to come in for their audience with the PM and pick out a nice pump in a red size 9 at the same time.

'Leeen, you look? Very nice. I think you like, look . . .' she's pointing at a striking strappy number with a little butterfly motif over the little toe, a criss-cross at the ankle to create definition, heels at just the right cheeky height to achieve a slender calf, and this very exclusive design is available to me in a selection of colours for the special price of 199 000 rupiah. Our English-speaking entrepreneur will also take the equivalent in US dollars for the convenience of her clientele. No sticky translation issues, money talks. Rita knows she's in a globalised world and she's opening up to the international economy — me.

To coordinate your outfit for best effect, handbags are also available to the shrewd shopper. A rainbow of colours and this season's latest styles can be shipped upon demand to your deskette before you can say Louis Vuitton. A darling little clutch in black? What about a half-moon tucking neatly under the armpit? Diamantés and a long chain for that company cocktail party? Funk it up with a backpack available in a profusion of pinks?

I don't want to be rude, so I guess I could get something that carries my notebook. That would actually be a work-related purchase allowing me to be professional and thus no work ethics are compromised, right? 'Rita, how long would it take for this tiny fake Burberry with the cutest handles to arrive? It's quite urgent that I have it, you see.' Shopping as I am, I feel like a drug addict having her first hit after months of cold turkey. I'm smiling maniacally, and . . . I . . . do . . . not . . . care.

Hey, I'm helping to build capacity. And this service puts paid to the knockers. All those critics who claim that this country is unable to achieve a capacity-built air-traffic control service, police force or government administration, have never seen the fantastic level of capacity here at the Prime Miniature's Shoe and Handbag Emporium, have they?

I am now in workplace heaven. They say you should make your hobby your job and I think I may have stumbled upon a way to make that possible. I've always thought of myself as staunchly dedicated to my politics and, frankly, I'm a dedicated capitalist. So I feel strongly that I've found my calling. 'Ten day, Leeen. You give me fifteen doll-ah!'

'And a kiss.'

'What? You crazy, Leeen.'

'No, I have never been so happy, actually, and you are responsible.'

'You crazy!'

They also say you should throw yourself into work in order to heal a broken heart and that's exactly what I'm going to do right now. 'How much for the kitten heel with red straps and white stitching, here, this one? Or what about these stilettos with the bow on the front? They come in nude, yeah? Oh, hang on, I love these mules, I must have them . . .' I knew this job would be a high point in my career.

37

ONE BANANA, TWO BANANA, THREE BANANA, FOUR . . .

It's pretty safe to say that Rita is one of the best connected people in Timor, as a result of touching people in the deepest place, their vanity. Rita isn't just tapped into the grapevine, she is the grapevine. So I ask her, 'Rita, do you know anyone who has a house available for rent?' She certainly does and so my lunch breaks see me heading off through the streets of the capital.

Dili is not built on a grid pattern but, rather, is a senseless collection of higgledy-piggledy dirt lanes and bumpy bitumen roads. It has no postal delivery service, which means there are no addresses and the only way to find a location is to follow directions — like 'Go past the cathedral and turn left at the crooked tree' — which wouldn't be helpful in most countries and, in Timor, with its proliferation of crooked trees and cathedrals, they have me bouncing aimlessly for ages.

Within the residences, when I find them, are walls brown with the stains of years; bare concrete floors; broken windows; ripped curtains filled with dust; cold water available only when the unstable electricity's on; non-flushing Indonesian squat toilets for strengthening those flabby thigh muscles; rudimentary kitchens with kerosene camping stoves; no fencing, which explains the curious neighbours following me from room to room . . . until the eccentric English flatmates on their revenue-raising campaign and the accompanying Portuguese perverts seem quite pleasant by comparison.

Maybe I should be thankful for what I have and remember that I am in a developing nation? People have it a lot worse than me I can see right now, as I look around and read the graffiti which has been conveniently and usefully written in an English of sorts on the inside walls of this current option.

Nah, bugger off. I'm from the developed world in which the accumulation of ever better circumstances is the primary *raison d'être* in a life. I expect comfort, privacy, respect and a substantial supply of mod cons, especially those trappings of a technological type. There is simply no place for compassion in a discussion about my luxury. Would it alleviate their poverty if I were to live like a poor person too? I mean, my compatriots at home are buying fridges in coordinating shades with Internet screens; wall-mounted plasma (which is what exactly?) televisions; digital surround-sound speakers to complement home entertainment systems the size of shoe boxes; mobile phones that apparently take photos (but I can't believe it); and cars that give directions with the aid of satellite positioning (I can see the value in this one). In reality, however, I'd accept a hot shower and some privacy.

While Rita may be the lynchpin of the Timorese grapevine, what we've seen thus far shows that the current matter is out of her league, so these days I cast my net into the luxury market and ask any malae I encounter if they know of vacant properties. I want my home to be a commerce-free zone and I'm fearful about the next venture Ann and Wayne will inevitably embark upon to prevent their financial ruin, because they are running out of space to co-opt in the house.

Despite the importance of my quest, I can only devote a certain amount of time to it: my two-hour lunch break. There are some things about the Latino influence in this country that I like very much. So, as the clock strikes two, I bounce back to the office and wait outside on the terrace for the unlocking that occurs at some point in the afternoon, 'Hello Leeen!' before wedging myself into the teeny receptacle between the wall and the deskette, and a maid brings me coffee while I update, yet again, the agenda for my introductory meeting with the PM, the first item on which is now: give the man a round of applause.

How persistent I am. I continue to have an unshakable faith that the great audience is coming any day now, maybe on this day. The Chimney is onto cigarette number ten or so and the room is under its customary grey cloud when I'm told that I've been bumped from the diary again. The Prime Miniature is simply too busy for me.

'Leeen, you come here.' Rita is emerging from the boss's office and she's beside herself with eagerness. 'Leeen, I must speak with you!' and I follow her out into the sun. 'Come, come, Leeen!'

'Okay, okay. What?'

'Leeen, the Prime Minister, he very angry with me.'

'Yeah, clearly, I heard all the fuss. What was that about?'

'Leeen, you must tell me. The Prime Minister he yell at me and he say that he have many meeting every day, too much. Ooooh, he very angry with me, he say no more, now I must put less meeting in diary and he only work morning to twelve then afternoon he work two and go to home at five-thirty. He say no leader of country work long hours but, Leeen, you from Australia, you tell me, this wrong?'

'Ah, well, Rita, let me tell you that the Prime Minister is

indeed wrong. Leaders of other nations work very long hours and unfortunately he has signed on for a job that requires him to work long hours, too, for at least five years. In fact, I can give you an example of the work ethic he needs to have: one leader of a nation had to take business calls at eleven o'clock at night while he was getting a blow job. That's the level of work ethic required, I'm afraid.' Yes, there is a marked contrast between Bill Clinton and Dr Mari Alkatiri.

Touring around the ministerial offices is also providing a fascinating look at the members of the elite in their positions of enormous power. Most fascinating of all are the introductions to Dr Alkatiri's comrades — the Old Fretilin allies that Dr Alkatiri has appointed to his Council of Ministers, creating a motley crew more comparable to Hanna-Barbera cartoon characters.

I'll start by introducing the Minister for Innovative Perspectives, aka Dr Rogerio Lobato, who has been jailed in Mozambique for diamond smuggling, which he claimed was required to fund the freedom movement and that made it all okay. He brings this skill to his actual role as Minister for Internal Administration.

There's the recently appointed Dr Roque Rodrigues, Secretary of State for Defence, a vitally important portfolio, who I couldn't possibly describe as anything other than the Minister for the Barking Mad because he is, thereby single-handedly demonstrating the problems inherent with nepotism. This man shows John Cleese's Minister for Silly Walks as alarmingly prophetic.

The legendary Minister for Justice, Dra Ana Pessoa, should be known as the Minister of the Frankly Intimidating; it's said that she could eradicate crime immediately if she dressed down every criminal herself. Certainly that would be punishment enough, striking the fear of God, too, into anyone sitting at home in their uninhabitable shack, tossing up whether to break the law '*ka lae* = or not'. I am thankful she is out of the country on unexplained extended leave which has lasted a couple of months already, and has left the faltering court system in chaos with people languishing in Becora Jail (unless they choose to check out for a protest) for months on end without a bail hearing, because at least I don't have to meet with her, a thought that frankly intimidates the shit out of me.

Dra Madalena Boavida is the new Finance Minister who was ensconced in this position after her predecessor, the independent politician Fernanda Borges, was sacked. Dra Boavida is a dedicated apprentice to her mentor Dr Alkatiri and to this end makes every moment of her time available to receive his wisdom — breakfast meetings, beachside tutorials, dancing at the Poy Cholor disco — merely to hear his insight into matters of gravity, receiving him at her house each night after he has dismissed his bodyguards, jumped into a little blue car and driven himself around there to continue tutoring her on the affairs of state.

The portfolio of Tourism has at the helm the loquacious and affable Dr Joe Teixeira as Secretary of State, a role too junior for his abilities, and to that end he needs to be promoted to the position of Minister of Ambition straight away. Dr Joe is on a campaign of self-elevation, but it's not that he is malicious, he's merely insecure, which is why he makes sure I am aware of all of his numerous credentials before I'm allowed to leave. Thankfully he happily speaks English with me, ingratiating himself with his claims that the imposition of the Portuguese language in Timor is ridiculous and problematic, and he points out that he was educated in law in Australia (reinforced a couple of times), and reckons that his contacts within the Australian body politic are blue ribbon, really they are, all of which shows an adept and adaptable political nous responsive to the context. To this end he is currently a new comrade within Dr Alkatiri's Old Fretilin faction.

Dr Gregorio José da Conceicao Ferreira de Sousa deserves his position of respect as Secretary of State for the Council of Ministers for having what must be the longest name in a country that provides a competitive field, although he might be a little more constructive in the public forum if he weren't the extremely quiet type. Still he's a party member and that says it all.

During my sojourn around I'm impressed at the remarkable prevalence of PhDs in the government, indicated by their prefixed Dr (masculine) and Dra (feminine). Well, to be clear, I'm impressed at the gall because it's not what it seems. Following the Portuguese example, anyone with an undergraduate degree here can call him or herself a doctor. That's demoralising enough for all those PhD students around the world working diligently to contribute to their chosen disciplines, but even bolder are all those ministers and secretaries of state who have no degree at all and do it because it is a symbol of the elite. Certainly, it's a creativity that means the Timorese Council of Ministers looks to be one of the most educated in the world, which is remarkable given where we are. But those Drs and Dras don't fool me, and if the UN is referred to as The Smurfs, as it is, then the government, such as it is, should be called the Banana Splits.

Anyway, it's a status quo that is likely to remain until the elite Portophiles forfeit their rule. Age alone will interfere, as most of them have already cheated the average life span in Timor, which currently stands at less than 45 years (another advantage of elitism and one of the few ways to get politicians to canvass the youth vote).

In the meantime, I need to get the Banana Splits talking to the media and the public. The ministers have listened with interest as I spoke of a media unit they could harness, and they have agreed to send their staff to a workshop which will use the expertise of a US consultant who is on her way to town. Individual media training will also be given to any ministers who make themselves available.

I'll admit that I was worried by the repeated requests to train them in how to 'manipulate' the media, but it's a starting point and I'm sure I can capacity-build them out of that rather undemocratic desire while I wait for the PM to meet with me and green-light a permanent unit with resources like desks, a Timorese counterpart, information accumulated via email from ministries for regular media releases, a telephone for liaising with the media, and a room with a patriotic and evocative flag backdrop for scheduled media conferences each week, which will all contribute to getting the Banana Splits into the lounge rooms of the nation, the protestors off the streets and the journalists off the staircase.

It's been an eye-opening and jaw-dropping exercise I'm thinking, as I head out to the house of the independent Foreign Affairs Minister, a committed and capable politician comparable with any international leader, especially Bill Clinton. Thus, Ramos-Horta's ministry suits him perfectly. And so, at the end of a day of prolific productivity in international relations, he's hosting a dinner for Ann and Wayne, to hear their experiences as investors and advise them on their problems.

'Hello Miss. How is the Midget Cop?'

'Fine, thank you, José. And you? How are you?'

'I am well. And how is his wife? Ann, you know about this wonderful love affair Lynne is having with a Midget Cop?'

'Oh, that, yes . . .'

'Ann, why don't you show José your glossy colour brochures?'

Luckily the scuba-diving company is a topic of mutual interest. It's not strictly his portfolio but the Minister loves his country and he has taken advantage of his travels to tell the world that this place is perfect for any holiday-makers looking for a new and exotic tropical destination. Obviously Ann shares in the hope that this can be a powerful contributor to the economy — Timor's and hers. Only the Timor Gap profits, they reckon, are likely to eclipse the allure of the beaches, palm trees and sunsets in this tropical idyll, and with missionary fervour she tells him about the other bounty beneath the sea.

Just off the coastline is one of the most beautiful underwater paradises in the world. A deep channel runs alongside Timor, so deep that US submarines are rumoured to travel up and down undetected by anyone but the whales that swim beside them. This underwater chasm is particularly appealing to scuba divers because it creates cool, recirculating waters that sustain healthy and lush flora which, in turn, entices lots of fauna, like the rare and spectacular whale shark. Even better, it means that divers can enter all this natural splendour from the beach, they don't even need to use a boat to get to the best spot, they just clamber to the edge of the abyss and dive in.

These rare and wondrous advantages make diving, therefore, an enticement to tourists, and the Minister listens to Ann's description of the joy of the deep blue, saying he'll think about her offer to take him and Xanana down there and that he is impressed at her enthusiasm for the company she runs with Wayne. 'Where is your husband?' José asks.

'Um, well, he's, um, out with a dive group but he, er, should be here at any moment.' She picks up her mobile and dials. It's not really worth the bother because she and I know that he is barely comprehensible at the best of times and right now he's undoubtedly at the pub, pissed, singing a song and unlikely to make it at all. What more could he contribute, anyway? I gleam from Ann's promotional pitch that scuba diving is a compelling pastime and that it will in all likelihood bring throngs of moneyed holidaymakers. I'm not convinced, however, and my cynicism has nothing to do with a fear of sharks. I just wonder if tourism in general is a realistic budget projection right now. As a rule of thumb, status as a peacekeeping mission should preclude any thoughts of that dream getaway. If soldiers bearing very large guns need to be stationed around a nation, it's fair to say that a place isn't a package deal delight.

Honeymooners should probably be deterred by the general disapproval of couples showing affection in public, and walking along the beach in the dark could result in theft or violent injury, especially if they're white. For families, I doubt that malaria would be a great addition to your child's holiday experience. Backpackers could probably find a number of other Third World nations to travel in without requiring a budget equal to the cost of a cruise on the *QEII*. Women would be best advised to pick an island on which they can wear the clothes of their choice and walk in the streets without lascivious attention. Then José interrupts my thoughts when he says, 'I want Timor to be a five-star destination, not for just anyone to come here, very classy.'

Beep, beep. Beep, beep. **1 new message. The big house at Dulce's is free. Call her.** It's José. I don't even want to think of the repayment terms. He knows that I'm looking for a house to rent and, once again, he has ministered to my needs. José's grapevine has far more cachet than Rita's. Now I'm reminded that there are three standards of living in Timor — that of the the Timorese population, the malae and the Timorese elites (in no particular order).

Next, to augment the point, I'm told by a consultant to the President's Office that Xanana has a house to rent in His compound, too. 'He wants someone trustworthy in there.

Really trustworthy because, you know, He's living next door now. You'd be neighbours with Kirsty. They'd been living in the house-for-rent while their own was being built, so it's got all the facilities you could want. You should move in there. Seriously.'

Now, this is an interesting choice. Forget facilities. Who of these two politicians should I align myself with — Xanana or Ramos-Horta? Which of these is the more powerful? What could be the benefit of each, in addition to the roof over my head and the trappings of a luxurious life? Surely this is a situation I could take strategic advantage of in order to assist me in a competitive workplace environment? On second thoughts, I work for the Prime Minister and he likes neither, so I need to decide: which of them does Dr Alkatiri dislike the least? Foreign Affairs Minister — President, Foreign Affairs Minister — President, Foreign Affairs Minister — President . . .

As I contemplate the ramifications of my choice, I head over to Dulce's to take a look at the 'big' house in the front of her compound which had, until recently, been rented out by six tenants. This is the same compound I lived in at the time of my arrival. Then I was sharing the family house out the back and the Minister was in residence, before he moved out to his manor house near the beach with the ant-eaten thatched roof. So there is a sense of familiarity when I arrive and it's as though I have come home. Dulce shows me through the door, putting her arm around me as she does so and saying, 'You know, Lynne, you are welcome. This is your home. You are like family to us, ye-es!'

Suddenly, political allegiances, professional gain and luxury facilities have no part to play in my decision. I want my house to be exactly what I have yearned for all this time: a home. I don't need a colour-coordinated Internet-connected refrigerator; I need a home with contentment and friendship, giggling children kissing me on each cheek, freedom from perverts, stalkers and obsessed police officers, and *hot-water* showers are a nice optional extra! And it's all for the very same amount of money that I've been paying for my tiny room and cold-water shared bathroom in the house-cum-entrepreneur's-supa-centa out in Comoro. It's a win–win situation when one can live within the bosom of a family and also, coincidentally, in a lifestyle to which the Timorese elite is accustomed. I always was interested in assimilating.

The 'big' house is that indeed, it is enormous. It has a sunroom with French doors out the front, a large lounge room with an imitation-leather couch, big-screen television, four bedrooms (two with *en suites*), a laundry area leading to a separate bathroom, a huge eat-in kitchen with a shrine in the corner, a 2-metre tall refrigerator (in a quaint white), tiled floors, large veranda, all of the house furnished with items such as wardrobes and double beds, and there's air-conditioning, a powerful generator capable of supporting the entire compound, a location across from Obrigado Barracks (making it easy to find) and there's the maid; it's Elsie, the very same maid, with her very same children, the very same ones who danced with me on the back veranda all those months before. Yes, I'm home.

That evening, I leave work to be picked up by The Missus — 'Ma'am,' he says — in his white UN Land Rover. The Missus has been a willing companion during all the nights I've needed to escape Ann and Wayne's, and a bond has been formed over oil-soaked codfish in any number of Portuguese establishments. On this day he drives along the oceanfront towards the Christo Rei. It's a well-worn path up the mount and we've hit the peak hour for all those trying to remove the evidence of too many nights of beer and chardonnay that are lodging firmly around their stomachs. I actually prefer the more sedentary pursuits, but I've been lured up here today by my friend who can't go any faster than a limping half-hop gait because he fell into one of those fetid-looking drainage ditches beside the roads.

'Guess what!'

'What's that?'

'The house is fantastic, it is huge and clean and it has malae comforts like *hot water*! There are two bedrooms with *en suites*, can you believe it? *En suites!*' I'm nodding in a manner that conveys the profundity of the moment. The Missus understands, he's smiling and nodding too. 'I know which one I want. I think you will love the room at the back, it is perfect for you!'

The sky is performing for us with a brilliant show of pinks to our left as we reach the beginning of the steep climb up. The Missus can't get up the steps to Christo Rei, which is fine by me, so we head back to Arieia Branca where we've parked the car. The temperature is cooler now and it is a gentle walk cocooned by a darkening sky.

Along the mountains the bushfires burn, always deliberately lit in the dry season, and we try to calculate how many shacks will burn down tonight. One blaze is hovering near the crest above the Caz Bar, as we head over the road and onto the beach where we sit down in the sand to catch the climax of the day. The subtle surf tickles the shoreline in front of us. All is peaceful. We have to leave soon. We can't be here at nightfall, it's not safe, but we don't want to leave.

'So what do you think? Should we take it?' I ask quietly with a very satisfied smile on my face and The Missus looks at me and opens his mouth to reply.

Before he's able to utter a word there is a crashing interruption: 'Fuck off! Ha ha ha ha!' We look over to the left to see that Mother Nature's magnificent show is not for us alone. No, there are three others just over there, drinking beer, lounging about in the sand, laughing uproariously. It does break the serenity somewhat but that's not the real problem because it's at this point one of them spots us and approaches, 'Hey, hey! Can you give us a lift back into town?' asks Ann.

'Sure, of course.'

'Meet my new friends, well, customers, actually.' She motions for her high-spirited playmates to join our group and, with an unsteady flourish, announces, 'These two are backpackers. Backpackers in Timor!' José's high hopes for the tourism industry seems dashed.

'How are you?' I throw at the backpackers who have chosen to include a peacekeeping mission on their itinerary Down Under. 'Um, what exactly do you mean when you say "customers", Ann?'

'Great news! Meet the very first customers to the Free Flow Backpacker Lodge!' She hoots at her obvious business flair. And, you know, I really have to appree-SEA-ate moments like this, moments when the crossroads in life come very clearly signposted.

38

VERB: TO DILI-DALLY

My toilet is porcelain and it flushes and it is mine. No other bottom is allowed to get anywhere near my shiny circle of hygiene. It gives me so much joy, in fact, that I will boldly suggest that I've never loved any object in my life as much as I love this toilet. But it was a close call, given the hot-water heater attached to my wall to stage right of the loo, which is second in my affections.

It's an exclusive retreat, my bathroom. Access is '*proibidu* = forbidden' for every organism but me. No boofheads. No perverts. The absence of open drains even means there are no cockroaches.

I wander out into my new bedroom on this evening, drying myself with a sarong, moving to a tallboy and wardrobe filled with clothes; I stand in homage and dress. I've kicked the suitcases away and I'm intent on living a civilised life from now on. Sure, this house isn't ostentatious, it isn't of Australian standard, but it is everything I could want here, a perfect balance of lifestyle and cultural appropriateness. And my room is private, pretty, clean and cool. But it's not quite finished . . . it's time to perform the most important duty of the day . . .

From the last box, I unpack the possessions that really outrank the toilet and hot-water shower for me, no matter where I am: the framed photos of my family and friends. I place them on the bedside cabinets, this side and that, and I look at them for a while, sitting on the edge of my double bed. There's my mum and dad, who've supported me even when it's hurt them; my nana and pop, who couldn't understand me leaving the First World for the Third; my brother, Brett, who didn't share my interest in East Timor; and there are my friends who think it's an eccentric adventure, captured in joyous scenes of us on my last night in Sydney when, in retrospect, I should have had a look of abject fear in my eyes. They are lovely images of a lucky life.

Still, there's no reason for melancholy because, finally, I am building a parallel life here. There has even been talk recently that Viktor's riot police will be returning to Timor. I've heard that the PM wants them back because he thinks them the most able to suppress dissent in this country. Sure, it is an alarming approach for a leader of a democratic government but I'm happy to place principle aside if it means Viktor will be back here, driving that car to me in my new home. So, it's with a spring in my step that I head out my door to see The Missus loading the fridge, 'Ma'am, it's a war zone, you know,' he says, as he places sun-dried tomatoes, olives and a selection of delicatessen meats on the shelves, while Dulce and Elsie peek in at the transformation occurring in each room.

'Bonoite!'

'Bonoite Lynne. We can look?'

'Please, look.'

'Ay! Very nice,' Dulce says, as she leans through my doorway.

Leaning over her, 'Nice,' says the Tetum-speaking Elsie and she laughs at her English.

'Kapas,' I repeat in her language.

'Kapas,' we all agree then burst out laughing, until Dulce looks at me and points.

'What?' I ask. Oh, no. I realise I'm in a tiny top. 'It's just that I'm inside the house and I thought it'd be okay.'

Smiling, she turns to Elsie and translates, pointing at my shoulders and telling the story of José's words all that time ago, merely days after the joyous photos were taken in Sydney's Chinatown. I'm mortified. Elsie nods and smiles too.

'You remember that?'

'Ye-es!' Dulce says. 'José say you not wear this.' She points at my shoulders again and I really wish she wouldn't.

'I know, I'm sorry. I have clothes that cover them up. I usually wear them, honest. I'll go change . . .'

'No-o! Lynne, you know sometime, José he is . . .'

'Cranky?'

'Ye-es, he is . . .'

'Conservative?'

'Ye-es!' and she laughs loudly. Thankfully she stops, I could go on all night with this exchange.

'Are you saying I can show my shoulders?'

'Ye-es Lynne, you are malae, you look nice.'

'Kapas,' says Elsie.

Right. I should have known better than to take fashion tips from a man who wore bow ties for decades.

Dulce is luckily from the more liberal younger generation, I'm thinking, as Marilyn flounces by, sensitive areas of her voluptuous body barely covered by a towel. 'Are you going out tonight?' I ask, as I follow her into her room, which is bedlam. Boxes, clothes, lingerie, electronic equipment, the detritus of her three years in the country, appear to have exploded over this space. It's no surprise to me. The Dili Queen was a controversial addition to our household because of her sheer largesse. Still, she needed to move out of her previous place after the word 'Fuck' was engraved in the duco of her scooter by a member of her landlord's family.

'Oh, course I am, honey. I'm going out with that gorgeous Portuguese soldier, the one I met the other night.'

'In such romantic circumstances.'

'Oh, come on. A woman these days has to be proactive. There's nothing wrong with going up to a spunky man and telling him that you want a fuck.' She does her hair and it falls in a whimsical, loose arrangement.

'Call me kooky but I actually like to be assured of greater compatibility. Can this man even speak English?'

'He can obviously understand it and that's all that's important. How do I look?'

She looks magnificent as always. She's all woman, of that there can never be any doubt. 'I'll daringly predict that you'll make his night and he'll tell you that you are beautiful.' She giggles with a high pitch, just like a girl. I find the *ingénue* in her incongruous with the heaving breast and sex-kitten affectations. I guess it all adds to the appeal. 'Where are you going?'

'City Café to start.' Ah, yes, there is no better way to augment a man's ego than to flounce, on his arm, into the busiest place in town where every single occupant will swivel and turn her way. Strategically brilliant opening gambit.

'So what was it about him that attracted you so much?'

She is applying lipstick now in a strangely provocative manner. 'He was leaning against a pole at the Purple Cow and looked gorgeous so I thought, "Wait a minute, cutie, you're all mine".' She smacks her lips together.

'And how did he react when you said, ahem . . .'

'Do you want a fuck?'

'Yes, when you said, "Do you want a fuck?"'

'He got me to repeat it.'

'Why wouldn't he? Although it could've been one of those language issues, I guess. Or comprehension issues, more likely; I doubt that many women in his country approach a man with a line like that.'

'Oh,' she shakes her head with disgust at such social ineptitude, 'I know. Madonnas.' She wiggles into a little ensemble.

'Indeed. So then what did he do?'

'Well, he opened his eyes really wide and I think he may have spat out his drink.'

'And you still found him gorgeous?'

'Of course, anyway, tonight I'll see if we're compatible . . . although really it's not that important,' says the queen bee.

A car arrives out the front in the dark. 'Look, he's on time, fancy that?'

'Oh goody!' She takes another long study of herself in the mirror, turning to examine her voluminous bottom and, approving of what she sees, goes out towards her Portuguese paramour.

'Hang on, what are you going to do about your room, you haven't even set up your bed?' A remarkable oversight for Marilyn, I'm presuming.

She looks over at Dulce and addresses her in Bahasa then turns back to me and says, 'Dulce will do it.'

'Um, Dulce's the landlord.'

'Whatever. She'd like to do it.'

In the lounge room now, The Missus has added his number to her audience which means he's just in time to hear her say, 'This house *so* needs to be christened,' as she flounces out the door.

Eventually I recover my composure, 'No wonder I'm single.'

'Yes, yes, yes,' says a clearly bemused Missus.

'She say to me she go with her boyfriend,' says Dulce. 'Namoradu.'

'Really? Did she?' Oh dear, Marilyn's behaviour at this early stage in our residency augurs badly. Mind you, Dulce has tolerated my shoulders, so she may even accept an overall drop in moral standards. Best not to test it on the first night, though. 'Oh, actually, I think he's more like a brother to her, she must have mistranslated. So then, Dulce, let me help you make up her boudoir, er, room.'

The Missus stifles a laugh and says, 'You're terrible, Muriel,' for me alone to hear.

39

TO EACH ACCORDING TO HIS NEEDS

It's 9.15 am which means The Chimney is onto her fifth cigarette of the day, creating a fog that's growing in its cumulonimbus-type consistency, I've been dropped from the day's diary, the bodyguards are up to lesson three in their English language textbooks and Jane is sitting patiently at the meeting table that's cutting off my circulation. A normal start to the working day.

Jane is a curious addition to the office, performing what I am coming to see as a sit-in. Most days she comes here and waits for a meeting because she has learned that the phone doesn't work, we don't have an IN tray, and meetings are rare privileges. Which all means that she has taken it upon herself to wait, determinedly, for a meeting that is required to save her UN capacity-building project.

I admire her tenacity. Her contract is ending soon and she wants to achieve the aim of setting up an independent electoral commission for Timor-Leste. She is one of those few humanitarians in town who works here because she wants to help the nation, not only her personal cash flow. Thus, she is sitting in this office, having placed her dignity aside once again to make it clear that she is available at any time for a meeting with the Prime Miniature, a man whose fondness for micro-managing requires him to sign off on a fantastic array of issues.

'Do you want a coffee, Jane?'

'No thank you, Lynne. I hope I'm not here for long.'

'Jane, I should pack you a thermos you're gonna be here so long.'

Jane wants the PM to sign off on the Timorese staff who were hired in an open and fair recruitment process and were trained during the elections held over the last few years in this country. These are the highest performing candidates, the ones who have shown the merit required to run free elections in the future, and as far as my understanding goes, elections are needed in a democracy. But the head of the Republica Democratica de Timor-Leste, Dr Alkatiri, won't go near that dotted line.

Watching Jane sitting silently at the table in front of me through the pungent smoke-filled air, I wonder if the PM's reluctance has anything to do with his place of sanctuary during the exile years. Like many of his Old Fretilin comrades, he fled to Mozambique where he was exposed to the pioneering political techniques applied in this other Portuguese colony, which had been left to its own devices in 1974, such as the introduction of a Marxist-Leninist single-party system combined with civil war. With the devastation of the countryside and economy complete, a cease-fire and multi-party system came along in the early 1990s and, from then on, politics in Mozambique was characterised by public exchanges of provocative accusations, culminating in allegations of a coup plot in 1995. Meanwhile, foreign nations bankrolled the whole game.

In '99, with Dili in ruins and discussions under way on who should head the Timorese transitional government, Mozambique's independent electoral commission was supervising an election for the very first time. So it's fair to say that, by the time of his touchdown at Dili airport, Dr Alkatiri had witnessed an idiosyncratic example of independence in a country that isn't known as a beacon for democracy.

Democracy, however, is precisely what the world was paying for in Timor, so the UN decided that the party of the resistance, Fretilin, was the most popular choice to represent the people, and therefore the leader of the party, Dr Alkatiri, found himself spirited up to the job of leading the government, administration, nation . . . even if it would require him to manifest a seismic attitudinal change because Fretilin was a pro-Marxist party. Whatever the reason, I'm concerned that Jane might sew her lips together or embark on a hunger strike in the middle of the office before the PM sees her.

Ring, ring. My phone. 'Hello.' It's the Australian Embassy. Once again they've heard on the frightfully efficient grapevine, the most effective public facility in Timor, that the PM is planning to drop into Australia and they need to be officially notified as a matter of protocol. 'Really? Again? I'd be the last to know but let me see what I can find out.'

'Rita . . .' Out of the corner of my eye I watch as The Chimney is called by Dr Alkatiri and she stubs out her cigarette with annoyance; I wished she'd exercise some sensitivity because there is an increasing number of individuals in this room waiting for just such an audience. 'Rita, is the . . .' and The Chimney resumes her position to my right, picks up her packet of fags, leans back in her tailor-made pantsuit with short-sleeved jacket (today's is white), then regales the room with the news in Tetum that the Prime Miniature asked her, again, if anybody's smoking in the office and she'd replied to him, as always, no, nobody's smoking in the office. Smiling, she gives a deep chesty cough and lights up again.

'Rita, is the Prime Minister going to Australia?'

'No, Leeen!' Her eyes roll.

I try another tack. 'Is he going via Australia to get to anywhere else?'

'Yes, Leeen!' Those eyes are very demonstrative.

'Well, you have to tell the Australian Embassy so the people there can organise the security escort that is required for every prime minister.'

'Leeen, is not my job.' I'm starting to wonder what her job is.

Dr Alkatiri is travelling to New York to attend the ceremony that will admit East Timor into the UN and it's in that foreign location that Jane can see her solution lies — the PM might not meet with her here but her bosses over there at UN headquarters may have more luck. As she sets her sights on international intervention I duck out of the office, click-clack down the stairs, pass Maluco, hop into the Governu Tata and bounce to UNDP headquarters in Caicoli because maybe I can get the highest-level influence for my project too. Yes, maybe force is exactly what's required to get him to be democratic.

'Hello, Lynne.'

'Bondia, Dulce.'

'Diak ka lae?'

'Diak los, obrigada! Diak ka lae?'

'Diak, Lynne.'

That's the extent of any Tetum dialogue between us because it's always at this point that we burst out laughing and revert to English whenever I sally out the back. Children come to look at me, 'Bondia, Lynne,' they say shyly, and one of them, Dudu, Elsie's youngest, leans up against me and I pat her knotted hair and my hand comes to rest on skinny shoulders that reach my hip.

'Lynne, mai han,' says Elsie, as I stand in the dark kitchen with its black-stained ceiling, large black pot of bubbling bean-and-pork stew, furious heat from the burning wood stove, and rough concrete floor, while Baby, her eldest, sits on my back step and throws rice grains up into the air from palm-frond baskets into which they land expertly again, allowing her to pick out the black ones from the top.

'Lae, obrigada.' I take a plastic seat and reach for the Timorese newspaper, *Suara Timor Lorosae*, opening it out on the plastic tablecloth, trying to read the Tetum section until I figure I may as well make my life easier and turn to the page in English.

'Lynne, you know, this week we put in new kitchen for you.'

'Really? Why?'

'Like kitchen in Australia, for you.'

'No?'

'Ye-es!'

'That's fantastic!'

'Ye-es!' I move my chair around to Dulce's side of the table. She knows exactly where to sit to enjoy the little breeze created by a wind tunnel that flows between the servants' shacks.

'Wow, now I just need to meet with my friend the Prime Minister and life will be perfect,' I say, as I use the newspaper as a fan. Fuck, this corrugated iron concentrates heat.

'You meet him?'

'No, I haven't met with him. I'm starting to think I should take out a bet that I'll get to the end of my contract without having met with him.'

'Not good.'

Elsie pours me a glass of chilled water. 'It's a waste of UN money, that's what it is. The good people of Ireland are generously paying for me to achieve nothing at all. Alkatiri has to accept that the money was allocated because the project is important. He has to talk to the media and the people whether he likes it or not.'

'Mmm, you know, Lynne, the people still say: why he not talk with us? And he say he have, how you say, mandate for five year.'

'And during those five years he has to be accountable.'

'Ye-es! But, Lynne, the people say he is not this. So they very angry with him, ay!'

'I really thought the protests would have given him a scare. He saw the people angry, desperate, I was standing beside him, I know he saw it, and I can't believe he'd ignore that. Crazy. Bulak!' We laugh and I fan myself as Dulce's youngest son, Mastoy, comes up and leans against her and she strokes his arm with an easy intimacy. 'I'm starting to believe that Alkatiri and I are different beasts. I grew up in a democracy, I understand it in every part of my mind and heart. I'm starting to believe that if a person has never really been exposed to it then maybe it's quite a foreign and complex concept.'

Dulce shrugs. She grew up under the authoritarian Indonesian regime here and yet she understands democracy. So maybe it's the electorate's responsibility to enforce democracy because any dedicated Marxist will release the inner dictator when handed power? 'He say to the protestor, in newspaper, the people protesting be careful or they wake, mmm, sleeping lion.'

'Who's the sleeping lion?'

'He is!'

'Alkatiri?'

'Ye-es!'

'Oh, so he does give public statements occasionally, does he? Although, as his adviser to his media adviser, if I'd been asked, I'd have suggested that threatening the voters isn't a guaranteed way of winning re-election. Or perhaps it is.'

A car arrives in the driveway and I wipe the sweat that's running down my face and accumulating at my collar. There are always so many people coming and going at Dulce's house. 'Lynne, you remember my sister, Gina?'

Not at all. It's impossible for me to remember all the branches of a vast Timorese family tree. However, 'Yes, of course,' I say, 'bondia, Gina. Oh, parabens, Gina!' Like many women in Timor, Gina is pregnant and her belly roundly announces that yet another child will be born into this fecund country with its knee-trembling fertility rate. The proliferation of women sharing Gina's condition and the collection of children in every single house is startling. Now I know why I've been told to not drink the water. 'How wonderful, Gina! When is the baby due?'

'October,' she says, as she releases her two little girls, Shania and Jenny, into the comings and goings.

'I have a friend who has a baby due in October and her name's Gina too! She's in Australia.' Which is where one would choose to be pregnant if given the choice. Certainly I couldn't handle such a condition with this heat. 'Dulce, the reason I came out here was to ask if the children want to go to the beach, maybe at two o'clock?'

This is a ritual that has become a favourite of mine. A weekend excursion out to Arieia Branca with children who are not mine. I just borrow them for the afternoon every now and then and give them back as the sun goes down before they turn into vampires or whatever it is that drives parents mad.

At 2 pm I load up the Popemobile with the inflatable beach toys I've accumulated in the new shops around town; there's a bright red lilo, an enormous white supertube and, the favourite of all the children, especially Mastoy, a big killer whale they can ride. The children come running up to me, 'Ikan bot!' they yell.

'Saida?' What on earth are they yelling about?

'Ikan bot!'

I think about it for a minute and laugh, 'Oh, ikan bot!' There's obviously no translation for killer whale in Tetum, so they're calling it the big fish. Simple yet effective.

With that established, everybody jumps in the car, the ikan bot taking pride of place with its head out a window. I count every head — eleven — and pull out of the driveway, heading down past Obrigado Barracks, over two sets of speed humps not unlike walls, past the new Balinese-style Tropical Bakery, then the shops, to the waterfront where we turn right at an ambling pig and drive east to the beach, hooray we all say!

The last sharp bend is negotiated and Arieia Branca opens out before us. Chatter reaches fever pitch and the car turns right into the Caz Bar carpark where we squeeze into a spot among the many cars representing a notable collection of international organisations that are here to save Timor (from Monday to Friday; otherwise they're at the beach) and unload the human and plastic cargo.

Crossing the road, we come upon the familiar sight of Timorese men lined up along the stone wall edging the sand watching the white-skinned girls in their bikinis. I lead our happy troupe past the appreciative Timorian audience, then the Brazilians in a dilapidated pavilion, and to a favourite tree that provides some cover from the sight lines of the onlookers. I sit on a sarong in the shade while the children throw off their clothes and run to the water's edge in a manner that transcends economy and race — the happiness of children is something that's universal, and even the First World can't harness it all for itself because it only requires the simplest of conditions; children will laugh even when they are poor — just so long as they have an ocean . . . and an ikan bot that's bigger than any of them.

'Hello Asim!' My big Bosnian friend lies down beside me.

'Hello Lynne.' One of the joys of a mission is meeting

people from around the world and the Slavs are an inspiration to me. All of them, Asim and his friends, have scars attesting to the wars in their countries, legs damaged by shot, shrapnel wounds on arms, a bullet mark in a head. All of them survived terrible things and yet they are here to help another nation, financially support entire villages back home, and enjoy their lives. These big men have suffered such horror that now they grab every moment of joy. Their pasts are filled with nationalist hatred but now they prefer friendship, especially in the karaoke bar in the early hours of the morning, arm in arm, Muslims, Serbs, Croats all singing 'We Are the World' or rather, 'Ve Are the Vorld'.

'Hey fellas,' I asked them once during a rowdy meal on the oceanfront, 'have you ever thought about the futility of war?'

They fell silent. After a moment, a hulk of an individual looked at me, put an arm around the colossus to his left, and said, 'This man, he is my brother, my colleague, my best friend.' It moved me immeasurably. 'But if ve vere in our country I vould shoot him.' And the table erupted in back-slapping laughter. Muslim, Serb, Croat, all of them agreed.

'Hey, Asim,' I say now, 'can you look after my things while I go in for a swim with the children?' I've been robbed at the beach before and I suspect that nobody will dare come near my possessions with him in proximity.

'Of course.'

I am grateful that it is a high tide, as I walk through a group of Portuguese peacekeepers playing soccer and they stop to watch me. Only a couple more metres to go on this terribly self-conscious journey during which I intuitively reach down to the bow on the left side of my bikini pants to find that it is unravelling. Jesus Christ! Grabbing the pieces of tie as they start to separate with a motor coordination I'll never take for granted again, I speed to the water completely aware of the momentous save I've made. There is simply no more dreadful an event that could occur here than my knickers dropping off while my butt's facing that human auditorium.

I drop into the water, catch my breath and cool my face before breaststroking to the boisterous children. They are never very far out, preferring to stay in the shallows where they can touch the bottom — swimming lessons are an indulgence of wealthy countries (together with string bikinis). They see me approaching, 'Lynne!' they squeal and cling to me. I might just drown under the weight of eleven children. Having extricated myself, Corrie takes my shoulders and tenderly pulls me horizontal. I float easily as she stands behind me, playing with my blonde hair, splaying it out in the water so it brightly ripples. 'Bonita,' she says, beautiful. I close my eyes, enjoying the fingertips through my hair, and the soft waves that undulate my body, listening to the chatter of the children in Tetum, Mastoy singing a ditty.

Making my way through the water, I walk quickly once I reach the beach (holding onto the knots in vice-like grips) to my place in the sand and I bend over (the Brazilians cheer) to grab my sarong, wrapping it tightly around me. Asim is asleep in the sand, turning pink, so I go over the road, ignoring Mister Whippy, which has hygiene issues I don't want to test in this place, passing the shuttle bus that the Portuguese military operates to takes its peacekeepers out to the beach, and entering the Caz Bar where I buy some chilled coconuts for Asim and me and some First World sustenance for the children. Back at the beach little Dudu runs over to meet me. 'Here,' I hand her two big bags of chips. She sticks her tiny arms down into each, grabs handfuls of loot and runs off to the water where she distributes it, then she returns and performs the very same chore; and again and again. I can tell she is the maid's daughter, she is already perfecting her humility, and I smile as she runs away with cans of softdrink too, pretty in the little bathers The Missus brought back from his last trip to Bali, pink with blue flowers. At least she isn't wearing the dirty shorts and T-shirt she normally swims in; she looks almost like a member of the elite except that she is distributing goods to the children who outrank her: Dulce's children, then her older sisters.

Settling down on a mat, flicking away fireants, I check on Shania who is playing on the waterline, picking at the sand, looking for pippies or crabs. Dudu is with her now, supervising even though she is only one foot taller. It's a beautiful scene and I watch it for a long time until eventually I open my book, Candace Bushnell's *Sex and the City*, which seems strangely appropriate in a mission (research I'll call it), and soon Asim rouses beside me.

'Always I am sweating in this country,' he says and his bulk is glistening as he props himself up on an elbow, blinking at the sun. 'Look at me, I am like your whale,' he indicates with his chin out to sea and laughs. 'I go for swim now, see if you can tell a difference, two of us in there,' and he heaves himself to standing, leaving an indentation of his shape in the sand.

This peaceful giant makes his way into the water, which is filled with people of all nationalities who are half the size of him (I expect the sea level will rise by approximately a foot when he sinks in), Latino pop music pumps from the Caz Bar and the Portuguese peacekeepers play their soccer between us, and that's when the screams begin, '*Lynne! Lynne!*'

The children are screaming. I only took my eyes off them for a minute, honestly. Oh God. Where are they? I run with every piece of my strength towards the water with not a thought about an untrustworthy bikini, discarding the sarong as I go. Where are they in amongst all these hundreds of people? Swimmers are standing now, looking in the direction of the screams, '*Lynne!*' Bloodcurdling screams. I can't see Shania. Where's Dudu? They were here just a moment ago, two girls playing in the sand.

I run over little footprints that walk straight into the water. In front of me is Asim, he's craning his neck, he takes off to my left and I see a Portuguese peacekeeper launch himself in the same direction into the sea as I splash deeper and deeper up to my hips then I dive, following them with my fastest freestyle.

Oh God, not the children, and I stroke with force, legs kicking, past Asim who stops when he sees me powering by and, peeking over the water level without adjusting my momentum, I see Baby as far out as she can stand and she's screaming, '*Lynne!*' her hand pointing outwards, into the deep. Where are the others? Oh, please, they can't swim.

I'm swimming with all my might when finally I see the focus of the anguish; I spot in the distance the cause of the screams: an inflatable toy that's floating away. Relief washes over me but it's quickly replaced by a patriotic competitive urge. The Portuguese peacekeeper is sprinting towards the killer whale and I'm right behind him now, stroke, stroke, stroke, breathe, stroke, stroke, stroke, breathe, and as we approach the ikan bot I pass him and lunge for it and I grab it, yes! And, as I do, I hear the children, the people on the beach, the Australians in the water all burst into jubilation!

Now out a long way from where we began, with the sounds of celebration in the distance, I turn to look at the peacekeeper, 'Thank you,' I say, holding onto the ikan bot's head. He is exhausted, I fear he will drown, so I pass him the inflatable whale, 'Here, have this,' and he takes it without a word, gulping air, which leaves me to swim easily and triumphantly back to the beach and it's there that I'm mobbed by eleven — count them, thank God, yes, eleven — ecstatic Timorese children.

40

ONE MUST IMAGINE SISYPHUS HAPPY

'Hello Missus,' I say, rubbing my eyes and dragging my bethonged feet.

'Mornin'. Coffee?' He fills my favourite mug. 'Toast? Vegemite today, Ma'am?' He reaches for the Smurf-blue United Nations helmet that serves as our breadbasket. Jesus, is this man always spritely and accommodating? Indeed he is and I ain't complaining because I'm not, so I nod as I plonk down into a kitchen chair and place my head on the table, moving it only when I register the coffee that's been placed beside my hair.

Every day I awake to the sound of the coffee pot bubbling on the stove and it spurs me out of my Bedouin tent-type sleeping arrangement, to this table, to this steaming mug with the lady beetle on the side. The morning chopper, in line with routine, whump, whump, whumps overhead, and The Missus regales me with a Camus philosophy for today and Marilyn flounces by in a handtowel, as custom requires, slamming her bedroom door. The Missus and I look at each other, 'Any idea?'

'None at all.'

'So what does Camus say about war zones?'

It's time for The Missus to ready himself for work at the Serious Crimes Unit so, while he's in his *en suite*, I take the opportunity to go out the front and write in the dust on the back window of his car: 'BITE ME.' I stand strategically in the way to obscure his view as he walks by and send him on his way with a salute goodbye. He drives off in the UN Land Rover, followed soon by me as I bounce my way towards work, down the road, singing a song to entertain myself in the absence of the looted radio, past the Tropical Bakery, I go, and it's right about here that I spot a sight that makes my heart skip a beat. It's a GNR car.

When Viktor and his contingent exited all those months ago they left their vehicles behind, which were promptly placed into storage, considered too valuable to end up like the Land Rovers and Tatas limping around Timor. Now, however, one of them is cruising the streets, I can see, as it turns in front of me and parks. I slow down, watching as I bounce by and the occupant dismounts. He is a tall, striking and, presumably, arrogant man in a uniform that is not Portuguese (what is that flag?) who believes that he can assume, by osmosis, the brave machismo that the car exudes. Fool. Look at him strut. He may have considerable height but I can't imagine that he'd be half the man of Viktor even if Viktor is literally half the man of him.

There had been talk that the GNR would return, but, alas, it was not to be. The UNPOL chief, a Canadian, opposed the move on the grounds of supposed cases of violence towards Timorese. So instead, some impostor has taken it upon himself to appropriate Viktor's car and that fraud has annoyed me significantly at a time when I'd really prefer to laugh in the face of my workplace trials. (I ignore Maluco as I stomp through the foyer.)

Sometimes it is hard to keep the spirits up, even with a hot shower, flushing toilet and wife at home. It's particularly hard when you're being treated like an idiot at work and all you want to do is help. I am here by my own volition and a broken heart is significant collateral damage as it is, let alone having to spend my time beating my head against that brick wall every day. Especially at a busy time. The media workshop is nigh with the international consultant flying in and the facilities waiting to be filled. I am nervously praying that someone, anyone, attends. Wedged behind my deskette now, I would breathe in deeply and count to ten but I'd be inhaling a thick cloud of smoke at 8.15 am, which seems rather unappealing even to me.

It wouldn't surprise me if the room at the workshop is completely empty. I dearly want the occasion to be a success because it could build support and commitment from the government in interacting with an independent media. Even more importantly, it could be instrumental, therefore, in making my work in Timor worthwhile. But short of forcing every ministry out at machete point (hang on, another resource I don't have), I can't see what more I can do to get them to the venue.

'Leeen, this workshop you do, I come too?'

'Rita, that would be so great, I'd like that!'

'And many kolega they say they come too. Okay?'

Quite a few of the saints in the building want to attend and, while I wonder at the usefulness of a random collection of the Prime Miniature's Shoe and Handbag Emporium clientele learning about the media (and getting the afternoon off from their jobs), I am happy to have a few participants to shroud the appearance of failure. 'They are welcome, please tell them they can come.'

The room is cavernous I notice, when I arrive in the afternoon and, even with the addition of the blessed sisterhood who wave at me, 'Botardi, Leeen!' I'm still concerned that the entire event will be a disaster. Pacing, darting looks at the entrance, then the doors swing open. In walks a José. Okay, one subscriber. A little while longer and another individual joins. I guess that's a start but glancing at the time I can see that it's just about scheduled to begin. I wonder if the flow of arrivals has stemmed, leaving me with a grand total of two genuine and impartial attendees who don't just want an arvo out of their offices (or maybe they do?). Hardly a winning result.

I'm not giving up yet, though, because I am actually praying for Timor time: the Timorian habit of being a leisurely half an hour or so late. Timor time is their firm belief that time is a fluid and flexible construct that depends mainly on their smoking habits. But even Timor time is running out ... dum dee dum dum ... I check my cuticles ... look up nervously, 'Hello Leeen,' the sisterhood waves again, clearly wondering if this thing is ever going to kick off, happy to gossip in the interim ... the international consultant is chatting to the American diplomat hosting her around town (she should avoid appetisers during her stay) near the podium at the front, and the delay seems to be escalating her already substantial level of impatience ... then, finally, the doors swing open again and there is an in-pouring of individuals with notebooks in hand, smelling of clove cigarettes. They keep on a'coming, too, until the venue is jam-packed to the rafters and I'm refraining from running around with my shirt pulled over my head like I'd just scored a goal.

Relief, smugness, elation remain jumbled up inside me when I give the closing address a couple of hours later. Standing there, I look at scholars representing every department, even the East Timorese Police Service, which bodes well for the future. At this moment I am enormously proud of them as they scribble notes because I see each and every one of them as representing the relationships that I have been trying so hard to build with the Timorese, my kolegas.

Today I'm click-clacking and swinging a handbag through the foyer, and I know this will be a very fine day. See, it's Maluco's day off, but more significantly, now that I have proven my bonafides and spread the gospel according to *moi*, I have no doubt that the Prime Miniature will have heard of my accomplishment which will cause him to green-light the media unit immediately and capitulate to every one of my requests for resources. In fact, I'm feeling so bold I think I'll even add stationery to the list instead of using the supply I brought from Australia, so I'm typing in: pens, staples, paperclips . . . go mad, Lynne, okay . . . notepad, I add. That's when Rita walks in. 'Good morning, Rita, darling,' I say.

Yes, I am spreading my joy, infecting those around me with my optimism. In fact, I'm in such a good mood I will happily shake the hand of every single individual who enters the room, a routine I normally loathe. See, most Timorese men who come here shake the hands of everyone in the room. And while I respect their culture, I am usually mortified when they follow it up by sitting at the meeting table in front of me and picking at their nostrils. Today, however, I am so buoyant that I intend to reach out to every individual who crosses the threshold and pump their hands with enthusiasm. God, I'll need to hold back from giving them all a kiss.

'Good morning, Leeen!'

'Bondia! Diak ka lae, Rita?'

'Diak. Diak ka lae, Leeen?'

'So absolutely diak, Rita, I can't begin to tell you.'

'Good! You know, Leeen, the Prime Minister, he say to me that he have no time today.'

'What?' Any motherfucker who comes near my hand today does so at his own peril. 'That's impossible!' Failure snatched from the jaws of success.

'Leeen, I sorry.'

'But he's going overseas soon, yeah?' The PM is about to leave for a lengthy trip. He spends most of his time out of the country, actually, and I'd hoped my project could be rubber-stamped before this latest departure to allow me to proceed in his absence. This is a disaster! It's important to capitalise on the momentum of the workshop. I mean, three ministers have now had one-on-one media training which indicates growing support within the Cabinet; still I need the support of the PM, a man who has ended up being as enigmatic as he suggested he was in my job interview.

'Leeen, is okay. Maybe tomorrow.'

'Yeah, everything in this country is "Finish, maybe tomorrow", even the Prime Minister's office.'

'Leeen, no problem.'

'It's a big bloody problem actually.'

'You, how you say, cranky?'

'Yes, we do say cranky. And no bloody surprise. Bloody godforsaken . . .'

'I say no problem because now you help me!'

How could I not? I conjure enthusiasm, 'Sure, possum, of course I will. I don't have any world leaders demanding my attention.' Beep, beep. Beep, beep. My phone. **1 new message.** Well, except for the usual communications from the Foreign Affairs Minister. **U miss me?** Doesn't he have any international treaties to sign onto today?

I reply, **If you'll excuse me, I'm a very important person and I'm very busy.**

Beep, beep. Beep, beep. **U have met PM?**

Who? I press SEND.

Rita hands me a letter to edit which is in English,

begrudgingly one can only assume. It is addressed to the UN and in it the PM slams the downsizing of the emergency services in Timor and insists on their immediate resumption. Oh dear, it's an angry letter, which needs more than grammatical assistance, it needs to mind its manners. It's the behaviour of a baby screaming at its mother when the breast is taken away.

Perhaps Dr Alkatiri is so accustomed to the international community subsidising Third World nations, such as Mozambique and East Timor, that he actually sees it as an obligation of the rich. I wish it was, but it's not, so the assistance that's provided here could go elsewhere. The West is more dedicated to exploring Mars than it is to ending poverty on this planet, that's the way it is. So let's have an honest think about it: a country of 800 000 people has received billions of dollars of help while many other nations with desperate need are left to fend alone.

The intention of the UN's contribution here was to administer, train, then wean Timor, giving it the ability to be a grown-up. With that achieved, the UN could then head off bravely to lend the very same assistance to the next devastated country in a world where there is always profound need. The government here doesn't want to cut the umbilical cord and share the love. But is dependency freedom?

I'm never going to get a Timorese counterpart, I'm thinking, as I look at this letter of demand. Clearly, the PM expects the UN to continue doing the work, which makes my job a little difficult to achieve and calls into question the mandate of the mission. It looks as though the UN's time in Timor will just have to be extended and extended . . . the government happy to be nursed, and the UN terrified of this nation descending into instability when it goes and besmirching the image of the Most Successful UN Mission, Like, Ever.

As dedicated as I may be, my time here is finite so I want to get this project up and running. Thus, I arrive at the UNDP headquarters in Caicoli, walk through the doors, flash the ID pass hanging from a lanyard around my neck and wander straight up to my project manager's desk. 'Hi, Terry.'

He looks up and I'm sure he stifles a groan. 'Hello, Lynne. What a nice surprise. What can I do for you today?'

'Can we talk in private?'

'Sure,' was that an impatient exhalation? 'Come this way,' and he leads me to the entry foyer with its noise and activity. 'It's the only place.'

'Why doesn't that surprise me?' A Timorese maid slowly mops the stairs and malae carry folders past us.

'Well, that's what you get when you work for a chaotic organisation in a chaotic place. What's up? It'd better not be a problem, I've had enough of them. You cannot imagine how fed up I am.'

Yeah, whatever. Speaking over the racket, 'I think I can imagine it perfectly well,' I say. 'But this is an emergency. The Prime Miniature, er, Minister is about to go overseas again and I'm still being bumped off his diary. He has to approve the media unit before he goes or I'll be wasting time until he gets back. I'm sure you don't want to misuse generous donor moneys like that.'

'Lynne, this is hardly the only problem we have in this place. Some Canadians have complained to their government about the failures here. Now that country and some others are demanding answers from us on how effective we're being.'

'How effective can we be if we don't have counterparts?'

'Hold on, before you get that far, six months into the mission and only six of you have been signed up.'

'What? So I'm a relative success story?'

'That's right, six out of 200 advisers have been hired. Only 194 to go.'

'That's a catastrophe.'

'Yes, it is. Particularly because this is the first time UNDP has had such a responsibility anywhere. They need it to be a roaring success, Lynne.'

'What's the delay in getting advisers on board?'

'The usual.'

'Bureaucracy.'

'And here's a great one — some Timorese ministers are putting their relatives up for the adviser positions.'

'Ah, nepotism, that old chestnut.'

'But do you get my point? Hiring a Timorese UN adviser invalidates the whole purpose. They are capacity-building positions. If a Timorese person is already capable of doing the job then we don't have to hire an adviser at all.'

'Oh yeah.'

'But they won't accept it. And . . .'

'There's more?'

'Some ministers are also demanding that the successful candidates get paid full P-position pay packets, not the UNV rate. How are we going to afford that? We're having to go to the countries funding this mission and ask them for ridiculous amounts of money to fund these positions.'

'Well, the UN does set a precedent with its huge wages. That's when greed enters humanitarianism.'

'Which is why some foreign candidates are being told by the government that they will only be hired if they pay a portion of the UN wage to the person recruiting them.'

'Bribery. Fascinating.'

'I know. The things that go on here. Boggles the mind.'

'Which is all the more reason why you should make sure that my project succeeds. At least I'm in position.' Here I am, a solution to their image problems. Someone who can go into the halls of power, of all places, and pull off a job well done. It'd be a public relations coup!

'For that to happen we'll need a miracle.'

Right. I get the feeling that I will be rolling rocks up a hill every day, day after day. 'I'll start praying immediately.'

Certainly, things aren't looking good. There must be something I can do. In the absence of a more concrete solution I project the message 'Get a life!' to Maluco who glares at me as I stomp past, at least he is a deserving target, and it does make me feel a little better. Then I arrive back at the office and walk straight into a mêlée. What's going on? Sorry?

How could I possibly have forgotten? It's delivery day at the Prime Miniature's Shoe and Handbag Emporium, an event that makes it all worthwhile!

'Oooh, I love them!'

'Rita, they come in black?'

'Can I try yours? Oh, so nice.'

'Kapas!'

It's like opening day of the Myer sales! There are boxes and excitement, chattering and products filling up the over-furnished, smoke-filled space. Shoes are delicately slid on to feet, handbags placed over shoulders, all of it to much acclaim!

The meeting table is filled now with women placing their orders for the next time around with a shrill glee. 'I want those ones!' says one woman in Tetum. A chorus lends its voice, 'I want red!' 'Size 36! Size 36! Rita!' 'How much for these?'

This puts paid to that rhetoric about town that neither the Prime Miniature's office nor me are functioning. We are. And I know that this is the perfect time to use my skills, which is why I send a message to José, **53 days till Christmas, get your order in now at the Prime Miniature's Shoe and Handbag Emporium.**

I'm bouncing down the road now, changing up through the gears, careful not to scuff my new stilettos, laughing at yet another typically absurd day, when up from behind comes an on-duty Portuguese military patrol, one of the open-backed trucks transporting peacekeepers in their camouflage uniforms who sit, guns in one hand, cigarettes in the other. It moves into the right lane, accelerates up beside me, its cargo enjoying a leisurely ogle, then drops back behind me.

I'm cursing as I look into the rear-view mirror filled with grinning faces when something else takes my notice. I adjust my focus, lean forward and closely observe a reversed image which seems to be showing me the outline of words that have been scrawled in capital letters in the dust on my back window.

Oh, no. I make a quick check of the road ahead for scrawny dogs and strolling goats then look back in the mirror, trying to read the back-to-front phrase, which pulls into stark focus now. Shit. The Portuguese peacekeepers on their chick patrol behind me are being told to: 'BITE MY UKRAINIAN BUTT'.

Right. It's war. I change down through the gears and turn off towards my house, knowing I have to drive past the busiest intersection in town, the one in front of the main UN base at Obrigado Barracks with this sign on my back window. Approaching the wall-like speed humps I don't slow down and instead I bang, bang my way over each (noticing, as I do, that it's actually easier on the suspension), pull into my driveway, stop with a little skid in the dirt thanks to the deft application of the handbrake, alight and stomp around to the back of my car, sticking my finger into the dust and adding an arrow between the words 'MY' and 'UKRAINIAN', and inserting a crucial word above it, 'TINY'.

There, I stand back and admire my handiwork: 'BITE MY TINY UKRAINIAN BUTT'. After all, if we're going to play this game we should at least be precise. So I turn on my heel and swan into the house, pledging to write 'GOAT APPRECIATION SOCIETY' on the back of The Missus's car the very first chance I get.

41

THE AWAKENING

I pad into the kitchen in the early morning, heading for the coffee and, as I do, the back door opens. It's Elsie, 'Bondia Lynne.'

'Bondia Elsie.'

There's nothing unusual within this scenario so far, it's all pretty routine. Every morning at around about this time I require caffeine and, hearing that I'm awake, Elsie comes in to begin sweeping the floors. I wish she didn't work such long hours. I've tried to institute fair workplace conditions but she continues to work for all the hours that I am awake. The only break in the pattern occurred yesterday when she didn't turn up at all. 'Diskulpa Lynne.'

Obviously, I accept her apology, I know there must have been a compelling reason and, hey, I owe her a lot of time in lieu. 'Lae problema,' I say, but she speaks very fast in Tetum at me and I'm having trouble following the words that are pouring out of her now with urgency, or is that distress? 'Hang on, hang on, slower, slower.' It's my turn to apologise now, 'Diskulpa Elsie. Hau la bele kompriende.' I don't understand what she's saying at all. It's a challenge being multilingual at this hour of the day.

Undeterred she continues. I catch Dulce's name. There's reference to an illness. Is someone sick? It appears to be serious but I can't keep up. Wait a minute, I haven't seen Dulce for a day or so either and I'm getting concerned now. 'What's going on? Dulce nebe?' Where on earth is Dulce?

'Dulce, something, something . . . ospital, something, something . . . tristi, something, something . . .' She's speaking at a million miles an hour.

I can only comprehend a word every now and then — a hospital is involved and it's sad and somehow Dulce is related to the story. 'Elsie, hau koalia ho Dulce.' I have to speak with Dulce, it's the only way.

Maybe my linguistic shortcomings are leading to misinterpretation? In my defence, studying the words relating to illness weren't a priority to me. Therefore, I can't pretend to know what on earth my last discussion was all about, so Elsie may or may not have gone to fetch Dulce who may or may not be nearby, ill or sad. I think it best not to assume the worst, and so I'm taking a draught of the coffee brewed by The Missus when the back door opens again. It's Dulce. Thank God. She looks perfectly healthy too. 'Bondia Dulce!' That's a relief.

'Lynne, bondia, you must do something for me.' She is upset.

'Dulce, what's wrong? Is everyone okay?'

'Gina's baby, he die.'

'What? Oh my God.' How terrible that she needed to learn the words for death in my language. 'I'm so sorry. Are you okay? And Gina?'

'Lynne, she sad, very sad. Lynne you speak with the Prime Minister, you tell him!'

'Tell him what? What happened?' Tears are welling in my eyes to mirror those in hers.

'The baby, he born and he have trouble, mmm, with his breathe and the doctor say he fine. No problem. Lynne, the hospital, we there, they have no nurse, the wall have blood,' she indicates up my kitchen wall which makes me flinch, 'the mattress no sheet, nothing, room have family in them, many, to nurse sick people, they are cooking and go to toilet and the smell. Ay! Lynne, you must tell the Prime Minister, the hospital, you must help!'

'Dulce, I am the last person able to speak to the Prime Minister.'

'But you are malae! You work with him. You must help!' She's beseeching me to help her.

'Of course, I will. Of course, Dulce, I will.'

'You will help?'

'Yes, I'll do whatever I can.' And to that end I'm planning to email her uncle, José, as soon as I get to the office, and I thank God that I have email access now because I am completely realistic that my nationality has no influence at all on the nation's leader, quite the contrary. 'Dulce, what happened?'

'The next day the baby he breathe difficult and we say to doctor that he do something. There is no facility . . .'

'Humidicrib?' I make a gesture that indicates a box then drop my hands away when I realise she might think I'm referring to a coffin.

'No! They take the baby. He is son,' their first son, a valuable child in a patriarchal society, 'and they come back and baby, they tell us, he have only one, mmm, lung.' She's overwrought, I'm having trouble understanding her and I'm trying to follow her words. Certainly, I can feel the pain she is in.

'Oh, Dulce, I'm so sorry. What did they do?'

'The doctor cannot do something. She and husband they can hold baby.'

'Until he died?'

'Yes, Lynne. He die.' I understood that point, her eyes alone communicated this part of the story, as they would. They tell the story of a woman who watched her sister holding her baby for hours on end until he inevitably died.

'Is Gina okay?'

'No! The walls with blood, mattress, we take some sheet, ay, smell.'

'Do they have any idea how the baby came to have the . . .' how do I say this? '. . . problem?'

'Maybe my sister she have some malaria some time but she did not know.'

'And there are no ultrasounds or medical tests during a pregnancy here to determine if a baby has problems developing in the womb?'

'No!'

'Nothing?'

'No, Lynne!' I realise that these are stupid, ridiculous questions arising from a life of opportunity but I don't know what else to say. How can I really understand lives like theirs, even if this is an elite family with many more opportunities than the average Timorese?

'Would you like me to come to the funeral?'

'Yes. You come?'

'Of course, nebe?'

'Santa Cruz.'

'Okay, I'll be there. What time?'

'Two.'

'Tuku rua, we'll be there. All of us in this house will be there, Dulce. Whatever you need we'll be happy to do for you and Gina.'

'You are good woman, Lynne.'

I'm shocked and deeply moved. 'God, thank you. It's the least I can do. Lae problema, Dulce.' We smile weakly and I hold her, this woman who comes up to my breast.

That afternoon I am sitting in the Prime Minister's office, having emailed José to tell him the terrible news, when my phone rings. 'Hello.'

'Mini!'

'G!' I move out onto the terrace, directly into a beautiful tropical scene and I'm struck by the insensitivity of nature's vanity. Here she lies, magnificently preening herself around me when she can't even sustain a newborn boy. Wresting my attention back to the task at hand, 'What are you doing? How is the little baby, moving around, kicking away?' I ask my pregnant friend in Sydney.

'Oh, it's incredible, I'm huge! But don't talk about me, you're the one in a peacekeeping mission! What are you doing over there?'

'Oh, nothing.' I am starkly aware that I am dressed in black and about to leave my work to go to a cemetery where a baby will be laid to rest, who lived for a day because he never stood a chance. 'Nothing really,' I say.

'Nothing? That can't be true. What's going on?'

What can I say? 'Sorry, I'm just, you know, working, nothing special, a bit busy, actually.'

'Oh, okay.'

Time to put on that sunny disposition. 'But hey, tell me about the baby! I'm never too busy to hear about the wee one. You must be getting nervous about the arrival!'

I can't tell her about her namesake, the Timorese Gina, who gave birth to a dying child, and I am immeasurably comforted to hear her talk of the obstetrician and the birthing centre and all the wonderful benefits of life in Australia, benefits that I will cherish forever because they will bring a healthy baby girl into the First World (we even know the sex!), and the Gina on the phone right now won't have to lie in a blood-stained room, on a mattress filled with body fluids, holding her baby while she dies. Disparate lives are brought into focus and while I am thankful for Medicare and wealth and medical services that give women respect and health and happiness, right now I'm also contemplating a mother and child denied all these things.

I'm terribly nervous about this funeral. I've been to these events in this country before, and they are noteworthy for the wailing that rents the air. This one is being held at the cemetery infamous around the world for the massacre of Timorese who were burying a compatriot killed by the Indonesian military, when they were fired upon and over 271 of them were murdered or disappeared. That massacre was witnessed by journalists, one of whom, Max Stahl, hid a videotape and managed to later distribute it around the world. It was evidence, finally, that atrocities were being perpetrated here. I've seen the footage many times and here I am, standing now at the gates, waiting for a funeral procession attended by people I've come to care about, and they will presumably be wailing in that terrible way — the poignancies combine.

I see a slow moving crowd in the distance, making its way down the street towards where I stand. As it moves closer I hold onto The Missus's arm to brace myself and I note the absence of wailing, thankfully, and as the procession approaches now I can't see Gina or Dulce.

The father of the child, Vincente, breaks away and he makes his way over to us, 'Thank you for coming,' he says.

'Of course. We're so sorry,' we reply and join the crowd, following him and them through the gates to a tiny plot among a random arrangement of handmade concrete headstones.

So many people whom I have come to know within the Timorese community say, 'Botardi Lynne,' and all of us watch as the sun descends in the sky and a priest recites his prayers of intercession, invoking God to protect the soul of this child that lived cocooned in his mother's embrace. The day is ending, spectacularly, in a tribute to a baby born to die.

Baskets are passed around, 'Lynne iha,' they tell me, and I take a tropical flower and approach the small hole in the ground. I throw a frangipani and it lands on the rough wooden box that is no more than one metre long and I make the sign of the cross, praying that the bud represents that he can exist for more than one mortal day, somehow.

Baskets pass again through the crowd. This time, as I balance between the scores of unordered concrete slabs, with a smell of decomposition filling my nose from a badly laid grave, I take a candle in my hand and, imitating the Timorese, go forward again and add mine to the line at the edge of the freshly dug site and light it too. Then, with the sky a vibrant red overhead, we make our way, silently, up the hill to Gina's house. She never did attend the burial of her child. She was lying sedated in her room, still is, Dulce beside her.

As directed, we help ourselves half-heartedly to buffet tables laid outside under the mango trees. 'Thank you for coming,' Vincente says again.

'Please Vincente, you should talk to your other guests.' There are so many of them who have come.

'You have enough food? You are comfortable? Please sit here,' he says in English.

It is an honour to have malae at a Timorese occasion, hence the attention, but I feel like a fraud. Because I am no better than them. I don't live their hardship. I've never had to experience the horrors they continue to endure despite their freedom. And I never will. My opportunity guarantees it. And as we sit here, the three of us white-skinned malae, poking without interest at our rice, side by side, we hear a wail.

42

CULTURAL INTOLERANCE

Marilyn is nude but for a towel. Moreover, as one does when clad in this way, she's enjoying a little stroll around the house. And it's during this latest of so many such promenades that she goes up to Asim for a chat, 'Hello, Asim, how are you tonight?' she purrs.

It's a purr that pierces the night-time air like a Scud missile, oh dear, and I can sense the clash of civilisations that is occurring right now, which is why I'm spurred down the tiled corridor and into the lounge room armed with the very best of my diplomatic skills to prevent an onset of hostilities. 'I'm ready, Asim,' I chirrup, as I try to move his massive bulk towards the door. 'Asim?' But it's rigid.

He was innocent! He was only waiting for me to choose my shoes from a substantial collection, that's all. Such a good man and this is what happens to him: a woman in an itsy-bitsy towel has proven that the bosom is mightier than the sword. My big Bosnian friend has lived through so much, this battle-scarred and hardened warrior has contended with terrible conflict, but right now he looks just like a mouse, a very large albino mouse because he's as white as a ghost. 'Asim?'

Thankfully, his dilated pupils narrow, his mouth closes, colour returns and six-foot-five worth of sangfroid is regained at precisely the same time as he barks, 'Let's go!' I'm swept out into the car in his wind-draft.

'She need to respect herself,' says my clearly disturbed Slav friend, motoring his UN police vehicle through the streets, 'vhat she think? I go veak at mine knees to see her in a towel? It's very sad, this voman. This is normal for Australian voman? You don't do this, I think?'

I think it my patriotic duty to defend my nationality, 'Um, actually, the handtowel is Australian national dress,' I proffer.

'It's bulak, I tell you, this act she put.' I love that he's using the Timorese word for crazy. In fact, I love that he and his compatriots make an effort to learn the local language, a detail that distinguishes them from most others. I guess it's because they know what it's like to have a UN mission in their country, a UN mission that waltzes into town with its National Balance of staff from around the world, ready to overhaul the place with its highly paid instruction of assorted levels of quality.

In the splintered former Yugoslavia it was particularly jarring because, sure, the place had been devastated by war but the capacity of the local workers was high. Pre-war they had been educated and professional bunches who were perfectly capable of running their own administration like the taxation department, media, roads and traffic authority, health system, schools, police forces . . . they'd just hated each other's guts. Now they are at peace and the tables have turned, which brings them here, far away from their no-man's-land and serving together under the flag of Bosnia-Herzegovina, in a place where they are seen as among the most skilled and tolerant of the national police forces represented under the banner of UNPOL. And they are skilled and tolerant, until confronted by cultural peculiarities such as breasts covered merely in a towel. 'Sometimes I don't understand some things,' says Asim.

I need to change the subject away from my compatriot's virtue(s), 'Yeah but you understand some Tetum, Asim, many Australian police officers don't even know how to say thank you in the language.'

'Of course I do this. It is respect. But my English is so bad.' English is the lingua franca of the UN here, despite the preference of the local government for Portuguese, and all staff need to have some proficiency in it so the many disparate peoples in the mission are at least able to communicate with each other, if not understand one another.

'No! Your English is great.'

'My English is not so good but vhen I come here I must learn more and my friends ve buy these VCD vith the karaoke and ve practise in our house.'

'You taught yourself English from music videos?'

'Karaoke. You sing vith it, the vords.'

'I know, I know, but that is amazing.'

'Vhat's amazing? Is the best vay.'

'What music? You have to tell me.'

'Vell, ve like to sing to Bee Gees.'

'All of you sat around singing aloud to the Bee Gees to learn English?'

'Sure.' And for my benefit, to dispel any incredulity I may have, he bursts into song, 'How deep is your love . . .' I think it's touching that ethnic division has been placed aside when Asim and his compatriots sit in their lounge room and sing, '. . . I really need to learn, 'cause ve're living in a vorld of fools, breaking us down, vhen they all should let us be . . .' He knows, more than most, how many fools there are in the vorld, '. . . ve belong to you and me, la da da dee da.' (I'm unsure about the linguistic value of the last bit.)

And so we motor down the road, dodging pigs, a Balkan Bee Gee singing a medley, with me marvelling at the insight I'm gaining into various cultures and the interaction between them.

Heading towards the scene of so many nights in the general assembly called the Purple Cow, the UN cars are parked for kilometres down the road as we approach and lined up along the fence are Timorians who surround us, 'Maria! Maria! Sekoority Maria,' 'Sekoority Mister.' 'Maria! Maria! Sekoority!' The children are desperate, jostling for front billing, pointing to their chests indicating that they want to earn US$1 for providing security for a UN police vehicle.

Some say it is a contravention of child-worker treaties to pay them, others are too tight to give them a dollar for anything at all, and me? Look, as useless as their service really is, I think it's better to pay them to perform a task, any task. It allows them to work for a living, it gives them pride in their accomplishments and it shows an alternative to begging and crime. Most Timorians live on US$1 a day, yet I'll spend four times that amount on just one glass of personality tonight. That's why I hand US$1 to a child whose prominent bones tell me he is starving and tell the little ones to '*ba toba* = go sleep', it wouldn't be good for them to be influenced by the bad behaviour here, and I'm referring to the cultural melting pot on the other side of the fence.

Which brings me to my favoured position near the dance floor. I'm drinking a warm glass of chardonnay soup, listening to music circa 1990 and watching the horde of weapons of mass erection and a smattering of Dili Princesses. And it's at this point that I notice someone who makes me double-take. It's a person I recognise — the man I saw driving Viktor's car. 'Who is that?' I elbow Asim.

He looks up and follows my gaze. 'He? He is Drasko. He is Bosnian Serb. He is friend of mine. You know him from somevhere?'

'No, not really. Just wondering, that's all.' Drasko. He's tall. Attractive. Arrogant. He surveys me and his stony eyes stare, confidently.

I look away to see the Drag Queen Strumpet is giving us a display, and it's with a sense of nostalgia that I watch her final cabaret performance. Yes, the Drag Queen Strumpet is ending her mission and, you know, I'll miss her. She has become a source of entertainment. Tonight she's wearing her hair flowing out in a thick black veil, stiletto heels like stilts that elevate her above the crowd, artfully applied make-up in substantial quantities, accentuating her every feature with melodrama, and she's squeezed into a little black number so tight it causes me to wince — it is a highly orchestrated look that really does enhance her beauty tonight in a characteristically flamboyant way.

What's going on? Have I been in the mission so long that I have adapted my idea of attractiveness, or am I recognising someone for what they really are — culturally specific? Sure, her outfits may not be seen on the catwalks of Paris or in the nightclubs of Darlinghurst (on second thoughts, that depends on the establishment), but she's not in those places, is she? She's a Portuguese woman headed back to Lisbon where, I imagine, she'll be one of many in technicolour jumpsuits. And, conversely, I imagine she thinks me rather plain.

Despite our differences, we — the Drag Queen Strumpet and I — have come to co-exist in a harmonious manner that tolerates diversity. It's a metaphor for the international context, I believe. And, let's be realistic, our differences were profound — fashion. So if *we* can come to appreciate our respective national idiosyncrasies then all the world's leaders can too.

There is a great deal of activity on the veranda. The electricity has cut out and the generator in my compound is out of order so everyone has emptied out ito the heat of the day. Children are playing elastics and eating packets of noodles (dry and uncooked as they do), while I sit on the veranda in the unrelenting humidity of the absent monsoon.

Ring, ring. My phone. 'Hello.'

'Lynne, something's happened,' says my mum. 'It's serious but I don't know how serious it is. It's Dad.' I move away from the sounds of laughter.

'Yours or mine?'

'It's Pop. He's had a heart attack.'

'Oh.'

'He's in hospital, it's, it's bad.'

'How are you?'

'Bad.'

'Where are you?'

'In Canberra.'

'Are you on your way down there?' My grandparents live three hours away from where my mother is now.

'No. Not yet.'

'Why?'

'Because I'm not. I'll wait.' Her voice is cracking on the other end of the phone and thanks to the distance I feel unable to comfort her.

'Wait for what?' I say softly.

'To hear some news. I don't know. I don't know.' She starts to cry.

'Okay, okay. What do you want to do, Mum? What would be the best thing for you?'

'I want to have never picked up the phone. I want the phone call to have never come through. I want my father to be all right.' She is sobbing. All inhibitions have left her as she sobs like a child.

'Hey, it's okay. Everything will be okay. He's a strong man, Mum.' I'm trying to be supportive, the roles are reversed, but my tears are falling too.

Still, he is a strong man. A man who endured Stalin then

Hitler, who spent years in refugee camps in Europe, who then sailed for a country called Australia with his wife and two small children, just them. Which makes this all the harder. See, refugees don't have large extended families, no uncles, aunts, grandparents and cousins like I've had. They only had each other.

I can only imagine the hardships my grandfather survived, leaving a homeland without choice, years of slavery, then making a new life in a foreign land with a different language. Yet he provided his family with comfort and gave me my obsession with the politics of a world like this. I wish the phone call had never come through too. I want it all to go away and for everything to remain as it was.

He's the reason I came here. Should he now be the reason I return? 'Do you want me to come home?' I ask.

'No, no. Don't do anything just yet.'

'Yeah, sure. I'm sure everything will be fine.'

At that moment, the town electricity comes back on and the children, the neighbours and the whole town of Dili cheers and I cover the phone so Mum can't hear it because she may have a continual supply of electricity but that's no cause for happiness right now.

43

STORM IN THE CITADEL

Bacon and eggs at the City Café is a tradition, as is the black hair garnish on my rockmelon juice which doesn't serve a delicate constitution well. The long black coffee, on the other hand, should see me right and in the interim I sit here with The Missus while old banana sellers ply their trade to us; they're not allowed inside the barricade so they stand on the outside looking in, 'Hudi Missus.' They move away with the local lope to be replaced by the fishmongers with their produce tied head-up and tail-down to a stick over a shoulder, 'Ikan Missus,' they ask, before moving along the uneven footpath with their decomposing catch of the day. The young and rather more assertive entrepreneurs with their pirate CDs walk up and down like cats trying to get into a gilded birdcage, 'CD Missus?' 'Jiggy jig Mister?' And the street children wash the UN cars, lifting up the windscreen wipers, standing on the bumper bars to reach the bonnets, running with bottles to and from a tap, jostling with each other to be the one who gets the US$1. Competition is fierce now that the mission is contracting and it's been exacerbated by the banning, for security reasons, of parking on this side of the street. My favourite tiny businessman is a boy who is cutting quite a swathe through his competitors with his big smile, good manners, multilingual skills and super-sized sponges. He'll even do the wheel arches and jump up on the roof to distinguish his as a quality service. Today he's painstakingly washing the back window of The Missus's UN Land Rover, particularly its message to 'HIT ME BABY ONE MORE TIME.'

This week's City Café breakfast has been convened with a sense of melancholy. Today there are only two of us here at this table, not the usual *ménage à trois*. Yes, it's with some sense of sadness that we rue the passing on of Marilyn. She conquered, she came, but now she's gone to accommodation more suited to her lifestyle, which means that I, for one, will miss heading out with her to AAJ's, the local karaoke bar, in the late hours of the morning to watch the crowd react as she flounces to the middle of the venue, takes the 5-inch microphone in her hand with a practised grip, and cooes 'Like a Virgin' to a spellbound crowd.

Looking to my right, I'm pleased to see The Missus wiping crumbs from his moustache, taking a sip of coffee number two and leaving a line of froth along the bottom of the ginger hair, which he removes with his bottom lip in characteristic fashion. Tradition, safety and companionship are important in this chaotic place. I'm glad I have all these things with him. We even have a pact detailing the protocols; it's called Article 36. According to Article 36, if we're single by the time I'm 36 then he and I will tie the knot. Clauses include that he shave off his moustache and I give up smoking. Obviously, Article 36 has been concocted over nights when we've lost the ability to speak English as a first language.

Why 36? Why not now? Well, that's because this article is subsumed by an article I'd instituted months earlier — the over-arching Article Zero, and this article outlaws any hanky panky in my life while I'm in this country, which would make

East Timor the biggest prophylactic in the world. One man, Viktor, was enough because now I have been here long enough to see that mission life is unlikely to facilitate many enduring sexual relationships. 'CD Missus?' 'Jiggy jig Mister?'

'How's your grandad?'

'Yeah, much better.'

'That's great.'

'Yeah, I'm sure he'll be fine. He's a strong man. I just wish I could be there. It's pretty hard. But, hey, I'm strong too. I've got some of his genes.'

'Then he'll get through it.' Yeah, I reckon taking sex out of the equation will lead to a relationship of a better kind — friendship.

I smile at his words and hold back the tears, 'Thank you. So, should we head off?'

'Fine idea.'

We leave and cross to a UN Land Rover on the other side of the road. I'm swamped, 'Maria! Maria!' by Timorese boys. Handing US$1 to my choice of service provider ('Thank you Missus Maria,' he says), I push my way into the front seat, careful not to close the door on any of the many reaching hands.

'God, they're getting desperate.' Their business plans obviously didn't factor in the volatile nature of the marketplace in Timor and, as the car starts, one of them punches the door, yelling, 'Maria no good!'

Following our traditional path, we proceed down to the waterfront, and turn left at the fish markets. 'Actually, you know, I'd like to go the un-scenic route today.'

'No, not Comoro Road? What's the attraction?'

'Obviously there's nothing attractive down there. I want to have a look at the Oz Embassy.'

'Ah, of course. Let's have a wave at our brave sons and daughters.'

'Brothers and sisters, thanks.'

I want to see what all the fuss is about. For days now the city has been under lockdown. Intelligence reports have suggested that Australian interests in East Timor are the targets of terrorists. As a result, we are not supposed to drive with our windows down in case a grenade is thrown in; we should also stay in at night and avoid large gatherings; shipping containers have been placed at either end of the road to Crocodile Alley, the main Dili military base; security checkpoints have been imposed in sensitive areas; cars are searched when they enter certain strategic locations; parking has been restricted in places vulnerable to attack; and sandbags surround the Australian Embassy, its residences, and the US Embassy as well.

I'd found out about it when my mum woke me up with a phone call, asking me to be careful. 'Why today more than any other day?' I'd asked, ignorantly. She'd heard media reports and I'd later emerged into a city of obstructions, guns, confusion and alarm.

It's enraged the Timorese leadership. The Banana Splits say that Australia is trying to ruin the nation's reputation as a safe tourist destination, and, look, I am sure countless jumbo jets have had to be diverted as a result. In addition, they say that international investors are being deterred by the idea of peacekeepers patrolling the streets of a peacekeeping mission, and, indeed, I'm sure the Dili Stock Exchange is taking a beating. But they also say that Australia has made no effort to brief them about the threats and the reaction, and, verily, I'd believe these comments that have made their way into the media here and in Australia if I didn't know them to be complete bullshit.

I have been fielding phone calls, not only from my mum but from the Australian Embassy, since that first day of fortification, during which requests were made for an urgent meeting between the Australian Ambassador and the Prime Miniature. I've taken each request as far as I can go, to the José who sits 5 metres away from me. Each time I have done so, he has put the request to the PM, and each time the response has come back to me that the request is denied. Dr Alkatiri is an important man, after all. Busy with all those matters that precede terrorism and international relations. Most recently, for example, Dr Alkatiri had to go home and ready himself for a function celebrating his political party, on a public holiday called Fretilin Day. For a PM who plays politics more than government, Fretilin Day was an event of greater importance than any security threat in his nation or a diplomatic breakdown with his closest benevolent neighbour.

The Australian Embassy ended up briefing the Minister for Internal Administration, Rogerio Lobato, I was told by a consular official, and that minister seems to have neglected to pass the information on, because the PM and his Banana Splits have come over all loquacious with the media (must have been the influence of my workshop, or perhaps Fretilin Day was a licensed event).

So while the Timorese leadership has been spinning their yarns and the media have been busily reporting them, I've been fine-tuning those receptionist skills. 'What about me?' I'd asked the Consul-General during one of his phone calls, 'Why don't I have a shipping container in front of my house? I'm an interesting Australian, honest.'

'Is that right?'

'Yeah, a virtual Aussie icon, mate. And given that Australians live in my house I think we should at least get a sandbag.'

'I'll see what I can do,' he'd replied laughing.

But it is a serious issue for a number of reasons, especially as it's highlighting the profound rift between Australia and East Timor. Dr Alkatiri is developing an antipathy for

Australia and its people due to the increasingly tense negotiations on the Timor Gap, and that's why he's unavailable and scathing. His diplomacy doesn't extend to the country that is gleaning profits from the oil and gas deposits under a sea that separates them. Conversely, any diplomacy he can muster is usually extended to Indonesia. His attempts to rebuild relations with that nation, the one that attempted to enjoy the spoils through occupation, have extended to his commitment to promote reconciliation, not prosecution. So, against the wishes of the Timorese people who lived through the horrors, the government refuses to support the work of the UN Serious Crimes Unit, which investigates the perpetrators and organisers of the murder and devastation that occurred here during '99. Timor prefers to forgive and trust Indonesia. Meanwhile, while I'd like to be a mediator in a truce between East Timor and the more benign Australia, my nationality precludes it.

Driving up to the Australian Embassy, we can see that sandbags and shipping containers sit at deliberate points along the roadway to prevent a car-bomb attack. It's closed for all but essential business now. Many of the staff have been flown out of the country. Armed and uniformed peacekeepers are stationed around the perimeter, holding combat-ready positions in the hot sun, with helmets and semi-automatic weapons, vigilant. Some are even lying prone in sandbag bunkers with machine guns propped and aimed towards the community. It is a strong presence, which suggests that this is not a facetious move, as the local government claims.

Anyway, let's be realistic. Security has been lax here. From the time I arrived, the government building, for example, has been peculiar for the congestion of cars that come and go or park right under the office windows of the most powerful here — the Prime Miniature and before him Sergio Vieira de Mello. The roadway right past the building has always been used by the public traffic, which includes every variety of dilapidated vehicle — overladen truck, doorless car, family scooter, Timor taxi and microlet bus with people hanging out the side. Cars are often parked on median strips out the front in a disorderly fashion. I'm regularly picked up or dropped off by The Missus right at the front door of the main foyer.

It's taken reports of terrorist activity in the region for complacency to come to an end. For some. The UN is taking the threats seriously too, so the area in front of the big white government building has now been spliced in two. In front of the UN office of the new Special Representative of the Secretary-General, Kamalesh Sharma, the carpark has been cordoned off and parking has been banned beneath the windows unless the car has 'UNMISET 1' or 'UNMISET 2' or a chosen few variations on the registration plate. However, in front of the office next door, the PM's, one can motor right on up with a bomb on board. Out the front of the portion of the building relegated to the Timorese Government, all sorts of modes of transportation continue to move around unchecked. It wouldn't seem right for the Prime Miniature to increase security on his side of the building when he is calling the whole matter an overreaction, now would it?

As an unarmed Australian civilian here, I reckon it's for the best that measures are taken to promote safety, which should be the paramount concern in a mission. So our car continues on past the embassy that's protected by peacekeepers deployed here, appropriately, as part of Operation Citadel, overtaking a family of five (including a breast-feeding mother) on a scooter then weaving through the madcap Timor taxis and Governu Tatas. Hang on, forget terrorists, the Timorese drivers are the real risk in this country.

The Timorese recently tried to make every fourteen-year-old taxi driver and the malae go for a local driver's licence, the price to the malae US$45. When ordered to do so I pointed out that I have an international driver's licence. I was told it wasn't recognised here. 'Er, right.' I ignored Article 45, as did most malae. Except for The Missus. He drove his UN car to the government department in question and waited his turn, watching on as Timor taxis crashed into witches hats. Finally, when it was his turn, he hopped into his car and did the course in reverse. Which is why I'm feeling safe with him turning the car now through the traffic, into the carpark of the Leader supermarket and department store.

We walk over the threshold, past the collection of Timorese men selling, 'CD Missus?' 'Telstra Missus?' and, once inside, The Missus goes in the direction to buy groceries. I, however, go to the section that's a cornucopia of novelty items such as imitation Chanel perfume and electrical equipment free of the constraints of a warranty. Indulgence has hit town and, like the hotels and restaurants that have been opening post-Independence, this department store is hitting its stride too late to capitalise on the vast numbers of highly paid UN and aid agency staff who were here during the UNTAET mission, so it's a playground made for me and the other malae who remain. Which is why I think it charitable of me to do my bit to help the economy of the foreigner who runs this concern undaunted by the peacekeepers in the streets. I also prefer to compensate for my fears and troubles by collecting an unauthorised UN sunhat, an unauthorised UN T-shirt, an unauthorised UN mug, an unauthorised UN baseball cap . . . 'Ready, Ma'am?'

'Hang on.' The final procurement of the morning is an ice cream. I'm scanning all the packets in the freezer chest, trying to read languages I can't understand, determined to find the closest thing to a Pine-Lime Splice. That would cheer me up. Purchases made, we walk out through the chant of Timorian street sellers, licking ice creams and carrying bags down the stairs, into the sunshine and to the car. 'Damn it! Tastes nothing like it! Why is this so hard? Pineapple and lime — they're hardly two obscure flavour sensations in this region. I'm not seeking out sauerkraut and pickled gherkins, am I?'

'Actually, you *can* get them in there, I just saw them. There's always next week. Don't give up.'

'The Pine-Lime Splice is a metaphor, don't you see?'

'I know it's hard here sometimes but keep your chin up. One day you'll be eating a Pine-Lime Splice again.'

'Yeah, I guess,' and I put my feet up on the dashboard, sulking, and we drive home, watching out for grenades.

44

INNOCENT PROMISE

'You are getting fat,' says the country's top diplomat.

'Actually, it's the fault of the restaurants in your country catering to soldiers and policemen with all that oil and cream.'

'I can see it in your arms. You are putting on weight, no?'

'How pleased I am to have come, Minister. How's your jogging going?'

He breathes his laugh. 'What? I've offended you, Lynnie? Oh, Lynnie, don't worry, you look nice with your big drumsticks.'

'I beg your pardon but I'll be forced to point out some physical deficiencies in reply if you keep on. So how is the nation-building going?'

'What's the matter? You have a nice, how do you say this in English, voluptuous, figure now.'

'You're enjoying this aren't you? So I'd just like to point out that you wore bow ties until recently.'

'Yeah, I know. God, what was I thinking. And for so many years, no?'

We've just arrived at José's house near the beach, having travelled by motorcade from the government building where he and I were working on a speech he'll be delivering this afternoon to an international audience at the university; the draft of which arrived at my house in his niece's compound last night with the instruction to rewrite at my will — an opportunity that had lifted my spirits. And so I'd worked on my laptop at the kitchen table until a second draft was ready this morning, then I'd driven it into his offices and discussed changes until he'd said, 'Lunch?'

'Um, okay. I guess we still have some things to go over.' I'm reticent because going to lunch requires me to get into Ramos-Horta's car at the entrance to the building. Sure, my job requires me to work with the Prime Miniature and the Council of Ministers, of which the Foreign Affairs Minister is one, but it wouldn't be prudent of me to be seen to do so because there is a minefield of political divisions in this country now. I walk through the foyer with José beside me. He's waving to people, smiling, being the statesman. Why is he taking so long? 'Hello, my friend,' he says to one of his many supporters, 'you have met Miss Minion?'

'Hi, great, nice to meet you.' Fuck. Why is he in such a good mood? Can't he be testy like he often is in the workplace? 'Hurry up,' I'm saying under my breath.

'What?' he says when we are safely inside his large Prado.

'Botardi Celestino,' I say.

José gives his driver instructions in Tetum and, as he does, his bodyguards leap into the car in front of us.

'I can't have anyone from the Prime Minister's office or any of his cronies seeing me going off with you, you know that.'

'Why can't you?'

'You know perfectly well why. The breakdown in your relationship with him is obvious. You don't have to spin your line with me. I know — I'm immersed in it. I have some horrid little ministerial adviser from Education who sits beside me making insults about you all the time, and he looks at me while he's going off with his slander, daring me to bite.'

'Who is that?'

'That's not important. And today when I went upstairs to tell Rita that I'd be working on a speech with you all day, there were shared glances. It doesn't do my position in the Prime Minister's office any good to be seen associating with you.'

'What stupid talk.'

'Really? Why don't we invite Alkatiri to join us then? If you and he are such good mates then maybe you can be the one to get me a meeting with the man.'

'You still haven't met with him?'

'No. Not once.' The oceanfront tables under the palm-frond shelters surrounded by banana trees are filled with people enjoying their two-hour lunch breaks as we drive past. Heads turn to watch José's motorcade and I want to slink down in my seat. Soon enough, though, the coast is clear, other than for a jumble of shanties along the waterline, and after a few kilometres of thin, wobbly road and a bit of goat dodging we reach an intersection and turn right up to his house with the big thatched roof. 'But obviously it is an honour to work on a speech with you, Minister. Thank you. At the very least it keeps me occupied.'

'What do you do with your time?'

'Well, I host international journalists, get them pissed, that sort of thing, tell them Timor is a tropical paradise. I edited a media manual — you got a copy, actually — and it seems to have made an enormous impact on you given that you have no idea what I'm referring to. And the pinnacle, at UNDP's behest, I drafted the program for a ministerial retreat that would bring together local and international experts to talk about media interaction and, what can I say, all the experts agreed to take part, and then the head of UNDP decided not to present the idea to the Prime Minister, didn't want to rock the boat. It's a shame because I'd even planned to include a video of you giving an interview in the 1970s to show that absolutely anyone can become skilled at interviews with practice.'

Seated at a table in his lounge room now, surrounded by memorabilia, and one of José's nieces brings us plates of food: rice, fish and a meat curry. 'Obrigada Lily.'

He serves me, sparingly, 'You should have the rice and some fish. Very slimming. Not so much of the pork.'

'Thank you for the advice, Dr Pritikin. On to slightly more important issues, the speech has a lot of talk about war in Afghanistan in support of the United States.'

'How many calories do you think are on your plate?'

'Do you think it's relevant to the audience?'

'Yes. It is important to speak of the international context; Timor now plays a part on the world stage.'

'Sure, but you're a Nobel Peace Laureate. Don't you have some requirement to remain peaceable? Isn't it a contravention of the award to spruik war?'

'No, I have no conditions applied to me with this award, of course.'

'But it was given to you because you advocated peace as the best way to liberate your people.'

'Yes, it was the best way, but Afghanistan is a different situation.'

'Or is it because Timor is now dependent on US money?'

'It is important to support our friends internationally.'

'Friends. But three of your brothers and a sister died at the hands of Indonesians armed with US-supplied weapons.'

'Yes, my sister was killed with bombs from American planes. We have just located her body.'

'Don't you find it a terrible irony, then, that you feel compelled to support their military and political actions in other countries now?'

'No, after September 11 we have to fight, unified, to rid the world of the scourge of the fucking bastards, the terrorists.'

This man does understand Realpolitik. 'Well then, you should support the Australian Embassy right now, even if your dear friend, the Prime Minister, is outraged.'

'You don't like mango, no?'

'No, I've tried, as you've told me to.' He talks in Portuguese to Lily who is clearing the table. 'I feel awful because the children pick them from the tree in my front yard and present them to me. It brings tears to my eyes. I feel like a cow when they go rotten in the fridge. I even take them to work and throw them in the bin there so the kids won't find out. What was that word you called me? You know, the crier in Tetum.'

'Tanis.'

Lily brings a platter of paw paw with segments of lime and places it in front of me. 'Yeah, that's it.' Timorese people cry rarely, only at times of great loss, like the death of a child, so the family says I am a tanis because I cry when I'm sad or happy. The struggle of their lives has made them more resilient than me and my sentimentality. 'I saw Gina smile for the first time since her baby died.'

'Yeah?'

'Yeah, I think she's getting a little better.'

'How is your grandfather?'

'He's better, it's been a terrible stress but obviously I decided to stay here. Oh, and my friend in Sydney, I told you about her, she is due to give birth to her baby any day now. Very exciting.'

'You want this one day.'

'Of course, you know my views on these things.'

'I think we should try.'

'What?'

'I think you should give a relationship a chance and we could try straightaway for a baby.'

'José, don't joke about things that are deeply important to me.'

'I mean it. I know this is important to you, so I have decided that we should start trying now because you want it. We can maybe have a future together. We should see how it goes. Maybe we can build something beautiful.'

'That's not funny. This is where witty repartee ends.'

'I have a proposition for you,'

'Indeed, you've just made it, again.'

'I need someone in my life. I have been approached by a coalition of opposition parties who want to get rid of the Prime Minister.'

'Okay, I can't quite see the link but please continue, by all means.'

'They have come to me and they asked if I would stand as the alternative prime minister. What do you think?'

'I think it's lucky there is no impeachment clause in your Constitution. But, seriously, I think it is your destiny. I think you would be a fantastic leader of this country. I think the local and international community would be relieved. I think it would make you the Nelson Mandela of Asia — Nobel Peace Prize winner goes on to be executive leader of his country.'

'That is not necessarily my aspiration.'

'Okay then, you'd be more powerful than Xanana.'

He grins. Widely. 'So you think I should do this?'

'Absolutely.'

'I will need someone at my side, someone I trust, who can provide support, political advice . . .'

'And I could. But I'm not taking your offer seriously for one minute.'

'What?'

'José, how many women have you proposed to this week?'

'Come on!'

The cynic in me simply cannot accept that a man could be

genuine in an offer of this kind. 'José, I don't trust you. I'll provide you with all the loyalty, support and advice you want, but I've told you before, I'm not prepared to take the risk.'

There's silence. He looks straight at me. Finally, he says, 'Imagine, Lynnie, that you had said everything I've just said to you to a man and he replied as you have to me.'

What should I say? Our conversations are always fey, and I can't see any reason to assume there has been a change. Plus, I have to maintain Realpolitik in my life. Nothing these days can convince me to contravene Article Zero, life just isn't filled with love and innocent promise. Ring, ring. Saved by the bell. 'I'm sorry, José, I have to get this in case it's Gina in Sydney . . . Hello.'

The words come through, 'Congratulations, you're a godmother,' and I can hear the snuffles of innocence and the voice of a mother welcoming her newborn child, the two of them acquainting themselves with each other, and I weep without restraint, as a man across the table passes serviettes to me, so I can dry my eyes.

'Tanis,' I say, looking over at him, crying with joy.

Beep, beep. Beep, beep. My phone. **1 new message.** I press OK. **Have you heard? Bomb in Sari Club. Hundreds dead.**

On the night that paradise was lost in Bali, the Portuguese peacekeepers here, coincidentally, went on a rampage, smashing chairs and throwing rocks at the Timorese who had been allowed into the Purple Cow.

The next day UNMISET frantically tracks its staff on R and R in Kuta — Australian police officers have been injured, a Portuguese peacekeeper is dead. Meanwhile, reinforced security in front of the big white government building means one can no longer park beneath the window of the Prime Minister of East Timor, Dr Alkatiri.

And all of it leaves me to wonder: at what point in life does our innocence end and the politics begin?

45

ON THE NOSE

Not only do Timorian visitors to the Prime Miniature's Shoe and Handbag Emporium come straight over to shake my hand, they also have a predilection for wearing thongs. Imagine it. You're dressing up to meet the executive leader of your nation and you're thinking about an outfit befitting the significance of the encounter and, so it is, upon contemplation, that you pull out your best thongs. I'm surprised Rita hasn't put her high heel down and stamped out the practice. At least it provides her with ample walk-in trade.

Other than the thong-wearing locals who wait around the meeting table, cutting off my circulation and flicking through mail-order catalogues, there is a daily visitor who paces back and forth ranting about an issue of political outrage for the day. He is a disruptive addition and no one really knows how he came to take up de facto residence in our space. He just turned up one day and he's been here, pontificating, ever since. And none of us can work up the courage to tell him to go away, not even the bodyguards, who prefer to study their English language textbooks and clear the toilet every two hours or so in preparation for the executive bottom.

All of us pretend that this man's very loud presence is perfectly normal and, when he focuses his attention on each of us, we nod and smile embarrassedly as he stands in front of our respective desks, waving a hand in the air to emphasise some latest grievance. It's at these times, if I'm the object of his evangelical exhortations, that I generally say something like, 'Excuse me, I have to try to fix the [insert printer/fax/air-conditioner/cistern/other],' very politely, of course, because our interloper is a very scruffy Timorese dwarf. Really.

Political correctness has taken a hilarious turn here these days, as each of us hopes some other bastard will tell him to piss off because he's a pest; instead we spend most of our days hoping he won't catch our eyes and he'll think we're ever so busy, too busy to talk, sorry, would if I could but, you know, the pressure. Unfortunately for Rita, she's actually genuinely nice, so she is usually the main recipient of each day's torrent. 'Uh-huh. Saida? Lae. La diak. Bain hira? Sin . . .' she says, disconsolately, her head propped up in her hand. She looks at me and rolls her eyes, lethargically.

Luckily, I am cocooned from most of his allegations and pronouncements by my own inadequacies: my language skills, which allow me to tune out to his rapid-fire outpourings. They simply float through one ear and out the other with no interference from my brain on their way towards The Chimney in her tailor-made short-sleeved pantsuit (navy today) with the fag in her hand. The maid empties her ashtray. It's 9.25 am.

This means I need to look very, very absorbed and, I'm afraid, surfing the *Sydney Morning Herald* website just won't cut it. Instead I take the opportunity to sort out a problem with the media here. I was given the role of overseeing the establishment of the Public Broadcasting Authority in Timor, a responsibility that hasn't been terribly demanding so far, as the whole thing stalemated some time ago, following the UN's choice to withdraw support to the media sector. And to match that, there seems to be a lack of enthusiasm emanating from the PM's desk towards the institution. Dr Alkatiri would prefer a government-controlled version, which would be an exercise in self-promotion on a par with Hugh Hefner's Playboy TV, I believe, as well as contravening democratic principles a bit.

But before East Timor's leader starts storyboarding his *Triumph des Willens*, the aid organisation funding the whole Public Broadcasting Authority project at great expense requires the intervention of a voiceover of reason. As usual, I have no alternative but to go to the most effective executive producer in the building — the one who understands the audience, whose office doesn't replicate a set from an Austin Powers movie, who is accessible to fans, who understands that media should be free from obligation, influence and legal constraint:

Dear Minister,
Greetings from the PM's Shoe and Handbag Emporium.
Please find attached the (Fondation Hirondelle) document on the suggested process for appointment of the Board of Directors for the Public Broadcasting Authority. It features in English and Portuguese. It relates to the legislation which clearly states that members cannot be ministers.
And don't forget, if you need a nice new pair of slippers, maybe some brogues, a sandal perhaps, a matching accessory, just

pop upstairs and one of our trained assistants will be happy to help.
Sincerely,
Lynne Minion

Although, a media controlled by the PM's office could have some residual social benefit by providing valuable free advertising for Rita's vital public service. Because if there's one compensation for lack of democracy, it's looking good while you're being oppressed — a point that, frankly, too few Third World nations have picked up on. So tune into the Prime Miniature's Home Shopping Channel for the chance to order that special kitten heel. With cameos by Mini-Me.

My alma mater has suggested me for an article in an Australian broadsheet newspaper on postgraduate studies and where they can get you and, looking around, I'm wondering if I'm a sensible choice. Especially as a photo is required that will adequately represent my work and I have mental images of me fixing the throne. Although, in order to put my best stilettoed foot forward I arrange for the media-friendly Foreign Affairs Minister to take part, the photo shoot confirmed for a time at the end of the day in his office.

Theoretically one needs a masters degree to work in the UN but all you actually require is the correct nationality or a friend in high places. As an alternative, there is the clique of young drifters who've plopped down in the country and are carving out quite a niche for themselves, smoking pot behind Timor Aïd and doing the odd freelance job for UN agencies. Nevertheless, for the purposes of the story I'm sure José and I can produce a picture that's erudite. If ever the photographer turns up.

UNDP couldn't provide the resources, of course, so I've had to arrange them from the open market and they're conspicuously absent right now. Until, a substantial time after appointed, an Englishman arrives at the PM's office in wet board shorts, hair windblown from the scooter ride in from the beach, bare feet covered in sand and no camera to be seen. 'What? You want me to get it?' he asks, incredulous.

'Ah, yeah, that's what all those messages I left you during the day have been referring to.'

'I was snorkelling.'

'Clearly. Best go get the camera now then and I'll apologise to the Minister and postpone for another half an hour.'

'What? You want me to go and get it *now*?'

'I imagine we'll need it,' I say, incredulous.

When proceedings finally begin, the photographer seems petrified to be in the company of the Minister, thus he hides behind his lens on one side of José's desk while we chat one-sidedly about issues of consequence on the other.

'So, how are plans going for Xanana's visit to Jakarta?'

'She is beautiful, no?' José says to the photographer who appears to be clicking away.

'Eek,' he emits, then hides behind the lens again.

'It'll be quite a historic moment, seeing he was jailed there. Are you expecting an awkward reception or do you think it'll be warm?'

'Warm, of course. Nice arse, what do you think?'

'Huh?' the photographer says and, oddly, holds the digital camera to his eye.

I stick my heel into José's leg under the table without interrupting my smile.

'Following that you're off to Singapore, yeah?'

'Singapore, others, many important meetings.' He wraps his legs around mine under his desk. I kick them away.

'Stop it,' I say continuing to look at the camera. 'It must be difficult to go away now with the tension rising in Timor.'

'No, this is not my concern any more. I am no longer

prepared to be involved in these problems. I distance myself from the Prime Minister. He can solve his own problems now.' He squeezes my knee.

I flick his hand away. 'Fuck off, I'm serious,' I hiss at him.

'Wow, look at that passion. Do you think she is passionate?'

'Yelp.' The photographer is completely overwhelmed.

'I think we've got enough now. Thank you for your time, Minister.'

'Are you free for dinner tonight, Lynnie?'

'No.' I stomp out of the door.

'Drink?' he calls after me.

Turning around in the corridor to face the photographer I make a request, 'Actually, we're not quite finished. There is one more photo. You don't mind do you?'

'Well, it's getting late.'

'It'll only take a moment. You'll be back in that bungalow out the back of Timor Aid in no time,' and I direct him outside to where I pose in front of my favourite work-related resource, my Popemobile. It shows that all the ambitions I had for myself when I threw that cap in the air have come true, in style! Or, on second thoughts, it could cause a dramatic decrease in enrolments.

In the end it didn't really matter, because the photographer never did produce a single shot.

It's a big day for the Australian community in East Timor. It's the Melbourne Cup and the Esplanada, a new hotel in Timor, is putting on a do to rival any marquee at Flemington racecourse. The race is even being shown live via satellite so many people are taking the afternoon off and heading down to the exclusive event at noon. I'm going to stay at work and be responsible (I assume the PM isn't a punter) until just before 3 pm, the traditional starting time, then I'll be there, in a hat as protocol dictates, and with my wallet in hand because this year I am betting on a horse I know will romp it in: Media Puzzle. That gee-gee will be racing with all my hopes on its back because I see it as prophetic; a win by that horse will predict success with my media puzzle too. So mid-afternoon, I'm eagerly pulling the handbrake on the Popemobile and sliding to a stop. I trip happily up the wooden stairs, emerging at the top primed to watch the race that stops two nations.

That's when I'm surprised to see a very dishevelled crowd over at the railing. What's going on? No! Of course. Damn it, there's a time difference which means the race was run two hours ago. And the winner? Media Puzzle. What impact does it have on the analogy that I was too stupid to make it on time? The impact is that I'm stuck at a debris-strewn once-posh now-despoiled affair with an unruly crowd drunk on champagne-and-fresh-mango cocktails.

'She made it! Donkey girl!' (I never should have compared myself with the donkey in the movie *Shrek*, trying to get the PM's attention by going, 'Hello, me. Me! Hello, yes, me!' because The Missus enjoys it far too much.)

'Um, hello. How are you?'

'Shsha great do.'

'So I can see.'

'Glashsh of pershshonality?'

'I would but I hate mango. I'll just have some chardonnay soup, thank you.'

'You're hungry? I'll bet you haven't eaten, I'll go and get you shshsomething, jushsh leave it to me, donkey girl.' Even when he's drunk he's still The Missus.

Seems I have some catching up to do. I am very unaccustomed to feeling like the grown-up in the room; it's a situation that needs to be redressed immediately. Who knows what sort of trouble I could get myself into if I'm the one who's sober. 'Lynne, how are you?' I turn.

'Joe, fine thanks and yourself?'

'Actually, it's José these days. I'm, you know, embracing my culture, and using my Timorese name is part of that.' It's Joe Texeira, the Secretary of State for Tourism, the young cowboy of the government whose political talent lies in his startling capacity for power shshmoozing.

'Great. That'll help you stand out from the crowd.'

'I have other ways to make myself stand out, Lynne.'

Er, the sheer magnitude of your ego? 'Of course you do. I've always thought of you as a stand-out in a number of ways. Another drink?'

'Sure, I could do with one. Been a bit of a difficult time, you know.'

'Really?'

'Yeah. My marriage.'

Right. Here we go. 'Oh my God, that's terrible. Are you okay?'

'Yeah, after seventeen years I had to tell my wife.'

'Anyway, sorry, I have to go to the bar.'

'I never expected this to happen, but she walked into my world and my marriage was, you know . . .'

'Spare me the details.' I can guess.

'I'm not telling you her name.'

'I'm not interested in her name.'

'All I'll say is she's American.'

Whatever. 'Congratulations, Joe.'

'José. It's hard going through something like this.'

'I imagine it must be terribly hard for your family.'

'Just breaks my heart.'

'Then why do you seem so happy, Joe?'

'José. Well, I am in love and that, okay, okay, is pretty great.'

'Well, there you go, you're moving onwards and upwards all over the place. Your career is looking good, you're right there in the inner sanctum. You've made it into the

Mozambiquean clique. They let in someone who spent the exile years in Australia. That's very gifted networking on your part.' This man has goals and he has set about achieving them by solidifying his position with the Banana Splits.

'Well I'm working hard to put myself in a good position.' And the PM could use the support these days.

'Sounds like you feel you should be more than a secretary of state.'

'What do you think? You know the other ministers. I'm an Australian-educated and trained barrister . . .'

So you've told me. 'Impressive skills.'

'. . . I'm young, multilingual, capable. I've worked at the highest level of Australian politics.'

Really? I had no idea. 'So what portfolio do you think would fit all those bona fides?'

'Do you think I'm stupid enough to speculate on that to a journalist?'

Absolutely. 'It wouldn't be speculation. I'm not asking you what portfolio you think you'll get, I'm asking you which portfolio you want. Justice?'

'Come on, I'm not saying a thing.'

Why stop now? 'Surely Justice is the only portfolio that would best utilise all your achievements.'

'Not saying a word,' he grins.

'I see it as a perfect fit. You must too. You've accumulated so much expertise to match your talent during such a successful career and they gave you Tourism, a junior ministry. I think Minister for Justice is where you'll end up.'

'Well, actually, so do I.'

'You want Justice?'

'I'm a lawyer. Of course I want to be Minister for Justice.'

'There's a lawyer currently in the position and she's a pretty formidable character.' So Joe's networking skills will be tested.

It's a contest I would never have the constitution for, but his ambition seems to preclude the interference of self-doubt.

'I'm biding my time.'

'You've been very clearly inserting yourself into the Old Fretilin faction; this surprises me.'

'Which raises an important point: we need to talk about your loyalty,' a point he announces with another bloody grin.

'My loyalty. To whom? What on earth do you mean? Have another drink, Joe.'

'José. You know exactly what I mean. Your loyalty is clearly in question and you need to be very careful about who you align yourself with.' My media puzzle has just morphed into one endless labyrinth.

'Or what?'

'You need to be careful, that's all. You are employed to do a job for the Prime Minister.'

'Indeed and the Council of Ministers.'

'Your loyalty has been noted as a cause for concern.'

'You've made that point. And I'd like to parry that I have made the utmost effort to be a trusted member of Alkatiri's circle.'

'That's the thing, the Prime Minister expects to be able to trust the people around him implicitly.'

'But he can't, apparently, because I've aligned myself with someone else from my very arrival; is that what you're saying?' My mind harks back to the protests that welcomed me into the office. 'Does this alternative individual have a name?' But I know.

'Just tell him that he has to start acting like the number two in the government and not number one.'

I feel that anything other than ignorance on my part right now would be an admission of guilt. 'And you would be talking about who?'

'The number two in the government.' Why so cryptic?

'Not you yet, Joe?'

'José. You need to pass on the warning that he has to start acting like number two in the government.' Okay, okay.

'Outside Timor?'

'No, inside.'

'Or what, Joe?'

'José. Or he'll be sacked.' What's with the grinning?

'That's a pretty serious threat.'

'That's right. And, as he is an appointed representative, he could be sacked tomorrow.'

'Tomorrow. You people don't muck around, you really want this to be a one-horse race. But why me? Why do I have to pass it on? Why don't you just tell him?'

'Because we know you will pass it on to him for us.'

'I have no idea what you mean. You're not making a great deal of sense to me. Anyway, if you'll excuse me I'll leave you to your conspiracy theories.'

Later, at the bar, with one hand holding a ham sandwich sourced by The Missus, 'They'd closhshed the kitchen but I convinshshed them to make a sandwishsh, donkey girl,' the other sends a text message to a certain minister who is overseas with the President. Both of those tasks done, I take a long draught of chardonnay and, ring, ring, my phone, 'Hello.'

'What do you mean?'

'It's Joe, I mean José Texeira. He gave me a message to give to you. He told you to stop acting like number one in the government or you will be sacked.'

'Stupid fucking idiot.'

'Look, he's drunk, I don't know what it's all about, José. All I know is that the threat was communicated via me. I've been told that my loyalty is in question. It appears that I'm seen as some kind of Mata Hari. Hang on a minute . . . sure Mum, yeah . . .'

A face presents itself in front of mine, 'Say hello to the

Foreign Affairs Minister for me,' says the grin.

'I don't know what you're talking about. It's my mum.' Joe moves away, stopping where he can watch me. I walk to the other side of the bar, smiling, pretending to have a lovely chat. 'Sorry, back again, just had a visit from your colleague, he says hi. Can't they just send you a text message like I did?' I smile and nod back at the grinning Secretary of State for Tourism.

'They say they will sack me?'

'Tomorrow, in fact, if they so choose. Look, now that you know, you can tell Xanana and work out some sort of strategy to put a stop to all this counterproductive bullshit.'

'I will resign before they can do this.'

'You're always saying that. Soon you'll be seen as the man who cried wolf. And you can't quit anyway. You can't allow a junior minister to intimidate you. He didn't intimidate me.'

The truth is he did. Of course he did. I'm not a politician, I'm just an employee who's been squarely placed in the middle of their high-level power war. And I don't have the constitution for it. I'm just a girl who ended up in this spot by naivety not design. I don't want to play with the big boys (albeit very small ones), and I'm rather shaken to find myself targeted by the Banana Splits' obsession with playing party politics, their paranoia, their willingness to trample over anyone who remains outside their faction. But, hello, I'm not Timorese, I can't vote here, and a couple of glasses of wine at José's house does not make a party. I wish they would put their energies into learning how to adequately administer a democratic nation. So I'm frightened and angry, although I'm loath to show either.

'See ya, Lynne, nice talking to you,' the junior minister says, walking past again.

'Yeah, pleasure, Joe.' You smarmy fucker.

'José.'

'Yeah, of course, José.' I smile sweetly.

I get an email the next day . . .

```
if I leave . . . one way or another . . .
how would XG react? who would he blame?
how would the bishops and priests react? who
would they blame?
how would the students, liurais [local
kings], the NGOs, etc react?
how would the common people react?
how would members of the US Congress react?
how would my many friends in the EU react?
how would key members in the MFAC [Ministry
of Foreign Affairs and Cooperation] react?
would they stay?
maybe you could ask these questions to the
fat opportunist gentleman . . .
maybe i should leave . . . and return one
day . . .
maybe . . .
```

Maybe it *is* time all those people told the Prime Miniature and his Banana Splits to concentrate on putting the pieces of their nation together instead of focusing on trivial pursuits. Regardless, I suspect that maybe my media puzzle will be far too complex for me to solve now.

46

I SPY WITH MY LITTLE EYE

I feel like I should be wearing a dark wig and glasses, and probably a trench coat too in the Prime Miniature's Shoe and Handbag Emporium these days. Do they have firing squads in East Timor? What's the penalty for being some sort of secret agent? How duplicitous of me to have infiltrated the halls of power with the very intention of passing on secrets to the number two in the government. How clever of me to have duped the UN, the executive leader of the nation and everyone I know to penetrate Fortress Alkatiri and glean top-secret information, like its roaring trade in accessories. It was all such an elaborate plan but it's been foiled! The whole accusation is ridiculous; and it's all because I have a view to a dill.

Shouldn't I be shredding or something? Shouldn't I have a locket around my neck containing a special pill? Shouldn't some co-conspirator be popping out of a bin with escape plans involving a helicopter and dashing men in uniform? In the absence of these things I'm worried that I'll be frog-marched out of here in handcuffs, accessories that will really clash with my outfit. Especially as it's really not the best time to be pissing off the Prime Miniature.

Why? Have I been privy to some terribly confidential plans? No, hardly. It's Ramadan. And even Rita, who is fasting as well, is manifesting the effects. 'Leeen, you dropping things all the time!' (Only when I want to hide from the Prime Minister on his way to the seat of government.)

'Sorry.'

'You sorry, Leeen. I sorry too because you give me ache in my head.'

'I know how you feel, I've got a four-foot-tall pain in the arse.'

Speaking of which, Timor may be a predominantly Catholic country but, in yet another testimony to Dr Alkatiri's political nous, the PM is a Muslim. As such, I am getting a close-up view of the effect of abstaining from food and fluid from 4 am until 11 pm in a dreadfully hot country.

'I go sleep, Leeen. I am tired very much.'

Me too because the whole drama of being outed as an undercover operative is draining and, more to the point, I can't bring myself to eat or drink in front of Rita, so I'm having a Ramadan by default. Which is probably why I feel like curling up under the deskette rather than facing another humiliating day of sitting here awaiting my fate.

However, to bring perspective, the universe sends an UNMISET staffer who has long been trying to get the PM to sign off on the recruitment of an international political adviser for this office. He is beside himself (the poor man), he's shaking (bless him), he is forlorn (I feel his pain), and today yet again he has been bumped from the diary. 'Can't he see that this will benefit him?' he begs of the room. I put my fingers in my ears and go 'la, la, la,' so no one can ever say I am eavesdropping. And that's when the real excitement happens because this man has decided to take matters into his own hands and, as the PM sweeps through on his way to lunch (must be 12.01 pm), shit there goes my pen, sitting back up again I see the UNMISET man sprinting down the corridor and he pushes his way through the Timorese bodyguards, and grabs the leader's arm, spinning him around: 'Here, you must sign this. All I need is your signature!'

Silence. All is still. The PM looks the man up and down and everyone watching out of doorways with wide-open eyes inhales with anticipation, and Dr Alkatiri finally, says, 'I'll do it in the afternoon' (he doesn't), before scattering the throng of journalists sitting on the stairs as he continues on his way.

Sure, I haven't resorted to physical intervention but later I bounce down the well-worn path to UNDP headquarters where my project manager greets me with enthusiasm and listens to my latest twist as we stand out the front. He smokes a clove cigarette and I drink a much-needed coffee while I beg him, 'I don't know what to do, Terry. UNDP has to help me here. I want to do my job. I want to work with whoever will work with me. If that's the Prime Minister then hooray. You've got to put an end to all the innuendo.'

'There's nothing I can do.'

'But it's undermining my position and causing me a fair bit of stress, I can tell you. There has to be a solution and it has to come from someone at a higher level than me.'

'We have advisers being sacked. Most of the 200 positions still have to be filled; money pledged by donor nations is yet to arrive, they're changing their priorities to other countries now; advisers, ministers and donors are screaming that nothing is being achieved; UNDP is frightened it'll be seen to fail; should I go on? You have no idea what we're dealing with, it's madness. And so, with all of this, I can't just go and give the Prime Minister a talking-to, I need to give half the people in this nation a talking-to and I'm not going to start with him.'

'Maybe you should? Maybe then he'll bring the other members of the government into line?'

'Yes, because prime ministers are known for taking criticism so well.'

'But you can't just allow projects to stall. You have a responsibility to ensure that they succeed.' The few advisers who have been hired are being put into offices without resources, support or advice. It *is* mad. We don't even have access to interpreters in a country that has switched official language. Imagine my state when I was told to produce a full-colour glossy brochure in Portuguese from a Portuguese draft by a committee headed by the current Minister for Justice, a woman known for insisting all communications with her be in Portuguese. She terrifies me as it is, and I was reluctant to explain that the UN provides me with no access to translation facilities at all, let alone budget, graphic designer or printing facilities. But when beseeched for assistance, Terry had replied, 'There's nothing I can do.' And it all has come to mean that I am unable to do my job any more. I've generated as much work as I can. 'Terry, I can't accept that my project will fail.'

'Wouldn't be the first.'

'Perhaps I have high standards but I really want to achieve this. It's the whole point of being here. I mean, I didn't think about my potential destinations and toss up between Dili or Monaco. I didn't come here for the lifestyle, I came here to work and contribute something to the Timorese.'

'And you're trying. But we can't force it on them. If they don't want help then that's their right. It's their right to fuck up their country if they so choose and we have to accept it.'

'Because it's an independent sovereign nation.'

'Precisely.'

I can't bear the thought of going back to an office in which dehydrated and hungry people believe I am a traitor, so I decide to use up some hours by sampling some of the free UN services. The UN dentist is located inside Obrigado Barracks and he's a popular chap. See, bad teeth are a sign of poverty and many people, representing many poor countries in the UN system, have their teeth done here, often for the first time in their lives.

I think the dentist will probably be relieved to see me, considering I grew up with fluoridated water, toothbrushes, toothpaste, orthodontic work, check-ups every year. 'Hello!' he says, 'Welcome! How are you? What can I do for you?' What a happy man this dentist is.

Walking into his surgery, I immediately spy the enormous jar filled with hundreds of brown teeth sitting on a shelf. 'That's your advertising campaign? I don't know if it's effective.'

'Oh, no! Every customers is very happy!' The chirpy dentist is a Filipino who has been working here for some time. Certainly, he hasn't lost his passion for his craft. 'What can we do for you today, Lynne? Lie back! Very good!'

'I've just come in for a regular check-up and clean. Nothing quite as drastic as your jar suggests. You know, Australian, good teeth,' I laugh awkwardly as he riffles through instruments on the bench. I look around for the sterilising equipment. I can't locate it and I'm hoping it's here and fully operational, just indiscernible to the naked eye.

He makes a selection and moves towards me. 'Let me see if that's all we can do! Open wide! We have some problem with some equipment so we will see what we can do today! Clean, no! You must come back for clean!'

'O-kay,' I say with a metal shaft in my mouth. That doesn't bode well and I'm contemplating how many diseases are transmitted via saliva, convincing myself it's precisely none.

'Ah-ha! Ah-ha! Oh!' I'm watching his eyes and I wonder if he can see that mine are filled with fear. 'Okay!' and he pushes away and sits up straight. 'The good news is we will becoming very good friends!'

'What's the bad news?'

'You will have thirteen fillings!'

'*Thir-teen* fillings!' His gusto is one thing in here that's catching.

'That's right! Thirteen fillings!'

'That's impossible! I had my teeth seen in Sydney before I came, X-rays, the whole bit, and I cannot imagine that I have developed the need for thirteen fillings!'

'It is possible! I am telling you! Thirteen!' He's saying this with far too much relish for my liking.

'I'm sorry but I refuse! I'd accept maybe one or two but not thirteen!'

'I show you! Open wide! You hold this mirror here and you see this dark spot here, this is very bad decay, see!' He scrapes it with his instrument and leaves white marks within a shadow of brown. 'Oh, okay, maybe not this one but this one here, this one, oh . . .'

I sit up, abruptly. 'They are coffee stains!' Man, now I know why I've always been told to do my teeth before I go to the dentist. 'I'm going to wait until I get home to Australia!'

'No, no! Don't go! I do eleven. Eleven fillings!' he says as I'm rushing out the door, determined to maintain control over my sovereign body no matter what that UN international says.

Rather than intervening in individual cases and because the problem is so all-pervasive, UNDP has decided to hold a conference at the Hotel Timor for the government and all advisers, UNMISET and UNDP, and I volunteer to sit on the front desk. 'Hello, good morning, what's your name, let me have a look . . . how do you spell that? . . . goodness, is that it? Good, thanks for coming, just down the corridor to the right. Hello, good morning . . .'

Hundreds of people are here representing both camps, the internationals and a few Timorese, within this sumptuous hotel where Viktor and I stayed. Sigh, I look at the stairway and remember climbing it with him, hand in hand, as I make my way past and enter the conference room.

I join my allotted consultative group and remain subdued, however, because I don't want to stand out at all, particularly as the Minister for Transport and Communications chairs my group of twelve. It could have been worse, there's the Minister for Justice over there; there's her heir-apparent (smarmy fucker); there's the Secretary of State for Defence . . . God help us, all the Banana Splits are here. Innocently, the other UN advisers are imparting their problems with relief and vigour. They have no counterparts, no resources, no support. They have extortion attempts on their wages, a Malae Syndrome, Timorese bosses who don't understand that the mission is about capacity-building . . . so I may as well keep my mouth shut, my contributions would only echo. And on they drone. There are a lot of people in the room who are somewhat fed up and they seem determined to use this opportunity to speak out . . . and out . . . and out. Man, and I thought I was pissed off. I'm positively Zen in comparison.

Hours later, there's a call to elect a group spokesperson, I slink down in my seat, looking away, placing a vacuous look on my face, and I drop my papers, sorry, bit clumsy, malnourished, that's all, at the point of entry of the PM who joins the top table, surrounded by the Banana Splits.

Summaries of the problems identified today present a pretty damning picture of the government, until we get to the Secretary of State for Defence who gives the views of his group to the accompaniment of silly walks, shrill tones, sentences that make no real sense, and gesticulations best left to music videos. Then the PM looks us all up and down and he provides the following research findings:

Rule #1 — Never criticise a prime minister
Rule #2 — Never criticise a prime minister in public
Rule #3 — Never criticise a prime minister in public in his country
Rule #4 — Never criticise a particularly cranky prime minister in public in his country during Ramadan

In Portuguese, Dr Alkatiri congratulates the Secretary of State for Defence for his positive and loyal contribution then, via translation, the rest of us are told, 'Let me be clear, the Constitution of this nation says the official language is Portuguese, yet I have had to sit here listening to presentations in English, including one by a Timorese!'

English speakers, all of us, look at the floor. Here it is again, the caveat, loophole, fine print that is always undermining our efforts. The heads of the UN look on awkwardly; the rest of us are disappointed. Still, the outburst doesn't last too long, I knew it wouldn't, because it's gone 5.30 pm. So, with knock-off time arriving and his point effectively made, he vacates, the Finance Minister trotting behind him.

'Terry, Terry, Terry, I've just had a phone call asking me to meet with the DSRSG tomorrow!' The Deputy Special Representative of the Secretary-General is the second-highest ranking UN representative here, he's also the head of UNDP, which makes him the very man I want to meet.

'Oh, already.'

'What? You knew about this?'

'Um, yeah.'

'I can't wait. I assume it means he'll be intervening.'

'Ah, you could say that.'

'What's going on? Your level of enthusiasm doesn't seem to

be matching mine.' Never has, truth be told.

'He needs to be the one to talk to you. I don't want to preempt him.'

This conversation isn't going the way I'd expected and I wonder if I should hang up, redial and start all over again. But life doesn't work like that, does it? I sense that I am hurtling along in the direction of an inevitable train wreck. 'Just don't tell me that I'm going to be sacked.'

'I'm not telling you anything; it's not for me to say but I think you should prepare yourself for the worst.'

I asked you not to tell me that. 'And if I hadn't called you? What would have happened then? I would have skipped into his office like an excited child, completely unprepared for the bomb about to drop out of the sky?'

'I suppose so.'

'And as my project manager I assume you've briefed him that there are far more constructive ways to move forward?'

'There's nothing I can do.' The old there's-nothing-I-can-do trick. And I'm the one being sacked.

'I so should have gone to Monaco.'

'I'll give you some advice: he's an extremely difficult character, you have no idea. He likes the sound of his own voice. Let him talk.'

'Bugger that. If I let him talk he'll just sack me. The only way I can have any influence over my future is to speak and get him to listen to how much I have tried and how much I care about this job!' But it's more than just a job.

At stake is my house, my ambitions, principles, my world as I know it, and so the next day The Missus appraises the fashion statement from his position on the couch. 'I'm going for strong, capable, feminine yet not too feminine, what do you think?' I ask him.

'Perfect. All of those qualities are conveyed accurately with that dress,' he replies.

'Is the big scorch mark down the front a benefit? Does it show that I, too, am living in a hardship mission, doing it tough, sacrificing for this country?' Elsie has had one of her ironing mishaps and I think it lends a certain authenticity and context to the look.

'Smart yet a little deteriorated. It's a good combination.'

'Soon to be seen on the catwalks of Paris.'

'Yes, yes, yes.'

'Hang on, were you referring to the clothes or me?'

He laughs out loud. 'Are we ready, Ma'am?'

'What time is it? Yep. Missus, we're needed. Hey, thank you for sneaking away from work, I really appreciate you driving me there.'

'It's the least I can do.'

'Does this mean I have to stop writing messages on the back window of your car?'

'Yes, it does.'

'Is all purpose being removed from my life?'

Despite the signs of bravado, I'm shaking as the car parks out the front of the big white building, and I look up at the terrace of the PM's office where I can see Rita gossiping with the maids as usual, and I get out of the car, trying to walk with steadiness to the left, to the UN headquarters next door, and I go through the security cordon, up the stairs and along the corridor, saying hi to extraordinarily well-paid people who don't answer, as custom dictates in these parts, to the office of the DSRSG, where I'm ushered in to see the man who holds my fate in his hands. 'Hello, come in,' says Sukehiro Hasegawa.

'Minion. Lynne, Minion.'

He is a Japanese man and he shepherds me in curtly, indicating the couch, where I sit, obediently, as he begins, 'Yes, Lynne, do you know why you are here?'

'Yes I do and I am so pleased to be able to meet you and discuss solutions to this stalemate.' And I table every document I have produced, project plans, manuals, memos and the ream of emails to UNDP inviting their assistance. Sometimes in life I have to believe in the strength of my convictions, that I have done my best, that the most effective course of action is not a dignified silence, that there's only one way to be heard and that's to talk until . . .

'I am so sorry to have to interrupt you. I have a Swedish diplomatic representative waiting outside for me but I have found this fascinating. I will talk to you again with a solution. Don't change what you are doing because you are wonderful.' Excuse me? What is it with that word? It harks back to my interview with the Prime Miniature, which I hope isn't an omen. Corridor, stairs, out into the daylight and, as I emerge, I see The Missus sitting just outside the doorway, his head buried in paperwork, waiting for me.

'He said I am wonderful!' What an outcome. I never imagined I could orchestrate a turnaround of this magnitude. I live to try another day.

'Calls for a celebration,' says my friend.

Realistically, the UN couldn't really have overruled the particularly irascible executive leader of an independent nation, so I guess it was inevitable that I would be sitting on my veranda, days later, staring out at mountains brown with drought, sacked from the Prime Miniature's Shoe and Handbag Emporium.

'Anything I can get you, Ma'am? Do you want to go for a drive or something?'

'No.'

'City Café? Brunch?'

'No.'

'Beach, take the kids?'

'No thanks. Look, I really just need to be alone.'

'Leader? Supermarket?'

'No, really. Please.'

I don't even say goodbye as he hops into his car. I don't even salute as he drives away. Instead I sit and think about the ceremony held recently in which the Australian police contingent members in Timor had medals pinned to their chests. And hours later, or however long it has been, the UN Land Rover with its back window free of phrase returns and The Missus climbs out of the driver's side, walks towards me and I don't even shift my gaze, preferring to continue staring straight ahead at mountains brown with drought as an arm reaches over me, to the table on my left.

It's only when he's gone inside that I look to the side and see the Pine-Lime Splice. Still, resuming my inspection of the mountains, I leave it there to melt.

47

NOBLESSE OBLIGE

'So what are you doing with your time these days?'

'I'm writing a book,' I reply, as I soak in the soft, still, cool sunset-time air. A drowsy ocean nuzzles the rocks to my right, the children run in front of us on this stroll to Christo Rei and back, and José returns the waves of passing joggers.

'Wow, what do you want? A Pulitzer Prize?'

'No, a Nobel.'

He looks at me, 'Oh, you mean Literature.'

'Actually, Peace would do.'

He breathes his laugh. 'Cheeky.'

'Well may you laugh now, my friend!' We are both laughing now.

'What about UNDP?'

'I told my program manager that I'm writing a book and he said, "Good for you!" Anyway, UNDP say they'll look after me, they refuse to sack me and send me home. They're looking for opportunities elsewhere in Dili. They have to, I mean, the Prime Minister doesn't take advice.'

I'd have thought the UN would have some say in how its staff are treated, how its money is used, whether the projects are allowed to succeed. If the mission is required to bring peace and security, if it is mandated to teach the government to govern itself, if it is all done with goodwill, then the UN must have control over its own operations. But for some reason this is seen as a threat to Timor's sovereignty.

Despite the money Japan is pouring into Timor, the DSRSG — Sukehiro Hasegawa, who is Japanese and has over 30 years' experience in the UN — is wary of falling out of favour with an ill-tempered PM, especially over little ol' me. I could have told him that he needn't be quite so concerned about a demand for his immediate removal landing on a desk in New York any time soon, because the Prime Miniature's office doesn't have an OUT box and Rita isn't at her most accommodating at the moment, so she's unlikely to pop down to get some stamps.

'I should have a Ramadan, no?' José pats his stomach.

'Warn me! I don't know if you have the disposition for it.'

'So you will stay?'

'Yes, I want to see what UNDP comes up with. And while I wait, with their blessing, I'll write and watch pirate DVDs of *Sex and the City* over and over.'

'I think you love it here, you will marry a Timorese man and stay in this country.'

'Really? And build a dream home on a stretch of sand near Dollar Beach and spend the rest of my life eating vodka-infused melon wedges in my very own plunge pool as whales breech on their way past and servants wave palm fronds to cool me in the tropical heat.'

The thing is, I do want to stay here. I love moments like this, walking under a pink sky, a bit of banter and a lot of laughter, watching the children in their bare feet running ahead then back again with their dog. Despite the menace, the filth and the poverty, there are so many times I cherish.

But I don't want to stay forever I'm thinking, as a

Portuguese patrol drives towards us. It slows upon approach. The peacekeepers on board stare, José waves, the teenage girls giggle and I pull down my cap, and it passes at a leisurely pace. No wonder I've had a T-shirt made up that says: 'Sim, sei que tenho olhos verdes', or 'Yes, I know I have green eyes'.

'Oi, girls, hati hati!' I tell them to be careful, pointing at the truck which is turning around now and, wouldn't ya know it, but it comes up beside us and adopts walking speed. Their lack of propriety amazes me. They are perving, they have no shame. The girls have transformed into coquettes! What did I just tell them? I'm pulling down my cap again, frustration growing as the minutes go by until I can't help it: I have to tell them to 'Piss off!' which is what's required to make them accelerate up and away — not protocol, not the Minister watching on, not their professional reputation. 'Sorry, Minister,' I say when they've gone, 'but with all due respect to your Portuguese blood, they are the one thing I really hate about being in this country. And I'm disturbed to see the girls flirting with them. If you're not careful, you'll have some broken hearts on your hands one day.'

'So how is the Midget Cop?'

The Missus and I like to hold cinema nights in our home and right now he is at Obrigado Barracks picking up pizzas and bottles of softdrink while I arrange chairs in rows in the lounge room and check the technology. The children love the novelty of these nights because there's no cinema in Dili. So, not wanting to disappoint them with a sub-standard show, I turn on the overhead projector and test that it has been correctly wired to the DVD player in preparation for our special presentation of *The Lady and the Tramp.* With the screening time approaching I press PLAY in order to focus the images that are being beamed up onto the big white wall, using whatever show happens to be in the machine at the time. This is when the children come running in the back door, early as usual thanks to their enthusiasm. 'Bonoite Lynne!' they yell just prior to their burst of laughter! They screech and point at the wall . . . which is when I look up and see *Sex in the City*'s Samantha *in flagrante delicto*, her fabulous butt 2 metres wide on my lounge room wall and a blow job being performed with a fair amount of flair.

I press EJECT in a hurry, press PLAY on the duty-free stereo I've bought from the Australian army base and try to entertain them in an appropriate manner by dancing, 'Come on, danca!' until The Missus walks in the door with his load of First World fare. 'Thank God, do you have any idea how hard it is to amuse eleven children with my appalling language skills and a house set up primarily for the entertainment of grown-ups?' So the children take their seats along the rows, The Missus and I pass around pizza, the lights dim and we watch a presentation that's designed for children's eyes; eyes that light right up, as the opening titles begin.

When it comes to grown-ups, Dili has a couple of discos, a karaoke bar, quite a few restaurants and a number of Australian pubs, but for those looking for an alcohol-free form of entertainment, there are the pirate DVDs available for the princely sum of US$4 each, VCDs come in a little cheaper at US$2 (or three for US$5) for the bargain shopper. These things are godsends to all of us here, they prevent profound boredom and alcoholism. And in my circumstances, waiting at home for news from UNDP, too humiliated to go out into gossip-obsessed Dili, they fill my hours with drama, intrigue, comedy — and that's just the production values. The movies are usually filmed by enterprising gentlemen in Asian nations who sit with their cameras in cinemas and capture the show which, therefore, includes more than the on-screen goings-on. You also get, thrown in at no extra cost, the conversations of surrounding audience members, sounds of popcorn consumption, oh and there goes some bloke in the front row on his way to the loo. But it adds to the narrative for me.

Which is why I am often heading down to the shops in the back of a cab, yelling at the driver to turn down the thumping Boney M, watching him cough up his tuberculosis phlegm and spit it out the window. Why am I taking these ear-splitting, consistently infuriating and occasionally dangerous Dili taxi tours again? Because I had to hand back my car.

My Popemobile had such personality in its endless and potentially fatal idiosyncrasies. And so I feel very real grief at having to revisit the very special service provided by the generic Timor taxi. Especially as Timor taxis can't be used at night, or for some destinations: I'm reliant on The Missus to drive me to the auto-teller machine whenever I need to withdraw money. He stands sentinel as I position myself inside the fortified shelter then emerge to be harassed by the bank's uniformed security guards, 'Telstra Missus?' who feel it acceptable to augment their wages by selling phonecards to the recently cashed-up. You are a pretty clear target if you go to the ATM. One Austrian police officer had a knife put to her throat by a driver and a couple of his kolegas who were lying in wait when she made a withdrawal in daylight hours, so I think it's best that I avoid tempting fate in such a way.

What am I going to do when The Missus goes? Yes, another tour of duty is coming to an end. He can't go! What about me? I'm facing such an uncertain future — who's going to feed me? is just one concern that springs to mind. I simply can't be expected to take care of myself any more, I'm as dependent as a newborn on him. I mean, I probably won't even wake up of a morning without the sound of bubbling coffee to rouse me and, ugh, what would be the point?

I have to be supportive of his home-going, though, don't I? 'Don't worry about me, Elsie has said she'll make me coffee in the morning,' I say.

'Oh, okay. Good, good.' Did his voice just taper off?

He's a good man, The Missus. He'll be missed by the malae staff at the Serious Crimes Unit for his raucous Friday night barbecues out the back in an entertainment area he constructed complete with UNHCR tarpaulin. He'll also be missed by the uniformed Timorese policemen and -women he trained in skills such as the exhumation of bodies, the very same Timorese police who drove him bonkers with habits such as snogging during class. And he'll be missed by The Family who trust this quiet and dependable man who brought them little pink outfits from Bali. And, all right, all right, he'll be missed by me but I'm buggered if I'm going to let him know it.

'I hope you packed the camouflage-print rubber ducky I gave you,' I say.

'Certainly have, Ma'am.'

'Good. So then, back to modernity, luxury, safety.'

'Yes but I'll miss the war zone.'

'Don't be bloody ridiculous. What's to miss? There's just dust, mozzies, the Portuguese and the heat here.'

'I don't know about that. Just ask Camus . . .'

'Stuff him. You are going home, Missus. It'll be great. Resuming your life and seeing your family and friends. There are barbecues to be conducted over there too, I can tell you. Australian society has fallen apart in your absence, I hear.'

He laughs. 'Well, I'd better get back there then, quick!'

But the reason that his influence has been strong is not only because he can cook a great steak; it's because he is an Australian police officer who cares for the Timorese and has done some remarkable work in this place, who chose to live within the local community and take the kids to the beach. He takes a lingering look back before he walks out the door.

'Homeward bound, you lucky bugger!' I say, as we drive together for the last time towards the airport, the chaos of the view appearing far more charming through my sentimental eyes, as I sit with my feet up on the dashboard of his UN Land Rover ('UNMISET 251'). 'Last chance to run over a $100 chicken.'

Too late. We pull into the airport carpark. 'I arranged to use the car to get to the airport,' he says. 'But it's going to be picked up in about an hour from out the front of the house, so when you get home just leave the key in the console. That's very important, I've arranged for the key to be in the console.'

'Yep, lae problema.' Soon enough, it's time for him to board his Airnorth flight and I employ all the techniques of the emotionless goodbye that I've learned before now. They're a part of mission life, after all. 'Anyway then, it's been great. Look after yourself. Have a good flight, See ya.' And I go to walk away from my BJ Hunnicutt.

'Don't forget the key, put it in the console,' he says vehemently. Jesus, he's even more pragmatic than I am at such a time.

'Yeah, yeah, yeah. Now get on that plane, go! Congratulations, you're going home! See you when I'm 36.' This time I do turn and leave. There. That wasn't so hard, was it? I'm fine, chipper, in control. Still, it's a lonely drive home, I won't deny. The end of an era. Who's going to buy me ice creams, take me to the bank, sit on the veranda with me night after night laughing about Article 36, sending me goodnight text messages after I go to bed?

After a little while I pull into the driveway of our house, my house, actually. I put the car into park and turn the key. The engine stops. I take a deep breath, straighten my back and ready myself for a new era that will, in all likelihood, be just as good as the one that's gone before.

Reckoning there's no point in being sad, I take the key out of the ignition and open the car door. Oh yeah, hello, moron, console. Turning back, I lift up the lid and, looking in, I uncover a beautiful green silk gift bag. What on earth?

Delicately pulling it out, I open it up to find, inside, a bottle of Poême. Looking at it in my hands in the stark sunlight that beats down through the windshield I can only think, 'My God, the man knows me. How did he do this in East Timor? And why?'

That's when my utterly false and wafer-thin bravado collapses and I sprint from the car, through the house, skidding on the tiles, into my bedroom, diving onto my bed where I hug my feather pillow and sob out loud, the bottle of perfume still in my hand. And I don't care if The Family can hear that I'm tanis.

48

THE PHOENIX FALLS

I'm watching TVTL and it's broadcasting ABC Asia Pacific. Now, this should have a certain appeal but, from where I'm sitting, the rhetoric of my politicians alarms me. For all of Australia's talk of identifying with Asia, we really don't have a clue. Thus, the deputy sheriff aims his barbecue tongs at the region's leaders and tells them to watch out or else. Talk of pre-emptive strikes seems boorish to those of us in the bullseye.

I cringe to think of such threats beaming into Asian lounge rooms via satellite, especially ones in the volatile nations to Australia's north. And they are volatile. Today, for example, began with the discovery of a Timorese woman's charred body on the beach in front of the American Ambassador's residence, and now protests are erupting again, as they have every day for almost a week.

Ring, ring. My phone. 'Hello.' It's an Australian media organisation asking me about the civil unrest and it heralds a flood of calls from former colleagues representing most networks who have been offered television images of the events in Timor and need information to explain what's going on — there are no correspondents on the ground. My phone's beeping and ringing and vibrating like crazy and to prevent me from getting into trouble by telling the truth, I refer them to the main UNMISET office for comment. It's just another day in the war zone for me and, thus, it's on to lunch.

Should I walk to the venue, I'm wondering. Don't get me wrong, I'm not worried about the protests, they've become the norm, it's just that it's not wise to walk on Dili streets at any time, even to a café 300 metres away. But I need to stretch my legs. I've been stuck in my house for too long watching DVDs, and so it is that I wander out the front gate and along the road. 'Malae, malae,' the Timorese say, although today they seem surprised rather than aroused. I walk by and they turn and watch. Where's the characteristic laughing and wooping? I'm a little disturbed by their propriety and in a couple of minutes I reach the Tropical Café to find it empty. I dial my phone, 'Hey, where are you?'

'I'm in the CARE compound, behind the gates. We seem pretty safe for the time being but there's a lot of uncertainty.'

'Really? Why today more than any other day?' The protests have become threatening in front of the government building, creating alarm. 'I'd best pop over the road to Obrigado Barracks,' I say.

Trotting through the gates I find hundreds of people inside, taking shelter, milling around, waiting to see if this is yet another day of civil unrest that causes no real harm. Although, there is a sense of tension that's quite odd. It's something I've never quite felt before, it's starting to seem somehow more sinister.

I join a table of people under the awning in the entertainment area and all of our phones are running hot by this time with calls and text messages from within Timor and around the world. For once my mother isn't the carrier of information, which makes me feel I should be responsible and tell her. I think it would be insensitive of me to allow her to hear about these security concerns from anyone else, such as a newsreader exclaiming: 'Fear and chaos in the streets of Dili as Indonesian-sponsored students go on a rampage . . .' or (in the case of commercial stations) 'Fear and chaos in the streets of Dili as Indonesian-sponsored students with possible links to al Qaeda go on a rampage . . .'

'Hi, Mum. How are you? Hey, I just thought you should know that you don't need to worry but you may hear some reports . . .' and I tell her precisely what she doesn't want to hear but has been expecting for almost a year, and I assure her that everything is absolutely fine, as I watch people stockpiling items in bulk — canned goods, bottled water. 'So there you go, Mum, everything's good. I'm completely safe. Okay then, yep, I will, see ya.' Still, I think I'd better get some essential provisions before they all run out, and a couple of minutes later I leave the supermarket checkout with a disposable camera, a must-have item in these situations, as far as I'm concerned.

Gasps and screams and, following people's gestures, I see smoke from the centre of Dili. Everyone rushes to vantage points. We are standing in our safe compound looking out over demountable buildings and palm trees to the sky where ominous black clouds rise, 'It's Hotel Timor!' 'No, it's the ANZ bank!' We're assuming the targets are foreign-owned. 'No, no, the ANZ bank is over there, I think it's the shops,' says someone else. 'But why would they burn down their own places?'

I am so disappointed. Anyone who is here working towards a democratic East Timor with heart and soul can only view this sight with despair. Our work, ambitions, principles are going up in smoke right now. If the Timorese are so desperate, if they can only communicate their discontent in this way, then it's all been a waste, hasn't it? We've failed/they're not learning. Whatever, it's a moot point now because this is a disaster that wasn't averted.

UNMISET staff are trapped in their offices down on the oceanfront, rocks are being thrown at the windows. Anarchy is imposing itself and growing in momentum. I talk to a friend who is in there and she's scared. 'What are the peacekeepers doing?' I ask. They are mandated to protect the country from outside invasion or matters of profound internal instability; they can't intervene in internal policing matters. 'And what about the police?' Some Timorese riot police officers have escaped into the building, terrified; they've taken off their uniforms or turned their shirts inside out, they're begging the malae for clothes to wear, they're cowering under desks.

Hearing this I think of Asim, who has been down on the frontline of the protests every day this week. I send a message, **I'm thinking of you. Take care of yourself.** A reply comes back, **I am fine. These people do not scare me.** I laugh out loud at the realisation that a huge Bosnian monolith who has fought in his own war would be fairly difficult to intimidate; his sheer height means that he could come waist to face with a machete-wielding Timorian, put his hand on the assailant's head, and a swinging weapon wouldn't even reach him.

Whump, whump, whump goes a UN helicopter above us. A UN briefing tells us that rioters — they've been upgraded from protestors — are moving through the streets, burning down buildings; hundreds of people are running amok, taking control of the city, throwing Molotov cocktails, spray-painting their taunts on walls, looting shops and terrorising the population, particularly the local police. Fear is mounting.

UN staff are being evacuated to Obrigado Barracks, swelling the numbers of people in here. The shelves of food are near emptied, jugs of beer are being emptied too, while the aid organisations, foreign business owners and Timorese have to look after themselves out there.

New arrivals are shaken, thankful to be safe, and they describe a Dili that is burning. Others pound at the gates, screaming to get out, 'I don't know where my baby is, you have to let me out, I have to find my baby!' The next UN briefing is firm: 'This is a non-family mission. You are all aware that this is a non-family mission and yet we've had people demanding to be allowed to find their partners, children. Our responsibility is to provide security for you and we've had to let people *out* into the riots.' As a result, the UN is arranging to evacuate family members from Timor to ensure their safety.

The rest of us, however, can stay in Dili. I'm pleased. I can't be evacuated to Darwin while The Family is out there, unprotected. I send Asim a message, **I realise you're not supposed to do this but it would mean a great deal to me if you could check on the family I live with whenever you can today.** They've been through so much already. They survived in the UNAMET compound during those last days of the militia violence of '99, after the Indonesian military took over their house. I often look at the children and wonder at the impact it had on them: I think it explains why Corrie takes care of the younger children; it's probably also the cause of Mastoy's preference for army-print clothing. And here they go again, too young to have to contend with an issue like survival, when their First World contemporaries worry about how many chocolate frogs they'll get in a $1 bag of lollies from the corner shop.

Calls continue to come in from the media in Australia. The journalists there are trying to get the details they need as time ticks towards each news bulletin. 'We've heard Xanana has been seriously injured. He's been hit in the head with a rock.'

'No, he hasn't.' Although it would be a great story. 'I've spoken to someone who saw him at police headquarters. He's shaken, that's all. I have to caution you, Dili is a town of gossip. Talk to UNMISET.'

'They won't provide a statement yet and we're approaching air time.' Riots make great stories, hence the interest.

The rule with the media is that it will broadcast and publish dramatic pictures. So the UN would be wise to provide the words that accompany the images. But what can I do? 'I'm sorry, I understand your constraints, but I can't speak for the UN.' Particularly given my current employment situation, although I can guess what any statement would say.

Cars are being set alight along the main café strip. Time is ticking on and it makes me wonder what my parents are hearing, so I log on to the Internet and read media reports from Australia. Some outlets are interviewing the cousin of someone's niece who once met a Timorian. And, look at that, apparently I'm being evacuated, best get my fake Fendi handbag. Others are saying that the riots have been caused by students — in a country with a literacy rate of 48 per cent that's quite a leap. But I know that the majority of the population is represented by those spirals of smoke because most Timorians know they could never aspire to a university education.

The truth is more complicated and it begins, unfortunately in this instance, with the President of East Timor. Xanana can be a powerful advocate for democracy, but a week ago he underestimated the emotion of the people during a speech commemorating the 27th anniversary of the independence of Timor that was declared prior to Indonesian occupation. He used the podium to enrage the population and incite them to stand up to the regime of Dr Alkatiri — he just didn't realise that their anger would spill over into a violent rebellion when they heard him say: 'The Government is mostly a Government of FRETILIN! Independence serves to care for the cadres of FRETILIN!' Of the Government, 'many of whom are constantly absent', he said: 'Unfortunately it seems that by creating problems, one can rise to become a Minister . . . The fact is that these problems have been accumulating.'

Xanana called on the Government to sack the Minister for Internal Administration, Rogerio Lobato, 'on the grounds of incompetence and neglect', and he claimed that 'The notion that the obligation or the legitimacy to govern Timor-Leste only belongs to some, not only reveals ignorance but also a lack of political maturity and a complete lack of understanding of the difficulties our country is facing . . . People become dazzled with "power"; whilst cadres of the Political Party, people became obsessed with being or having to be the ones to reign . . . regardless of their technical capacity, regardless of whether they contributed at all towards the struggle or not, but by virtue of being a cadre of the Political Party.' But his impact came with the point that: 'this is the disease that dragged many political parties and many recently independent countries into disarray, inefficiency, corruption and political instability, where the members of the Government are well off but the people live in misery.'

With his words, Xanana validated the experiences of people living in increasing poverty and inadvertently gave them a call to arms. The protests that followed have seen demands for the dismissal of the Prime Minister, prompting Dr Alkatiri to respond that he has been mandated for five years, that he is omnipotent, and that he doesn't take kindly to attempts to force his hand. Thus, faced with the idea that democracy can be a matter of personal interpretation, the protestors decided that their interpretation includes the right to force his hand, which is what they're trying to do out there with the weapons they have to theirs.

A hotel has gone up in flames and with it a newly arrived, day-old Canadian police contingent's entire personal belongings. I'm even more convinced that international issues really are so much more complex than they appear to be. Stereotypes, idealism, bigotry, wealth and arrogance colour our view into these troubled countries. In their First World offices I'm sure the right wing is saying that those of brown skin are predisposed to the very violence that is occurring right now. Conversely, the left wing will invariably counter that brown-skinned people are oppressed innocents and that any violence is the fault of the World Bank or the UN. The Timorese leadership will tell the world that the rioters are pro-Indonesian renegades, reinforcing the idea that this country continues to be the innocent victim, a message that will pull at the heart strings, deflect criticism and guarantee many more years' worth of aid contributions. The UN, I imagine, will say there's nothing going on and that this remains the most successful mission of all time.

For me here, my prejudices are falling away, as I see that all of these interest groups are wrong as much as they are right. The Timorese are oppressed and starving; they are being oppressed by their own; they are predisposed to violence given the legacy of decades of occupation; and maybe this *is* the most successful mission of all time.

Dili has been closed off to all transport in or out, martial law has been declared. Boredom has set in for me, broken occasionally by someone becoming hysterical with fear. Beyond the gates, rioters are gathering pace, running around town following a plan, burning down specific targets. What's the pattern? Some malae buildings are being destroyed, although they seem to be the exception to the rule — such as the brand new Harvey World Travel office, which opened yesterday and lies trashed today. 'The ANZ bank is safe.'

'I just spoke to someone who reckons they're headed towards Pertamina.'

'No, they're not going to blow up the petrol plant, are they?'

'What else is down there?'

The path chosen by the rampaging mob seems deliberate, not random. So what point are the rioters trying to make? 'They're burning down Alkatiri's house!' yell people with phones to their ears. 'It's in flames!' The executive leader of a nation's house is collapsing into cinders at this point, and, as far as protest messages go, this is much more effective than any placard I've ever seen. I can't conceive of this occurring to The Lodge, the White House or Number 10 Downing Street. I'm not talking about security, either. I'm talking about the will of a people to take such symbolic action.

'The ANZ house is being looted!'

'What? Why?'

'It's owned by Alkatiri's brother,' someone yells.

Regardless of the breadth of the Alkatiri real-estate portfolio, why won't the peacekeepers intervene? Doesn't a violent attempt to destabilise a nation's leadership satisfy the mandate? The place is mad I'm thinking, as I sit in the bar and wait for the news on a TV that is showing Australia's Channel Seven. And what about the Prime Miniature? Will he now accept that dialogue will get people to communicate in more constructive ways? Can peaceful debate find a place in East Timor's society?

Phones ring and buzz again and this time the news is of a tragedy made immense by its very uselessness. It's an echo of the past, and so people of disparate nationalities are crying in Obrigado Barracks. All of us feel sorrow to hear that events have escalated into new, yet familiar, territory. The Timorese riot police, those who have remained in their uniforms, have opened fire on a group of rioters. They've shot into the crowd indiscriminately, mowing down their countrymen.

UN police officers tried to stop them, they shouted for their Timorese colleagues to lay down their weapons, instead the fear has spilled over into the most terrible of violence, not shops, not houses, but people. Broken and bloodied bodies are being carried through the streets now — five dead, many more wounded. The wails of mothers are poised to rent the air.

It's so soon after '99 for wounds to be opened with this bloodshed. Again these scenes will be broadcast around the world. Once more, the Timorese people must rebuild. And, inexplicably, they have to mourn their dead one more time.

Helpless and hopeless, those of us in Obrigado Barracks spend our time sitting in despondency, sharing updates and comfort, or attending UN briefings. Now and then we embrace those who have been working to control the situation out in the streets and have come here, seeking rest. Whump, whump, whump goes another UN helicopter. Some Slavs arrive and they hold me in their big strong arms, 'Are you all right?' they ask me with genuine concern.

'Of course I am. I've been in this Club UN the whole time, perfectly safe. What about you?'

'It's anarchy but they are slow down.'

'I'm sure the riots won't last much longer. They'll need a sleep soon.'

'Yeah, ve think so.'

Around me, men in full riot regalia from various forces are searching for any leftover food. After all this time in Timor, I'm familiar with military and police uniforms from around the world. I can pick a nation's camouflage print without seeing the shoulder flag and recognise the epaulettes, slides and insignia that represent any rank, but today even I'm impressed at the weaponry, bulletproof vests, berets and batons milling around the pizza counter. They look capable and impressive but, really, they're exhausted and depressed. Maluco glares at me and points to his gun.

'Ve should leave them to themselve,' my friends say with exasperation.

'That's an argument that could have been employed in Yugoslavia.'

'That's for sure!' they boom. 'But now ve have peace and ve must rebuild our countries.'

Timor too, again.

Finally, after 10 pm, a UN briefing tells us that the situation has settled. We can go home if we want, but only to those places back from the roads and behind gates, and with car parking inside to prevent the torching of vehicles. My home satisfies all of these requirements and I am eager to leave.

In the passenger seat of a UN Land Rover that emerges into streets black and empty, there is an eerie pall as we drive along. Then, entering the compound, I leap from the car and run around the back to The Family's house. Spotting Dulce, I go to her and hold her, 'Thank God you are okay.'

'Ye-es, Lynne.'

Breaking away, 'And happy birthday. I wanted to get you a present but all the shops were burned down!'

She laughs, 'Lynne, no problem! Today is very good birthday present!' The Timorese seem to have stronger constitutions for this sort of violent chaos than me.

'Really?'

'Ye-es!'

'So you've been okay? I told my friend to come by and check on you, did you see him?'

'Your friend, he come here.' God (or Allah, more to the point) bless Asim.

'Who were the rioters, Dulce? I'm hearing so many different things?'

'Ay! You know, Lynne, they think no one here can make militia.'

In the morning, I make coffee for the people who stayed with me overnight, taking every available space, their homes deemed unsafe. Then curiosity urges two of us to drive around town to observe the aftermath. Buildings lie in ruins, still smouldering. The white government building has sustained cracked windowpanes but is otherwise undamaged. The Prime Miniature's house is a destroyed and mangled mess, the charred wreck of a police motorcycle out the front. A burned-out Tata sits in the middle of the road of the main café strip. I take photos with my disposable camera of a country that has turned on itself.

Still, I'm hopeful that from these riots all parties will take responsibility, adopt humility and recommit to working better towards a common goal. Surely this was the wake-up call everyone required? It's time to face the truth, free of agenda, with the world's democratic institutions acting in concert for the good of the Timorese people.

Ring, ring. My phone. 'Hello.'

'I've tried to call you three times.'

'Who is this?' It's an Australian radio producer. 'Hi there, I think I should mention that it's pretty lucky that you can get through to me on my mobile phone in a Third World country at all.'

'I've been dialling the number over and over. It wouldn't go through. I even called Telstra. What a waste of time. Every time it . . .'

'You've got me now, how can I help you?'

'I want to know what's going on now, an update of the situation.'

'I've just been for a drive through town and all is calm. I'd even describe it as tranquil.' I have no doubt the UN would approve of my description.

'It can't be. We've just had the news go to air saying the riots continue.'

Right. 'As I said, I've literally just been around town and it is completely calm, tranquil in fact.'

'It can't be.'

Meanwhile, the UN says it had no warning of what was

something like a mardi gras through the streets, during which martial law was never declared at all. It's a mystery to me, therefore, to find people at Obrigado Barracks with mounds of luggage beside them. 'Why do you have so many bags?' I ask a UN staffer.

'Because I go from here. Enough! I have enough!' Indeed they have been paid enough and still they're outraged at the audacity of the joint to be unstable. They obviously took the term peacekeeping very literally.

In the days that follow, peacekeepers move Dr Alkatiri into a new oceanfront casa he's been having renovated, from where the lion, presumably wide awake now, bites the hand that feeds him when he blames the UN for allowing the carnage. Then he warns the pro-Indonesian enemies of a democratic East Timor against provoking him, which leads Indonesia to respond that this time Timor's going to have to do some introspection. And the ANZ manager receives a call, directing the bank to refurbish the house it rents from the Prime Miniature's brother. It's pointed out, with all due respect, that the bank rebuilt the property at great expense post-'99, that an inability to insure a property in Timor means the investment went up in smoke when it was destroyed thanks to its link to Alkatiri, which leaves the PM with no choice but to have the manager's passport seized.

So everything's back to normal. Everyone continues to focus on their own agendas, without thought to the real story: the day-to-day misery here. Which brings me to the woman whose charred body was found on the beach. Remember her? It had nothing to do with the riots at all, actually. She was killed by her husband for producing a substandard lunch. Which to me is more illustrative of the situation than any smouldering house, even if it is the Prime Miniature's. Yes, it was just another day in the war zone.

49

BE CAREFUL WHAT YOU WISH FOR

I have to say, for the record, that I love riots. Well, to qualify, I am thankful for these latest ones because I've heard from Viktor and he's worried about me because he loves me and had feared I'd fallen victim to the rampaging rioters. I kiss you and i miss you . . . he goes. Still?

That communications have resumed makes me as excited as a teenager! What's with the niggling doubt then? Is it best to leave the memories unstirred?

For a while now I've looked back on that episode in my life as a pocket of happiness designed to showed me that I can love and that I can be lovable too, thanks very much. All due to Viktor's sheer charisma and sensuality, which caused me to drop the guard constructed years before — and I was rewarded for my bravery. So I remember him now as a man who taught me more than I'd known about relationships. He mended wounds and led me by the hand into uncharted and wondrous territory. Yes, I loved him.

Now that he has chosen to re-enter my life, though, I have

thoughts and feelings coursing through that heart again, and my brain, long since silenced, is demanding answers once and for all. Isn't it enough that we were happy? Yes, that's what I'm going to do, I'm going to leave well enough alone, that's the sensible thing to do.

So it makes no real sense then (yet all the sense in the world) that I'm at a party at Obrigado Barracks thrown by the African UN staff and I weave my way over to a Canadian woman who was a good friend of the Drag Queen Strumpet while she was here. 'Hi, how are you, I hear you're ending your mission on Wednesday, and, hey, anyway, I was wondering if I could, like, ask you some questions?' I smile. And hiccup.

She looks at me and I wonder if she's going to punch me (which is why I chose this point in proceedings because I wouldn't feel a thing), but instead her eyes seem to express compassion and she replies, 'I thought you would one day. Let's go outside.'

'Hang on, hang on,' I make sure my glass is full to the brim, 'okay,' and we move through the crowd of African men and women wearing enormous head adornments that are matched in magnificence only by their backs and, once outside I think we should dispel the silly suspicions up front: 'Is Viktor married?'

'Yes.' My left ventricle ceases to function thanks to a dagger plunged right through it with striking precision.

'Are you certain?' And am I coughing up blood?

'Yes, I was in Bali and I saw him with his wife. She'd flown over from Portugal. He didn't see me. They were in a restaurant and I watched them for a while and they seemed affectionate, happy.' That one got me in the guts and I have to check to make sure I'm still upright and not doubled over as I should be.

'Why were you so interested?'

'Because he'd told Maria he was going over there with some of his contingent members.' That's right, the Drag Queen Strumpet's name is Maria. And I could swear I've been slapped across the face.

Shaking my head to remove the stinging pain, I need to clarify this, 'Why would he tell her that? What was the connection?'

'They were having an affair.' Okay, I'm not enjoying this at all. I should never have awakened the dead. Denial had me living in far greater happiness — with some doubt in the back of my mind, sure, but it didn't have the power to strip away the meaning of everything that was. Now, however, I've exhumed a relationship that should have been left to rest in peace.

And this is what I get. It was inconceivable, wasn't it, that I would hear the reply, 'Oh no, Viktor's not married, he's completely devoted to you and turn around, here he is, he's come back for you.' Love never seems to unfold in that way. Are you happy now, Lynne? That's right; it was nothing. It was a lie. You were one of many, a notch, a trophy, a player in a game . . . oh, God, for some reason I find this agonising process strangely compelling in a sado-masochistic sort way.

'Oh,' I reply. Is that all you have to say? All you can say is, 'Oh,' like a woman who believes she deserves every single bit of this. 'Ahem, when?' I can't seem to bring myself to stop the torture.

'For a while. She was seeing him when she went to the party at the GNR camp and then he met you there. She was devastated.'

'He just discarded her like that? I remember them having words on that night but I couldn't understand what was being said, they were speaking Portuguese.'

'She was pretty upset, as you can imagine.' Imagine? I'm living it right now and it feels like a cardiac arrest.

'I had no idea,' I say. 'Although, everything makes sense now. How could he do that to her?' Hello, *her*?

'I know. He told her he was married but he said it wasn't working out with his wife. He talked about the future, marriage, all of that.' Why on earth am I putting myself through this?

'Marriage. Yeah. I got that one.'

'You know, I think he did love you. I think you caught him off guard.'

'That's very nice to hear and I'll take whatever scraps I can, but I guess it's irrelevant now.'

'He didn't sleep with Maria after he met you; she tried, desperately, really devastated that he could leave Timor without one more night with her.'

'But why did she want one more night with him after what he had done to her? He'd humiliated her publicly.'

'She loved him.' Ouch, ouch, ouch.

'Love, huh? There was a bit of that going on.'

'He is very practised. He knows what women want to hear.' Flagellate yourself, Lynne, why not. Is this some old African ritual? No, it's actually a ritual performed by women around the world every day, a special brand of witchcraft we perform on ourselves.

'All men know what woman want to hear, it doesn't take a PhD to work it out, but no one should ever abuse that. To use women's vulnerabilities makes him a predator. I told him that he had a duty of care to me. That my heart was fragile. I asked him so many times if he was married and every time he said no. He told me that my paranoia would ruin our relationship.'

'I suppose he knew that if he told you he was married you wouldn't be with him.' Indeed. Instead I am bleeding from internal wounds.

Damn it, why couldn't I be unic? And Maria wasn't the only one. There was another Australian in Dili, she loved him too and he went to her to say goodbye after he'd said goodbye to me and I'd sat kneeling on that beach; then she'd never heard from him again. Three broken hearts and counting . . . Meanwhile, I need a triple bypass and I realise that I may even have caught him during a phone call with one of them, maybe even his wife.

That night, in the dark of my room, surrounded by the mosquito net, I send him an SMS. I know the truth. The phone rings immediately and I hear his caramel tones crooning to me that it's all lies, that he loves me alone, that he doesn't know 'this Maria'. Why do I want to believe him so badly that I will ignore all evidence to the contrary? I suppose it's easier because the alternative is simply too painful.

Night after night he calls me, soothing me with his words. But even *my* capacity for denial isn't strong enough. 'How could you lie to me?' I ask him, eventually.

'I love you, we have a fairytale, Lynne Maria.'

'Don't call me that. My name is Lynne.' How could he?

'Lynne, okay, Lynne, I love you.'

'Don't, Viktor. Don't. You have no right to manipulate my heart any more, you never did. How could you do this? Stop the lies. Just be honest. Be a man and admit it to me. Take responsibility for what you've done.'

He's crying. 'I loved you, my green eyes . . .'

'Viktor. They're not your green eyes any more.'

'Okay. I love you. I do. I never feel this before. I don't know what's gonna happen. I want to be with you in my life. I come back to Portugal and it was terrible this place without you. I leave my wife for two month and I tell my family about this and they tell me they cannot understand.'

'Why should I believe you?'

'You must believe in this. They tell me I cannot leave. My sister, my mother; they say if I leave my family I never see them. They hate you.'

'Great, people I've never met hate me. They can't tell you what to do with your life, Viktor, and they most certainly cannot judge me. I never chose to be a mistress.' I have always loathed them, but right now I can see that mistresses are victims too, just like wives; the men, however, they're the ones betraying their vows before God, harming those who love them and there is no excuse in the world.

'But you don't understand, I am a very sad man. My wife she . . .'

'Viktor. I'm gonna stop you right now because I've heard it all before. It's always the same.'

'But I am condemned. I never feel the happiness that you have in your life some time.'

'You poor thing. You find it very easy to blame your wife, don't you, but a marriage can never be successful when one partner is off chasing other people. It's a very simple rule. You're a grown man. You can leave but instead you choose to devastate the people around you.'

'This is not Australia. I wish at that time I am from a country where this is possible to choose my life. In Portugal, you don't understand, this is not possible. Divorce is not possible. I talk to some of my guys who have done this and their family has stopped them from their children. I cannot do this. My daughter, I love them. I love you and I love them and I cannot do this.' He's sobbing now and I am too. I'm sitting naked on the tiled floor of my bedroom, my back against the door of the wardrobe, weeping.

I wouldn't want him to do this either. That's the thing. I would never have chosen to involve an entire extended family in my life. I feel like a bystander who's been embroiled in a story that has nothing to do with me.

I look at my phone and press END, and my head leans back onto the wardrobe door. So that's it. It's over. The relationship, the uncertainty, the fantasy. It's all over. And it wasn't what I thought it was at all. It was doomed and immoral. It was murky and painful for more than merely me. I sit in the dark. I only wanted to love and be loved. The purest motivations in the world and they amounted to nothing in the end, which is why I lean forward and cry now, hugging my stomach, tears falling on my legs and shining in lines of light filtering in from the cracks around the air-conditioner, and I cry.

At least for me, healing can begin. Obviously, I'd have preferred that the answers to my questions hadn't reaffirmed all of my cynicism about men, but at least I know why my future with Viktor became my past.

Standing up, I dress and go out to the room next to mine. 'Hello, J-Lo? Are you awake?' I say, as I push open her door. 'J-Lo?'

My new housemate answers me, 'Hey, sure, come in,' she says through a sleepy voice. 'What's up?' She's lifting herself up on an elbow and checking the time. It's 3 am.

'Hey, sorry, I was just talking to Viktor. He confessed that he's married, always was. So who's the moron?' I laugh and cry at the same time, sitting down on the end of her bed.

'Hey, hey. Let's have a cup of tea.' She gets up and puts her hand on my shoulder. 'Come on,' she says softly, looking down into my teary eyes. She shuffles from the room. I follow her.

'It hurts,' I say.

'Ah well, Miss Lynne, be careful what you wish for,' she replies, walking down the corridor, and I'm reminded of that night on a beach so many months before when she and I had wished on a shooting star.

'I'd forgotten about that. That's what I get for dreaming of the impossible, hey? I guess it was inevitable, then, the call tonight.'

She puts the kettle on (the electricity's operating), and hunts for mugs. 'Now you know why I call them Portuguesa sobre messa — Portuguese dessert,' she says, turning to face me, 'because they look good but they're bad for you.' And, despite the pain I feel, I can't help but join her as she giggles.

50

TOUR OF DUTY

We strap ourselves into a UN helicopter for a flight to Oecussi, to where we saw that shooting star. J-Lo's going there for work. Me? I'm cheering myself up, which is an appalling misuse of UN resources, but the situation's dire.

'Seems to me that friendships last longer than relationships,' I say.

'They do here. But Viktor was only one man. As wonderful as he seemed to be, you'll find someone who deserves you. We get what we deserve in life.'

'No we don't. We get less. The arseholes get more.' This time our giggle is cynical.

The Russian pilot tells us to put our earplugs in, then the rotors start up. I hear a muffled whump, whump, whump, and soon we're suspended above the ground. I can see our house over there and the cathedral at Villa Verde; the landmarks of the city are below me now, as the chopper rotates around, dips its nose and heads west and up into the sky.

Looking out I feel relieved that Timor is dropping below me, the city of Dili fading into the distance, the mountains looming alongside us to the left, the coastline marking our path, and the troubles left behind.

Days later, I'm sitting in a UNDP truck J-Lo's driving. 'I'm thinking of going home.'

'Really Miss Lynne?'

'Yeah. It's just a thought. I might wait out my contract then go back to where I belong.' The road is bumpy. I don't know how J-Lo can handle the vehicle over this terrain. Practice, I guess.

'You're feeling demoralised about it all.'

'I guess. I tried hard but . . .'

'But I thought you wanted to stay.'

'I did. I was going to stay for years but, come on, police and peacekeepers come here for six-month tours of duty, I'm about to double that and what have I achieved? What can one person really achieve?' We descend into a rut and I hit my head on the roof.

'It's all of those one persons who amount to something powerful.'

'Humanitarianism requires humanitarians?'

'Exactly. And it's hard work. I've been here for three years. You should have seen the accommodation when I arrived and the only food you could get was canned tuna.'

'Which is why you'll never eat it again.' We giggle and J-Lo stops the vehicle, asking a group of churchgoers in her fluent Tetum if they'd like a lift.

'And there have been many times when I've wondered why I've put myself through it.' The women and children hesitate and, realising why, I jump out and open the back door — they don't know how to use a handle.

'Why do you?' I say, jumping back in the front.

'I still don't know,' she says. 'But, generally, I think it's a good thing to do.'

'Maybe I don't have the strength you have?'

'Or maybe you've had a particularly bad run or maybe you can do good work from Australia or maybe you're not mad like the rest of us who stay here or maybe you'll decide to stay? I'll get you a list of all the aid agencies here and I want you to talk to them. Don't rush into any decision.' She's an experienced humanitarian, J-Lo. She's remained committed when others have long since left. So I should pay attention when she speaks.

'Yeah, because maybe I have PMS.' And looking back at a truck that's full now, the women smile at me as they're jolted around, and I realise I'd hate to have PMS if I was stricken with poverty too. 'It's not all bad,' I turn back to J-Lo and say, 'I only have 138 PMSs left in my life.'

'You count down your PMSs?'

'Sure, I have to be aware that I still have 138 more opportunities to make catastrophic decisions that would never be made on the remaining 23 days of any lunar month.'

'I've changed my mind, you are mad.'

'Only for the other five days.' So rather than allowing hormones to make my decision, I think it's probably best that I take J-Lo's advice and wait a while until it's safe, like at menopause.

In an attempt to sort out my direction, I take the ikan bot and, together with some friends, we pile into a car with a big blue flag flying from the front representing the International Organisation for Migration — the precursor of which settled my family decades ago — and we journey eastward and onward towards the nose of the crocodile, the symbol of East Timor and the shape of the island.

The window is open and my left hand plays in air that's thick with humidity. Goats, ocean views and coffee bushes blur in my vision as we pass through the terracotta village of Manatutu, a sleepy and dusty hamlet, and onwards to the metropolis of Baucau, with its street market, the grand Portuguese architecture, and a café on a hill where one can sit under a tree and watch the Timorese washing their clothes in the public fountain. It's a picturesque surface that belies the rebellion bubbling beneath. This is the nation's hotbed of dissent and so I keep a careful eye out. That man selling boxes of chickens in the sun seems questionable. The woman selling clothes donated by Australians to charities for Timor is clearly not trustworthy. But that's not on a par with what this place is known for.

Despite statements that all was calm on Independence night, the police station here was stormed and overrun. It has happened since then too. Murders are a community hobby. Even the local police and military have been involved in some settling of violent scores. With that in mind, we proceed with caution, which means that any branches lying across our way are a sign to speed up — roadblocks are the popular choice of bandits. Exiting the wicked city, we continue on past gnarled trees (the scenery seems wicked too) and groups of bandana-wearing men who stare as we break through to the countryside.

After hours of passing palm-frond shacks and clusters of people sleeping under bamboo village gazebos, Com Beach lies to the left and so it is that the car comes to a stop at the edge of white sand stretching for miles. I walk to the shore with an ikan bot under an arm. The big inflatable fish is bait. I float in the shallows thanks to the buoyancy provided by my water retention and look out to sea until, right on cue just 20 metres away from me, an enormous whale moves slowly through the sea water. It seems to be the size of a bus as it goes by, in no hurry at all.

Down the road, the area of Los Palos is lush and fertile, subsistence farmers tend their crops; a disabled man smiles as he rides his old bike around town; 'Hello Missus!' people call to me in sincere greeting; from an abandoned pousada on the end of the crocodile's nose I witness a panorama of ocean and cliff merging; there's a traditional place of worship with an enormously high thatched ceiling; a shack has a satellite dish attached, presumably for the soccer; women balance wicker baskets or buckets on their heads, as they walk along the dirt roads; and markets sell live dogs, trussed up, bones ready broken, bloodied and whimpering, ready to be bought, cooked and eaten.

East Timor is a complex place. It can be innocent and it can be cruel, charming and horrible, beautiful and ugly. The world sees one dimension: that it is an inspiration. In some ways it is, but looking around at the Timor that's passing by me now, I'm thinking of all the freedom movements in the world that are invoking the name of Timor, calling on the international community to give them independence too. And what happens then?

This country has had billions of dollars poured into it, a massive amount for half an island with a width of 100 kilometres and a population of 800 000. Thousands of aid organisations and the significant resources of the UN have spent years dedicated to helping this place become autonomous. Yet Timor's still stumbling as it gets to its feet.

Is it possible for the rich in their world to really help the wretched? Despite the failures within the most successful UN mission in history, I've come to see that humanitarianism is the only enemy of evil. More so, it's the responsibility of those of us with wealth. With reform and the support of those of us in honest democracies, the United Nations can be the best we have in a world that continues to go to war, in which people live in abject poverty and nations further their interests in places they don't understand for dubious gain. I know this now. I've lived it to the extent that I've been able and I've tried to understand it as much as I can, which is more than many.

Watching the landscapes of this troubled new nation, I curse that the UN is a bureaucratic mass of overpaid, sexually distracted fat cats, and that soon the Timorese will be left to fend for themselves. But that's when I wonder: had the UN, such as it is, not stepped in as the transitional administrator, peacekeeper and capacity-builder of this nation, what would have happened here?

Approaching the outskirts of Baucau again, we slow down and proceed towards a crowd of men who approach us on foot. We're creeping along, and we enter a mass that swamps the vehicle. We move bit by bit. They stare inside, walking by. Then a man comes up beside my window and his eyes connect with mine and he raises his arms above his head and that's when I see the machete above me. There's no time to react because he collects his strength and brings the weapon down with force. The blade stops centimetres from my wrist. And the Timorian bursts into laughter.

51

MELLY CHRISHMUSH AND A FELIZ ANU NOVU!

Quite frankly, I'll never have a kitchen again without an enormous shrine in it. There is something oddly comforting about staggering, half-dressed, mascara under the eyes, cursing the banging in my head while the Virgin Mary, or Saint Fatima, or Saint Therese, or Saint Philomena watch on. Where's Saint Jude, I'd wonder on these occasions — the patron saint of lost causes.

I've become rather partial to my iconography during my time in Timor. Why not get a bit of divine intervention working in one's favour? And whenever the urge to pray takes me, I don't have to venture any further than my own house and its 2-metre-high wooden monument complete with holy water, statues of the martyrs and Bibles in a selection of languages.

Inspired, I have also ventured to Dili Cathedral at 7 am on Sundays to add my number to that of the Timorese, with the kids in tow, dressed in a sarong (trousers are banned) and covered up nicely in a top that obscures a shoulderblade or two. Well, I did. But I gave it the flick. Not because I had a crisis of faith, no, but because there is one very tangible effect of poverty: poor dental hygiene. So imagine being in a cathedral building with thousands of the Timorese devout. When the hymns began I'd have to hold my nose. (And they don't have access to the UN dentist, which may or may not be a bad thing.)

Still, for as long as I was able to make the sacrifice, I had the chance to observe the devotion of the Timorese, which is absolute. I understand why they need to believe in something omnipotent, but I have also watched and reflected on the influence Catholicism has had on a people who have little capacity for analysis. Religion may have been the first manifestation of globalisation but it seems ludicrous when the Timorese add money to the collection plate.

It's such a powerful influence the UN even tried to harness it by producing a public information campaign telling Timorese men that if they abused their family members they'd go to hell.

But there is some local interpretation. In the more remote regions, the Catholicism has a mix of animism to it, so the graves are marked by the crucifix plus a goat's skull suspended on a stick; and in the city there is a mix of traditions too. Right now, at Christmastime, each street is decorated with ornate palm-frond thatched nativity scenes with the white-skinned Holy Family attending to the numerous mangers under flashing lights. But sometimes I wonder if I follow the same religion at all, like when I see a sight through my windows that makes me recoil. I go out the back to where Dulce and the servants are preparing a feast. 'Um, Dulce . . . there is a cow being killed at my front door.' Peals of laughter, as always, for the malae.

'Ay, Lynne, it's for Christmas!'

'Well, it's just that in my country we don't kill cows, we just have these meat portions turn up magically in supermarkets, so I find killing rather traumatising.' There's that laughter again. It's a culture clash that confirms for The Family that I am an alien.

I have sufficiently recovered hours later, by the time I enter the malodorous cathedral for Mass. I'm with twelve Timorese girls who are dressed in remarkable brand new pink taffeta confections. The children carry a chair to me, fan me with a piece of paper and put their arms around me, their hands in mine throughout the hot, steamy service. 'Lynne diak,' 'Lynne bonita,' 'Hau gosta Lynne,' they say to me as they always do, and I look at their little brown faces and feel that I am truly privileged to share a pocket of my life with them, and for that I thank God.

I am in the right place to do so, of course, and I know that I am giving to them too, not with my altruism, my selfless philanthropy and extraordinary humanitarianism but, rather, because, as the only white-skinned woman in attendance, the children are gaining enormous cachet for having their very own personification of Mary with them. We go up to receive Communion and all eyes in that congregation are on me and them, and strangers stroke my white arms, they stare up into my eyes, and everyone forgives me benevolently when I refuse to kiss the statue of the baby Jesus (see: dental hygiene above).

We skip arm in arm back to the compound, through the crowds of church-goers, along the dark streets illuminated only by the flashing lights of nativity scenes, as the little girls sing a Christmas carol in English for me, 'We wish you a melly Chrishmush . . . ' as we dodge pigs and open drains and turn right into the compound and the adults in The Family rush to meet us with firecrackers exploding in welcome, one of them careering towards me, I duck, it lands right in Grandma's hair and off she runs, screaming, hitting her head.

Asim speeds into the compound in his UN police car to Holy Spirit me away through flashing streets, fireworks exploding along the way, and onwards to the Croatian party, where people of every denomination and nationality are celebrating throughout the early morning hours in a particularly Western way. Cocktails, singing, salsa. Ah yes, these religious festivals are all a matter of interpretation, so I twirl . . . straight into Drasko. 'Oh, hello,' I look up into his hard steel-grey eyes and they stare straight back at me with his characteristic intensity. 'Sorry about that,' I say to the man who drives Viktor's car around town. I can tell that he isn't accustomed to people stepping on him. He surveys me for a moment, 'No problem. Listen, I can get you a drink,' he says.

Most malae have flown home for Christmas, especially those from rich countries who don't need to save up their monstrous wages to provide for desperate families and entire towns. Many of them had trysts with mistresses in Darwin or Bali on the way to meet up with wives and children. Others didn't bother going home to all that responsibility; they ended their marriages and chose the tryst instead. But in a back room of the City Café, those who decided to stay and work are taking time out to gyrate wildly, paying homage to the birth of the Lord with the fervour of the devout.

Timorese priests would hold their crosses aloft, but after the fourth caipirinha I believe that everything seems simply heavenly . . . even Drasko. He's not as arrogant as he has seemed to be, or is it his skill in making explosive cocktails that has created the fireworks in here? I just hope he trashed Viktor's car.

Muslims, Buddhists, Hindus and Christians of different kinds have joined together tonight in peace and friendship. It's an appropriate tale for yuletide. A unified world represented on the dance floor in the private bar behind City Café. Unity and harmony spreading through each of us, no matter what our differences may be. Sure, it's all frightfully profound when you look at it that way but, really, all it shows is that the caipirinha is the solution to war.

Yes, make love not war I'm thinking, as I awake on Christmas Day, and out I go into the kitchen while my mother sings an indistinguishable carol on the phone; the children peek in the windows and bang on the doors, they want to get to the presents that sit wrapped under my Christmas tree; roosters crow, they're not on holiday; and the fireworks bang away even though it's daylight now, and I glance at my shrine convinced that the saints on this day, of all days, will perform a bit of that divine intervention and cure my hangover, just this once.

Where I am, there is a startling absence of wise men and, while I'm more accustomed to turkey and trimmings followed by a game of cricket, on this afternoon I'm at the Dili Club being entertained by compatriots of mine who are dancing on the furniture and swapping clothes. A man in a black dress with reindeer antlers on his head is up on a rickety table, his VB is thrust into the air, and he's going, 'Oi, oi, oi!'

With that bit of cabaret as my milieu, I turn my attention back to Asim and the Slavs, who are arriving in ones and twos and taking chairs, including, next to Asim, Drasko. 'Ooh, it's a bit hot,' I say.

'You think is hot? Vhat you think ve are feeling? Is minus tventy for Christmas vhere ve come from,' says someone.

'Of course, sure, yeah, a-ha,' and I take a swig of beer to cool myself from the inside out, which is where the heat is being generated. I awkwardly pull on the red ribbon I have tied in a big bow around my neck and it strikes me that it may make me look like a Christmas present and I know whom I'd like to open my wrapping. Lynne! That's right, I'm celibate. Yep, that's me. Going home soon. No point in any messy attachments. Men here can't be trusted with a precious gift like my heart. Nope.

Timorese people gather at the fence to watch our peculiar variety of Christmas cheer. For the viewing pleasure of them and anyone else in the vicinity, an inflatable pool sits just inside the venue catering to those who need to wash off the humid heat; and right now it's filled by a number of people, including a man in a black dress and reindeer antlers. 'Watch the beer!' he yells to the woman in the white T-shirt who's splashing water his way.

'Lynne, she celebrates the Orthodox Christmas as well.' It's Drasko and I'd like to contribute to the conversation because he's making an effort to include me and, hey, we're just shooting the breeze, you know, hanging out as friends do, but I know that I can't open my mouth because I'd squeak.

Eyes are on me and I take another swig of beer and slide down behind Asim's huge protective bulk. 'Australians celebrate on December 25th, Ukrainian Catholics follow the Orthodox calendar. I choose to do it all,' I speak then, looking to my left, I quickly get up to go to the loo with the intention of regaining my composure. Standing in the filthy cubicle, I try to read the English-language graffiti but I can't focus and I think I'm going to faint. That's when it occurs to me that I haven't inhaled since Drasko walked in.

'Damn it!' I say out loud. Damn it. I would kick a wall but I don't want any part of me coming into contact with my surroundings. I would count to ten but I really don't want to breathe too deeply in here. In fact, I would just hide in here all night but the mouse-sized cockroaches chase me out.

Walking out into the bar area and towards the large table, I continue to curse a body that's conspiring against me. *Why am I feeling like this when I'm going home?*

'Lynne, this is Australian, this voman?' one of the Slavs asks me.

I look over to see the latest addition to the dancers on the table, 'Yes, she is.'

'This is normal for Australian voman? To do this?'

'What? Have fun? Sure. Dancing on tables is harmless enough. You should try it yourself.'

'Yeah?'

At that minute the show comes to us and upon our table clambers the woman in question and into the mayhem jumps Asim, and we are all utterly amazed. I mean, who'd have thought the table would hold him?

'You don't do this,' says Drasko, assessing me.

'Well, I'm in a dress.' A particularly lovely black dress with beige stitching, fitted bodice and an A-line skirt.

'She is in mini-skirt, come on!'

'Okay, I'm shy.'

He booms his laugh, 'I think you are not so shy, I think you are elegant.'

'Really? Oh goodness,' I undo my red bow.

Drasko is the leader of the Slavs and it's not a matter of rank; the man carries himself in a way that commands respect. Men want to obey him, women want to appeal to him, oh, yes, we do . . . and he stands above it all, tall, seemingly arrogant, immeasurably confident, with a straight back and unflinching stare.

I need to avoid looking into those eyes because I know they will turn me into a pillar of salt, and yet I feel myself weakening to their temptation. I am being drawn into the ice-cold intelligent gaze that cuts right though me and leaves me naked and . . . ahem, luckily, this is the perfect day to be reminded of the values of self-sacrifice and chastity.

I take another swig of my beer, which calls into question his assessment of my elegance. 'So, it's not really your Christmas today then, is it? Serbs are Orthodox, yeah?' I did not squeak, honest.

'Okay, but here we have them all, Muslim, Orthodox, Catholic,' his arm sweeps indicating all around the table.

'I am very happy to join in on all the other celebrations too. I see it as my duty as an employee of the United Nations.'

'You think this.' Drasko doesn't ask questions, he makes statements of fact. He is all-seeing, all-knowing, and I wonder if he knows what I am thinking right now while we're sitting on a railing now, a flimsy wooden structure away from the table by a few metres, side by side. Then our knees touch and I feel energised.

Drasko has the chiselled face of his people, a straight nose, angular chin, one eyebrow that arches up handsomely whenever he looks at me with curiosity (I really must ensure that I am curious often in future) and he, characteristically, has his sunglasses across his forehead. When I can bring myself to remove my eyes from his gaze I see that he's wearing a sky-blue, sleeveless T-shirt which highlights his arms and their dark olive tan; bandages cover injuries from an accident he had on the motorbike he rides around town.

Forget the beer, I may as well drink in a chemical concoction that comes from the combination of us right now and my hand brushes up against his leg and I'm sure I'm about to turn white and crystalline when he launches himself from the rail, which I view as a rather strong reaction, but, following his trajectory, I am aware of my surroundings again and I notice a melee of people, screaming, pushing, throwing punches, smashing glasses on the concrete floor, and Drasko separates the drunk pub brawler in the dress with his swinging arms from the Slavs. 'Come on, we go!' and a group of us extricate ourselves from the pack of cross-dressing revellers who've enjoyed a few too many Christmas spirits and, thank God, I am rescued from my own unholy urges.

José was in Madrid in the middle of a trans-continental official trip when he got word of the riots and, cancelling all engagements, he jumped on the first plane to Dili.

'Were you frightened?' he asked me when he got back.

'Nope. There was no reason for me to be frightened. And you? How do you feel?'

'Disappointed, depressed. Fucking stupid idiots.'

For an elite politician, issues hit this man hard. He seems to care too deeply to be in a job that requires a thick skin. To raise him from his malaise, though, The Family kitchen out the back of my house was transformed into a hub of activity, all hands contributing to producing platters of food for a birthday party to be held at his house with the new ant-proof roof.

'Happy birthday, Minister,' I say, as I arrive and give him a kiss, kiss on each cheek.

'Be careful, you're the one who is aging more than me.'

'Thank you. Good to see you are getting your humour back.'

'Who's joking?'

'Did Dulce give you my present?'

'Yes.'

'Did you open it?'

'No. I know what it is. Everyone gives me books.'

'It's a Harry Potter DVD, actually. The new one. It's just come into the pirate DVD shops.'

'Oh, really?' A smile!

I can understand the despondency, but tonight is a night of celebration with the officials of the UN, Foreign Affairs staff, some political allies, friends and family. We all sit with our laden plates in his partially landscaped courtyard, around the huge concrete garden feature, listening to the speeches (it is Timor, after all) and applauding the 53rd birthday of this man who has lived his life well, with feeling.

Is it enough to lift his mood? Days later I find a contemplative Minister when I meet him for lunch on New Year's Eve at Sagres on the Beach, the venue formerly known as the Purple Cow, which had to be sold off after the Portuguese peacekeepers went on the rampage and the UN banned their lucrative attendance. It has been bought by José's cousin, and so we sit down in the near empty restaurant on the beach.

'We will have the fish, no?'

'More fish and rice. Great.'

'They do a very good fish here. And prawns, what do you think?'

'Prawns? What's the occasion, José?'

'It's always special, Lynnie, when I am with you.'

'How many people do you think are called José in Timor?' I add in a particularly adept attempt to change the subject.

'Why did my father call me José? Such a common name, everybody here is called José, God. Don't change the subject, Lynnie.'

'Who, me? I don't know what you're talking about. So, the rioters have taken Christmas off, hey?'

'I think we should talk about getting married,' he says as he takes my hand in his.

His security staff look on with open mouths. I liberate myself and reply, 'I've told you, get down on your knee and I'll think about it.'

'I won't get on my knee.'

'Tell Dulce and your family then. Go on, legitimise your intentions if they are honourable.'

'Why should I do this?' He's squirming and I'm enjoying it very much.

'What's the problem? I think they would be very happy. I'll tell them.'

'This is not necessary!' I still remember the time, at a party, when José was asked what dowry I should get (in the Timorese custom) and he'd replied: a chicken, a goat and a scrawny dog.

'It is to me. What's the problem? If you mean what you say then let's tell the world!'

'God!'

'See, I have every reason not to trust you. How many women are you text messaging at the moment?'

'What? None! One!'

'Why don't I believe you?'

'I message you.'

'And various other women around the world whenever you've got some spare time in hotel rooms and airports during your travels.'

'I have had some long relationships in my life, you know that, and then I have had some not so long relationships.'

'Indeed.'

'Yes, I have had a very good life and I have enjoyed all the opportunities, any man would do this, but now is the time for something more.'

'Actually, I've decided to go home, José. Back to Australia.'

'What? No, you won't go.'

'Yes, I will. I'd be very surprised if I change my mind. And changing my mind for a man would require a miracle.'

'Have you booked your ticket?'

'No, but I will.'

'You won't go.'

'Talk to Bishop Belo. Get him out of retirement to perform the ceremony and I'll think about staying.'

52

INDISCREET RETREAT

'I've been warned away from you, I'm told you are Ramos-Horta's.'

'What? You're joking?' I'm looking straight into Drasko's eyes, holding his stare.

He is assessing me, I can tell. He assesses everyone, every situation. And he clearly believes that by looking into a person's eyes he will discern the truth. 'No, I was told to stay away.' He continues to stare.

'That would not have come from him, it's clearly just gossip, yet more gossip.' I'm telling the truth so he can stare all he wants.

'I won't get some violence for being here with you.' A question as a statement. It's an idiosyncrasy that suits him.

'Ooh, yeah, you're right. Be careful. You never know who's watching. I wouldn't want you to get kneecapped or anything.' And we laugh. 'Somehow I think you can look after yourself,' and now I'm completely serious.

We're sitting in the elevated restaurant of the Esplanada, and the spectacular Balinese architecture includes no walls to interfere with the view of ocean from the wicker and wood furniture. The Espy is my favourite place in Timor, so here we are, at a table for two. A candle flickers between us in the breeze, palm trees stand sentinel out front, UN Land Rovers rush by at tremendous speed, Governu Tatas hop along, and women cook cobs of corn on wood fires nearby. While up here in the first-floor dining room neither of us is eating our meal.

'I was surprised when you say you will have dinner with me.' I'm starting to see that he's not arrogant at all. 'I am surprised that you have no man in your life,' he says, and his grey eyes flash with intensity. Does he ever blink?

'Well, according to gossip I have actually slept with every man in Timor. But there's no one. Unless you count the entire Portuguese contingent, I've done all of them, of course.'

He smiles. 'So you have no one.'

'No. Timor is one of those places where you're surrounded by people but you can be very lonely. The attention isn't always fun or flattering. Some men can get angry, as though it is some sort of an obligation of mine to reciprocate.'

'Listen, just tell them to fucking fuck off!' I jump at the vehemence in his voice. Some protective instinct has been set off in him and I am pleased that I've never had to encounter him on a frontline, like Asim.

'Not quite so easy. I don't take on anyone who's armed these days. Anyway, it just means I don't trust any of thc men here.'

He booms a laugh. 'Any.'

'Yes.' I hold his gaze.

'Some men should see that it is not so easy access. I see this. They need to respect you.'

'Bless you. You are a rare man.' He does seem to be a rare man. He speaks his near perfect English with the hard, exotic Serbian accent influencing a voice made deep of timbre by the Marlboro Lights he smokes unrelentingly. He is twice the height of most men in this country. And he appears to be quite respectful of women.

'These men who treat you like this, you call me.' We laugh, although I suspect he might be telling the truth because he doesn't seem to take quite as much pleasure in the company of men.

'I wish I'd known!' I say, even though I think it best that I didn't. 'The other day, one bloke was in my kitchen and he put his arm under my T-shirt in front of my maid and she dropped her mop, bucket, the lot. I was furious!'

'Listen, Lynne, I teach you some defensive moves so these arseholes can only touch you if you want.'

'Like during self-defence lessons.' Did I just say that out loud?

He smiles. 'Yes, like during self-defence lessons.' Oh dear, I did. I hide my eyes from his to prevent him from seeing into my leaping insides and look down at the barely touched plate of Pan-Euro-Asian-Arab-fusion food provided by the new Australian chef. Drasko is dangerous for me. He is achingly attractive and the chemistry I feel when I am around him replaces the need for the city of Dili to have an effective electricity system; we light up the whole town.

No I'm thinking, as I shift around on my seat and cross my legs, I will not break my vow of celibacy. I am Sister Bertrille. I shouldn't have come out with him at all. It would be easier for me and him to stay in separate places — like me in Sydney and him in Dili. Yes, that should prove effective.

'They would start serving world-class gourmet food here just as I leave, wouldn't they?' I say.

'You're changing the subject,' he observes.

I really must improve my skills in this. 'Well, I was just thinking, you know, about my imminent departure . . . for no real reason,' I say, and he leans back in his chair, never taking his gaze from me and, lifting his head, he bangs the table and roars, thankfully, with laughter.

Looking around and raising his hand, 'Please,' he says to the maître d'hôtel, 'here, bring us some more wine, thank you.' Turning back to me he says, still chuckling, 'Listen, don't worry, I want to spend a time with you, talk, drink some good wine,' he drains the rest of the first bottle into my glass. 'Laughing, anything you want. You won't have any problem with me. I like you, that's all.'

'Oh, okay, thank you. Great. It's a deal,' and our glasses clink.

'So this is true. You are really going,' he says.

'I'm afraid so.'

Therefore, I am unable to explain quite how we came to be in the pool an hour later. Sure, I know that we were the last table exiting the restaurant and we were walking down the stairs when Drasko had spotted the pool and said, 'We should go for swim.'

But neither he nor I ever expected that I would say, 'Okay!' and run forward, throwing off my clothes (but for my knickers), and jump in. He gallantly left his underwear on too then dived in before surfacing in front of me where he stroked the water, suspended, staring at me.

I'm holding onto the side and smiling in reply and he swims slowly in the water towards me. 'You're not going to perform a human rights abuse, are you?' I ask.

'I am Serb,' he replies with a smile, as he encircles me in his arms and our mouths touch. With eyes open we explore each other's lips . . .

After some time I come up for air. 'This is a surprise,' I say, looking at him and my arms rest on his shoulders. The warm water laps at our necks and I feel weightless.

'You think this is a surprise, fuck!' he roars, throwing back his head.

Bringing it down again, we're kissing through our laughter, which is quite hard to do, but we're managing quite effectively in the moonlight and it feels as though this hotel resort was built for our amusement alone until, suddenly, we spot the maître d' walking under the canopy of palm trees and along the pathway towards us. Quickly, we separate as though we are just having a bit of a swim at night, as you do, near nude. And in the darkness the intruder nears, then, bending down, he places two glasses of chardonnay on the edge of the pool and says, 'Compliments of the house,' before beating a discreet retreat.

53

PRIVATE MINION

Rounding up today's news . . . The owner of City Café has shot a waitress, the man claims he was just fooling around with a gun, the case is expected to get special treatment in the courts . . . A man has been found dead tied to a tree near the town of Atsabe, it's the latest in spate of murders in the isolated central district . . . Locals continue to clash with members of the Indonesian Colimau 2000 gang at markets on the border with West Timor, the death toll rising . . .

Pleasant place, isn't it. And these are only a few of the crimes. The vast majority are never reported to police. No surprise, really. You'd have to wake them up first. Plus, there is a historical distrust of them. And there are some competency issues too, unless you'd like them to simulate sex or meow. Which is why, in a reinterpretation of their mandate, peacekeepers are rounding up youths in bandanas and locking them up without charge in a move designed to prevent a return to violence.

'Do you think it is the job of peacekeepers to do this sort of work?' I ask Major-General Tan Huck Gim, the Force Commander of the peacekeeping mission, at his house one night during pre-dinner drinks.

'Good question.' He is a smiling, hospitable and charming Singaporean man and he says he's enjoying the chance to talk to someone who doesn't work for him. 'It's a diversion from our normal operations,' he says while shaking the hand of a man wearing a beige look on this uniform-free, smart-casual occasion.

'Don't you think you're becoming the pawn of the Prime Minister? I mean, suppressing dissent isn't generally thought of as a very democratic approach, is it?'

'No.' He shakes the hand of another in beige.

'Do you think he has Small Man Syndrome?'

They're high-level discussions indeed at this catered event in honour of something or other. (Ah, yes, I'm so accustomed to the luxurious lifestyles of the UN elites now that I'm wondering how I'll readjust to Australia's relative paucity.) I'm the only civilian in attendance (other than the Timorese who carry the trays) and the rest of the group is made up of men of the highest ranks indeed.

My exposure to military leaders has shown me many important lessons: (a) that officers rarely advocate war, it's politicians who do; (b) that their sacrifice includes not only time spent away from family, but a frighteningly high divorce rate too; (c) that their loneliness is intensified by a rule against lower ranking personnel talking to a higher ranking officer, even for social reasons, unless invited; (d) that the small proportion of women in the military means that these men talk to relatively few in their lives, which led one officer to comment to me on the beach, 'Gee, for a woman of your age your body's held up all right'; and (e) that even though they all wear hot and tedious camouflage-print uniforms in the humid heat, when they're at ease conformity is something they choose.

These men are officers and gentlemen. They have class that Australian police contemporaries don't even aspire to I'm thinking, as I watch General Tan shake another respectful hand. 'I'd like to have a rank,' I say.

'What do you mean?' he asks.

'Well, General, you have a rank, and Justin's a brigadier, there's a colonel and a couple of lieutenant-colonels here and I feel somewhat left out. That's why I'd like a rank.'

'Why, Lynne, you have a rank and, in East Timor, Miss outranks us all.'

The meal is a sit-down affair inside the Force Commander's house with wine and a buffet meal but it's not your average dinner party, no, and I am trying to take note of the protocols but I'm in alien territory. Military environments at this level of seniority are peculiarly free of spontaneity. They inhibit egalitarianism, irreverence, and exuberance. I'm unable to fathom how they came up with the term Officers' Mess.

I listen in to snippets of enthralling conversation. It's fair to say that the focus is on Australia's preparation for deployment for an allied invasion of Iraq. It's very intriguing hearing this shoptalk but, hang on, don't I come from a democracy? 'The government is denying this in the media. It's saying no decision has been made,' I challenge an officer at some point.

'I don't care what they're saying. I'm telling you. We're getting ready to go, the plans are advanced. It's a done deal.'

'Yes, sir.' Doesn't he know I outrank him? Be beige, Lynne.

The compulsory speeches tell me that we are here tonight to honour two officers who are ending their missions and going home and I listen to them speak about this bubble, this peacekeeping mission. And with all of their rules and codes of conduct they've done it harder than most, and probably been paid the least. Sure, they've actually signed up to be posted from bubble to bubble, the Gulf being the next on the agenda, but by the time they've told of babies newly born whom they've never seen and their anticipated emotional airport reunions, I have tears in my eyes.

Later, out on the back terrace again for post-dinner drinks, 'I'm ending my mission soon,' I say.

'You're going back to Australia?'

'Yes, to Sydney.'

'Oh, that's a shame for us here.'

'I don't believe you for a minute, General, but thank you.'

'You'll miss it, I'm sure.'

'Do many of your officers miss it when they leave?'

'Good point. But you have learned a lot?'

'I don't think I'll ever be the same person. I hope it makes me remember, every day, just how lucky I am. I don't think I'll ever be able to care about superficialities and trivialities again. Too many people get caught up in complaining about their lives and yet I've seen Timorese people smiling through their poverty. It seems I'm the one who's been capacity-built since I've been here.'

'Well, you have learned some important things.'

'Yeah, I won't be recognised when I get home. Oh, but I might still care about fashion because I haven't had a lobotomy since I've been here.' He laughs and, looking around, I see that I'm one of the last to leave and, unfortunately, it's time to go. 'Goodbye General,' I say, kissing him on each cheek.

'Goodbye Miss,' he replies. This affable and refined man clearly leads by example and it occurs to me that his famed dinner parties are a positive way for him to dispel the loneliness. It's a curious life, military life. It's all very isolating, especially when you're the person in charge.

So I hop into a UN vehicle and, as it's heading slowly out of the compound, I pass by the General who's standing on his back terrace, waving, and I feel it necessary to salute him when, of course, it's not appropriate at all. But, perhaps thanks to my higher rank, he salutes me in return.

54

GOING OFF

'Congratulations on yet another year.'

'Thank you, Minister. How kind of you,' I say into the phone, while I walk around in the dusty driveway out the front of my house, a house Dulce's recently had painted bright pink.

'How do you feel now that you've passed your use-by date?' he says.

'Fine, José. Thank you for your concern. It's very touching of you but, surprisingly, I'm coping remarkably well.'

'That is a surprise. You must be losing count with . . .'

'Yes, I get your point. Now, I believe the words you're searching for are "Happy birthday, Lynnie."'

'Am I? Okay, happy birthday dear Lynnie.'

'There, that wasn't too hard, was it?'

'So what are you doing on your birthday?'

'I'm opening presents, they arrived today from my family.'

'Presents. Why did your family send you presents when you're going home?'

'They were actually sent for Christmas, they only just arrived. Anyway, my mum doesn't believe me. She thinks I'll stay.'

'I told you, you will stay.'

'That's not what I said.'

'Yes, I know this. You will stay. You will not leave.'

'José, I'm serious and you more than anyone can't expect me to stay after everything that's happened.'

I can feel the eruption before I hear it, despite the five kilometres separating us. 'You blame me, don't you?' he yells. There goes his notorious temper.

'Yes! Yes, I think I do!' I'm yelling now too, about something I've kept to myself for weeks now. 'You could have intervened with the Prime Minister, with the UN. You were the only one who could have, and you chose not to!' Finally, it comes out.

'What could I do?' He seems to have been expecting the accusation because he seems resigned rather than angry now.

'I was caught up in your political dramas and then what? I ended up as collateral damage. You didn't want to stick your neck out!'

'I don't know what I could have done. I emailed Hasegawa and it bounced back.'

'How coincidental. Don't you have his phone number? I do. I'll give it to you!' The bottled disappointment has exploded in fury.

'Lynnie, I can tell, you don't want to go.'

Okay, the whole truth is coming out now, isn't it? The floodgates have opened. 'No, I don't want to leave Timor, okay?' I look up at the blue sky, I will not allow myself to cry. 'But I may as well go! Why would I stay if I'm not contributing a thing? I'm not here for my own entertainment, I can tell you!' Noticing big brown eyes watching me from out on the street, I realise I'd better lower the volume, which makes me take a deep breath and concede, 'Anyway, what does it matter now.' Then there's silence except for honking Timor taxis, crowing roosters, chirping geckos, and whooping locals beyond the gate. Thankfully, there are no tears. I won't be tanis about this.

'So, what are you up to?' I ask him, trying to change the subject.

This time he lets me, 'I am getting ready to fly out, long trip, official visits.'

'Oh, really?' I reply, quietly. 'Then I won't see you again in Timor.'

'Yes you will,' he says.

Heading out to the beach, the UN Land Rover turns right from the road to Arieia Branca and mounts the hill past José's house. 'Hang on a minute. Do you mind if we stop? I'll just be a minute,' I say to the driver, as I open the door, jump out and rush through the gate.

'Botardi Missus Leeen.'

'Botardi Celestino.' The security guards look up then back down at their cards in a poker game under the little thatched roof built for them out the front. Inside the grounds, José is in his dining hut with an Asian delegation armed with cameras which they're wielding at him and his house.

'Hello Minister,' I say mounting the steps. 'Am I interrupting?'

'Hello Miss. Come here in the photos . . . Ladies and gentlemen we have a very special surprise visitor.'

'Don't you dare, José.' They turn their cameras towards me. 'Please, please, there's no point photographing me,' I say.

'This woman is a very important woman,' he says to them. 'For historical record you should make sure you take many, many photos.' He puts his arm around my waist and pulls me against him; the paparazzi go mad, click, click, click.

'Let go,' I hiss at him through my gritted smile.

'That's right, many photos,' he smiles and nods at them. 'What?' he says as he looks at me beside him. 'What's the problem?'

I'm pulling away while careful to maintain my diplomatic countenance. 'I'm sorry, José, but I have to go. I have someone waiting for me in a car out the front. I just wanted to say goodbye, properly.'

He looks towards his gate, sees the UN vehicle there and points for the delegation to go around the back to where something more fascinating than me is available for the cameras. The delegation continues its click, click, click and his level of agitation rises. He barks words in Portuguese at his niece, Lily, who shepherds them out.

'I was driving past and I saw that you were here so I thought I'd stop in.'

'Oh, you were driving past. Well, thank you for coming. I am very humble, such an important woman coming here to my home.'

'Stop it. No need to be caustic. I just wanted to see you one more time.'

'Don't be melodramatic. I'll see you in Sydney.'

'Yeah. Of course. Okay.'

'So, thank you for coming to my country to do all of your important work.'

'José, there's no need.'

'It has been a gift to my people.'

Taking a deep breath, 'Talking about my work, thank you for the job reference. Your office went to a lot of trouble, printing it on coloured cardboard and formatting it beautifully.'

'The reference, God. Complete garbage, of course.'

'Yes, of course. It must be, it even mentions that I'm intelligent.'

'Does it? I didn't even read, I just signed.'

'That's a shame because it's actually a marriage certificate and now I own half of this,' I sweep my arms around.

He looks at me, 'Is it?' he says. Is that the faint beginning of a smile?

'Yeah, I'm going to take you to the cleaners,' I say. Finally he breathes his laugh and I join him. 'Anyway, thank you, José. For everything. I mean it.'

'I did nothing,' he says.

We lean towards each other and kiss, kiss on each cheek then, embracing, arms around each other, we stay that way for a minute, then, disengaging, I quickly walk away.

In the car now and it takes off up the hill and, as it reaches the crest, I turn in my seat and look down into José's compound. People wander around the circumference of his traditional house, photographing, probing, invading his privacy, revering him; meanwhile, the Foreign Affairs Minister of East Timor, the Nobel Peace Laureate, José Ramos-Horta, is seated on a chair in the dining annexe, alone, his head in his hand, staring out before him at the landscape of his country.

I know you're avoiding me and sometimes it hurts. I am. It's an SMS from Drasko. I've been determined to leave Timor and equally determined to maintain my detachment until that point of departure, and being around him is simply not going to work in with my objectives, hence my evasion.

Tonight, however, I'm having a birthday celebration with friends that's very delightful yet, for some reason, I'm watching the time. Sitting at Sagres on the Beach, we order food and chardonnay and settle into the night, and there is a soft wind playing and coconut trees swaying and waves lapping and all that and another hour passes and, look, it's lovely but something is missing. Looking around, I notice that the rest of the place is quite empty. The ban on peacekeepers coming to this location remains even though the place has changed hands. I chose it for tonight's dinner for that very reason, so the seclusion is not the cause. Then my heart flutters when I hear the words, 'Here come the Slavs.'

Car after car arrives, dramatically. 'Hey!' I yell, standing to greet them, coming up to their stomachs.

'Happy birthday!' they say and Asim gives me a present.

'Thank you,' I say, looking around his girth. But there's no Drasko. 'Come, sit down.'

'How old are you becoming?' a foolish man asks.

'Tventy-five!' most of them answer in tandem and I am pleased to see that I am a capable agent of propaganda.

Tables are placed together, booming voices begin their banter and soon we are consumed by hilarity. Yes, this is the perfect birthday, I'm convincing myself. Why is it then that the butterflies start again when a solitary car pulls up beside the others with a skid? Ah, my void seems filled as Drasko emerges from the dark.

'Hey, this motherfucker was supposed to tell me when he was leaving,' Drasko says, pointing to Asim. He takes a seat, 'Happy birthday,' he adds, staring with smiling eyes that penetrate me. I look away, I have to just in case he and everyone else at the table gets a clear view of the longing I feel.

'Have you all been at the same place?' I ask.

'Tonight ve have a party. Vun of our colleagues, he is ending his mission,' says Asim.

'Thank you for coming to my little soiree then.'

'Is no problem. But I must go soon, party is in my house.'

'Even more reason to thank you for coming!'

I hate myself for feeling relieved that Asim must go but in an hour's time I find myself, relatively guiltlessly, dancing at the disco *du jour*, Poy Cholor, in Drasko's arms. 'Hey you,' I say in his ear.

'Hey you,' he replies.

We move to the new hit in these parts and the immeasurably romantic words of 'The Ketchup Song'. But who cares right now because everything seems romantic: Timorese prostitutes being mobbed by Portuguese peacekeepers, US$4 glasses of chardonnay, fluorescent lights designed to highlight women's underwear, Pakistani military observers who hover behind women on the dance floor, shit-faced Australian police officers, Dili Princesses sweeping past with adoring coteries in tow; all of it seems perfectly wonderful while I dance in one man's embrace.

As we move in an Eastern European interpretation of the salsa, it's clear to see that we are perfect together. 'You're are perfect together!' says a friend over the music.

'Are we?' Staring into each other's eyes we know it's true. How could we have taken so long to see what is obvious to everyone else? Yes, we were made for each other.

'But, you know, as true as that may be I'm afraid it's too late because I'm leaving.'

'Don't go.' His breath caresses my neck. 'Come, I show you some place,' and he grabs my hand and pulls me out through the crowd, the gate, and within minutes I find myself in his car.

'Oh, I don't know if I can. I should go home.' I should *so* go home.

'No, I must show you this.' I'm sure it'll be a spectacular display, particularly as I'll be seeing two. He directs the car the other way from my house and out of Dili we go, down towards the airport, then along a bumpy track until he says, 'We are here,' and the car slides to a stop in the dust.

I open the door and step out of the car. He leads the way and on unsteady feet (stilettos are not all-terrain footwear), I walk towards a small cliff face and see a remarkable sight. 'Oh my God!' I yell. Throwing off my sandals (red leather, silver buckle), I jump down into Drasko's strong, outstretched arms and onto the sand and look out at an enormous full moon reflecting on the expanse of ocean before me. There is no sign of land, we are on a point out to sea. 'It's the end of the earth!' I squeal. 'It is beautiful, so beautiful!'

Whoever imagined that a place so perfect could exist? With my arms out wide, skipping in the sand down to the waterline, I'm marvelling at Mother Nature, when this man comes from behind and gathers me up. 'You like this,' he states as he always does.

'Thank you. Thank you,' I say, staring up over my shoulder into eyes that are also a gift from nature.

'For this.'

'For bringing me here. For everything. For making me so happy.'

'It's for you. For your birthday.'

I turn and look straight at him and the reflected moonlight illuminates his substantial presence. God, he's extraordinary. Happy birthday to me! How did I deserve my life? I am a truly lucky person. And in this place at the end of the earth we kiss.

'Thank you for the night of my life,' I say to him, while we sit out the front of my house, and we look into each other, intensely, and I need to gather up every piece of my resolve to exit the car.

Opening the front door I turn and wave, 'Bye you.' I hold up my hand. He drives out the gate.

Turning and walking inside, singing to myself, I'm halfway through the room before I see the mess. I didn't realise I'd left in such a hurry. Look at all this jumble, how embarrassing. Dancing down the corridor I go into my room and I'm shocked at the disarray. That's very unlike me, I'm a Capricorn I think, happy birthday to me I giggle. Hang on, my drawers are upended on the floor.

'Dulce, Dulce!' I'm pounding on her bedroom door out the back of the compound now. 'Dulce!' It opens. 'I'm sorry to wake you so late but I've been robbed!' I've instantly sobered up. There is activity and faces are peeping out of doors around the place. The UN police are called and, while I wait, we roam through the house. The wardrobe contents have been thrown across the floor, most rooms have been trashed, especially mine. The intruder even found my pepper spray and I know this because it has been sprayed around the room, the red marks colouring the walls and door, and I hope he got himself as well.

Hours pass and I'm looking in a traditional Timorese basket sitting in the middle of the lounge room which holds the DVD player and my entire *Sex and the City* collection. I obviously disturbed him when I came home because he's left this bounty he'd collected of what he thought were jiggy jigs and I would laugh except that some pieces of my jewellery have been taken and Aveda products that I'd received this morning in my birthday package. 'Lynne,' I hear, 'police.'

'Where are they from?' I ask.

'Ghana,' comes the reply.

'Oh, great.' I make my way out unenthusiastically. Two big men stand there. 'Do up your shirts,' I say. 'Don't you have any respect for your uniform? It bears your flag.' They've clearly just woken up, they were presumably asleep at their desks and, therefore, being capacity-built by the Timorese. They look me up and down and spend more time investigating my chest, mistaking it for the crime scene. Satisfied with what they've seen, they leave. I waited up four hours for that? They didn't even bother walking into my room.

'Lynne.' It's Elsie. She holds out a bundle of items. It seems the burglar ran off through the sunroom door with the possessions he could carry and he dropped some — FCUK jeans, some Havaianas thongs, cosmetics and cigarettes, even a thong of his own. It shows the priorities of the Timorese thief, and I marvel at the thought of a man walking around town in a pair of women's Audrey-cut, flared denim pants, and smelling like Aveda's exfoliating bodywash. That would make him stand out here. But all he actually got away with were a pair of earrings and they were priceless to me, they were gifts from my mother.

The sun has risen on a new day and I'm sitting on a wicker chair on the veranda. Within all the debris I've found a birthday gift that must have been placed on my bed the previous eve, while I was out celebrating the night of my life. It sits on my knee now. It's been a long time since I've slept and I'm feeling violated, so maybe a gift is what I need to cheer me up?

Dulce comes and sits beside me. 'Lynne,' she says, placing an arm around my shoulders, 'we take the thong of this man. Okay?'

'Okay.'

'We take it to some person here. He can see thong, tell who does this.'

'Okay.' Identified by the vibrations from a thong. It sounds more effective than DNA testing.

But I can't joke as tears well in Dulce's eyes and she says, ' I do everything, even pay dollars, to get this jewellery of your mother.'

'Oh, Dulce,' and I hold her hand.

'Should I open my present?' I say, to lighten the mood.

'Ye-es,' she says.

It is a large photo album with a dried flower arrangement on the cover. There's a card too. Inside it says: 'Congratulations? With affection and friendship in spite of everything . . . José, 18.1.03.' On the other side it's inscribed, 'To Auntie Lynne . . . as you fast approach menopause, I want to wish sexuality and optimism . . . Don't feel bad, there are millions of nice old single ladies like you around the world . . .'

And looking at his niece I smile. In spite of everything.

55

DANCING IN THE RAIN

I hear it arriving before I see it. Drasko's motorbike parks in my driveway in the early morning sunlight and, sashaying out of my house, I go out and hop on the back. He takes off, speeding through the streets, wind flying through our hair and my hands holding onto his sides, tightly.

Down to the waterfront and right we go, past the big white government building, the Hotel Turismo, the World Bank and on to the thin, winding bridge over the ghetto of dirty children and pigs, then out towards the Christo Rei. 'Woo hoo!' I yell.

It's a spectacular day, as always, and the heat of the day is yet to set in when Drasko pulls over to a new café on the beach. Exhilarated, we hop down to the ground, order black coffees, two each to start with, and take our places at a table with a view. But who cares about the picture postcard scene in front of us when he and I have the three dimensions of each other to explore and very little time to do so.

Drasko is leaving in a couple of hours to go to Bali on R and R. By the time he returns to Dili I'll be gone. Which makes this our goodbye.

'How long are you going to stay here?' I ask.

'I will apply for extension. I work here to pay for security for my family. My job in our war was protection for the Serb leaders. I know things and some people they know this. My mother, she was killed. I live with this. I have to protect the rest. The UN is the only place I can get the money to pay these motherfuckers.'

'Drasko, that's horrendous.'

'You have no idea the stress I am under because of these fucken people. They have sprayed my family's car with bullets,' he drags deeply on his cigarette and I notice the collection of scars on his hands, arms, legs, 'and now they are demanding some more things. I have some problems.'

'That's shocking. I had no idea.'

'No, I haven't told you these things but it is a stress for me.'

'But you're a police officer. You work for the United Nations. Isn't there anything you can do?'

'Listen, some countries aren't like Australia. Guns and violence are the way of business for some people in my country.'

There are so many stories in Timor. People from around the world have converged here for myriad reasons. That's what makes a peacekeeping mission a source of endless fascination. 'Yeah, I've come to see how lucky I am.'

'So you go back there and we have a Dili without you.' He stares at me.

'You won't even notice I'm gone.'

'I'll notice.' We stare at each other. 'You have your seat booked,' he asks.

'No, but I know when I'm going. I'll get out on the UN flight to Darwin. They prioritise repatriations.'

'You don't confirm this.'

'I like leaving things to the last minute.'

He throws his head back and roars, 'This is bullshit.'

'Are you laughing at me? Do you think I am avoiding it, that I'm being weak?'

'No! You are a strong woman, determined. This is what I know about you. You will do what you decide.' His insight must come from all that staring. He sees beyond my words. He understands me. He was a rare find in the world. The needle in the haystack . . . 'I will notice if you're not here,' he says.

Drasko is the one with a flight to catch and I don't want to go but we must. On the back of his bike again, he accelerates then brakes sharply which makes me thump into his back. 'Careful,' he says, taking my hand and pulling it around him, where he places it on his chest, over his heart.

The wind plays with us as he pulls at the accelerator and off we speed again, weaving through meandering goats and scrawny dogs, then he flicks the brakes again and I thump into his back again, my arms gripping his body tightly now and he looks over his shoulder and says, 'I can't believe it's you. If only I'd known,' and we zoom past palm trees lining the seafront and into the city, left, right, left, right, travelling the back way through town among all the people, taxis, bikes, scooters, wildlife. I never want this ride to end! Soon, however, we're emerging near my compound, which he turns into, then stops.

Reluctantly I swing a leg over the back of the bike and stand beside him. We stare one last time in a moment I've been dreading. He's clearly been dreading it too because he kisses me on each cheek, places the motorcycle into gear and then he's gone, and I'm left standing in his dusty wake, listening to the roar carrying him away until I can't hear it any more.

I'm walking into the house, trying to hold in the tears which are welling, when two little children run up to me, 'Bondia Lynne!'

'Bondia, bonita meninas!' I say, and my nose starts to run and I wipe my eyes as the beautiful girls jump into my boxes and I concentrate on the task of packing my possessions and they try to surprise me whenever I place anything inside. I feign shock, 'Hey, bulak!'

In my room, the girls are getting in the way so I decide to distract them. I place a tiara on Dudu's head and give my camera to Ruth. I've loved simple moments like this, teaching them how to take a picture. As the final trick to keep them occupied and out of my boxes I start singing a song that stirs Australians of every colour who feel a connection to that place. It's a song that promotes unity and reconciliation and so I sing it with these two, teaching them the words to 'My Island Home'. They nod and giggle. 'Okay?' I ask.

'Sin!' they screech, as they bounce in my Bedouin tent and I press PLAY. At the tops of their voices they sing what sounds like: 'Wah, wah, wah, wah-ah-ah-ah-ah,' which is close enough, and so the three of us sing a song that bears little resemblance to the real one but it retains the power to profoundly impact on someone who's going to her island home, particularly if she is hearing it through the laughter of children.

I'm working my way through the belongings I want to take with me. I am lucky that my equipment has withstood the unstable electricity here. When laptops were blowing up around me, mine was endured. My beloved stereo too. Surge protectors don't work and I try to focus on topics like this, free of sentiment, taping up a box, children dancing around me and Christine Anu's voice . . .

That's when I hear a momentous sound from outside. Moving out through the lounge room to the front door, I look out to see a monsoon that is blanketing the city. Ah, the drought has broken and I lean against the doorframe. It's a magnificent force, the monsoon, and it soothes and comforts me. The hammering on the corrugated-iron roof drowns out my thoughts. And then I see Baby. She's dancing in the rain.

She's oblivious to anyone watching on and she spins around, smiling, without self-consciousness, her face held upwards and her clothing drenched. I don't think I've ever seen an act any freer in my life. This teenage girl is a servant's daughter and her stained dress clings to her frame as she spins around and around until, dizzy, she falls onto her back on the ground and, saturated, holds her arms out to embrace the monsoon, laughing. I don't know why Baby's expressing such joy but I know enough of the females here now to know that their cheerfulness defies explanation. 'Lynne!' she yells, looking over at me as the water beats down on her, calling me to join her. Goodness, should I? The monsoon ends as suddenly as it began and in the new sunlight everything seems clear and fresh.

Ring, ring. My phone. I run through the house, chasing the sound of the ringtone. I know exactly how long it lasts before diverting to voicemail and I'm running out of time. Where is it? Why are they so hard to find? Found it, 'Hello,' I exhale, pressing it to my ear.

'Hey you,' says Drasko.

'Hey, where are you?'

'I'm through passport control, in departure lounge.'

'Oh, okay. Well, um, have a great trip.' What more can I say?

'Lynne, listen, I have to tell you something. This morning I want to say this but, like always, you make me speechless.'

'I do?'

'Yes! Come on, you know this!'

'No! I don't, I didn't.'

'Listen, I'm in here and I won't see you again and I want to tell you something. It's important to me. I can't leave without this.'

'Okay.'

'I have to tell you, I have enjoyed all my times with you. Every time. More than you know. I think you are a very special lady and we've had special times, the best for me. In Timor, I can't believe this. I want you to know it.'

He never made flippant promises of marriage, he never reflected on my relative beauty, he never remarked on the colour of my eyes. And as a result he's communicated the depth of his feelings to me. And I wish it wasn't too late, still it is, and that makes it all the more sincere. I feel the very same way, but I can't tell him, I am unable. 'Oh my God. Thank you. Thank you for calling.'

'No problem. I'm going now, the plane is . . .'

'I know. Bye you.'

'Bye you.'

56

IN ESSENCE

'Man, I'm so sick of fish and rice.'

'So what are you going to do? Go to Sydney or Bali?' she asks, following it up in timely fashion with a giggle. Yes, J-Lo's back from Melbourne, where she has spent time in hospital with cerebral malaria, the very worst kind. She's recovered though and I, for one, am not surprised. It'd take more than a deadly tropical disease to keep her down. Still, it was a relief to have her back and we welcomed her with a sign on the front door drawn by me and coloured in by the little girls: 'WELCOME BACK J-LO!' then, 'FROM RUTH AND DUDU', added below which they'd taped up back-to-front because they can't read their names.

She'd enjoyed the surprise and is happy to be back but there's the tiredness, the sweats, the sleeping. In spite of that, she's committed to continuing on in the mission. And she's landed back in time to see me packing up.

'I think it's really sweet of Elsie to cook us lunch but I don't have the heart to tell her that I never want to eat fish and rice in my life again.' In the run-up to my departure, Elsie has decided to cater and she obviously remembers the time when

I'd first arrived and I'd told her that her fish and rice was 'kapas'.

'So, Miss Lynne? Sydney or Bali?'

'Who do you think you are? Cupid? Sydney. Via Bali. And I don't think I'll miss swamp cabbage either . . .'

'What? Hang on a minute, go back! What did you just say? You're going to Bali?'

'Yeah, I think I should. And I'm looking forward to a culinary feast at Ku De Ta.'

'Lynne! Shut up! What are you sitting here for? Come on! You're going to Harvey World Travel now!'

The city is under lockdown today because of a public protest forum and many streets, including ours, are blocked to public traffic, which gives us a rare opportunity, 'Let's walk! Maybe that's just what the doctor ordered?' The travel agent is only about one or two kilometres away, but it is incomprehensible that a malae woman would walk this far generally, and certainly not if she preferred her day to be harassment-free. Today, however, the streets are empty but for some peacekeepers on patrol and a Tata police car every now and then. 'I've missed being able to go for walks to the corner shop or anywhere, really,' I say. 'It's been bizarre being vehicle-dependent. It's going to be a readjustment leaving here. I mean, I'll even have to wear seat belts and obey laws. Shit, I'll be in a place that even has some laws that are not arbitrary.'

To illustrate all of the points above, an overladen Timor taxi, in defiance of the lockdown, drives towards us as we're crossing a road then swerves deliberately in our direction; we leap out of its path. 'Ya fucken wanker!' we yell simultaneously, having barely survived, before collapsing into peals of laughter.

'Ah, you can never take the girl out of Australia,' J-Lo says. 'So when are you going home, Senhora?'

'Maybe in six months. I don't know. Yes, six months, then I

will have had enough. When I finish this contract.'

'Sure,' I say and smile at her.

'Anyway, what would I do at home?'

'You are an impressive and dedicated professional. You should be bloody proud of the work you do here and I've got no doubt that you'll be in demand when you go home.'

'Yeah? But what work could compare with this? I feel that I help people here and, you know, I like it.'

'Ah, well there lieth the real issue. It's a shame when your career depends on war and suffering, hey.'

'Yes!' There's the giggle.

'Although, there's enough of it in the world to keep most UN workers cashed up for some time to come. Especially with Iraq in the firing line.'

'It's a lucrative business, humanitarianism.'

'There's not likely to be any dot.com-type crash. So are you interested in going somewhere else?'

'Ah, remember, I'm an Australian.' No giggle this time.

'Ah, yes, good old National Balance,' I say. 'Marry a Portuguesa sobre messa and get another passport.'

We laugh so hard, out on the street, and I can't help but watch J-Lo and it reinforces to me that peacekeeping missions attract some remarkable people, and they're often not the peacekeepers at all. They're the civilians who've volunteered to do this work, for myriad reasons, none of which is to enrich themselves. These are the humanitarians who suffer the hardships, contend with the loneliness, learn the language and help rebuild a society from its ashes because they want to help. 'You'll be here for years. Hope you've stocked up on mosquito repellent.'

'No, six more months,' she replies. 'Until the end of this contract. Then I'll go home. Honest.'

57

BUT NEVER FORGOTTEN

I pour myself a mug of Elsie's black coffee for one last time. Am I really leaving this place? How will I readjust? I've heard about the post-mission depression suffered by those who go and I know I'm a prime candidate because I'm unlikely to have ball boys during tennis games for US$1, or cigarette sellers who come to my car window, or indeed a maid when I get home.

'Bondia Lynne.' I turn and see Elsie entering through the back door. I used to say that she was my most vital capacity-building project in Timor because I'd found it hard having no privacy — she walks in day and night. You know those times when you really want to be alone? Impossible here, sheer self-indulgence. I tried imposing some conditions to stop her working quite so much; with as much success as I had capacity-building in the office of the Prime Miniature. Anyway, I realised I had nothing to complain about when Elsie caught J-Lo having sex in one of our showers.

So sex and morning moods are not permitted here because Elsie hears my radio turn on each morning and straight in she comes. And I've come to enjoy her company and cheerfulness.

Thus, 'Bondia!' I reply. 'Elsie, neba,' and I lead her towards the laundry. 'Ba ita bot.' We laugh as I address her in the respectful tense and tell her that these piles of clothes are for her and The Family.

'Obrigada barak,' she says but, to be honest, she needn't be thanking me because I've offloaded my lilac. Then I ask her to wait and I rush into my room and emerge, carrying a big box. I hand it to her and inside she finds my cherished possession: the stereo. 'Thank you, Lynne,' she says in English, then out the back she goes, leaving her gifts behind. Have I embarrassed her? Great. After all this time I still don't get this place.

I've tried. I've tried to view her circumstances with sympathy, not pity. I respect that she's a single mother of three happy children, that she lives with them and her niece in one small room out the back, that she hasn't had any of the opportunities handed to me by an accident of birth. I've never felt that my comparative wealth makes me any better than her. I've always viewed her as my equal, my contemporary, and she is because we are the very same age.

But there is a gulf between me and the Timorese, I know, as I lean up against my kitchen bench, thinking of the day before, Australia Day. A day spent out at a peacekeeper event with J-Lo, the children and a collection of inflatable toys, floating in the sea and watching the sky, or handing out sausage sandwiches. Then little Mastoy had asked to go to the toilet. 'Come on, mai,' I'd said, leading him to the Portaloos. He was perplexed. I'd given him a demonstration and I'd told him, don't touch anything, 'Foer,' I'd said, dirty. I'd ended up posted out the front for longer than is seemly, while the rest of the children joined in the fun of running from cubicle to cubicle, flushing and washing, as though I'd taken them to an amusement arcade. For all of their usefulness, it had simply never occurred to me that there was any entertainment value in two rows of blue plastic portable toilets.

By the time I'd walked into the Australian Embassy's party held at the Hotel Timor that night, I was still laughing. 'Hello Lynne,' said my Ambassador, shaking my hand.

'Hello Paul. Happy Australia Day, good turnout.' The place was filled with Australians and I'd thought it rather nice of my government to put on a going-away do for me. (It's also sending my boxes home through the free peacekeeper post but it doesn't know about that one either.)

'Lynne's leaving,' someone said.

'How do you know this?' That well-worn grapevine.

'You're an old-timer,' came a contribution.

'Gee, thanks.'

'No, we thought you'd be one of the few to stay,' said someone else.

'Really?'

'You've been here since I arrived,' the Ambassador said to me.

'Oh, yes, I guess have.' I hadn't thought of it like that.

'So? Are you going to Bali?' asked the chef of the Esplanada, the maître d' beside him, waiting for my answer.

'What? Does everyone know about this too?'

'So? Come on, girl, tell us! You're not going to go coy now, are you?'

It was a bit late for that. 'I am going to Bali and you'll be pleased to know that he's booked a villa with its own private pool.' There was applause.

This morning, by the time Elsie re-enters, I'm standing at the kitchen sink, washing my collection of shoes in line with the requirements of Australian Customs, and the smell of roasting coffee beans comes in with her through the open door and she looks at me with displeasure. What have I done now?

She gestures to take over, 'Lynne, lae! Hau halo.'

'Okay, okay!' I smile as I'm shunted out of the way. She doesn't see me as an equal, she's willing to clean my shoes and do it for the pauper's sum of US$20 that I've been paying her per month. And so she takes a big basket of shoes out the back. Watching her go, it strikes me that I don't have the grace she has. I have a hard enough time being dignified as it is; I'd never be able to have dignity in poverty.

And, sure, many people don't. Desperation manifests in terrible ways in a traumatised people, but there are the many others, like Elsie, who persevere, cheerfully, who contain their crying and contend with circumstances that most in the First World can barely comprehend. She gives me hope in this country, that it can grow into a robust and fair democracy, and then maybe her children will be of the first generation to have opportunity. And stereos.

The back door opens again and Elsie reappears, carrying a single pair of shoes. I have no idea why she's bringing them to me, each laid out in a palm of a hand. Are they ruined? She walks towards me. 'Lae problema,' I say, don't worry about it, there are many more where those came from, I can tell you, which is when she says to me in Tetum that these are the shoes I was wearing the day I arrived. My God, was I? Thinking back to a time long ago, I can recall a frock with shoulder straps and little mother-of-pearl sandals, 'Elsie, sin, sin!' Yes, yes! I can't believe she remembers.

Yes, she tells me, I remember, 'Hau hanoin-hetan.'

Boxes line a wall of the hallway now; it's quite a collection, filled with tais, palm-frond baskets and memories . . . and the pair of Scanlan & Theodore trousers I brought with me — ah but that was a long, long time ago; a time when I thought hipsters looked good. My room contains bare furniture and I look into an *en suite* with a flushing toilet which gave me such pleasure. It's been a journey that began upon arrival. Now it's about to end.

'Lynne!' I go out the front to find Dulce there. 'Lynne, I come to say goodbye.'

'Oh, Dulce, goodbye. Thank you. I'll miss you and your family, you know.'

'I will miss you.'

'No.'

'Ay, ye-es, Lynne! You come to Timor again, you are our guest.'

'That would be lovely.' Though highly unlikely.

'Here. Is for you,' and she hands me a little package and inside is a gold pendant in the shape of a traditional Timorese house with a sky-high thatched roof, just like José's.

'It's beautiful. Thank you.'

'Is okay, Lynne.' We embrace and hold each other.

'Atelogu,' see you later, I say to her, smiling, as we break apart.

'Atelogu,' she says, too, smiling at me and she hops into a car and her husband, Agos, drives it out the gate, they're both waving and yelling goodbye. I watch them go and I know that I've shared my life with these people — they are the true story of Timor to me. I've been granted intimate access to their lives and I am grateful for everything they've taught me, and I'm wondering if I'll ever see them again, when I notice a blondie head bobbing on its way here, attached to a characteristic walk.

'J-Lo!' She's arrived back from work to send me on my way. 'Look at what Dulce gave me!'

'Do you know what this is?' she asks, holding it up.

'A symbol of Timor, I'm assuming.'

'Yeah, but more than that, it was worn by the Timorese during the resistance years. This is a special gift, Lynne. You should be flattered.'

'Oh, really? God, I am.' More than I can say.

My boxes are being carried out to a car by an armed and

uniformed Australian peacekeeper now, and I walk through the house one last time. That's when I see that the stereo no longer sits on the kitchen table. It's been taken out the back, finally.

I have to go and, walking out now, I hear a sound in the lounge room. What on earth was that? Looking towards the windows I see a little figure half obscured by the curtains, holding a mop. It's Elsie. And she's tanis. I go to her and take her into my arms. I never noticed she was so small. Her body is wracked with sobs. 'Hey, it's only a stereo,' I say, and I lean down and kiss her tear-stained face.

Moving out the door, I pick up my hand luggage and get into a car with J-Lo and forward it drives and, as it does, I see Elsie standing inside the doorway, peeking out, leaning against her mop.

I stare ahead, I have to, and we enter into streets filled with chaos. We negotiate pigs and potholes beside the remnants of burned-out buildings in the dust. Vandalism paints the picture of years of political struggle. The tiny, malnourished Timorian men sit in the shade of frangipani trees, picking their noses; women lope slowly, small groups of them, arm in arm, black hair swaying down their thin backs; scrawny dogs stagger out in front of us, as UN Land Rovers go tearing by; Timor taxis honk and scooters carrying extended families add to the fray. Much appears as it was when I arrived. Except that now Timor is free. It is free to be the country it wants to be.

Pulling into the airport carpark, scruffy children yell, 'Hello Missus!' 'Dollar Missus?' and the forecourt, with its new café, is filled with uniforms from around the world. It's a chance for one last gossip, a bit of sexual harassment, a view of people from around the world gathered ostensibly for the good of one tiny half an island. Then I have to leave.

'I hate goodbyes,' says J-Lo. 'I'm not going to say goodbye. I'll see you in Australia, yeah? So go and have a great shag,' she says, knowing she's going back to the house in which Elsie stalks the halls, and she giggles.

By the time I go through passport control the plane is boarding and I run out onto the tarmac, inhaling the familiar fragrant air, and I'm click-clacking in my high heels, trying to catch up to the line of people filing before me to the flight, simultaneously typing in a message on my phone to The Missus, my BJ Hunnicutt and best friend here, who should be a part of this moment. **And then she was gone**, is all I can write because I wonder if my contribution was really any greater than that, than this.

I've only moved on a few steps in the blazing humid heat when the reply comes through, Beep, beep. Beep. Beep. My phone. **1 new message.** I press OK. **But never forgotten**, he says.

The tears run down my face, I can't stop them, and I step up onto the gangplank of the plane. 'Botardi, obrigada,' I say for the very last time to a uniformed Timorese man who stands there and he waves. 'Thank you for coming to my country,' he says, then adds, 'Goodbye Missus.'

I'm tanis now, walking up the steps and, stopping at the top, I turn around and survey this place that has captivated me. Palm trees sway, as always, mountains rise above the city of Dili, locals line the other side of the fence, and I know that I've changed profoundly since I gazed on this scene for the first time. As foolhardy as it had appeared at the time, I should have come: to learn to dance in the rain.

Be careful what you wish for? I'm thinking, as I stand up on this platform. No. Because if I'd been careful I'd never have come here. I'd never have fallen in love with Viktor, I'd never have met a multitude of friends and nationalities along the way, and I'd never have come to know Timor, my muse.

Crying in my window seat, ingoring the safety demonstration in Bahasa, I look on the bright side: toilets that flush each and every time, no cockroaches on my toothbrush, never another day spent with perverts or midgets, killer mosquitoes or relentless roosters, not even riots; instead on the other end of this flight a remarkable man, a needle in a haystack with a private pool, because I've learned that my impulsiveness comes with so many rewards. Then it's on to a place where I belong with *my* family. And all of it confirms to me that I really am one of the lucky few who can have it all. Finally, I can see that my life always was a dream come true, and the dream wasn't even mine.

The plane's taxiing along the runway and, gathering speed, it soars. As we circle around there's the cathedral in Villa Verde, there's my house, there's the grand white proportions of the government building and, as we ascend, there's Christo Rei in the distance. Goodbye East Timor I whisper, and, yes, Goodbye Missus, because it's back to a life of opportunity for me. A life in which I'll never have to wear lilac again. But somehow I think I'll miss it.

In fact, I think it's fair to say, I'll never forget.

Before Lynne Minion worked for UNDP and UNTAET in East Timor, she was variously an Australian broadcast journalist and a media adviser to multinational organisations involved in humanitarianism or social change. She has an MA in international relations and lives in First World luxury in Sydney.